A COGNITIVE PSYCHOLOGY
OF MASS COMMUNICATION

Second Edition

A COGNITIVE PSYCHOLOGY OF MASS COMMUNICATION

Second Edition

Richard Jackson Harris
Kansas State University

LAWRENCE ERLBAUM ASSOCIATES, PUBLISHERS
1994   Hillsdale, New Jersey   Hove and London

Lawrence Erlbaum Associates, Inc., Publishers
365 Broadway
Hillsdale, New Jersey 07642

Library of Congress Cataloging-in-Publication Data

Harris, Richard Jackson.
    A cognitive psychology of mass communication / Richard Jackson
Harris. — 2nd ed.
        p.   cm.
    Includes bibliographical references and index.
    ISBN 0-8058-1264-4
    1. Mass media—Psychological aspects. I. Title.
P96.P75H37 1993
302.23'01'9—dc20   93-23939
                                                    CIP

Books published by Lawrence Erlbaum Associates are printed on acid-free
paper, and their bindings are chosen for strength and durability.

Printed in the United States of America
10 9 8 7 6 5 4 3 2

CONTENTS

To four women of four generations

My grandmother Anne Roberts Harris (1890–1974)
  who modelled an unconditional love and an intellectual curiosity

My mother Helen Sellers Harris (1917–1970)
  who modelled exceptional parenting and was always there for me

My wife Caprice Joan Becker (1955–   )
  whose love for me continues to amaze and sustain me in the present

My daughter Natalie Becker Harris (1991–   )
  who, with her brothers Clinton and Grady, have opened up new horizons
  of being a father and balancing home and career

PREFACE TO THE FIRST EDITION

This book evolved from developing and teaching a course "Psychology of Mass Communication" at Kansas State University yearly since 1981. I am grateful to the students in this class over the years for their enthusiasm, inspiration, and challenge; their ideas and responses to my material have affected the book throughout. Some research on the cognition of deceptive advertising in the late 1970s originally challenged me to think seriously about mass media consumption as information processing. Thanks are due to Tony Dubitsky and Kristin Bruno for contributions to this research. The support of the Psychology Department at Kansas State University during the writing has been tremendous. I also greatly appreciate the Fulbright Visiting Lectureship I held in Belo Horizonte Brazil in 1982; this experience gave me an internationalist perspective that I have tried to bring to this book.

Particular thanks are due to John Bechtold, Sherry Wright, Jean Peters, and Ty Callahan for their helpful reactions and conversations about this material. Jennings Bryant and the reviewers for Lawrence Erlbaum Associates have made exceptionally helpful comments that have improved the book immeasurably. Working with them on developing the manuscript could not have been more helpful and pleasant.

Finally, I thank my parents E.R. and Helen Harris for modelling such effective media use in the home I grew up in. I am sure that many conversations over the television or the evening newspaper provided some intellectual seeds that bear some fruit in this book.

Richard Jackson Harris
August 1988

PREFACE TO THE SECOND EDITION

Seldom does the content of a textbook become obsolete so fast as when it deals with the media. Of course there are the predictable changes in what television shows are popular and what changes the latest telecommunications technology has brought. Far beyond these, however, the changes in the world in the time between the completion of the final draft of the first edition of this book (summer 1988) and the completion of the final revisions of the second edition (winter 1993) have been nothing short of astounding. Never in recent history, with the possible exception of 1941–1945, has the world changed so much in 4 years. In all of these changes the media have played a central role.

In many ways, 1989 was a watershed year, when the "springtime of democracy" in Beijing would culminate in the brutal repression of the Tiananmen Square massacre of June 4 and following. Later in the year, one by one the communist nations of eastern Europe threw off their authoritarian governments, using very different methods, ranging from the "velvet revolution" of Czechoslovakia to the grisly televised execution of Romania's Ceaucescu on Christmas Day 1989. The new year of 1990 brought the unexpectedly quick reunification of Germany, the independence movement in the Baltic states, and Saddam Hussein's invasion of Kuwait. The 6-week Persian Gulf War of early 1991 brought together the most unlikely allies of Saudi Arabia, Syria, Israel, the United States, and much of Western Europe to fight a war marketed through media as a struggle against a Hitler-like figure. By the end of that incredible year of 1991, the reforming Soviet Union had survived an attempted August coup by hard-liners and, most incredibly, voted itself out of existence. The end of the Soviet Empire and the Cold War initiated a massive realignment of nations and a revolution in the way we will all need to learn to think of the world.

As if these events were not cataclysmic enough, South African Whites voted to end apartheid, Israel and the Palestinians sat down together to talk peace, Yugoslavia disintegrated in a civil war no one seemed able to stop, and troops were sent to Somalia to distribute famine relief in a country with no government but lots of televised pictures of starving children whom the world could no longer ignore. Within the United States, opinion moved from massive support of a take-charge president during the Gulf War to massive disillusionment in the face of the worst economic recession since the Great Depression. Late 1992 saw the election of the first U.S. president (Bill Clinton) born after World War II; perhaps even more significantly, he was the first U.S. president to grow up with television from his childhood.

In all of these events the media were central. More than telling us the events, although that in itself was a landmark undertaking, the media participated in the changes. Two dominating visual images of 1989 served as a sort of extreme anchors for that unforgettable year. The lone protester in front of a line of tanks in Beijing represented both the hope and despair of Tiananmen Square. Considerably more uplifting were the images 5 months later of dancing on the Berlin Wall as it was literally dismantled piece by piece. For many who shared that image worldwide the triumphant strains of Beethoven's Ninth Symphony will forever evoke that historic moment.

Even as events reshaped the world, they also reshaped the media. The Persian Gulf War was the best thing that ever happened to Cable News Network (CNN). Ted Turner's upstart all-news cable channel became the industry standard, providing its footage to the big three networks and establishing itself as the source even world leaders watch to help them plan their policy.

In 1993 the nations of the Soviet Union, East Germany, Czechoslovakia, and Yugoslavia are no more, while new nations of Slovenia, Croatia, Slovakia, the Czech Republic, Belarus, Ukraine, Latvia, Lithuania, Estonia, Moldova, Armenia, Azerbaijan, Georgia, Kazakhstan, Uzbekistan, Tadzikistan, Turkmenistan, and Kyrgyzstan sent people worldwide running to their continually outdated atlases. Other events of immense import receive relatively little coverage in competition with these cataclysmic changes; for example, the moves toward economic unity through the European Community (EC) and the establishment of the North American Free Trade Agreement (NAFTA).

Surely the book is not closed on these events, especially the rapidly changing situation in central and eastern Europe. My hope is that reading and studying this book will sensitize you to the psychology of the mass media, how they connect us as persons. Although it is almost a cliché to talk of our becoming a smaller and more interdependent world, it nevertheless is profoundly true. The media make us all neighbors, and faraway events affect us personally. For example, I personally have friends in my small town who were eyewitnesses present at the Tiananmen Square massacre, the abortive Moscow coup, and the Desert Storm campaign in Kuwait and Iraq. My personal stake in the continuation of a good livable world has increased since the publication of the first edition, with the birth of my three children in March 1989 and January 1991. Expecting the birth of twins about at the UN deadline for Saddam Hussein to pull out of Kuwait on January 15, 1991 caused a strange juxtaposition of the hopes and fears of both personal and world events. As we spent the evening after bringing two new babies home watching CNN show us the beginning of a massive air war, we were left with all sorts of mixed emotions and second thoughts about things ending and things beginning. The media were the messages as well as the messengers.

Finally, thanks are expressed to editor Hollis Heimbouch and the other people at Lawrence Erlbaum Associates for having the confidence in doing a second edition of this book. Thanks also to Jennings Bryant, Alan Rubin, and some anonymous reviewers who taught from the first edition and offered very helpful comments for revisions. Many of their suggestions are followed in this edition, especially an inclusion of a greater amount of theoretical materials and research from the field of communication.

Richard Jackson Harris
February 1993

1

MASS COMMUNICATION
IN OUR LIVES

Q: Why did the U.S. Coast Guard receive many telegrams from viewers of "Gilligan's Island" in 1964?

A: Because people were asking them to go pick up those stranded castaways (Fore, 1987).

Q: What leisure activity do people spend the most time on?

A: Watching television. Residents of the United States spend almost half of their total leisure time watching television, making it by far the most popular leisure activity. Every day people worldwide spend over 3.5 billion hours watching TV. Only work and sleeping take more of our time (Kubey & Csikszentmihalyi, 1990).

A young BBC news reporter was sent to cover the Vietnam War in 1969. Not being very experienced or knowledgeable about what he was observing, he led off his first televised report of an American attack of a Vietcong stronghold with "My God! It's just like watching television" (Bogart, 1980).

People very frequently take portable radios, or even televisions, to the stadium with them when they attend a sports event. When asked why they listen to the play-by-play when the game is going on right in front of them, a common response is, "so I can know what's really happening."

In 1984, a 13-year-old boy died instantly after shooting himself in the head with a handgun while he and a friend were re-enacting a scene from *The Deer Hunter*, an Oscar-winning film depicting American POWs in Vietnam being forced by their captors to play Russian roulette. The boy and two friends had recently seen the film. He had later taken the handgun from under his father's bed. The county coroner ruled the death accidental. He was the 31st person known to have died reenacting that climactic scene from *The Deer Hunter*.

These three examples concisely suggest the major theme of this book, that our experience with the media is the basis for building our knowledge about the world. We may call this a *cognitive* approach to mass communication because the emphasis is on the way that our minds create knowledge, indeed, create a reality about the world based on our experience with the media. This mental reality then becomes the basis for all sorts of behaviors and has numerous effects on our lives. Instead of television being a more or less accurate reflection of some external reality, it has *become* the reality against which the real world is compared. The media view of the world has become more real than the real world itself.

Mass communication in the form of print media has been with us almost since Gutenberg's invention of movable type and the printing press in 1456. However, the nature of mass communication, indeed, of life in general, has been radically changed in the 20th century by the advent of electronic media, especially television. Television has transformed the day-to-day life of more people in the last 50 years than has perhaps any invention in human history. Radio and the print media have been greatly changed by TV as well. In one U.S. poll (Handler, 1987) 68% of the participants reported that watching television was their main source of pleasure, followed by spending time with friends, helping others, and taking vacations. Besides changing the way that we spend our time, television has also revolutionized the way that we think and the way that we view the world. These effects on our perception and our cognition are particular emphases of this book. The media are not only the "magic window" through which we view the world, but also the way in which we learn about the world.

Media are far more important than merely serving as conduits of knowledge, although that is no trivial role. The act of transmitting that knowledge may itself become the event of note. When the U.S. and Saudi Arabian governments and military blocked press access to the war front during the Persian Gulf War in 1991, the nature of the war coverage became one of the major news stories of the war. The media were not merely communicating the news, they had become the news. In the case of the Vietnam War, scholars, heads of state, and the general public are still debating a generation later the role of the media in the declining public acceptance of that war over the years 1965 to 1973.

We have come a long way from Gutenberg to the 1,657 daily newspapers, 1,611 television stations, and 10,128 radio stations in the United States in 1987 (Friedrich, 1987, see Box 1.1 for some further background on print and broadcast media). In this chapter we introduce mass communication and our use of the media from a psychological perspective. We conclude with an overview of the rest of the book.

BOX 1.1: A PRIMER ON ELECTRONIC AND PRINT MEDIA

Mass media are of two basic types: print and electronic (or broadcast). Print media (newspapers and magazines) provide information through the production and distribution of copies. In contrast to electronic media, print media tend to be more permanent (at least before the advent of widespread video and audio taping) and depend on the literacy of the audience. There are also no channel limits in print media—although there have traditionally been a finite number of possible television channels (today rapidly increasing in number), there is no inherent limit to the number of newspapers that may be published. Print media also lend themselves better to detailed treatment of subjects than do electronic media.

In contrast to print media, electronic media are technologically more recent, less permanent, and less dependent on formal literacy or accessibility to urban infrastructure. This last point becomes especially crucial in the isolated regions of the world. One can have a portable radio without any access to electricity, schooling, or urban life. From its beginnings in a Pittsburgh garage in 1920, radio grew phenomenally in its first 10 years in a manner parallel to the rise of television in the 1950s and VCRs in the 1980s. With the advent of television after World War II, however, the character of radio changed drastically, away from prime-time programming to music/news formats and later to more specialized (especially FM) stations like country and western, classical, gospel, or all news.

Because of its use of the public airwaves, which are sharply limited in capacity, radio and television typically are regulated by governments much more tightly than are print media (e.g., assignment of television channels by the U.S. Federal Communications Commission [FCC]). The more authoritarian the society, the easier it is for the government to control radio and (especially) television in times it deems to be unduly threatening. Although television networks, both private and government owned, tend to be national in scope, they often have influence far beyond their country's borders. Because broadcast signals do not respect political boundaries, most Canadians are able to receive U.S. television. One of the major influences in the 1989 democratic revolutions in Eastern Europe was exposure to Western television.

WHAT IS MASS COMMUNICATION?

What makes mass communication *mass*? First of all, the audience is large and anonymous, often very heterogeneous (Wright, 1986). Individual viewers, listeners, readers, or even groups of individuals can be targeted, but only with limited precision. Second, the sources of the communication are institutional and organizational (Wright, 1986). Some, such as television networks, newspaper chains, or wire services, are among the largest and richest private corporations. Third, and perhaps most importantly, the basic economic function of most media in most nations is to attract and hold as large an audience as possible for the advertisers. In one way or another, advertising pays a high percentage of the costs of commercial television networks like CBS, NBC, ABC, and Fox; even public television and government-subsidized networks like the Canadian Broadcasting Corporation (CBC) or the British Broadcasting Corporation (BBC) are far from immune from commercial pressures.

In spite of all the high-sounding rhetoric about serving the public, the bottom line of commercial mass media is money, which comes from advertisers at rates directly determined by the audience or readership size and composition, which in turn determines the content. Thus there are tremendous pressures to be as entertaining as possible to as many people as possible; this principle also holds for nonentertainment content like news. All of this is not to say that editors and programmers have no concern about responsibly meeting the needs of the public. They do, but such needs must necessarily be considered within the constraints of the economic realities of the media industry.

Print media also have the pressure of numbers. Newspapers and most magazines receive a majority, though not all, of their income from advertising. There are economic pressures, and sometimes political and ideological ones as well, to control the content of media. For example, magazines that accept tobacco advertisements print fewer stories about the health risks of smoking than those that have no cigarette ads (Lee & Solomon, 1991). See Box 1.2 for a further discussion of blatant and subtle censorship.

In spite of its mass nature, there is more than *mass* to mass communication. There is also *communication*. In true communication there is a reciprocity, some kind of response from the audience. Although the TV viewer is often characterized as being extremely passive, mindlessly absorbing the program content, such a picture is far from accurate. The meaning of a particular program certainly depends heavily on the content of that program, but it also depends on what is in the mind and experience of the viewer. A TV movie dealing with rape will have a very different effect on, indeed a different meaning for, a viewer

---

BOX 1.2: THE ISSUE OF CENSORSHIP

A major philosophical and legal issue with regard to media is censorship, which varies greatly across different societies. Prior censorship (i.e., requiring approval of all content before broadcast or publication) occurs in some totalitarian societies, but more subtle forms of censorship exist in all nations. Even in democracies, press freedom has never been absolute, but rather operates within certain constraints. One may not print or broadcast material that is libelous, classified, obscene, incites people to violence, or infringes on copyright laws.

(Continued)

In the United States, the FCC assigns channels and issues licenses. Although it has the power to deny renewal of licenses, less than 150 radio and TV renewal licenses (out of 70,000) have been rejected in over 50 years of operation. The FCC also insures application of the Equal Time rule (and, until its demise in 1987, the Fairness doctrine as well) to insure that opposing points of view on controversial issues and political campaigns are aired.

There are pressures toward censorship, although it often is not called that, especially in the United States, where *censorship* is a very dirty word. The National Association of Broadcasters (NAB), a professional organization of radio and television stations, has a fairly rigorous ethical code that it expects its members to adhere to, although court challenges and appeals, an atmosphere of deregulation, and changing social standards weakened adherence to the NAB code in the 1980s. Some content, which may not be illegal per se, may nevertheless not appear on television because it is not in accord with NAB guidelines or because broadcasters fear public outrage (e.g., graphic and explicit sex, violence, or surgery). Also, certain words (e.g., "shit," "fuck," many racial epithets, and religious expletives stronger than "Oh, my God!") seldom occur on U.S. prime-time television. Incidentally, these standards change: 30 years ago we did not hear the words "damn," "hell," or "pregnant," although we may have heard "nigger" in the early days of radio.

Real or feared reaction from advertisers is another subtle source of self-censorship. Television networks and stations are very loath to risk offending those who pay the bills for their livelihood. Advertisers occasionally threaten to withdraw their ads in protest. In 1979 General Electric was unhappy with ABC's Barbara Walters' plans to interview Jane Fonda about her antinuclear activism and pulled their ads in protest. However, ABC still aired the interview. Not so noble have been magazines' frequent failure to run articles on the health hazards of smoking for fear of alienating their lucrative tobacco advertisers (Lee & Solomon, 1991).

A democratic government may exert influence even in cases where it has no formal censoring authority. For example, the British government requested the BBC not to run a scheduled documentary on Northern Ireland in August 1985. This documentary included extensive interviews with two extremists, one Catholic IRA member and one Protestant extremist. The government argued that this gave those whom it called "terrorists" an undeserved platform and hearing. After extensive discussion, BBC management decided to honor the government's request, although this decision evoked a 1-day strike by BBC employees in protest.

Concern over the public's reaction may be another source of self-censorship. In 1985 two of the three U.S. commercial networks refused to run an antismoking PSA that showed a fetus smoking a cigarette in the womb. Similarly, we seldom see ads for contraceptives on U.S. television, although they have appeared in magazines for years. In fact, commercials are the most conservative component of television. Advertisers are extremely loath to offend viewers; from an economic perspective, the worst sin a broadcaster can commit is to air something that causes viewers to turn the set off.

who has herself been a rape victim than on someone with no such personal experience. A violent pornographic video may incite one man to sexual violence because of the way his mind interprets and interacts with the content of the video, whereas another man who sees the same video may be repulsed by it and show no antisocial behavioral response.

The nature of the media consumption experience must also be considered. Watching television or listening to the radio may be done alone or in small groups. Reading newspapers or magazines is typically, though not always, a solo activity. Although this is not always a concern of the communication source, it can greatly affect the psychological experience of using the medium. For example, consider the difference between watching an exciting ball game by yourself or with a group of friends. Consider the difference between watching a horror film with someone who either shrieked in fun, cried in severe distress, laughed, or made no obvious reaction at all (Zillmann, Weaver, Mundorf, & Aust, 1986). Within the family, each medium may either promote family harmony and interaction or be a divisive force, depending on how it is used (Bryant, 1990; Lull, 1988).

Now let us turn to how we use the various media of mass communication.

MEDIA USE

Television

Although experimental sets existed in the 1930s, television was practically unknown among the general public at the end of World War II in 1945. Although only .02% of U.S. homes had TV in 1946, that figure rose to 9% by 1950, 23.5% by 1951, and 90% by 1962. By 1980, televisions were found in about 98% of U.S. homes, and that figure has remained there since that time (Andreasen, 1990). Although most of the programming over the years has been by networks or local stations, the rapid growth of cable and satellite technology in the 1980s greatly expanded the offerings. How networks and their affiliates deal with this competitive challenge may dramatically alter the face of television in the 1990s.

The television phenomenon is almost as pervasive in the developing world. For example, in 1984, 86% of Costa Rican homes had TV (95% in the more urbanized Central Valley; Lobo, 1991). Over three fourths of Brazilian homes had TV, although only 20% of all homes had refrigerators (Marquez de Melo, 1991). Even the worst urban slums of the Third World sprout television antennas. No nation on earth is beyond the reach of television. Over 1 billion people have seen recent Olympics and World Cup soccer finals on TV. See Box 1.3 for a look at an anthropologist's views of the stages of a society's acceptance of TV.

The bulk of mass communications research has been on television; the main reason for this is that we spend so much time watching television. On average,

---

BOX 1.3: STAGES OF TELEVISION IMPACT

Drawing on his studies of television use in several Brazilian communities with varying lengths of exposure to television, cultural anthropologist Conrad Kottak (1990) identified five stages of societal interaction with television. In Stage 1 the medium is new and strange and attracts people with glued gazes to whatever the content. "The medium rather than the message is the mesmerizer" (Kottak, 1990, p. 139). Stage 2 is usually the next 10 to 15 years when people begin to interpret TV's messages and selectively accept or reject them. Due to its high status, television ownership becomes a source of conspicuous consumption and a source of privileged information. In Stage 3 the community is saturated with television and the length of exposure increases. By Stage 4 adults have spent their whole lives in a culture permeated by television, whose lifelong impact on members of society is taken for granted. Finally, Stage 5 occurs with the widespread appearance of cable TV and VCR ownership. At this stage there is much more individual control of TV, in terms of both "time shifting" and abundant selection of programming. Marketing is increasingly done to homogeneous segments, not to the mass audience.

Although Stages 1–3 no longer exist in developed countries, at least Stages 2 and 3 are still present in more isolated sections of Third World nations.

---

a TV set is on in U.S. households over 7 hours each day (over 8 hours for homes with cable and subscription services), with the typical adult or child watching 2–3 hours per day, more time than they spend on any other activity except working and sleeping (Kubey & Csikszentmihalyi, 1990). The average child has spent over 2 years of his or her life watching television by age 18 (Hearold, 1986). He or she also sees over 9,000 scenes of suggested sexual intercourse or innuendo on prime-time TV each year (National Federation of Decency report, in Liebert & Sprafkin, 1988). In 1985 the National Coalition on TV Violence reported that the average U.S. child would see 50,000 attempted murders on TV by age 16 (Van Evra, 1990), still years away from being old enough to vote or legally drink beer. Frequently an infant's first coherent sentence will be an advertising jingle learned from television.

Group Differences. The amount of television viewing changes through the life span. It rises sharply between ages 2 and 4, from about 15 minutes to 2.5 hours per day. It then levels off until about age 8, rising again to a peak of around 4 hours a day by age 12 (Liebert & Sprafkin, 1988). It then starts to fall, especially during the high school and college years and young adulthood, when people are busy with dating, studying, and rearing young children. There is another rise, however, in older adult years after one's children are grown. In fact, the elderly are some of the heaviest viewers of television (Condry, 1989). Other relatively heavy viewing groups are women, poor people, and African Americans

(Condry, 1989). It is interesting that many of the groups that watch the most television are the same groups that are the most underrepresented in TV programming, whose characters are disproportionately middle class, White, male, professional, and affluent. We return to this issue in chapter 3.

Time-of-Day Differences. Television viewing also changes sharply throughout the day. Typically the largest audience in the United States is in the "primetime" hours of 8–11 p.m. Eastern and Pacific time (7–10 p.m. Central and Mountain). These are the hours of highest advertising costs and greatest investment in programming efforts. The most obvious pinnacle of such efforts may be seen in the prime-time "sweeps" weeks in February, May, and November, where Nielsen audience size over a 4-week span is used to calculate advertising charges for the next several months. These are the weeks when the networks outdo themselves presenting blockbuster movies, specials, and landmark episodes of top-rated series.

Other Media

Radio. The other major electronic medium, radio, rapidly permeated society in the 1920s much as television did 30 years later. The current TV pattern of entertainment programming was borrowed from radio, which reorganized into a primarily music-and-news format in the 1950s following the advent of TV. Radio is highly age- and interest-segmented (top 40, classical, country, easy listening, album rock). Demographically, it is little used until pre-adolescence but then becomes a central part of adolescent and young adult culture. It is also extremely important in isolated, nonliterate societies, because it depends neither on literacy nor on the relatively expensive purchase of a television set.

Newspapers. In terms of numbers of dailies, newspapers are in decline, although total readership is probably more stable. In large markets, morning papers are dominant, but afternoon papers are the rule in suburban areas and small cities. More than television or magazines, newspapers have a local identity and are the preeminent source for local news and gossip. In the United States, newspapers are almost totally regional, with the exception of *USA Today*, although large national papers are the rule in many nations (e.g., *Guardian* in the United Kingdom, *Le Monde* in France). In spite of the regional character, newspapers are becoming increasingly similar due not only to purchases by conglomerate corporations, but also due to increasing reliance on a few international wire services as news sources (especially Associated Press [AP] and Reuters).

Demographically, the sports section is the most read, and heavy readers are generally those groups who are light TV viewers: they are older, White, better educated, and have higher socioeconomic status. A newspaper reader is generally engaged in many other activities and likes to keep up on the news. He or she is more likely than a nonreader to also watch TV news; it is probably not the case that the increasing use of TV news has been at the expense of newspapers. Those who consume news usually use both sources; those who do not read newspapers do not watch TV news either (Bogart, 1981; Stone, 1987).

Magazines. These are the most narrowly targeted of all the media, having become increasingly so after an earlier period of popular general magazines (*Life, Look, Saturday Evening Post*) ended in the 1960s. They combine the permanence and opportunity for greater depth of newspapers with the photographic appeal of television. Reading magazines is primarily an adult activity, but there are children's magazines (*Boys Life* and *National Geographic World*) that are useful in enticing children toward reading and print media. At least for girls, certain magazines (*Seventeen* and later *Glamour*) are part of the female adolescent experience.

Other Media. Not everyone agrees on what other media, if any, are included in mass communication. For example, there is increasing use of personal media (Ganley, 1992)—such as VCRs (see Box 1.4), computer networks, and fax machines—in ways that have many characteristics of mass communication. Movies have a similar role in mass communication in popular culture (Jowett & Linton, 1989), especially now that the technology of the VCR allows them to be viewed on television. Although we make occasional reference to film and personal media, they are not emphasized in this book. However, readers should bear in mind that they function like mass media in some ways.

OVERVIEW OF THE BOOK

This chapter introduces mass communication from a psychological perspective. The next chapter explores in some depth the different theoretical bases of studying mass communication, drawing on models from communication, psychology, sociology, and other fields. Chapters 3–11 are topically organized to explore several different content areas. Because of both the greater amount of time spent watching television and the greater amount of research on that medium, it receives the major, though not exclusive, focus in the book.

Chapter 3 explores the issue of group portrayals in the media. The emphasis here is on how media portray various groups of people and what the effects of such presentations are. We see that media's portrayal of groups may become a stereotyped reality in the minds of the public, especially in cases where the viewer has limited real-life contact with members of that particular group. Two groups examined are men and women. Are they portrayed in stereotyped fashion? What are the effects of such portrayals on the socialization process of

BOX 1.4: STUDYING THE VCR REVOLUTION

One of the major video revolutions of recent years has been the rapid growth of the VCR industry and the near-record-time penetration of this appliance into homes. Starting from the slow introduction of $2,000-plus machines by Sony into the U.S. market in 1975 (5 years later less than 1% of U.S. homes owned a VCR), growth took off in the early 1980s, until 64% of U.S. homes owned one by 1989 (Andreasen, 1990). Today many shows are routinely recorded for later viewing (time shifting), with the most-recorded genre of TV shows being soap operas, which the VCR has now opened to viewing by those who work regular hours (Hickey, 1988).

Although bitterly opposed to videotaping at first, Hollywood studios have now joined forces to forge a very symbiotic and lucrative relationship between movies and VCRs. Videocassette sales and rentals have helped to bring additional income and interest to the movie industry, making 1984 and several later years the biggest-grossing years ever for the major studios. The widespread renting of movies on cassettes has raised some new ethical and legal issues. Although the U.S. film rating system (G, PG, PG–13, R, NC–17) can have some force in theaters, it has very little in rental stores, where 13-year-olds generally have no trouble renting an R-rated movie. More recently, increasing numbers of films are being produced solely for cassette distribution, bypassing both theaters and the need to have a rating.

One segment of television still distressed by VCRs is advertising. The capability of time shifting by taping TV shows and watching them later while zipping through the ads has encouraged a new creativity in the ad industry, in an attempt to produce ads that viewers will be reluctant to fast forward by (Harvey & Rothe, 1986; Yorke & Kitchen, 1985). There are also increasing attempts to create ads in which highlights can be noticed while fast forwarding (Freedman, 1988).

Because of the relative newness of widespread VCR ownership and use, there has been relatively little empirical research on VCR use (see Levy, 1987, for a discussion of the issues). There have been a few studies of VCR use in the uses-and-gratifications and cultivation-theory traditions discussed in the next chapter (Dobrow, 1990; Gunter & Levy, 1987; Levy, 1980; Lindlof & Shatzer, 1990; Williams, Phillips, & Lum, 1985).

children? Also examined are African Americans, the portrayals of whom have been more carefully studied than any other group in the history of TV. The portrayals of Hispanics, Native Americans, Asian Americans, Arabs, the elderly, and occupational groups are also examined. What are the effects of unrealistic or even nonexistent portrayals on the public's perception of these groups?

Chapter 4 examines the world as created by advertising. We view advertising as a type of information to be processed, one very important way that we learn about the world. Techniques of persuasion are examined, focusing on various types of psychological appeals, especially as they involve persuasion through the creation of a new reality that then becomes real for the consumer (e.g., a reality full of danger where one needs to buy locks and weapons, a reality where most people are very thin and suntanned, a reality of status-conscious people that one has to continually impress with one's dress and possessions). The issue of subliminal advertising is also discussed to see if it is possible to unconsciously persuade through subtle messages or embedded sexual implants.

Part of our media-created reality involves values. Chapter 5 looks at values communicated by television and other media and examines how these values affect society. One area of considerable comment and some study is "family values." We examine what this means and how media teach in this area. Then we turn to economic values, and finally to the topic of religion, which, more than sex or other controversial topics, seems to be the most taboo. Contrary to the popular belief that looser moral values and permissiveness are rampantly increasing, we shall see that, although some values are clearly becoming less strict (e.g., profanity, sexual explicitness), others are actually becoming more restrictive (e.g., expression of racism, sexism, or violence toward women). Many traditional values, such as family solidarity, patriotism, and abstinence from drugs, continue to be stressed.

Chapter 6, on sports and media, examines how television not only transmits results and play-by-play of sports contests, but also influences and changes the ways that these sports are played. We look at ways that rules and practices of sports have been changed by the demands of television coverage, and also at the effects of media coverage on the public's interest and tastes in sports. Finally, the psychological fulfillment of viewing sports on television is explored, looking at how media coverage encourages competition, cooperation, gender-role development, hero worship, and violence.

Chapter 7, on news, examines how the media's coverage of news affects our understanding and attitudes about events in the world. This is perhaps the area where people are most likely to believe that media merely reflect and report the reality that is "out there." The argument is made that such is not the case, that in fact news reporting is by no means such a "reality transmission," but is necessarily a somewhat "distorted" interpretation of that reality, based on what is newsworthy more than what is important. Simply by choosing what to cover and what not to cover, media are setting an agenda. This necessarily involves only a partial presentation of reality, but this partial reality becomes the basis of our knowledge about the world, even affecting foreign policy.

Chapter 8 examines ways that a politician can manipulate media coverage to convey his or her intended reality. As practically all of our information about political candidates and officeholders comes through the media, the importance of mass communication in this area can hardly be overstated. Such issues as image building and the necessity of an "electronic personality" are discussed. The impact of televised candidate debates is particularly examined. A final topic in politics and media concerns the appeals and effects of political advertising.

Types of appeals in political advertising and its effects on attitudes and voting behavior are examined.

In chapter 9 we look at television violence, the most heavily researched issue of the book. Different effects of televised and filmed violence are examined, including modelling, catharsis, reinforcement, desensitization, and the cultivation of fear. In addition, we explore different factors that may interact with media violence to enhance or lessen its impact. The question of the effects on children of viewing violence turns out to be more complex than is frequently admitted by partisans on both sides of this controversial issue. The effects are substantial but usually in interaction with other factors.

Chapter 10 examines the character and effects of sexual content in media, focusing both on mainstream media and pornography. The creation and transmission of sexual values through media, as well as the socialization of sexuality, are addressed. Recent research on and concern about effects of sexual violence are considered in some detail, raising the possibility that viewing sexual violence may be more damaging than viewing either sex or violence by itself.

Chapter 11 examines media that are specifically designed to teach skills or persuade people to change attitudes and/or behaviors in a more health- or safety-oriented direction. One section discusses children's prosocial television (e.g., "Sesame Street"), whereas another section focuses on prosocial media targeted at adults. The media's role in social marketing campaigns to increase prosocial behaviors like stopping smoking, exercising more, or wearing seat belts is also considered. Public service announcements (PSAs) and other social marketing uses of media face greater obstacles in many ways than does commercial advertising.

Finally, chapter 12 ties together themes from the entire book and explores how a greater knowledge about media and its impact can help you to gain more from television and other media without having your reality distorted in destructive ways. Comparative studies of different media are examined, as well as some ways that we may influence the media and develop skills for becoming a more critical media user and help mitigate the negative effects of television on our children.

2

RESEARCH AND THEORY IN MASS COMMUNICATION

Q: What was John Hinckley's stated reason for attempting to assassinate U.S. President Ronald Reagan in 1981?

A: He thought that would cement his parasocial relationship with actress Jodie Foster, with whom he was obsessed, although they had never met. (Note: In his trial Hinckley was found not guilty by reason of insanity and was ordered to a psychiatric facility.)

Q: During 5 years of the TV medical drama "Marcus Welby M.D.," how many letters did actor Robert Young receive?

A: Over 200,000, most of them asking for medical advice.

In some sense everyone is a media critic. Far fewer, however, have the answers to the questions and concerns that are so easy to raise. The answers to many questions about the media come from scientific research. The results from such research are cited throughout this book, but in this chapter we look at some of the theoretical frameworks and assumptions behind such research. It is easy to raise concern about violence in the media; it is more difficult to precisely assess the effects of seeing that violence. It is easy to bemoan the lack of family values on TV; it is more difficult to identify exactly what those values are and to understand the relation of television to their formation. Our relationship with the media is so profound precisely because it meets some of our deepest psychological needs and contributes naturally to our ongoing psychological development.

In terms of both the level of public interest and the amount of social science research on media, there is far more study of television than of radio and print media. Many of the psychological issues discussed in this book apply equally well to all media, although most have typically been specifically studied in regard to television. We begin by looking at some general approaches to studying the media scientifically and then move to examining specific theories, drawn from the disciplines of psychology, communication, sociology, and elsewhere. Finally, we return to the construct of perceived reality for a more precise look.

MEDIA RESEARCH FRAMEWORKS

As well as being of great concern to the public, the media are also objects of considerable study among both commercial interests and scientific researchers. There are different perspectives that are used in studying media (see Heath & Bryant, 1992; Lowery & DeFleur, 1983; McGuire, 1985b; Roberts & Maccoby, 1985, for reviews). Much of that research has been done by or for TV networks, publishers, corporations, or ad agencies for commercial purposes. For example, the Nielsen ratings of the television audience (see Box 2.1) or marketing research studying the public's taste in colas is done for the purpose of increasing the profits of a corporation. The other general type of scientific study is usually performed by independent scientists with the goal of explaining the effects of media and studying their role in society and in people's lives (Davis & Baran, 1981; Lazarsfeld, 1941). For example, studies of the effects of media violence or analyses of the allegedly sexist content of ads are generally done with no commercial motivation. It is this noncommercial research that is the primary focus in this book.

We begin by looking at three general ways of focusing on the media. Then we move on to look at specific theories.

Looking at Content

One very straightforward way to study media is to study the content. This is often an important precursor to exposure or effects research. For example, there are studies counting the number of characters of different racial, ethnic, or gender groups in TV shows. If we are going to argue, for example, that television ads or shows are sexist, then we must carefully define what we mean by *sexist* and then study the ads or shows to see if they fit those criteria. Studies of the effects of sex or violence make use of content-analysis studies to provide data on the prevalence of such themes and changing trends over time.

One research approach to examining content is the use of *discourse analyses* from linguistics, anthropology, and text analysis (Van Dijk, 1985a, 1985b). This careful investigation of the messages communicated through media has often been neglected because of the traditionally stronger connection of mass communications research to social, rather than cognitive, psychology. The more cognitive emphasis in this book may help restore some balance here.

BOX 2.1: THOSE ALL-IMPORTANT RATINGS

The Nielsen ratings are the all-important barometers used to measure the audience size for network television programming in the United States. It is on these ratings that programs, careers, and even broad social trends rise and fall. The A. C. Nielsen Company has for many years selected approximately 1,700 American homes to have "Storage Instantaneous Audimeters" hooked up to their TV sets. This machine measures when the set is on and what channel is on and relays this information back to a Nielsen computer. It does not measure who, if anyone, is watching the set, how intently he or she is watching, or what else he or she is doing at the same time. Another sample of homes, frequently changed, keeps weekly diaries of programs watched.

In the late 1980s, the method of data collection of Nielsen ratings began to change dramatically. The advent of the new technology of "people meters" promised to give Nielsen more accurate information on exactly who is watching when the TV is on. The people meter is a remote-control-like device whereby the viewer punches in the exact time of beginning and ending of viewing and information on who is watching. It should provide more accurate information on viewing than merely a global on–off measure. Some questions have been raised, however, as to whether Nielsen families, especially children, are actually entering all of the required information. Some evidence suggests an over-reporting of viewing commercials and an under-reporting of young children's unsupervised viewing.

The Nielsen "ratings" are in fact two types of information. The rating proper is the percentage of the potential audience that is viewing a program (e.g., a rating of 30 reflects that 30% of the homes with TV have that program on). The "share" compares that program's performance with the competition on at the same time. In the United States, commercial programs with much less than a one-quarter share are very ripe candidates for cancellation. Network advertising charges are usually based primarily on the Nielsen ratings and shares measured during the three 4-week "sweeps" periods, usually in February, May, and November.

Advertising charges are based primarily on the number of homes reached by an ad, ranging all the way from very modest charges for a spot on a local late-night show to well over $1 million dollars for a 60-second national spot on the Super Bowl. Charges of over $100,000 for a 30-second prime-time spot are not unusual. The cost for a 30-second spot on the Super Bowl rose from $125,000 in 1975 to $800,000 in 1993 (Lever & Wheeler, 1993). The even more lucrative 15-second spot typically sells for 55%–60% of the 30-second price. Most U.S. networks or TV stations sell around 9.5 minutes of advertising per hour during prime time (8–11 p.m. Eastern time zone) and 16 minutes at other times, with charges per minute typically much higher for the prime-time slots.

The audience is also a factor in terms of advertising costs. An audience of heavily 18- to 49-year-old upper middle-class viewers is worth more to advertisers than one in which the same size consists largely of the elderly, the unemployed, and children. In this sense one of the most successful talk shows on American TV was "Late Night with David Letterman." Some shows can survive with modest Nielsen ratings because of the buying power of their upscale audience.

Looking at Exposure

A second general way to study media is to study the amount of exposure; see Webster and Wakshlag (1985) for a review of methods of measuring exposure. Who reads how many newspapers or watches how much TV and when? Demographic information about different groups of people watching different shows comes from this type of study. This type of information is useful, but purely measuring exposure is a gross measure. Just because the radio or television is on is no assurance that anyone is devoting much attention to it or being affected by it, nor can we conclude that, merely because they are not paying conscious attention to it, that they are unaffected by it. Often people are simultaneously doing something else besides listening to radio or watching TV when it is on. Sometimes they leave the room altogether for some periods, especially during commercials. To understand the cognitive processes involved in experiencing media, it is crucial to take seriously the amount and nature of attention devoted to the medium; we return to this issue later.

Looking for Effects

Probably the most common general perspective in studying the media is a search for the *effects* of exposure to mass communication. In the general public, probably the major concerns about the media center on their effects. The nature of these effects can take different forms.

The crudest form of a theoretical effects model is the *theory of uniform effects*. This model argues that individuals in a mass society perceive messages from media in the same fashion and react to them strongly and very similarly. Media messages are thus "magic bullets" piercing the mind of the populace. Such a model was used after World War I to describe propaganda effects. Lasswell (1927, 1935) suggested the "hypodermic needle" metaphor of media (i.e., that viewers were "injected" with some dubious message that brought out their worst behavior and thoughts). The assumption that media purveyors are evil thought controllers who manipulate a passive and helpless population is no longer a serious theoretical position among communications researchers and is largely seen today only in strident popular media-bashing critics (e.g., Key, 1976, 1978, 1981, 1989; Mankiewicz & Swerdlow, 1978; Winn, 1977).

We still believe that media can have substantial effects, but often they occur only under certain conditions and in less dramatic form than imagined by the most vocal critics. This is a model of *selective effects based on individual differences*. Different people perceive the same message differently and respond to it in varied forms. For example, a violent TV program probably will not incite all of the viewers to go out and commit mayhem, but it may reinforce the already existing violent tendencies of a small sample of the viewers and slightly dull the sensitivities of many others. Certain positive or negative aspects of television may affect exceptional children more than normal children (Sprafkin, Gadow, & Abelman, 1992). A major effort of this type of research has been to discover other interactive variables that mediate or moderate the effects. These may be demographic variables classifying the individual or they may be properties of the message or of the context of its reception. The fact that the effects are not uniform does not denigrate their importance. For example, even an effect on .01% of the viewers of a certain TV program may still impact on 4,000 people out of an audience of 40 million!

In looking for any sort of effects of media exposure, we must also always keep in mind the importance of cumulative exposure. Most media messages or images are seen or heard dozens, if not hundreds or thousands, of times. Such exposure is difficult to simulate in a laboratory setting and difficult to control in a field study.

Behavioral Effects.   There are four general classes of effects that may be measured. Probably the type most people think of first is behavioral effects, where somebody does something after seeing someone else do it in the media; for example, acting violently, buying a product, voting in an election, or laughing in response to a comedy. This is particularly the emphasis of social learning theory (Bandura, 1977; Tan, 1986), discussed later. Although this is in some ways the most obvious type of effect, it is in fact often very difficult to measure and even harder to definitively attribute a causative role to the media. For example, we can know if somebody sees a certain commercial and we can check to see if that person buys that product, but knowing for sure that he or she bought the product because of seeing the ad and not for other unrelated reasons is very difficult to demonstrate. In a case like the deaths of young teenagers playing Russian roulette after watching *The Deer Hunter*, it is very difficult, in either a legal or scientific sense, to demonstrate a cause-and-effect relationship between seeing the movie and a subsequent tragic death.

Attitudinal Effects.   A second general class of effects of media is attitudinal effects. For example, an ad might make you think more highly of some product or candidate; whether this attitude would be followed up in actual buying or voting behavior is another question. For example, U.S. and Japanese moviegoers viewing the film *Roger and Me* showed a more negative attitude toward General Motors in particular and U.S. business in general (Bateman, Sakano, & Fujita, 1992).

Although attitudes consist of an intellectual component (e.g., reasons that you favor one candidate's position over another's), much of the psychological dynamic in attitudes is emotional (e.g., liking one candidate more than another). Sometimes the intellectual and emotional components may be inconsistent with each other, as when most U.S. voters in 1984 disagreed with President Ronald

Reagan's positions on issues but voted for him anyway because they liked him and trusted him.

Positive feelings about products or candidates may be taught through the process of classical conditioning, whereby a conditioned stimulus (a product) is associated with an unconditioned stimulus that naturally elicits some positive response. For example, a beautiful model paired with some product may teach us positive attitudes toward that product by associating the product with the sexy model that naturally elicits a positive response. The precise processes by which this occurs are discussed in more detail in chapter 4.

Media may teach us a whole constellation of attitudes on a given subject. For example, a dramatic TV movie or documentary on AIDS may sensitize people to the problem and make them more sympathetic to AIDS victims. Seeing R-rated slasher movies in which women appear to be sexually aroused by being raped or assaulted may lead viewers to believe that women derive some secret pleasure out of being victims of sexual violence (Donnerstein, Linz, & Penrod, 1987). Attitudes are easier to measure than behaviors and sometimes are of great importance, for they influence behaviors that may follow.

Attitudes may have influence beyond one's opinion on a particular subject. Sets of attitudes may form a sort of mindset through which we view the world. These attitudes color our selection of what we perceive in the world and how we interpret it. The interaction of this knowledge gained from media with our experience in the world can lead to what is called *cultivation* (Gerbner, Gross, Morgan, & Signorielli, 1986; Signorielli & Morgan, 1990). For example, if we accept the cop-show image of large cities being very dangerous places, that knowledge colors our attitudes about cities but also can affect cognitions and behaviors indirectly in ways that are difficult to measure experimentally, although methods have been developed to test such effects.

Cognitive Effects.   The third class of effects is cognitive effects (i.e., changing what we know or think). The most straightforward example here would be learning new information from media (e.g., facts about chimpanzees from a *National Geographic* article). There are other more subtle kinds of cognitive effects, however, that overlap with attitudes. Simply by choosing what news stories to cover, for example, media "set the agenda." By covering presidential primary campaigns much more thoroughly than complex but abstract economic issues like the Third World debt crisis or the shift from domestic to export agriculture, the media are telling us that the political minutiae of all those primaries is very important, whereas the other issues are less significant.

Different media may stimulate different types of cognitive processing. In a fascinating series of studies comparing cognitive effects of radio versus television in telling stories, children produced more original endings for incomplete stories heard on the radio than they did for stories seen and heard on television. This offers some research support for the intuitive claim that radio stimulates the imagination more than TV does. Children remembered verbal information from radio better but visual, action, and overall information better from television (Greenfield & Beagles-Roos, 1988; Greenfield, Farrar, & Beagles-Roos, 1986).

Physiological Effects. The fourth class of effects is probably the least often measured but is being increasingly used; this effect is the physiological changes in our bodies resulting from exposure to the media. For example, sexual arousal resulting from viewing pornography may be measured by heart rate, skin resistance, penile tumescence, or vaginal lubrication (Malamuth & Check, 1980a). Watching a scary movie or an exciting ball game results in physical changes like rapid breathing and heart rate. Even such mundane material as television commercials can induce changes in the heart rate and orienting reflex (Lang, 1990) and the blocking of alpha waves given off by the brain (Reeves et al., 1985). See Zillmann (1991) for a review of the effects of television viewing on physiological arousal.

THEORIES OF MASS COMMUNICATION

Now that we have looked at different media research frameworks and types of effects measured, let us turn to some specific theories that have guided mass communication research.

Social Learning Theory
(Observational Learning, Modelling Theory)

This approach grew out of behaviorist (S–R) psychology and was primarily developed by social psychologist Albert Bandura and his associates in the 1960s (Bandura, 1977; Bandura, Ross, & Ross, 1961, 1963; Bandura & Walters, 1963; Tan, 1986). We learn behaviors from observing others performing those behaviors and subsequently imitating them. The relevance to media appears when the media model becomes a source of observational learning.

For social learning to occur, someone must first be exposed to the media example and must attend to it. Second, he or she must be capable of remembering the behavior and thinking about it ("cognitively rehearsing"). Finally, the person must possess the cognitive ability, motor skill, and motivation to perform the behavior. The motivation would be sustained by some sort of internal or external reinforcement for performing the behavior.

Social learning theory was initially developed in the context of studying the effects of violent media models on behavior (see chapter 9). Although that is clearly the most salient and most studied application, the model has other applications as well, as in the modelling of sexual, prosocial, or purchasing behavior.

Cultivation Theory

This approach looks at the way that extensive exposure to media (especially television) over time gradually shapes our view of the world and social reality. It was initially developed by George Gerbner and his colleagues in the Cultural Indicators research project. See Gerbner, Gross, Morgan, and Signorielli (1986, in press) and Morgan and Signorielli (1990) for overviews of the theory, and Signorielli and Morgan (1990) for a collection of papers using the approach.

One of the major constructs of cultivation theory is *mainstreaming*, the homogenization of people's divergent perceptions of social reality into a convergent "mainstream." This apparently happens through a process of construction, whereby viewers learn "facts" about the real world from observing the world of television. Memory traces from watching TV are stored "relatively automatically" (Shapiro, 1991). We then use this stored information to formulate beliefs about the real world (Hawkins & Pingree, 1990; Hawkins, Pingree, & Adler, 1987; Potter, 1989, 1991a, 1991b). When this constructed world and the real world have a high degree of consistency, *resonance* occurs and the effect is even stronger.

In terms of methodology, cultivation research usually compares heavy and light viewers of television through correlational methods. A typical study finds that the worldview of heavy viewers is more like the world as presented on television. For example, people who watch a lot of violent TV believe the world to be a more violent place ("mean world syndrome") than it really is (Signorielli, 1990). There is also a greater variance of views among the light viewers, suggesting that an effect of watching a lot of TV is to inculcate a sort of middle-of-the-road view. For example, people who watch a lot of TV are less likely to be either extremely liberal or extremely conservative politically, whereas the political views of light viewers run the entire ideological spectrum. Mainstreaming pulls deviants in both directions back to the middle.

The social reality that is cultivated through mainstreaming takes many forms, including understanding of sex roles (Morgan, 1982; Preston, 1990), political attitudes (Gerbner, Gross, Morgan, & Signorielli, 1984; Gerbner et al., 1986; Morgan, 1989), science and scientists (Gerbner, Gross, Morgan, & Signorielli, 1981b), health beliefs and practices (Gerbner, Gross, Morgan, & Signorielli, 1981a), adolescent career choices (Morgan & Gerbner, 1982), and views of the elderly (Gerbner, Gross, Signorielli, & Morgan, 1980) and minorities (Gross, 1984; Volgy & Schwarz, 1980). Cultivation theory has also been applied cross culturally (e.g., Morgan, 1990; Morgan & Shanahan, 1991, 1992).

There is considerable methodological and theoretical study and discussion about the specific nature of the cultivation process. For example, Potter (1991b) argued that the cultivation effect really involves several components, some of which operate differently. Shapiro (1991) looked at the process of the formation of memory traces from television and the later effects on the construction of the worldview. Tamborini and Choi (1990) looked at the frequent failure of non-U.S. data to strongly support cultivation theory and to suggest some reasons for this. Data are still being analyzed from a massive content analysis study of all news and entertainment programming broadcast on all U.S. major networks during 1 week in December 1987 (Morgan, 1990). Cultivation theory generally focuses on the cumulative effect of many repeated images. It is also argued, however, that some images are far more influential than others. For example, Greenberg's (1988) drench hypothesis says that a highly respected popular character like Bill Cosby's Cliff Huxtable can have far more impact than a dozen other African-American sitcom fathers seen and identified with by fewer viewers.

In spite of being very influential, cultivation theory is not without its critics. Several studies show that careful controls of certain other sociodemographic and personality variables tend to reduce or eliminate cultivation effects (Carveth & Alexander, 1985; Doob & Macdonald, 1979; Hawkins & Pingree, 1981; Hirsch, 1980; Hughes, 1980; Perse, 1986; Potter, 1986; Wober, 1986). Secondly, cultivation studies have been criticized on conceptual and methodological grounds, including response biases and problems with the measuring instruments (Hirsch, 1980; Hughes, 1980; Perse, 1986; Potter, 1986, 1993; Schneider, 1987; Schuman & Presser, 1981; Wober, 1978; Wober & Gunter, 1986). There have also been criticisms of some of the assumptions underlying cultivation theory. For example, it seems to assume, without demonstrating, that the messages of TV are essentially uniform (Hawkins & Pingree, 1981) and that viewers accept what they see as perceived reality (Slater & Elliott, 1982). See Rubin, Perse, and Taylor (1988) for a review of the methodological critiques of cultivation theory and Potter (1993) for a review of conceptual critiques.

To deal with some of these concerns, there has recently been some tendency to reinterpret cultivation theory in line with a uses and gratifications approach, stressing the active mental activity of the viewer while watching TV (Levy & Windahl, 1984; Rubin & Perse, 1987; Weaver & Wakshlag, 1986). Whatever cultivation in fact occurs then grows out of the active information processing and the construction of reality performed by the viewer.

Socialization Theories

Taking a similar approach to cultivation theories, various socialization theories (see Heath & Bryant, 1992, for discussion) stress how prolonged exposure to media comes to teach us about the world and our role in it. For example, Meyrowitz (1985; see also Postman, 1982, 1985) argued that children are socialized into the role of adults far earlier in the age of television than had been the case for several hundred years previously. Television is the window through which children learn about the world of adults, which is no longer kept secret from them. The effect of television thus is a homogenization of developmental stages; children become more like adults, and adults become more like children. Similar "blurrings" of the dichotomies of masculinity–femininity and politician–citizen are also posited and attributed to electronic media, with the effects of increasing androgynous behavior and holding political candidates to personal standards.

Another socialization theory focuses on conditions leading to maximal media socialization influence. Van Evra (1990) argued that the cumulative media effects on children are the greatest when the purpose of viewing is diversion and when they perceive the media content to be realistic, perhaps due to a lack of a "critical thinking" mode present during the viewing. Socialization effects are especially strong on frequent viewers who have few information alternatives available. For example, a boy who watches lots of sitcoms for entertainment and perceives as realistic the portrayals of ethnic groups with whom he has little personal contact is likely to be heavily affected.

The media, particularly television, are extremely important socializing agents for national and cultural socialization (Rosengren, 1992). Children's perceived reality about the culture they live in is, in part, a media creation. This socialization role of television may be especially crucial in cases where a child lives in a different culture than he or she was born in. In an interesting study comparing U.S. children and foreign children residing in the United States, Zohoori (1988) found that the foreign children found TV more interesting, spent more time watching it, identified more with TV characters, and used TV more for learning than did their U.S. counterparts. Consistent with cultivation theory, they also expressed stronger beliefs in the social reality portrayed by television (i.e., the perceived reality of TV seemed to them more real, consistent with the fact that they had fewer real personal experiences in that culture on which to draw). There is also evidence that adult immigrants draw heavily on television to learn about the United States, both before and after their arrival (Chaffee, Nass, & Yang, 1990; Littwin, 1988a). See Box 2.2 for some examples of how four very different societies use television as a socializing agent.

Socialization theories discuss the impact of media in very broad strokes. As such, they have been useful in helping us to appreciate the complexity and pervasiveness of media and their effects. They have, however, been criticized for needing greater specificity and more serious consideration of prevailing social and historical trends. See especially Kubey's (1992) critique of Meyrowitz (1985) for a careful development of this sort of argument.

Agenda Setting

This theory, growing out of research on political socialization (Rogers & Dearing, 1988), defines *agenda setting* as the "ability of the mass media to structure audience cognitions and to effect change among existing cognitions" (McCombs

BOX 2.2: TV AS SOCIALIZING AGENT IN FOUR CULTURES

Singapore. One of the emerging East Asian economic powerhouses explicitly uses television to further its social ends. Proud of its peaceful multicultural, multiracial, multireligious society, Singapore censors its television in four areas—racial, religious, moral, and political. No criticism of any race or religion is allowed. No sexual expressions that might offend the Buddhist or Muslim communities are allowed. No religious programming at all is allowed. News of religious or racial strife elsewhere is played down to avoid inflaming latent local grievances. An orderly and harmonious society is deemed to be a higher priority than Western-style press freedoms (Hickey, 1988).

India. One of the most popular programs on Indian television uses the new medium to tell ages-old Hindu stories. "Ramayana" uses live actors to dramatize the ancient Hindu epic of the same name. Devout Hindus place garlands and incense on the TV set every Sunday at 9:30 a.m. when the show comes on (Panitt, 1988). This show is performing an ages-old anthropological function of cultural continuity (Dorris, 1988), whereby each generation participates in the telling and relearning of the archetypal tales of that culture. The only difference is that the modality has changed from oral (or written) to broadcast tradition.

Ivory Coast. The West African nation of Ivory Coast (Côte d'Ivoire) has two government-run TV stations. As well as importing French movies and serials and U.S. programs, Ivorian TV increasingly produces its own programming to meet the unique needs of its developing society, (e.g., documentaries on traditional African life, health documentaries on AIDS, and music videos of local reggae star Alpha Blondy). Although not a large country, Ivory Coast is nonetheless a multilingual nation only superficially unified by the national language of French. To deal with this diversity, the TV broadcasts the first nightly newscast each evening in a different African language each night of the week, followed by a French broadcast. Although most educated Ivorians understand French, the station attempts to reach more than merely the upper socioeconomic status people (AP Wire story, 5/4/87).

Belize. A small (population 150,000), English-speaking Caribbean country on the northeast coast of Central America, Belize had no daily newspapers or television until a local entrepreneur bought a used satellite dish antenna in 1981, set it up in his backyard, and began selling retransmissions of his pirated signals from Chicago television. Some favorite shows were U.S. sitcoms and Chicago Cubs baseball games. Radio, which was listened to by 95% of the population, aired news mostly from the BBC, *Newsweek*, and the Voice of America. There were seven small weekly newspapers, with mostly local news. Almost all of the media content was foreign, especially from the United States (Snyder, Roser, & Chaffee, 1991).

& Gilbert, 1986, p. 4) or, more intuitively, "creation of public awareness and concern of salient issues by the news media" (Heath & Bryant, 1992, p. 279). The media do not necessarily tell us what to think, but rather what to think about. For example, through heavy coverage in a political campaign, media may tell us that marital infidelity of candidates and whether they smoked marijuana in college are important issues on which to base our vote. Other issues covered in less depth, such as their positions on dealing with the federal deficit, are thus seen to be less important. See chapters 7 and 8 for further discussion of agenda setting in regard to news, and McCombs and Shaw (1993); Rogers, Dearing, and Bregman (1993); and Kosicki (1993) for recent theoretical conceptualizations.

Although it has been explored more fully in regard to news and politics, agenda setting is also relevant to other issues. For example, in its basic ignoring of religion, mainstream television in the United States is sending a message that it is not an important factor in people's lives. Soap operas and dramas that continually show characters engaging in presumably unprotected casual sex without regard to the consequences like HIV infection or pregnancy are subtly telling us that those concerns are not important.

Uses and Gratifications Theory

The uses and gratifications approach places much more emphasis on the active role of the audience in making choices and being goal directed in their media-use behavior (Blumler, 1979; Blumler & Katz, 1974; Boeckmann & Hipfl, 1987; Palmgreen, 1984; Rosengren, Wenner, & Palmgreen, 1985; Rubin, 1986, in press; Rubin & Windahl, 1986). The experience and effects of media depend in part on the uses one is putting those media to and the gratifications one is receiving from them. For example, watching a horror film will be very different to one who is experiencing much empathy with the victim than to one who is being superficially entertained by the suspense of the plot. Watching CNN "Headline News" or reading *USA Today* may be a very different experience for someone trying to be entertained and someone trying to be seriously informed on the details of a political candidate's positions.

Although the motivations to be entertained and to be informed are perhaps the most obvious reasons for media use, they are not the only ones. Television is often turned on more for company than for any other reason. With radio, this is an even more common reason. People are often home alone and want somebody to listen to, even if not to talk to. We think of Bryant Gumbel and Katie Couric more as our breakfast companions than as news spokespersons. Dan Rather or Peter Jennings are regular dinner guests, not merely people who read the news. It is not unusual for people to respond audibly to a greeting from the tube, as in responding "Hi, Tom" to news anchor Tom Brokaw's greeting to start the evening news.

A feeling of connectedness with entertainment series characters may be even stronger; when Gary Shepard on "thirtysomething" was suddenly killed in a car accident in early 1991, the show's faithful viewers felt a genuine emptiness and loss. Such *parasocial relationships* (Rubin & McHugh, 1987; Rubin, Perse, & Powell, 1985) have many of the characteristics of real interpersonal relationships (Perse & Rubin, 1989) and are one of the best predictors of television viewing motivation and behavior (Conway & Rubin, 1991).

We may watch television for many other reasons as well. Perhaps it is to avoid studying or some other activity. Perhaps it is to escape into a fantasy world or be turned on by a particular sexy star. Maybe it is to find out what "everybody's talking about" on some popular show. Maybe it is to conform to others who are watching. Sometimes we will watch a program we strongly dislike simply to have some conversation and make us feel less alone. For most solo drivers, the radio is a constant traveling companion. Fenigstein and Heyduk (1983) argued that most of the research about television has focused primarily on the effects of TV and much less on the attraction of TV. What draws different people to consume different types of media may be a critical issue; for example, factors that cause some people to watch violent pornography. See McGuire (1974), Rubin (1981, 1984, in press), and Conway and Rubin (1991) for discussions of psychological motives in uses and gratifications research.

The relationship of media use to mood and personality variables also bears on the issue of reasons for media use. For example, does heavy TV viewing cause one to be an escapist, or do factors of temperament and personality cause one to seek escape through heavy TV viewing? Kubey (1986) investigated this issue and concluded that heavy TV viewing is more likely an effect rather than a cause of mood and personality factors. We have uncomfortable and unpleasant feelings and seek an escape from these through television.

Schema Theory

An important general cognitive principle is that information processing is constructive; that is, people do not literally store and retrieve information they read or hear in the media (or anywhere else). Rather, they modify it in accordance with their beliefs and the context in which it is received. The way we comprehend a program we watch on TV is through a constant interaction of the content of the program and the knowledge already in our minds. The mind thinks in response to what we see and those thoughts become an important part of the constructive process of comprehension (Hoijer, 1989).

Part of what guides the comprehension and any later memory of the information are *schemas* (Brewer & Nakamura, 1984; Rumelhart, 1980; Thorndyke, 1984). The concept of schema refers to knowledge structures or frameworks that organize an individual's memory for people and events. The schema is a general construct that acts on all forms of information, irrespective of the mode—

visual or auditory, linguistic or nonlinguistic—to which it is exposed. A person holds mental schemas based on past experiences. One consequence of this for information processing is that the individual is likely to go beyond the information actually presented to draw inferences about people or events that are congruent with previously formed schemas (Graesser & Bower, 1990; Harris, 1981; Rojahn & Pettigrew, 1992; Singer, 1984). For example, someone with a very negative schema about Mexican Americans might respond very differently to a new TV show set in Chicano East Los Angeles than would someone without those prejudices. Much of the content in schemas is typically culturally specific. The schema that members of one culture may hold may cause them to interpret the same story very differently than members of a different culture (Harris, Schoen, & Hensley, 1992; Lasisi & Onyehalu, 1992). Cultural differences must be carefully considered by TV producers in international programming sales (see Box 2.3).

In mass media, activation of a schema in the mind of the audience member may be triggered by some particular information in the program or article. It may also be triggered by the content of certain formal features of the particular medium; for example, flashbacks, montage, or instant replays. Young children do not understand these conventions and will interpret the input literally (e.g., taking a flashback or instant replay to be continuing new action). Part of the socialization to the use of a medium like television is to learn these formal features and how to interpret them (Abelman, 1989; Calvert, 1988; Condry, 1989; Huston & Wright, 1987; Kraft, Cantor, & Gottdiener, 1991; Lang, Geiger, Strickwerda, & Sumner, 1993; Rice, Huston, & Wright, 1986; Smith, Anderson, & Fischer, 1985; Wilson, 1991).

Scripts. Borrowing a concept from computer science and experimental psychology (Bower, Black, & Turner, 1979; Fayol & Monteil, 1988; Schank & Abelson, 1977), we may speak of learning scripts from television (Janis, 1980; Luke, 1987). *Script* here refers to a schema about an activity and is *not* the same as the meaning of pages of dialogue. For example, when we watch a TV drama about a woman who discovers she has breast cancer, we may acquire a script for dealing with that particular situation. The viewer may learn specific activities like breast self-examination, how to tell her husband about her illness, how to seek out information about possible treatments, and how to cope with a mastectomy in terms of her own self-image and sexuality.

Scripts are acquired from the media, among other sources. Through exposure to samples of activities following some script, that abstract script is inferred and gradually becomes a part of our permanent memory (Ahn, Brewer, & Mooney, 1992). This skeleton structure of some activity is then used to interpret future instances of that activity.

The potential consequences of learning scripts from media becomes especially clear when we consider a situation for which readers have little prior

BOX 2.3: AMERICAN TELEVISION IMPERIALISM: FACT OR FICTION?

The rapid diffusion of American movies and television throughout the world in the last few decades has been well documented (Lee, 1980; Read, 1976; Tunstall, 1977). Although the United States is the world's largest exporter of television programming ($1 billion a year, 75% of worldwide revenues [Bernstein, 1990; Mele, 1987]), whether those media completely dominate local sources is considerably more questionable. Recent studies (Cantor & Cantor, 1986; Schement, Gonzalez, Lum, & Valencia, 1984) suggest that no country is able to dominate media today, if indeed this was ever possible.

The United States itself is a market as well as a producer. Cities with large Hispanic populations receive channels from the Spanish International Network (SIN), which is a satellite export from Mexico. Mexico's Televisa earned $4 million in 1986 exporting its soap operas, 70% of the sales going to the United States (Michaels, 1988). British television, notably the BBC and Granada TV, have exported programs to America's PBS for years.

The four largest networks in the world (CBS, NBC, and ABC in the United States and TV Globo in Brazil) export their programs to dozens of other nations. Millions of people around the world may know virtually nothing about the United States besides what they see on such programs as "L.A. Law." Conversely, many Americans' impressions of British people is unduly colored by televised imports like "Masterpiece Theatre" or "Fawlty Towers" on PBS. Mexican television programs from the Televisa network are seen throughout Spanish-speaking Latin America and the United States, as well as in Spain. How we learn about other groups of people from media is the subject of chapter 3.

Some countries, like Japan, Mexico, and Brazil, formerly imported much more American TV than they do today, with most of their programming now being locally produced. Indeed some foreign producers are major exporters. Brazil's TV Globo, for example, earned $12 million in profits in 1987 selling its popular soap operas (novelas) throughout Latin America and Europe, in spite of the fact that they are produced in Portuguese, which is spoken in few other places (Michaels, 1988). Sometimes the television empires fall along linguistic lines. For example, Francophone Africa and French Canada generally buy television from France. American and other non-French sources typically must go through Paris to dub their programs in French before selling to French-speaking markets.

knowledge or scripts. For example, suppose a child's knowledge of dealing with muggers has resulted from watching TV adventure heroes trick and overpower the robber. If that child were to try that script on a real mugger by attempting the same moves as seen on TV, he or she might be considerably less successful than, for example, MacGyver would be. For another example, consider a TV movie dealing with incest. A preteen in the story is being sexually molested by her father and is sufficiently troubled to mention this to a school counselor, a revelation that sets in motion a sequence of events that eventually, but necessarily, brings this event "out of the closet." Because this subject has been so taboo until quite recently, most viewers, including those who are currently or were formerly victims of incest, may have no mental script for how to handle it. In this sense, such a movie, if done sensitively yet realistically, could help such people come forth and seek help. It could provide information on how one may expect to feel about that experience, where to seek help, and, through the context of the drama, could offer a scenario of what the effects of such a revelation might be.

In a more general sense, media fiction may use very abstract scripts such as "overcoming adversity." This implicit knowledge may be reflected in a story about a slave escaping from servitude in the antebellum South, a child learning to cope with alcoholic parents, or a burned-out police officer coming to terms with a vicious crime syndicate (Janis, 1980). The same script is used in many human interest news stories, such as the North Dakota teenager John Thompson whose arms were severed in an agricultural accident and later reattached. News consumers were regularly kept apprised of his progress for several weeks.

Biocca (1991) combined cognitive schema theory with some notions from the semiotic study of language (Biocca, 1990) to develop a model of how TV viewers "model the flow of information and imagery" (Biocca, 1991, p. 81) as they watch. These processes include the basic understanding and organizing of information and the drawing of further inferences. Also, one infers about ideologies represented by the program and how it all relates to the self as viewer. The schemas and constructed interpretations are both constantly changing.

The Narrative Script.   There is also a very general script/schema for stories in Western culture (Kintsch, 1977). This "narrative script" is learned implicitly from the earliest days of young children hearing stories from their parents. Such stories are composed of episodes, each of which contains an exposition, complication, and resolution. That is, the characters and setting are introduced (exposition), some problem or obstacle develops (complication), and that problem or obstacle is somehow overcome (resolution). We grow up expecting stories to follow this general script. Children's stories (e.g., fairy tales) do so very explicitly ("Once upon a time there was a . . ."). Adult stories also follow the script but often in a more complex fashion. For example, some of the complication may be introduced before all of the exposition is finished or there may be two subepisodes embedded in the resolution of a larger episode.

Television and print media fiction also draw on the narrative script to make their stories more readily understandable. Children's cartoons follow the script very explicitly. Most TV sitcoms and action-adventure shows do so as well, although perhaps in a bit more complicated fashion; for example, two interwoven episodes (subplots), each with its own narrative structure. The use of schemas enhances our information-processing capabilities. Meadowcroft and Reeves (1989) found that children had well-developed story schema skills by age 7, and that such skills led to better memory for central story content, a reduction in processing effort, and a greater flexibility of attention-allocation strategies.

Soap operas traditionally hold an audience by concluding each day's story just before the resolution. Because we have this sense of our narrative script being incomplete, we return the next day or the next week to complete it. This was used in some of the most spectacularly successful marketing techniques in the history of prime-time TV. The producers of "Dallas" left viewers hanging a whole season to find out "Who shot J.R.?" in the early 1980s. "Cheers" viewers waited a whole summer to find out if Sam and Diane would actually get married. Prime-time soaps, as well as ensemble drama shows like "L.A. Law," often leave critical complications unresolved at the end of the week's show.

Even many ads draw upon the narrative script. For example, a nice young fellow is ready to go out on a hot date (exposition), but alas, he has "ring around the collar" (complication). But his mom and her amazing detergent come to the rescue to wash the shirt in time (resolution). Because of our familiarity with the narrative script, we are able to comprehend such a commercial readily, which is of course to the advertiser's advantage. Also, because it fits the story structure of many programs, it seems more entertaining and is thus more likely than a traditional sales pitch to hold viewers' attention. The narrative script is a deeply ingrained knowledge structure; Esslin (1982) went so far as to argue that the 30-second story of an unhappy hemorrhoid sufferer has the same dramatic structure as classic Greek tragedy!

Now that we have examined some major theories of mass communication, let us turn to some additional psychological problems and issues that must be considered in any comprehensive and ultimately correct mass communication theory.

OTHER PSYCHOLOGICAL ASPECTS OF MEDIA

Attention

The nature of mass communication, especially electronic media, is such that we typically must select some information to attend to and process and neglect other information (Zillmann & Bryant, 1983). Although there are many ways, some very sophisticated, of measuring exposure to media (von Feilitzen, Strand, Nowak, & Andren, 1989; Webster & Wakshlag, 1983), attention must also be paid to what is being cognitively processed from those media. It is simplistic to assume either that viewers are fully processing everything that they hear on radio or TV or that it is not affecting them at all if they are not paying full conscious attention. The issue is also relevant to print media. For example, how much do we process the typical newspaper ad as we read through the paper?

Merely measuring when the television is on is not really enough to tell us how much is being understood or what influence it is having. A big question in the study of television is how much attention viewers are paying to the tube at any given time it is on. Clearly the TV is often on when it is receiving less than total undivided attention. Research studying videotapes of people watching television show that the typical older child or adult attends to the TV about 70% of the time it is on (Anderson, 1985; Anderson & Burns, 1991; Anderson & Field, 1991), depending on the time of day and the program. For example, early morning news shows receive less attention and weekend shows such as sports and children's cartoons receive more attention. Children initially allocate more attention to a difficult segment but quickly fall in attention invested if the material is beyond their level of comprehensibility (Hawkins, Kim, & Pingree, 1991). Both structure and content factors help determine amount of attention allocated (Geiger & Reeves, 1993a, 1993b). Sometimes we may not be looking at the screen very much but may nonetheless be monitoring the sound for items of interest and can redirect our vision toward the screen if necessary.

Emotion

What Is Emotion?   We can't observe emotions directly; we do not see anger or hear happiness. We see violent behavior and feel anger; we hear laughter and feel happiness. Emotions themselves are internal states and must be inferred from behavior. Sometimes such inferences are unwarranted. We may see someone crying over a TV movie and infer that they feel sad, when in fact they might be crying for joy, or for that matter, they might have an allergic condition where the crying does not reflect emotion at all.

Emotions are an integral part of the appreciation of media, especially television; most notably sports, action-adventure shows, soap operas, game shows, and comedies. What we feel while watching these shows is a central part of the whole psychological experience. If the emotional aspect is absent, we seem to be missing an important part of the experience. Consider the unsatisfying experience of watching a ball game between two teams when you could not care less who wins.

There are two components of emotion: the physiological and the cognitive. When we are aroused, there are certain changes in our bodies, such as increased heart rate, sweating, and change in skin resistance (GSR). We also *think* about our feelings and attribute causes and interpretations to them. For example, if you feel very "hyped up" just after being offered a new job, you would interpret the same state of bodily arousal differently than you would if you had just consumed 10 cups of coffee or had just escaped from the clutches of a crazed killer. Thus the emotions we feel are a product of both our bodily state and our cognitive interpretation of that state (Schachter & Singer, 1962; Zillmann, 1983, 1991a).

Media as Vicarious Emotional Experience. Watching a crime show on TV allows us to experience some of the emotion felt by the characters without putting ourselves in any physical danger. Thus we can become aroused safely through this vicarious experience. This allows us to focus on the excitement of a police show or the humor of a sitcom. If we actually experienced those situations in real life, the danger or embarrassment might overpower the positive aspects and they would not be nearly as much fun as they are on TV (Tannenbaum, 1980).

Other types of emotions are enjoyable to experience vicariously. Many comedies show people in embarrassing situations that are more humorous when happening to someone else. TV characters may do things we would like to do but have moral or ethical proscriptions against. We can, however, with a clear conscience, watch them have extramarital affairs, verbally insult their boss, or drive recklessly. One type of programming where participants are particularly encouraged to be highly expressive emotionally is the game show; see Box 2.4

BOX 2.4: GAME SHOWS AROUND THE WORLD

One type of TV show where emotion is often expressed far more freely, even excessively, than in real life, is the game show. These range from the popular "Wheel of Fortune" to the sleazy "The Newlywed Game" to the quasi-intellectual "Jeopardy." Although a majority of quiz shows worldwide are American or American inspired, each nation has its own domestic offerings of this genre.

U.S. shows by no means have a monopoly on bad taste. One French show had contestants take off an article of clothing for each question answered correctly, down to their underwear. Another Gallic effort had blindfolded couples identify their partner from a nearly naked group of people. The Philippines held a "grandmother Madonna" competition, where elderly women dressed like the singer Madonna and danced to the song "Like a Virgin." On the Australian "Newlywed Game," husbands estimated their wives' chest size. Perhaps the most outrageous of all is Japan's "Ultra Quiz," where losing contestants faced punishments like fighting off 25 pounds of bees dumped on them, washing dishes in the kitchen of a cruise ship, or being left alone on a high butte in the Utah desert.

Some game shows are a bit more sedate, even if not exactly uplifting. Muslim Saudi Arabia's "In the Shadow of the Koran" gave cash prizes to young boys reciting long passages from the Koran. Malaysia used to have a show where contestants composed rhymes on a given topic of national social importance, like family planning or good nutrition. Dominican Republic TV held a contest open only to the poor with a prize of a new house. Britain's "Treasure Hunt" had contestants decipher clues and thus direct a helicopter to find the hidden treasure. In the Russian "Let's Go Girls!" attractive young women competed at question-answering, vacuum-cleaning, cow-milking, and rolling the thinnest dough (Kalter, 1987b).

for some examples of game shows around the world that allow vicarious expression of emotions.

Occasionally a particular live media event is so emotionally compelling as to make a lasting impact. When the U.S. space shuttle Challenger exploded in January 1986, this event was seen live at the time on TV or later that day by 95% of the population of the country (Wright, Kunkel, Pinon, & Huston, 1989). In a study of the reactions of school children to the event, Wright et al. found strong evidence of emotion evoked by the tragedy, especially among girls, reflecting the gender stereotyping of girls admitting to feeling more emotion.

Emotional Expression and Media.   Mainstream North American and Northern European societies often discourage direct expression of emotions. Television, however, sets some new rules with greater flexibility. It is more acceptable to yell and shake your fist at a referee in a ball game on TV than to do the same at your boss. Although sports is probably the only arena where adult men may show physical affection toward other men without intimations of homosexuality, some of the same license is transferred to viewing sports on television. Thus, two men may playfully slap each other or even embrace after watching a spectacular play in a televised ball game.

The social situation of watching TV also makes a difference in our cognitions and experience. Watching a ball game or scary movie might be very different by yourself versus at a party with friends. There might be more expression of emotion in the group. The scary movie might be scarier alone and funnier with the group. Even though the stimulus of the TV show is the same in both cases, the experience of it, especially in terms of emotion, may be quite different. The social experience of teenagers going to a horror film together is often very different than one might predict purely from considering the content of the film; for example, laughing at graphic horror (Oliver, 1993; Tamborini, 1991; Zillmann, Weaver, Mundorf, & Aust, 1986).

Children may learn from TV, helpfully or otherwise, how to deal with emotions they feel in various situations. Young children learning to play tennis may curse and throw their racquets in imitation of John McEnroe, whose antics on the court are carried on TV as a model for dealing with frustration in sports. In an even more serious case, if TV regularly portrays men who feel frustrated with women as expressing such feelings through violence (battering or rape), children may learn that these antisocial ways of dealing with those feelings are acceptable.

Suspending Disbelief

Like movies or theater, television involves the social convention of the *suspension of disbelief*, "for a brief time accept the characters we see . . . as real human beings so that we can identify with them to experience their joys and sorrows" (Esslin, 1982, p. 33). We know that actors Roseanne Arnold and John Goodman are not really married to each other but we agree to suspend our disbelief of that and accept them as Mr. and Mrs. Connor when we watch "Roseanne." Because of the continuing nature of a television series (often several years for a successful show), this suspension of disbelief is a far more enduring fantasy than it is for a 2-hour movie or play. Producers in the early days of television may have doubted the ability of the public to suspend that much disbelief. Many of the early series featured real-life spouses playing TV partners (Lucille Ball and Desi Arnaz, George Burns and Gracie Allen, Jack Benny and Mary Livingston, Ozzie and Harriet Nelson). This phenomenon has been rare since the 1950s, however.

Sometimes disbelief is suspended so long that the fantasy–reality distinction becomes blurred. Young children clearly have difficulty understanding the difference between actors and the characters they portray (Dorr, 1980). This problem is not limited to children, however. As any series actor knows, adult fans frequently ask an actor playing a doctor for medical advice or hurl epithets at an actress playing a villain on a soap opera. Such fantasies are covertly encouraged by spinoff series, where the same character moves from one series to another (e.g., George and Louise Jefferson originally were supporting characters on "All in the Family"). Children's cartoon or puppet characters like Mickey Mouse, Big Bird, or Pinocchio may reappear in commercials, toys, and kid's meals at restaurants, all of which support a belief in their reality apart from the show.

Sometimes television may provide such a salient exemplar of an unpleasant reality that it is difficult to maintain reality in suspension. Box 2.5 explores the feared and actual effects of a much-hyped TV movie on nuclear war.

Identification

The emotional involvement that we have watching a TV show will depend in part on how much we *identify* with the character (i.e., mentally compare ourselves to and imagine ourselves like that character). It is easier to identify with characters with whom we have more experience in common, although that is not a prerequisite for identification. There is a certain universality in most good drama. For example, a huge number of Americans, none of whom had ever been in slavery and most of whom were White, were moved by the landmark miniseries "Roots" in the late 1970s. Apparently the basic humanity of the characters was portrayed so well that viewers could identify emotionally with the characters at some level without having experienced similar situations themselves. The perceived reality of media is greater if our identification with the characters is such that they become significant persons in our own lives (Potter, 1988).

BOX 2.5: NUCLEAR WAR ON TV

One of the most hyped television events of all time was the 1983 ABC TV movie *The Day After* (TDA), the drama of the aftermath of a nuclear attack on the American Midwest. Its anticipation became such a media event in itself that competing CBS' "60 Minutes" took the unprecedented step of covering TDA hype as one of its feature stories 1 hour before the movie's airing. It also became a political event. Antinuclear groups encouraged people to watch it, whereas conservatives decried it as an unfair move in the battle to mold public opinion on arms control issues. Mental health professionals worried over its impact on impressionable young minds and warned people to watch it only in groups and to not allow young children to see it at all. All of the heavy media coverage of course insured a large audience, which numbered over 100 million viewers, the largest to date for a TV movie.

Psychologists Janet Scholfield and Mark Pavelchak (1985) decided to study exactly what impact this controversial film's airing had actually had. Contrary to some fears or hopes, the movie actually did little to change attitudes about arms control and related issues. Arguments such as the possible failure of a deterrence through strength policy had been widely discussed in the media and were not really new ideas to most viewers. Many viewers reacted that, horrible as it was, TDA's portrayal of the effects of a nuclear attack was actually milder than hype-weary viewers expected and in fact was somewhat akin to many disaster and horror movies. The movie did have its effects, however. Viewers were more likely to seek information about nuclear issues and become involved in disarmament activities, and they reported thinking about nuclear war twice as often after seeing the film as they had before.

Empathy

When we have the "ability to understand and feel what another feels" (Myers, 1992, p. 641), we experience empathy. Empathy may be seen as emotional identification, and it is a very important factor in the enjoyment of media. We enjoy a comedy more if we can feel something of what the characters feel. We enjoy a ball game more if we have played it ourselves and can relate to the tense feelings of being at bat with two outs in the bottom of the ninth and our team down by one run.

In the case of media (Zillmann, 1991b), empathy is diminished somewhat by the relatively omniscient position we occupy relative to the characters. We generally know more of what is going on than they do. If we know the final outcome, it is often difficult to become as emotionally involved as if we knew as little as the character. Such enjoyment varies a lot depending on the genre, however. Audiences for reruns of sports events are almost nonexistent, whereas audiences for reruns of comedies and some dramas hold up quite well. Apparently the loyalty to the characters and show and the empathy and degree of parasocial interaction with them are crucial factors (Tannenbaum, 1980).

Empathy is composed of cognitive and emotional components. Cognitive empathy involves the ability to readily take the perspective of another, whereas emotional empathy involves readily responding at a purely affective level. Davis, Hull, Young, and Warren (1987) showed that the level of both of these types of empathy influenced emotional reactions to viewing the films *Brian's Song* and *Who's Afraid of Virginia Woolf?*, but that each type of empathy influenced reactions in different ways.

More recently, empathy has been conceptualized as a three-factor construct (Zillmann, 1991b). One factor may override another that initially predominated. For example, suppose the initial natural, unlearned response to the victim of violence in a news story or cartoon is one of empathy. This may, however, be overridden by a less empathic response to the next news story, commercial, or cartoon action quickly following. Thus what might otherwise elicit considerable empathy does not do so, in part due to the nature of the "sound-bite" nature of the medium of television. This could explain why it is so difficult to become caught up emotionally in a TV movie broken up by commercials.

Another approach, not extensively examined in the research is the extent to which media, especially television, teach empathy to children or could potentially do so were more sensitivity given to such issues by teleplay writers, directors, and networks (Feshbach, 1988).

Suspense

Suspense is usually characterized as "an experience of uncertainty whose . . . properties can vary from noxious to pleasant" (Zillmann, 1991c, p. 281). The suspense we feel in an adventure show or drama is maximal if some negative outcome (hero is about to die) appears to be highly likely but not absolutely certain—everything points to disaster with just a slight hope of escape. If the negative outcome is either not very likely or is absolutely certain, there is not much suspense (Zillmann, 1980, 1991c). We experience a high level of suspense, for example, if our hero appears about to be blown up by a bomb, with just a slight chance to escape. The physiological excitation of suspense is relatively slow to decay and may be transferred to subsequent activities (Zillmann, 1980, 1984, 1991a, 1991c).

Humor

One particular type of emotion that we can feel while consuming media is the enjoyment that comes from experiencing something funny (Brown & Bryant, 1983; Zillmann & Bryant, 1991). But what makes something funny? Why is one line of comedy so hilarious and a very similar one not at all funny, and perhaps even offensive?

Most comedy involves some sort of incongruity, inconsistency, or contradiction, which is finally resolved, as in the punch line of a joke (Long & Graesser, 1988; McGhee, 1979; Suls, 1983; Wyer & Collins, 1992). Neither the incongruity nor resolution by itself is usually very funny. Although the joke "Two elephants got off the bus and left their luggage by the tree" is very incongruous, it is not particularly funny because there is no resolution. Although "Two soldiers got off the bus and left their trunks by the tree" has a resolution, it is not very funny either, because there is no incongruity. Only "Two elephants got off the bus and left their trunks by the tree" has both.

The best jokes offer some intellectual challenge, but not so much that we cannot "get it" or have to work too hard to do so. Some of the most satisfying jokes are very esoteric "in jokes" involving knowledge from a particular group, such as a profession. What is an adequate challenge for one person may not be so for another. For example, many children find certain very predictable, even "dumb," jokes funny, whereas adults do not. They are simply not novel or challenging enough for adults.

Another important concept in understanding media humor is the notion of *catharsis*, the emotional release of tension we feel from expressing some repressed feelings. For example, if you are very worried about some problem but talk to a friend and feel better just for having "gotten it off your chest," what you are experiencing is catharsis. Humor is often seen as a healthy and socially acceptable outlet for dealing with some of our darker feelings. For example, we may be able to deal with some of our own hidden sexual or hostile impulses by listening to a caustic comedian or talk-show host insult people or brazenly ask someone about their first sexual experience. We would never say those things ourselves but might secretly want to; hearing someone else do it partially fulfills our need to do so. Catharsis is often invoked to explain why people appreciate racist, ethnic, sexist, or sexual jokes. It is also frequently put forth as a socially beneficial outcome of consuming sexual or violent media, although research has failed to confirm such a conclusion (see chapters 9 and 10).

Social factors can make a lot of difference in the experience of humor (Apter, 1982). Sometimes the presence of others watching with us enhances our enjoyment, particularly for broader, more raucous humor. Consider watching a film like *Revenge of the Nerds* or *The Rocky Horror Picture Show* on the late show by yourself or in a group. The presence of others may genuinely enhance our enjoyment, or we may outwardly appear to enjoy it more due to peer pressure to conform; if we are in a room full of people laughing uproariously at some TV show, it is hard to avoid at least a few smiles, even if we are not at all amused. This is the principle behind the inclusion of a laugh track on some sitcoms. The person who tells the joke is also an important factor. A joke making fun of

Hispanics may be much funnier and more acceptable if told by a Latino than if told by an Anglo or an African American.

There are individual and cultural differences in appreciation of humor. Some people prefer puns, others prefer physical humor or practical jokes, still others prefer sexual or ethnic jokes. Cultural standards change over time. In the very early days of television (early 1950s), "Amos and Andy" could make fun of African Americans being slow-witted; a few years later Ralph Kramden could playfully threaten his wife with physical violence on "The Honeymooners" and everyone roared with laughter. Now we have the chance to laugh at more sexual innuendo on TV than we could then, but Andy and Ralph somehow do not seem quite so funny.

Different cultures find different themes and approaches funny. In North American society, for example, certain topics are off limits or very touchy, at least for prime-time humor (late-night TV and some specialty cable programs are a little more permissive). Jokes on U.S. TV about racism, feminism, or mainstream religion are risky; such humor does exist but people are likely to take offense and thus producers and comedians are very cautious. A popular Brazilian TV commercial for a department store chain during a recent Christmas season showed the three wise men walking to Bethlehem. Suddenly, to a rock beat, they threw open their ornate robes and started dancing in their pastel underwear, which was on sale at the store. It seems unlikely that such an ad would be aired in the United States.

One function of television humor is as a sort of leavening in the context of a more serious offering. A little so-called "comic relief" in the midst of a serious drama is much appreciated, although if done badly, it runs the risk of being in poor taste and thus offending people. If done well, it can increase motivation and interest and make the characters seem more human. If done too well, it may distract from the major content. This is particularly a concern with commercials. Some of the funniest and more creatively successful TV commercials have not been too effective at selling because the humor overshadowed the commercial message. People remember the gag but forget the product.

MEDIA AS PERCEIVED REALITY

Now that we have examined some of the theories and psychological constructs used in the scientific study of the media, let us return for a more careful look at the theme introduced earlier: the reality created by the media.

The Reflection Myth

Often people think of the media as vehicles for reflecting the world around them. News stories report what happened in the world that day. TV sitcoms reflect the values, lifestyles, and habits of their society. TV dramas and magazine fiction reflect the concerns and issues that viewers are struggling with. The presence of violence and offensive stereotypes merely reflects the ugly reality of an imperfect world. Advertising reflects the needs and wants that we have. Media, in this view, are a sort of window on reality.

This is not the only way to view mass communication, however. It may be that we think certain events and issues are important because the news tells us they are. Sitcoms may portray certain values, lifestyles, and habits that are then adopted by society. TV dramas deal with certain issues that then are considered and dealt with by the viewers. Stereotypes seen on television implicitly teach young viewers what different groups of people are like, and the presence of much violence on TV teaches that the world is a violent place. Advertising convinces us that we have certain needs and wants that we did not know we had before. In this view media are not merely reflecting what is out there in the world. Rather, they are constructing a world that then becomes reality for the consumer. This world may be accepted by TV viewers, who are often unaware of such a process happening, as they feel they are only being entertained. Soon the world as constructed by media may become so implanted in our minds that we cannot distinguish it from reality.

Do the media reflect the world or create a new reality? Certainly media do in many ways reflect what is out there in the world. However, they also choose what to tell us about what is out there in the world and we then accept that interpretation, which then becomes part of our memory and our experience. In this book we examine how television and other media create a world that then becomes our reality. This cognitive perspective focuses on the mental construction of reality that we form as a result of our contact with print and broadcast media. This constructed reality often differs significantly from objective reality in ways that are not always understood. The plan of this book is to examine various content areas from a cognitive psychological perspective, while focusing on the theme of how media create a reality.

The Study of Perceived Reality

Each of the theoretical approaches discussed earlier has something to say about studying the perceived reality that we cognitively construct through interaction with media. For example, agenda setting (McCombs, 1981; Rogers & Dearing, 1988) tells us what is important to think about to begin with. Social learning theory (Bandura, 1977; Tan, 1986) examines how we learn the behavioral component of this reality. Cultivation theory (Gerbner, Gross, Morgan, & Signorielli, 1986; Signorielli & Morgan, 1990) focuses on the construction of a world view. Uses and gratifications (Palmgreen, 1984; Rubin, 1983, 1986; Windahl, 1981) looks at the uses we make of media and the gratifications they give us, increasingly connecting this research to an examination of the effects of media (Rubin, 1986). Socialization theories stress how this knowledge becomes a part of how we learn what it is like to be an adult member of our society. Schema theory looks at the knowledge structures that we create from exposure to the media.

When we speak of the reality perceived from the media, this is actually a more complex concept than it may first appear. At least three components are involved (Potter, 1988). The central factor in perceived reality is what has come to be called *magic window*. This is the belief in the literal reality of media messages. This reality can either be conveyed at the level of style or content. The style of news reporting, for example, may convey a message of factual correctness more strongly than the style of an entertainment program (Altheide, 1976; Lippmann, 1922; Tuchman, 1978). The content of action-adventure shows presenting a world that is very dangerous may cultivate a view that the world is also like that (Gerbner, Gross, Signorielli, & Morgan, 1986; Signorielli, 1990).

A second component of perceived reality is *utility*, which refers to the perceived applicability of the media to one's own life. For example, a viewer with a strong belief that soap operas present very real-life situations would expect more application to their own life than another viewer who feels that soap operas present wildly unrealistic and purely escapist content (Rubin & Perse, 1988). Because of their much lesser degree of life experience, young children often see greater utility than adults do in television content.

The third component of perceived reality is *identity*, the degree to which a viewer feels that a character is active in the viewer's real life. Sometimes a media character becomes a significant person in the viewer's life, constituting a *parasocial relationship* (Levy, 1982; Rubin, Perse, & Powell, 1985). In extreme cases there is a tremendous outpouring of grief for someone people have never met, such as what occurred following the death of ex-Beatle John Lennon in 1980. The character need not even be real. When the network "killed off" Col. Henry Blake of "M*A*S*H" on his way home from Korea, they were deluged with letters from grief-stricken and irate fans who did not appreciate that intrusion of wartime reality in their sitcom. See Potter (1988) for further discussion of the construct of perceived reality.

CONCLUSION

The meaning that something in the media has for us, at either a cognitive or an emotional level, depends on how that information is processed during our experience of interacting with the medium. Each of the theoretical perspectives reviewed in this chapter has something useful to say about the formation of this meaning and its consequences. They should not be seen as mutually exclusive, but are rather, in many ways, complementary. Elements of the different theories are brought in as appropriate in discussion of the topics in the rest of the book.

The media create a reality for us in many different areas, drawing on different psychological processes as they do so. Now we turn to the first set of those perceived realities created by media, namely, our knowledge of what different groups of people are like.

CHAPTER

3

PORTRAYALS OF GROUPS: LEARNING ABOUT PEOPLE

Q: When 293 high school teachers were asked to name any heroic or humane Arab characters they had seen in movies, how many could not think of any?

A: 287 (Shaheen, 1992).

Q: What TV show had the highest audience rating ever in Poland?

A: *Escrava Isaura* (*Slave Girl Isaura*), a Brazilian soap opera set in colonial Brazil (Marquez de Melo, 1991).

What do you know about Mexican Americans? Arabs? Farmers? Aging people? One of the major perceived realities that media help create for us involves information about groups of people. Through TV and other media we are exposed to a much broader range of people than most of us would ever encounter in our own lives. Not only are media our introduction to these people, but often they are practically the only source of our information about them. Sometimes *everything* that we know about some kinds of people comes from television. Some rural White North Americans have never seen any African Americans or Jews in person. Many urbanites have never met a real farmer. Most people of the world have never met someone from the United States. In such cases the TV portrayal of African Americans or farmers or North Americans is reality for them. Even in a study done many years ago, children reported that most of their information about people from different nationalities came from their parents and television, with TV becoming increasingly important as the child grew older (Lambert & Klineberg, 1967).

In this chapter we examine primarily the U.S. media image of a variety of groups of people and look at the consequences of such portrayals. The concerns in some of the areas are widely known and discussed (e.g., women, African

Americans), and, in the case of some minorities, have been widely examined in research (e.g., Graves, 1980; Greenberg, 1986; Greenberg & Atkin, 1982; Greenberg & Brand, in press). Similar concerns about portrayals of other groups have received relatively little attention (e.g., farmers, Arabs, police officers). Although the issue is relevant to all media, television is the primary medium of concern, considering both programming and commercials. The focus here is on television of the United States, although the same principles, if not all the same specifics, hold true for any nation's broadcasting. Before looking at minorities, let us focus on gender portrayals. What do TV and other media say about what it means to be a man or woman? For reviews of research on gender portrayals, see Busby (1985), Durkin (1985a), Fejes (1989, 1992), and Gunter (1986).

PORTRAYALS OF THE SEXES

The View of Women

We have heard a lot in recent years about stereotyping of women by the media (e.g., Baehr & Dyer, 1987), but what, exactly, are the concerns about the way women are portrayed? Some of these concerns are very familiar, whereas others are more subtle but just as serious. For a review of content analysis studies of the image of women in advertising, see Courtney and Whipple (1983).

Perhaps the most basic gender asymmetry is that there are far fewer women than men. Content analyses of characters on television shows in the 1970s and early 1980s show about three times as many men as women in prime-time dramas and four times as many in Saturday morning children's shows (Fejes, 1992; Greenberg, 1980; Kimball, 1986). Even on "Sesame Street," most of the classic characters are male (Bert, Ernie, Big Bird, Cookie Monster, Elmo, Oscar, etc.). Photos of men outnumber photos of women everywhere in the newspaper except the lifestyle section (Luebke, 1989). This situation may be due to the far greater numbers of men than women among editors, writers, and producers or to a belief that women find the opposite sex more interesting to watch than men do.

There is some evidence that a better balance is emerging. Until such mid-1980s shows as "Cagney and Lacey," "The Golden Girls," "Designing Women," and "Kate and Allie," shows with all-women leads were largely nonexistent in the United States, with infrequent exceptions like "One Day at a Time" and the arguably sexist "Charlie's Angels" of the 1970s. Virtually all-male shows have never been unusual, however (e.g., "Bonanza," "Barney Miller," "My Three Sons," "Simon and Simon"), and most shows over the years have had predominantly male casts. The commercial success of several all-female shows has probably insured the existence of at least some such programming for the foreseeable future.

Still, all is not equal. Although women appear almost as often as men in commercials, the voiceover announcer, a sort of authority voice, is still a male 83% of the time (Ferrante, Haynes, & Kingsley, 1988), virtually unchanged from the early 1970s (Dominick & Rauch, 1972). One of the newest forms of media, the music video, shows at least twice as many males as females (Brown & Campbell, 1986; Sherman & Dominick, 1986; Vincent, Davis, & Boruszkowski, 1987). On radio, disc jockeys, newspersons, band singers, and voiceover announcers all are still overwhelmingly male, although increasing numbers of female voices are being heard (Melton & Fowler, 1987). A minority of news anchors and weathercasters are now female, although almost no sportscasters are. In a content analysis of guests interviewed on ABC's "Nightline" from 1985 to 1988, Croteau and Hoynes (1992) found that only 10% were women.

Another concern is that women are too often portrayed as youthful beauties whose duty it is to stay young and attractive to please their men. Once a woman is no longer so young and attractive, she becomes an object of ridicule. Support for this criticism comes especially from all of the subtle messages that a woman must not allow herself to age, a message transmitted especially, although not exclusively, by advertising, the media content with the most stereotyped gender portrayals. *Seventeen*, the most widely read magazine among teen girls, devotes two-thirds of its editorial content to fashion and beauty topics, with most of the remaining articles about relational topics like finding boy friends and being popular (Phillips, 1993). Wrinkles, gray hair, or a "mature" figure are to be avoided at all costs. At least until recently, women obviously over 30, and especially those over 50, have been grossly underrepresented on television and, when they were present, were often seen as stereotyped "old folks" that no one would want to grow up and be like (Davis & Davis, 1985). Women in TV ads were disproportionately younger than men (70% vs. 40% under 35, respectively), in ratios unchanged from the early 1970s (Dominick & Rauch, 1972; Ferrante et al., 1988).

Media women are disproportionately seen as homemakers and mothers, with their business, professional, and community roles minimized or nonexistent. This is especially true of advertising (Culley & Bennett, 1976; Knill, Pesch, Pursey, Gilpin, & Perloff, 1981; Schneider & Schneider, 1979), although there is some evidence that the range of occupational roles for women in ads is increasing (Ferrante et al., 1988). Not limited to the United States, the stereotyping of women in advertisements occurs in many societies (Gilly, 1988).

Another concern is that women are seen as dependent on men and needing their protection. Even relatively egalitarian TV families like the Taylors of "Home Improvement" generally show the wife deferring to the husband more often than the reverse, although the behaviors showing this are much more subtle than those of 20 years ago. Women are not seen making important decisions or engaged in important activities as often as men. Advertising often portrays women as terribly perplexed and even neurotic about such matters as dirty laundry or yellow floors. Women squeezing toilet paper or berating others about soiled clothing also make this point. Early sitcoms showing women playing bridge or gossiping with neighbors all day also illustrate this concern. Newspaper cartoons, particularly strips like "Blondie" or "The Girls," also frequently show traditional women primarily preoccupied with trivial concerns, although changes do occur even here, as when Blondie started her own catering business in 1991. Brabant and Mooney (1986) found that gender images in Sunday comics had changed little from the mid-1970s to the mid-1980s. Some of the most heavily sex-typed TV shows are children's cartoons, which contain far more male characters than female characters. Often the few females who do appear are rather frilly and wimpy characters like Smurfette of "The Smurfs" or April O'Neill of "Teenage Mutant Ninja Turtles," who mainly seem to nurture and support their male colleagues (Canzoneri, 1985; Crimmins, 1991).

Sometimes the power that women do exercise is used in very underhanded and conniving ways, often directly or indirectly involving sexuality. The soap opera businesswoman who sleeps her way to the top is a good example. There are subtle messages that it is not ladylike to confront men (or even other women) directly but it is perfectly acceptable to deviously trick them. Portraying sexuality as a weapon of power subtly de-emphasizes and even degrades its tender and relational aspects. A woman like Alexis of "Dynasty" may at first appear to be a very strong and nontraditional role model because she is a powerful executive. However, a closer examination of where her power seems to come from and how it is used suggests a very different situation from that seen in her male counterparts (Fiske, 1987). Female uses of power are not confined to adult media; Lucy, in the cartoon "Peanuts," dominates the boys through intimidation (Canzoneri, 1985).

A more recent concern, focusing on the unrealistic "superwoman," is directed specifically at a relatively new media portrayal that has arisen in an attempt to represent modern women more accurately and fairly. Most TV series women characters are employed full time (64% in the new shows of the 1986–1987 season), 61% of those in professional or managerial positions, compared to only 23% in such positions in real life (Kalter, 1988a). Many, most notably sitcom moms, are also mothers. Although characters like Clair Huxtable ("The Cosby Show") are positive role models of professional women, they seem to handle the demands of career, wife, and parent with amazingly little stress and difficulty. Real women in two-career families need such positive role models but they also need some acknowledgment from TV that the great difficulties they experience balancing all of those responsibilities are not abnormal. Clair Huxtable and her sitcom counterparts ("supermoms") make it look all too easy. Viewers for whom that life is not so easy may feel inadequate by comparison (Maynard, 1987).

The superwoman myth is also reinforced by some advertising. For example, one perfume ad says that a woman can "bring home the bacon, fry it up in a pan, but never never let him forget he's a man." In other words, a woman can (or at least should) work outside the home all day, come home and cook dinner for her husband, and still have enough energy left to be sexy for him that evening! Are these realistic messages to send to young girls about what it means to be a woman in today's society? Are these helpful expectations to send to young boys about the women they will eventually marry?

A final concern is that women are subtly linked with violence, especially as victims of male violence. Some commercials or programs playing on the seductiveness of women also suggest that they are animals to be tamed, something wild to be brought into line by men. A high fashion ad selling negligees by showing a scantily clad woman being playfully attacked by two men, or an auto magazine ad showing a woman in a bikini chained inside a giant shock absorber subtly link sexuality and violence. Perfume ads may stress the wildness, the toughness, and the challenge of women and imply the need for an attack from a man in response to this irresistible fragrance.

Although we may not find Ralph Kramden of "The Honeymooners" threatening his wife with violence ("One of these days, Alice, pow! Right in the kisser!") as amusing in syndicated reruns as we did in 1955, more graphic instances of violence toward women are common, especially in the so-called "slasher" films (*The Texas Chainsaw Massacre, Friday the Thirteenth, Nightmare on Elm Street,* and *Halloween* series) aimed at teenagers and in violent pornography allegedly aimed at adults. Association of women with violence is a lesser concern on most network television series, although it does occur. When Luke and Laura on "General Hospital" fall in love and marry after he rapes her, a message may be sent to men that, when a woman says no, she may really mean yes. In fact, this image of a woman resisting but secretly wanting a man to force himself on her has a long cinematic tradition, including such classics as *Gone with the Wind* and various John Wayne westerns. The sex–violence link is also a major concern on rock videos shown on MTV and other cable channels (Brown & Campbell, 1986; Vincent et al., 1987). Possible desensitization effects of such portrayals (e.g., Donnerstein, Linz, & Penrod, 1987) are examined in chapter 10.

Although we have so far focused on women, there are also some serious criticisms of the portrayals of men in media. Although these have received less general attention and scientific research than portrayals of women, unrealistic stereotyping is also a problem here.

The View of Men

Men are seen as calm and cool, self-confident, decisive, and emotionless. Although this may be positive in many ways, it sends the message to young boys that this is what men are supposed to be like and if one cannot, or chooses not to, deny his feelings, he is therefore not a real man. The "Marlboro Man" is the quintessential TV man, but many classic TV fathers come in a close second. Who could imagine Ward Cleaver ("Leave it to Beaver") or Jim Anderson ("Father Knows Best") shedding a tear? This picture has changed somewhat; modern TV dads like Tim Taylor ("Home Improvement") are allowed to cry occasionally, although they are generally somewhat embarrassed and ashamed to do so.

Men are still portrayed as high achievers and are dominant over women, although the domination today takes more subtle forms than previously. Although J. R. Ewing of "Dallas" was obviously domineering over his women, so was Dr. Cliff Huxtable, although much more benignly and sensitively. He is clearly a stronger personality than his lawyer wife, who very frequently giggles and acquiesces while her husband expresses his opinions and makes the important decisions. Men with "subservient" jobs like housekeeper are frequently the object of some ridicule (see Box 3.1).

Like women, men are portrayed as young and attractive, but the rules are a little different. A study of images of men and women in heterosexual erotic magazines found that photos of women were more sexualized and idealized than photos of men (Thomas, 1986). It is not quite as bad for a man to age on TV as for a woman (Davis & Davis, 1985). A little gray hair may make a TV man look "distinguished" or possibly even "sexy," whereas it is to be avoided at all costs by women. It is not unusual to see a man with some gray hair giving the news, sports, or weather, but seeing a woman with gray hair in these roles is unusual.

BOX 3.1: THE MALE TV HOUSEKEEPER

There have been from time to time some very nontraditional men on the tube. Some male domestics appeared on early television like "My Three Sons" (1960–1972), where William Frawley and later William Demarest played crotchety older men taking care of a widower and his three sons. The Asian housekeeper on "Bachelor Father" was another such example. However, these characters tended to be older or at least desexualized to permit them to fit into these emasculated roles, which never really allowed them to be fully rounded characters.

The mid-1980s introduced several shows starring male housekeepers. "Charles in Charge" starred Scott Baio as a college student earning his way through school taking care of three children of a couple of wealthy but dim-witted yuppie parents. Charles' relationships with the kids was interesting and fairly believable but the show was cancelled from network TV after one season. "Mr. Belvedere" featured a stately English butler who held together a family of incompetent parents, sultry teenagers, and an obnoxious brat. "Who's the Boss?" drew the highest ratings of this group and starred the ultra-macho Tony Danza working as a housekeeper for a divorced female executive. Charles, Tony, and Mr. Belvedere were allowed to be strong males even in these traditionally female occupational roles. In fact, all three were clearly the competent parent figure in their respective households.

In spite of this, the message to stay young is still a strong one for men. One example is baldness. Although a sizable proportion of men lose their hair to greater or lesser degree starting in their 20s, few sympathetic leading male characters in TV series or even in commercials ever have even the slightest receding hairline. A bald character, when he does appear at all, is usually an object of at least subtle ridicule (e.g., the pompous George Jefferson of "The Jeffersons," the stupid husband who needs his wife in the commercial to find him the right laxative), or at best a "character" like the eccentric chap who doesn't believe oatmeal really could have all that fiber. Baldness in a TV series character is an indication of villainy, unfashionable eccentricity (e.g., Yul Brynner's King of Siam), or, at best, a sort of benign asexuality (e.g., Capt. Stubing on "Love Boat"). Even middle-aged or elderly male characters usually have full heads of hair. The occasional man who wears a hairpiece (Howard Cosell, Willard Scott of "Today") is the butt of tired old toupee jokes. The few apparent exceptions like Kojak, Picard of "Star Trek, The Next Generation," and some of Ed Asner's characters are clearly middle aged if not older.

Although images of friendship are common for both males and females, the nature of those friendships is different (Spangler, 1989, 1992). Women show a greater degree of emotional intimacy in their friendships than men do. TV images of male bonding go back to the Westerns of the 1950s, where a cowboy and his sidekick went everywhere together. Sitcom friends like Ralph and Ed on "The Honeymooners," Andy and Barney on "The Andy Griffith show," or Hawkeye and B.J. on "M*A*S*H" were clearly close emotionally, although that was never explicitly discussed, unlike the more overtly emotional friendships of Lucy and Ethel on "I Love Lucy," Mary and Rhoda on "The Mary Tyler Moore Show," or Kate and Allie of "Kate and Allie." This gender difference may fairly accurately reflect real life in terms of different communication styles of the sexes (Tannen, 1990). See Box 3.2 for a closer look at the masculine socialization messages in one specific form—beer commercials. Although men are generally portrayed as competent professionally, they are often seen as bungling nincompoops in regard to housework and child care. TV fathers of year-old infants often do not know how to change a diaper; this is unlikely to be true in even the most traditional real family. Men in commercials often seem to know nothing about housekeeping or cooking and have to be bailed out by their wives, who, in the domestic sphere, are portrayed as very knowledgeable experts. In the late 1980s a fad emerged for TV shows and movies portraying the ineptness of men dealing with small children ("Full House," "My Two Dads," *Three Men and a Baby*, *Mr. Mom*). Although they always learned and grew as persons from the experience, their initial ineptitude would seem to suggest that child care is not a part of the normal male role.

BOX 3.2: MESSAGES OF MASCULINITY
IN BEER COMMERCIALS

In a content analysis of TV beer commercials, Strate (1992) argued that there is strong socialization occurring about what it means to be a man. Specifically, he claimed that five questions are addressed by such ads:

1. *What kinds of things do men do?* First of all, they drink (although they cannot by law ever be shown actually drinking on television). This almost always occurs in the company of others in the context of good times. Beer is seen as a reward for a job well done and is a common marker for the end of a work day, such as stopping for a drink with friends after work.

2. *What kinds of settings do men prefer?* Beer is identified with nature and the outdoors, through images like a cowboy, animals, or a mountain stream. The second popular setting is the bar, which is always clean, smokeless, and full of polite and noninebriated, upper middle-class people. Also, no one ever seems to pay for a drink, either in cash or consequences.

3. *How do boys become men?* Beer serves as a reward for a challenge or an initiation or rite of passage.

4. *How do men relate to each other?* Men relate to each other primarily in groups (interestingly enough, a contrast to the frequent "loner" image of masculinity). Beer drinking is the shared activity that brings the group together and is never seen as being harmful.

5. *How do men relate to women?* Although women are largely absent in beer commercials, they are occasionally there as rather passive and peripheral accessories. The male group is clearly more important.

Anybody watching sports events or other programming with many beer commercials receives a heavy dose of such messages. What are boys learning from beer commercials about the use of alcohol and what it means to be a man?

In a similar vein, men are often portrayed as insensitive and rough interpersonally (e.g., not knowing how to talk to their children about sensitive personal issues). This is changing but is still a problem. Tony Micelli, on "Who's the Boss?" was extremely awkward when trying to talk to his daughter about her need to wear a bra and shoved the responsibility off onto his female employer. Cliff Huxtable turned his child's request for advice into a little joke to avoid having to deal with the serious issue. In a study of African-American Upward Bound high school students' reactions to episodes of "Good Times" and "The Cosby Show," Berry (1992) found that a majority of the youth found the more authoritarian James Evans of "Good Times" a more positive role model than Dr. Cliff Huxtable of "The Cosby Show."

Effects of Gender Stereotyping

Although it is relatively easy to describe gender role portrayals on television, the question of their effect is a far more difficult research problem and largely remains unanswered (Durkin, 1985b; Fejes, 1992). Negative or restricted gender images become a serious concern if they are seen as reflective of real life. Although no single exposure to a sexist commercial or sitcom episode is likely to irreparably harm anyone, the huge number of multiple exposures to commercials (100,000 or more ads seen by one's high school graduation) is unlikely not to have some effect. In general, effects of repetition are often underestimated; if the same themes about how men and women are supposed to behave and think keep recurring on show after show, that is perceived as reality. For example, women may expect men to dominate them and to be relatively insensitive, or men may expect women to be submissive to them and to be preoccupied with their appearance.

Not only may we take the television portrayals of the opposite sex as reality, but we may take the portrayals of our own gender as cues to the ways we should look and behave. When we fail to meet these standards, that "failure" sets us up for experiencing low self-esteem. For example, a woman feeling frazzled meeting the demands of career, family, and homemaking may feel very inadequate comparing herself to the superwomen on TV who do all three so well. Similarly, a man losing his hair or a woman losing her girlish figure may feel like a loser when using video bodies as the standard (Myers & Biocca, 1992).

Such concerns are especially important when considering children. Children who are heavy viewers of TV hold more traditional sex-role attitudes (Beuf, 1974; Freuh & McGhee, 1975, Lemar, 1977; O'Bryant & Corder-Bolz, 1978). Using an argument similar to cultivation theory, Kimball (1986) found that sex-role attitudes of children were less strongly sex typed than normal in a town with no access to television until 1974; however, their attitudes became more sex typed after the introduction of television. Wroblewski and Huston (1987) concluded that repeated TV appearances of women in traditionally male occupations can lead to more open attitudes by preteen girls to consider those occupations. Other studies have shown that advertising portraying women in more egalitarian fashion may be followed by more accepting attitudes in young viewers (Geis, Brown, Jennings, & Porter, 1984; Jennings, Geis, & Brown, 1980).

Obviously we cannot expect any given type of portrayal of the sexes to have a uniform effect on the public. For example, McIntyre, Hosch, Harris, and Norvell (1986) found that less traditional men and women were more sensitive to and more critical of stereotypic portrayals of women in TV commercials, in contrast to more traditional subjects. Men more prone to use violence often are affected much more by violent media (see chapters 9 and 10). The perceived reality differs across individuals.

Now that we have looked at TV's view of the sexes, let us turn to minorities, starting with a developmental model of the portrayals of minorities in media.

THE FOUR STAGES OF MINORITY PORTRAYALS

Some years ago, Clark (1969) identified four chronological stages of the portrayals of minorities on television. The first stage is *nonrecognition*, in which the minority group is simply excluded from television. It is not ridiculed, it is not caricatured, it is simply not there. Someone from an alien culture watching the programming would never know that such people even existed in that society. For example, until quite recently this was the position of homosexuals on U.S. television. To a large extent, Asian Americans are still absent.

The second stage of minority portrayals is *ridicule*. Here the dominant group bolsters its own self-image by putting down and stereotyping the minority, presenting them as incompetent, unintelligent buffoons. Very early television programs like "Amos and Andy" and characters like Stepan Fetchit or Jack Benny's Rochester reflect this stage in terms of portrayals of African Americans. On the current scene, Arabs are a good example of a group at the stage of ridicule; we seldom see positive or likeable Arab or Arab-American characters on U.S. TV.

A third stage is *regulation*, where minority group members appear as protectors of the existing order (e.g., police officers, detectives, spies). Such roles were typical of the first positive roles open to African Americans in the 1960s; one sees Hispanics in the same types of roles on U.S. TV today.

The final stage is *respect*, where the minority group appears in the same full range of roles, both good and bad, that the majority does. This is not to say that there is never a stereotyped character or that the characters are all sympathetic, but just that there is a wide variety—good and intelligent characters as well as evil and stupid ones.

Now let's turn to looking specifically at the media's portrayal of several particular minorities, starting with African Americans, the minority receiving the most study for the longest time.

AFRICAN AMERICANS

How Are They Portrayed?

The most studied group portrayal in U.S. media has been African Americans. Up until the 1960s, there were almost no African Americans on U.S. TV commercials (Colfax & Steinberg, 1972; Kassarjian, 1969; Stempel, 1971), and the only African Americans in prime-time programming were limited to a few stereotyped and demeaning roles, such as Jack Benny's servant Rochester or, most notoriously, the two affable but dim-witted African-American friends on "Amos and Andy." At least, however, the TV series employed African-American actors; the earlier radio version had used White actors speaking their interpretations of Black English.

Television was not the first medium to be criticized for stereotypical portrayals of African Americans. In the United States, media reflected this prejudiced viewpoint before radio or television were ever conceived. One of the earliest movies was *Uncle Tom's Cabin* in 1903, a film that highly stereotyped African Americans. This trend persisted in films for many years (Bogle, 1973). In 1942 the NAACP convinced the Hollywood studio bosses to abandon the characteristic negative roles for African Americans and try to integrate them into a variety of roles; this agreement did not produce overnight change, but advances did come eventually.

With the civil rights movement of the 1960s came changes on the tube as well (Berry, 1980). African-American models were used in commercials, with none of the resulting feared offense taken by Whites (Block, 1972; Schlinger & Plummer, 1972; Soley, 1983). African Americans also appeared for the first time in leading roles in prime time as well, most notably "I Spy" (1965–1968), with Bill Cosby, and "Julia," the first African-American family drama. In addition, there were African Americans as part of the starring ensemble on 1960s drama programs like "Mission Impossible," "Peyton Place," and "Mod Squad."

In the 1970s and 1980s, there were usually some African-American characters on TV, although they tended to be heavily concentrated in sitcoms and largely absent in daytime soap operas and children's programming. Some of these characters were more rounded than early TV African Americans but still retained some stereotypic characteristics, such as the buffoonery and posturing of J.J. on "Good Times" and George Jefferson on "The Jeffersons." A landmark occurred with the phenomenal commercial success of "Roots" in 1977. This miniseries was based on Alex Haley's sage of his ancestors' journey from West Africa into American slavery and later emancipation. Although widely praised both for its artistic and entertainment value and its effectiveness in widely publicizing key aspects of the African-American experience, "Roots" was also controversial. Some called it biased for presenting few sympathetic White characters, whereas others took it to task for making the horrors of slavery acceptable for audiences by "transforming a national disgrace into an epic triumph of the family and the American dream" (Riggs, 1992).

The current media situation is vastly improved from "Amos and Andy" days, although some argue that there are still subtle indicators of racism on television (Gray, 1986; Greenberg, 1986; Pierce, 1980; Poindexter & Stroman, 1981; Waters & Huck, 1988) and still very few realistic portrayals of typical African-American life (Riggs, 1992). African Americans are still underrepresented in most TV genres except sitcoms (see Box 3.3) and are largely absent in high-level

---

BOX 3.3: SUCCESSFUL AFRICAN-AMERICAN SITCOMS

Two of the most successful U.S. sitcoms of all time have been shows about African-American families, "The Jeffersons" (1975–1985) and "The Cosby Show" (1984–1992). In one sense, both are unstereotyped and atypical of African Americans; both families were quite well off economically, although not among the super rich. However, some African Americans have argued that "The Jeffersons" retained some earlier racial stereotyping in a more subtle way. The African-American characters were mostly rather loud and brassy, not very bright, and often acted rather foolishly. Still, George Jefferson is a vast improvement from Amos and Andy (Gray, 1986).

Cliff Huxtable and his family, on the other hand, are the epitome of upper middle-class gentility. In fact, some African-American critics have argued that their wealth and high status are so atypical of African Americans that it is inaccurate and even offensive to consider "The Cosby Show" an African-American show at all. Some have argued that the show is a sort of neo-tokenism in that it is a show at heart about Whites with African-American faces. Bill Cosby, although stressing that his show was primarily a show about families, not a show about African Americans, disputes that claim. At one point, a year after the start of his show, a consistent ratings topper, he threatened to leave the show if the network adhered to its intent to remove an anti-Apartheid poster from the wall of teenage son Theo's room. Although the producers were afraid that the poster might offend some White viewers and not be realistic on the wall of a teenager's room, Cosby replied that it would be very realistic for an African-American teen's room, even an affluent one. The poster stayed, and so did Cosby. The next season, in one of the series' most moving episodes, the Huxtable parents and grandparents taught Theo about the work of Martin Luther King, Jr.; the episode closed with the family watching a documentary of King's "I have a dream" speech, themselves epitomizing the fulfillment of that dream.

---

creative and network administrative positions. Although the phenomenal success of "The Cosby Show" (1984–1992) presumably laid to rest any commercial concerns about Whites not watching "Black" shows, its relevance to the experience of the large majority of less affluent African Americans continues to be debated. Cliff Huxtable and his family were clearly both positive role models, but they also enjoyed a lifestyle that is beyond the reach of most African-American families (and for that matter, most Caucasians and other races as well).

Research done in the 1970s shows about 8% of prime-time TV characters to be African American (Gerbner & Signorielli, 1979; Seggar, Hafen, & Hannonen-Gladden, 1981; Weigel, Loomis, & Soja, 1980), with less than 3% in daytime soaps (Greenberg, Neuendorf, Buerkel-Rothfuss, & Henderson, 1982), compared to 12% of the national population. Comparisons of African-American and White characters in the same show reveal many similarities and some differences, specifics depending on the study and programs sampled (Reid, 1979; Weigel et al., 1980). Barcus (1983) found cartoons to be the most ethnically stereotyped of all television genres. Some blatantly racist cartoons from the 1940s are still widely sold in the 1990s in inexpensive video cartoon anthologies; the villains have dark skin, big lips, and speak in Black English. Sometimes the bias may be more subtle. For example, two ugly and stupid regular characters in one cartoon are Rock Steady, named after a Jamaican musical genre of the mid-1960s, and Bebop, which was a form of jazz with origins in African-American music (O'Connor, 1990).

Blacks as Viewers

African Americans of all ages watch more television than Whites, even when controlling for socioeconomic status. They especially watch more sports, action-adventure shows, and news. They watch the so-called "Black" shows ("The Jeffersons," "The Royal Family," "Good Times," "227") in relatively greater numbers than Whites do, but there is no evidence that Whites avoid such shows because of the African-American characters (Comstock, Chaffee, Katzman, McCombs, & Roberts, 1978; Graves, 1980). Children of both races tend to identify more with characters of their own race (Eastman & Liss, 1980; Greenberg & Atkin, 1982). Overall, African-American children prefer sitcoms, whereas White children prefer action-adventure shows. Heavy viewers believe that African Americans and Whites are more similar, African Americans are more middle class, and racial integration is more widespread than do light viewers (Matabane, 1988). This may be interpreted in terms of cultivation theory to suggest that television mainstreams viewers into the optimistic view that African Americans have "made it" and that segregation and racism are no more.

Effects of African-American Portrayals

One focus of research has been on the effects of African-American portrayals on TV on both Whites and African Americans (see Graves, 1980; Greenberg, 1986; Greenberg & Brand, in press, for reviews). Like anyone else, African Americans are more likely to identify with and emulate TV characters who exhibit personal warmth and high status and power. Often these models have been White characters, yet African Americans will readily identify with media African Americans as role models, especially with the more positive ones (Ball & Bogatz, 1970, 1973; Bogatz & Ball, 1971; Jhally & Lewis, 1992). This can have important positive effects on African-American children's self-esteem, especially with regular viewing and accompanied by appropriate parental communication (Atkin, Greenberg, & McDermott, 1983; McDermott & Greenberg, 1985). Sympathetic characters like the Huxtable children or the students on "A Different World" thus become potentially very important models for young African Americans.

Studies on White children have shown that prolonged exposure to television comedies or "Sesame Street" with regular African-American and Hispanic cast members influences the attitudes of these White kids in a more accepting, less racist direction (Bogatz & Ball, 1971; Gorn, Goldberg, & Kanungo, 1976). Similar results have been shown for White adults' exposure to certain aspects of television (e.g., there is no evidence that White consumers react negatively to African-American actors in ads [Soley, 1983]).

Even a very positive portrayal developed with the best intentions may contribute to misconceptions, however. For example, some White viewers of "The Cosby Show" cite the Huxtables as examples of why affirmative action is no longer necessary (Jhally & Lewis, 1992). If the affluent Huxtables have attained their share of the American dream and they are assumed to be representative of African Americans, then African Americans who "haven't made it" must not be trying very hard. Armstrong, Neuendorf, and Brentar (1992) found that White college students who watched a lot of entertainment TV believed that African Americans were relatively well off socioeconomically.

There is some tendency for TV to unexpectedly reinforce existing stereotypes. For example, more bigoted White viewers tended to identify with Archie Bunker of "All in the Family" and accept his racist views, whereas less prejudiced people decried these views and found Archie's attitudes offensive or laughable (Surlin, 1974; Tate & Surlin, 1976; Vidmar & Rokeach, 1974; Wilhoit & de Bock, 1976). In Armstrong et al.'s (1992) study, White college students who watched a lot of TV news believed African Americans to be relatively worse off economically.

In contrast to this picture of some progress in the portrayal of African Americans, the media image of another American minority almost as large is far less developed.

HISPANIC IMAGES

The second largest, soon to be the largest, minority in the United States are the Hispanics, a diverse group of Americans with ethnic origins in Cuba, Puerto Rico, Dominican Republic, Mexico, Central America, South America, or Spain. Actually several different groups, Hispanics are racially and culturally diverse. Although many Puerto Ricans or Dominicans are African American or part African American, most Mexican Americans are mestizos (mixed White–Indian) but seldom African American. Many New Mexicans are pure White of Spanish descent, whereas some recent Guatemalan refugees are pure native Americans who speak Spanish only badly as a second language.

The histories of different Hispanic groups are very different. Although some

White ethnic Spaniards have lived in New Mexico since before the Puritans settled Massachusetts, many Mexicans and Central Americans are very recent immigrants. They are economically diverse, from wealthy Cuban Americans of South Florida or the "Spanish" New Mexicans of Albuquerque and Santa Fe, to the poor illegal immigrant underclass of southern California and Texas. Ironically, the economically poorest Hispanic group, the Puerto Ricans, are almost entirely urban and are all American citizens. Hispanics are politically diverse, from the staunchly Republican and conservative Cuban Americans in Florida to the politically liberal Mexican Americans starting to flex their voting muscles in Texas and California.

With such a large and important set of groups in the United States, what is the image of Hispanics on American television (Arias, 1982; Greenberg et al., 1983; Zoglin, 1988a)? The answer seems to be: largely nonexistent, with perhaps a few signs of coming change. According to one study cited in Greenberg et al. (1983), only 1.5% of all characters in TV programs during a sample period were Hispanic, compared to 9% of the population at the time. When they did appear, they were usually as crooks, cops, or comics and tended to be concentrated on a few shows, primarily unsuccessful series that did not last long ("Chico and the Man," "a.k.a. Pablo," "I Married Dora," "Trial and Error"). Five-sixths of the Hispanic characters were male. Almost no Hispanic characters appeared on Saturday morning television (only two characters in the 3 years of the study). Mention of Hispanics in the news tended to focus on the group as a social problem, especially in connection with the illegal immigration issue (Greenberg et al., 1983). In a discussion of television with Hispanic leaders in New York, Rivera (1987) reported people identifying only Victor Sifuentes on "L.A. Law," Lt. Castillo and Det. Calabrese on "Miami Vice," and Lt. Calletano on "Hill Street Blues" as prime-time Hispanic characters. All were involved in law enforcement or the legal system (Clark's regulation stage), none were leading characters, and only Sifuentes and Castillo were even strong supporting characters.

Historically, the current stereotyping of Hispanics follows an older tradition in films of the greasy Mexican bandit of the silent film era and the sensual and musical, but slightly laughable, "Latin lover" of the 1930s and 1940s (Amador, 1988). Although extremely blatant stereotypes like the Frito bandito are seldom seen on U.S. television today, they do exist elsewhere. For example, the stupidity of the servant Manuel on Britain's "Fawlty Towers" sitcom (also seen on PBS in the United States) is usually explained by the throwaway line, "Oh, he's from Barcelona."

By the late 1980s a few signs suggested that Hollywood and the TV networks were beginning to discover the largely untapped Hispanic market. Spanish cable channels offered popular options to Latino populations. The unexpectedly great commercial success of the 1987 films *La Bamba* and *Born in East L.A.* inside and outside of Latino communities allowed several new Hispanic films to be released in 1988 (Corliss, 1988), although this trend did not continue.

As of this writing, U.S. television has been an even more dismal story. Following the commercial failure of several very short-lived Hispanic-oriented sitcoms, the networks appear to be gun-shy about more such shows. When a TV show achieves the "crossover" success that *La Bamba* had in the theaters, we will no doubt see changes (Waters & Huck, 1988; Zoglin, 1988a).

Overall then, in many ways Hispanics on television are at the point somewhat similar to that of African Americans 30 years ago (i.e., largely invisible and tending to be negative or in regulatory roles when they do occur). Greenberg attributed this at least in part to the low level of minority employment in the broadcast industry, not necessarily due to overt discrimination but often more to the low entry-level salaries that are not attractive enough to the relatively few qualified well-educated Hispanics, who typically have numerous job opportunities. Because the management level and decision makers are mostly Anglo, it is their world that tends to appear on television.

NATIVE AMERICANS

Surprisingly little attention has been paid to the media portrayal of the original inhabitants of North America. Clearly the most maligned and persecuted groups in the history of the United States and Canada, Native Americans were largely the objects of extermination campaigns in the 18th and 19th centuries. Negative images persisted into the media age, starting with the bloodthirsty and savage Indian of old Western movies. Westerns were one of the most popular genres of television through the early 1960s. Indians were at the very best seen as lovable but simple and primitive sidekicks to White men (e.g., Tonto and the Lone Ranger [Morris, 1982]).

Native Americans who did appear in the media (usually in Westerns) were almost always Plains Indians, and behaviors like living in teepees and hunting buffalo came to be identified with all Native Americans, although they were no more characteristic of the northeastern Iroquois or northwest Tlingits than they were of the English or Africans. The overemphasis on Plains Indian peoples is still seen in a few recent and otherwise nontraditional films like *Dances with Wolves* (1990) and *Thunderheart* (1992). Women seldom appeared, and when they did, they were passive and rather dull background figures. The powerful women in matriarchal societies like the Navajo and Mohawk have never been seen on TV. Most media Indians are seen in the historical setting of Westerns; the few modern characters are usually presented as militant activists or alcoholics. There is hardly any Native American news and what does appear is usually about some land claims litigation or demonstration, such as the 1991 protest at Oca, Quebec.

The implications of this lead to great confusions in the socialization process for Native American children. There is almost a complete lack of Indian role models. When Native American children play "cowboys and Indians," they are as likely as Whites to want to play the cowboys (i.e., the "good guys"). To add to the confusion, one of the few places that their ethnic identity appears is in the names of school and professional sports teams (see Box 3.4).

The oppressed history of the native peoples is by no means unique to North America. They have been similarly marginalized in European-oriented Latin American countries (e.g., Argentina, Chile, Brazil, Costa Rica), Australia, New Zealand, and elsewhere. A particularly notable and interesting exception to this pattern is Mexico, which, unlike the rest of North America, has always had a very large urban indigenous population. At the time of the Spanish conquest in 1521, the Aztec capital Tenochtitlán was one of the world's most populous cities. In spite of early severe oppression by the Spanish conquistadors, the Indian identity has come to be fused with the Spanish into a unique culture that is the essence of modern Mexico. It is the last Aztec ruler Cuahtémoc, not the conqueror Cortez, who is the Mexican hero.

BOX 3.4: NATIVE AMERICAN NAMES
FOR SPORTS TEAMS

A currently very controversial issue in many places is the use of Native American names and themes for sports teams (Atlanta Braves, Washington Redskins, Cleveland Indians). Although the most visible examples are names of professional teams, the same issue exists at a local level where many high schools and colleges use Indian names. Mostly named many years ago before much consciousness of media stereotyping existed, they probably arose to suggest the strong, fighting, even savage nature associated with the Indian image from Westerns.

Now it is time, so argue many, to replace these names with others that do not demean any ethnic or racial group or co-opt and cheapen its cultural symbols. The issue first came to a head during the 1991 baseball World Series. Fans of the Atlanta Braves had a hand motion called the "tomahawk chop" done to support their team. Critics argued that the use of comparable symbols or names from any other minority group would not be tolerated; could one seriously imagine teams called the "Chicago Jews," "Washington Wetbacks," or the "Dallas Orientals"? Why was there this moral blind spot regarding the oldest ethnic group in the country?

As of 1993, few, if any, teams had changed their names; old traditions die hard. However, others were taking stands. In February 1992, the Portland *Oregonian*, the state's largest daily, announced it would no longer publish names or nicknames of sports teams that used racial or ethnic stereotypes. The teams would only be referred to by their city. Some radio stations or broadcasters in different places announced similar intentions to stop using the offending names. Predictably, many called the whole flap much ado about nothing, but Native Americans were almost uniformly pleased. Is this a case where it is time to change some traditions in response to an increased sensitivity to minority concerns in a multicultural society?

ASIAN AMERICANS

The fastest-growing minorities in the United States and (especially) Canada in the 1990s are Asians, although their immigration history goes back to large numbers of Chinese brought over to work the railroads in the American West in the 1800s. In more recent times, large numbers of Chinese have migrated to America, particularly to centers like Vancouver, British Columbia. As the projected date of 1997 for returning Hong Kong to Chinese control approaches, there will almost surely be massive emigration to North America and elsewhere. Japanese emigrated to the United States (as well as Brazil and elsewhere) in the early 20th century. These Japanese-American U.S. citizens (but not German Americans) were rounded up and put into concentration camps during World War II. Although the official justification was national security, the decision has more recently been attributed to racism. Koreans and Filipinos are coming to America in increasing numbers, some as spouses of U.S. military formerly stationed there. Vietnamese and other southeast Asians came in large numbers to the United States following the fall of Saigon in 1975. There are also a substantial number of South Asian Americans, from India, Pakistan, Bangladesh, Sri Lanka, and Afghanistan, as well as Iranian refugees from the 1979 Islamic revolution.

Like the Native Americans, there is a long history of media stereotyping of Asians in movies, such as Fu Manchu and Charlie Chan, characters often played, incidentally, by White actors (Iiyama & Kitano, 1982). On television there have been few Asian Americans. A "Kung Fu" series had the Asian lead played by David Carradine, who is White. The 1970s and 1980s saw some improvement, with the addition of some minor Asian characters in shows like "Hawaii Five-O" (1968–1980) and "M*A*S*H," although they were often villains or in stereotyped occupations like Chinese running a laundry. Perhaps the most well-rounded Asian-American character was played by Japanese-American actor Jack Soo on "Barney Miller" (1975–1978).

Often the villains of choice on entertainment TV follow news events. After the 1989 Tiananmen Square massacre, Chinese officials from the People's Republic of China (PRC) were villains on action-adventure shows. During waves of U.S. concern about Japanese commercial power and ascendancy, Japanese businessmen were portrayed as "buying up America" in a sort of "yellow scare." Newspaper stories about Asian immigration use headlines like "Asian invasion" or "containing Japan" (Funabiki, 1992). Parallels of Japanese economic ascendency are drawn with World War II militarism.

Overall, Asian Americans are probably portrayed more positively than other minorities on U.S. media. In fact, there is one positive stereotype that is increasingly troubling Asian Americans; that is, the "model minority" image of the group that succeeds academically, commercially, and socially. Sometimes this perceived success image is used to ignore problems that the group has or to criticize other minorities for doing less well and seeming lazy. Such treatment engenders deep feelings. For example, in the 1992 Los Angeles race riots, some of the major targets of angry looters and arsonists were Korean-American-owned businesses. The University of California system and others have set an "Asian quota," a limit on the number of Asian-American students that can be admitted.

ARABS AND ARAB AMERICANS

A much smaller American minority offers a look at a seldom-discussed stereotype, but one that is currently among the most unsympathetic and derogatory portrayals on U.S. television; that is, Arabs and Arab Americans. This stereotype is seen both in news coverage (Suleiman, 1988) and entertainment (Shaheen, 1984a, 1984b, 1984c).

According to Shaheen, there are several stereotypic ways that Arab men are portrayed, all very negative. One is as the terrorist. Although only a minuscule fraction of real Arabs are terrorists, there are many of them on television, especially among Arabs identified as Palestinians. A second stereotype of Arab men is the wealthy oil sheik, who is often greedy and morally dissolute. His wealth, often suggested to be undeserved, is spent on frivolities like marble palaces and fleets of Rolls-Royces. Sometimes he is portrayed as madly buying up land in America and erecting garishly kitsch homes in Beverly Hills. A third stereotype is that of sexual pervert, often dealing in selling Europeans or Americans into slavery. This is an older stereotype, perhaps originally arising from medieval Christian Europe's enmity against the Moslem "infidels," who were, incidentally, primarily non-Arab Turks. Although probably less prevalent than the terrorist or oil sheik portrayal today, this image does appear occasionally.

A fourth stereotype is the Bedouin "desert rat," the unkempt ascetic wanderer far overrepresented on TV in relation to the approximately 5% of Arabs who are Bedouins. Jokes about camels, sand, and tents are frequent in connection with U.S. media Arabs. Finally, Arab men are generally seen as villains, a stereotype especially rampant in children's cartoons (e.g., Daffy Duck being chased by a crazed, sword-wielding Arab sheik or Heckle and Jeckle pulling the rug from under "Ali Boo-Boo, the Desert Rat"). These barbaric and uncultured villains are not usually balanced by Arab heroes or "good guys." One of the few exceptions is probably Lebanese-American Corp. Max Klinger on "M*A*S*H." He is a sympathetic and rounded character, yet (especially in early episodes) he still comments about his relatives in unnatural relations with camels and other such stereotyped images.

How about Arab women? They are seen far less than Arab men on U.S. TV, but, when they are seen at all, it is usually in an oppressed situation and often in highly stereotyped roles such as a belly dancer or a member of a harem. The reality about harems, as Shaheen (1984a) pointed out, is that they were never common and today are nonexistent in Arab countries. The public veiling of women is presented as the Arab norm, rather than a characteristic of some Islamic traditions.

Arab children are practically nonexistent on U.S. television, even though the negative adult Arab stereotypes are perhaps more prevalent in children's cartoons than on any other type of programming. Even as we routinely see African-American, Hispanic, and Asian faces on programs like "Sesame Street," few Arabs appear.

Islam as a religion is often portrayed as cruel and vicious, in total contrast to the Judaeo-Christian faith and civilization. Because most North Americans know very little, if anything, about Islam except what they find in the media, this may easily become their perceived reality about one of the world's major religions. Although many Americans have sufficient knowledge to recognize a Christian extremist on TV as very atypical of Christians, they may not have the necessary knowledge to so critically evaluate a media presentation of an Islamic fanatic, whom is thus taken to be typical of Muslims.

Historically, Arabs may be the latest villain in a long list of many groups who have been maligned by the U.S. media. The vicious Arabs of the 1980s and 1990s have been preceded by the wealthy but cruel Jews of the 1920s, the sinister Asian villains of the 1930s, or the Italian gangsters of the 1950s. Each of these stereotypes has been tempered and balanced as a result of protests from the offended groups and other concerned citizens. Such media portrayals can provide unwitting social support for racist and discriminatory policies and legislation, such as the network of Jim Crow laws and racist practices against African Americans in the century following the American Civil War of 1861–1865.

Recent historical events have probably encouraged unflattering media portrayals of Arabs: the OPEC oil embargoes of the 1970s, hostage-taking incidents, the Lebanese civil war, the Iran–Iraq War of 1980–1988, the Persian Gulf War of 1991, and continuing Arab–Israeli conflicts. Ironically enough, the media Arab may have suffered the most from the action of their fellow Muslims, the non-Arab Iranians, for their actions following the 1979 Islamic revolution, especially the holding of the U.S. hostages from 1979 to 1981. This protracted tragedy produced a wealth of bad feelings about the Islamic faith in the United States, even though the Ayatollah Khomeini was in no way a typical Muslim and not an Arab at all.

The concern is not that there are some negative portrayals of Arabs and Arab Americans. The concern is that such portrayals are not balanced by positive portrayals to feed into the perceived mental reality constructed by TV viewers. There is very little programming on Arab culture or society. The Arab world was more intellectually and technically advanced than Europe in the Middle Ages and gave us many of the basics of modern science, mathematics, and music, but how many Americans know that? Nor do the close family values and other positive features of the Islamic faith and Arab culture receive much press in the United States.

The concern about stereotypical portrayals of groups is not limited to gender, race, and ethnic groups, however. Now let us look at the media portrayal of one of the fastest growing demographic groups in our society, the elderly.

THE AGING PERSON

One of the most underrepresented demographic groups on U.S. television throughout most of its history has been the older adult (Davis & Davis, 1985). According to 1982 census data, 15.7% of the U.S. population was age 60 or over, yet content analyses of the characters on U.S. television have showed only 3% of over 3,500 characters in prime-time series that were over 65, with an even lower percentage of older adults in commercials (Greenberg, Korzenny, & Atkin, 1979). Other studies examining different types of programming have yielded figures in the 1%–5% range (Aronoff, 1974; Harris & Feinberg, 1977; Northcott, 1975). Only daytime soap operas had a higher percentage of older people, 16% judged to be over 55 (Cassata, Anderson, & Skill, 1980).

Even that relatively small number of elderly people who did appear on TV were not particularly representative of the population. For example, two thirds of the TV elderly were men, as compared with only 43% men in that age population. A disproportionate number of the TV elderly were in sitcoms, with very few in action-adventure or children's shows. Studies of print media also show underrepresentation and stereotyping in portrayals of the aging (Buchholz & Bynum, 1982; Nussbaum & Robinson, 1986; Robinson, 1989).

Often, the older adult who is portrayed is more of a stereotype than a fully rounded character. These stereotypes are of several forms:

1. *Physical and mental weakness and poor health.* Overall, older people on TV are often seen as quite healthy, perhaps even unrealistically so (Cassata et al., 1980; Davis, 1983; Kubey, 1980). Those who are sick, however, are ailing very badly, often seen as infirm, feeble, and sometimes senile. Although in terms of numbers of stories, newspapers do the best job of any medium in covering the elderly, a high percentage of such stories are obituaries (Buchholz & Bynum, 1982; Robinson, 1989)!

Moreover, the elderly are usually sexless. The major exception to this is the other extreme, the so-called "dirty old man" (or woman), the older person who is preoccupied with sex and usually is a highly ludicrous character (e.g., Mona on "Who's the Boss?"). The very active and healthy senior citizen may be an object of ridicule (e.g., the grandmother who rides a motorcycle or cruises bars to meet men).

2. *Crotchety and complaining.* This is the narrow-minded older person who is constantly complaining, criticizing, and generally making a pain of him or herself for everyone else. Such characters as Mama on "Mama's Family" are examples. As with the physically weak stereotype, the crotchety complainer is usually at best a laughable buffoon and at worst an object of scorn and derision.

3. *Stereotyped positions and activities.* Older people tend to be seen doing relatively trivial things like playing bingo and sitting in rockers on the front porch. Such identifying "tags" of an older person are especially common in advertising. The woman in a magazine ad for cookies is placed in a rocker to make sure we recognize that she is a grandmother.

4. *Physically unattractive.* Unlike most of the unusually attractive young adults on TV, television's elderly are often stoop shouldered, mousy haired, badly wrinkled, and usually wearing long out-of-style dowdy clothing. Such marks may be given to them so that we do not mistake them for younger people. Intentionally or not, it also contributes to their being perceived as buffoons. Seefeldt (1977) found that elementary school children viewed physical signs of aging as horrifying and saw the elderly as infirm and incapable of doing much.

An interesting class of exceptions to these generalizations can be seen in commercials. Although the elderly are as underrepresented here as in the programs, the characterization is a bit different. The elderly in ads often appear as the "young-old," with few of the stereotypic signs of aging, except the gray hair, which is almost always there. Although they suffer more health problems than young people in ads, they retain their vigor. It is as if the producers give the character gray hair so we all realize that he or she is supposed to be older but allow that person to show very few other signs of age that our society finds so distasteful. Baldness, wrinkles, and otherwise general dowdiness is unseemly (Davis & Davis, 1985; Harris & Feinberg, 1977).

Even in cases where the elderly are portrayed very positively, they tend to be in rather a restricted and stereotyped range of roles. They are almost always in relation to family, very often a grandparent but also often as the antagonist in a relationship with their adult child. We seldom see an older executive or professional.

What was in one sense a truly new type of sitcom, NBC's "The Golden Girls" (1985–1992, succeeded by its sequel "Golden Palace") featured four single women (three widowed, one divorced), aged about 50 to 80, sharing a house in Florida. What was new was the age of the stars. Never before had a sitcom, or perhaps any U.S. TV show, had its regular cast consisting entirely of older adults. There were no precocious children, no squirrely teenagers, no "hunks" or bathing beauties, and no yuppie couples, yet the show had consistently high ratings. Nor were the characters the stereotyped TV old ladies. Three of the four were working professionals, and all showed depth of character beyond the typical TV grandma. However, they have been criticized for being excessively interested in sex, although the criticism may more reflect the traditional bias against accepting sexual interest in the mature adult. Also, the humor of the show sometimes perpetuated stereotypes of aging by poking fun at counterstereotypical portrayals (Harwood & Giles, 1992). As the U.S. population ages sharply over the next few decades, a greater variety of portrayals of older adults is practically assured.

In spite of some inadequacies in their portrayal on TV, older people are heavy users of media, especially television. Robinson (1989) offered a Uses and Dependency interpretation of this. A reduction in the number of friends and family seen regularly, in part perhaps due to decreased mobility from health limitations, leads to a proportionately greater reliance on media, especially television, with its high level of redundancy in the visual and auditory modalities. If one sense is impaired, the other may partially compensate. In the case of the sound track, the volume may be turned up, so some elderly TV viewers may actually hear more from TV than from people.

OCCUPATIONAL GROUPS

Finally, in this look at portrayals of groups, our attention focuses briefly on another large area of group stereotyping on television, namely, various occupational groups. Presence of positive media models in certain occupations can greatly increase the numbers of those entering that profession. For example, the number of journalism students (and unemployed journalists) mushroomed after the Watergate scandal of the early 1970s, where investigative reporters became the heroes. The number of medical school applicants surged sharply in 1962–1963, apparently due to the debuts of the popular medical TV dramas "Dr. Kildare" and "Ben Casey" (Goldberg, 1988). Events of media portrayals of occupational groups are not always so dramatic, however. We examine a few especially interesting groups and see how television presents these professions.

One important group to study in regard to stereotyping is police officers. This group is especially interesting because (a) police officers are greatly overrepresented on television relative to their numbers in the population, and (b) most of us have relatively little intense contact with police in our daily lives. Thus a high percentage of our knowledge about cops is likely to come from television. Indeed, some research by George Gerbner shows that heavy TV viewers greatly overestimated the percentage of the population working in law enforcement. Real police officers and trainees see the TV police shows as unrealistic portrayals of their profession (Simon & Fejes, 1987). See Box 3.5 for some thoughts of a prominent lawyer about TV's portrayal of the law as an abstract system.

Some controversy has arisen around the "realistic" courtroom TV shows like "Divorce Court," "Superior Court," and, especially, "The People's Court." All of these shows present legal proceedings—either dramatization of real cases (e.g.,

---

BOX 3.5: TV MYTHS ABOUT THE LAW

Attorney Alan Dershowitz (1985) noted two myths about the law that he believed were very prevalent even on the best cop shows of the time like "Hill Street Blues," "Cagney and Lacey," and "Miami Vice." The first myth is that the law is unambiguous, unforgiving, and controlling, although the people who administer it may be complex, forgiving, or ambiguous. However, Dershowitz argued that, in fact, real-life law is much more subjective and ambiguous than the police shows portray. For example, plea bargaining and decisions about bail and sentencing are seldom spelled out precisely in the law but leave considerable latitude to magistrates and attorneys. TV cop shows often present a judge or attorney's hands in such issues as being completely tied by the law.

A second "myth" pointed out by Dershowitz is that the Bill of Rights to the U.S. constitution and Supreme Court decisions like the Miranda rule are to blame for freeing lots of criminals. Cop shows would have us believe that "silly" legal technicalities are undoing the valuable work of the police every day, such as critical evidence obtained illegally causing a conviction to be thrown out or overturned, allowing an obviously guilty person to go free. It sometimes may appear as if the Bill of Rights and the Miranda rule are inconsistent with adequate law enforcement. A study done by the General Accounting Office showed that, during the period of the study, only .5% of all serious Federal criminal prosecutions were thrown out by exclusionary rule violations (inadmissibly gathered evidence). If this frequency had been represented accurately on the TV crime shows, it would have come out to one episode on one show every 2 years!

"Divorce Court") or actual court proceedings (e.g., "The People's Court," Court TV cable channel). In "The People's Court" an actual judge presided over small claims court cases where both parties had agreed to have their case settled on the show in lieu of a more traditional setting. The cases were real, as were all parties in those cases.

On the one hand, such shows have been praised for making the court system more available to the public, who now can better understand how this phase of our judicial system functions. In fact, the number of small claims cases has risen considerably since the advent of "The People's Court" (although not necessarily because of that show). Speaking to this point, however, critics argue that many such cases are frivolous, now that the public realizes that redress is so "easy" via the small claims route. Furthermore, some judges report that litigants have become more contentious, dramatic, and emotional in court, apparently following the model of the parties on "The People's Court." Is the public well served by such shows? Do we have a more accurate perception of how courts function, or is our reality colored by some "Hollywoodizing" of the courtroom by the producers of these "real-life" judicial programs? Even less clear is the impact of newer innovations like the cable channel Court TV or the extensive broadcasting of sensational trials like the Willie Smith and Mike Tyson rape trials in 1991.

Many other occupational groups are the object of media stereotyping. For example, see Box 3.6 for a look at TV's portrayal of farmers and rural America.

CONCLUSION

The concern about group portrayals may extend to any sort of group; the ones we have discussed are only some of the most maligned and most studied. Many other groups still struggle with achieving a balanced and realistic treatment from television and other media. See Boxes 3.7, 3.8, and 3.9 for three such examples.

We talk a lot in this chapter about rather narrow and negative portrayals from media, especially television. But what is the impact? Although we have already discussed some effects of research in regard to gender and race images,

---

BOX 3.6: DOWN ON THE MEDIA FARM

As a rule, farmers and rural life in general are not highly visible on television, but the few rural shows that have existed have been among the most extremely stereotyped and unrealistic of the airwaves. In earlier days it was "The Beverly Hillbillies" and "Green Acres," then later "Hee Haw" and "The Dukes of Hazzard." All of these portrayed rural people as uneducated and stupid rubes totally lacking in worldly experience and common sense. True, there was also "The Waltons," perhaps the most popular rural show of all time, but its historical setting detracted from its use as a model of modern rural life. Many, if not most, of the farm shows have been set in rural Appalachia, one of the poorest and most atypical of rural regions nationwide. There is an occasional other extreme of the rural refuge of the very wealthy, although "Dallas" and "Falcon Crest" are as equally unrepresentative of rural America as "Hee Haw," although for entirely different reasons.

This stereotype is not limited to television. Use of Grant Wood "American Gothic"-type figures in advertising to reach a rural audience reflects an archaic (if ever accurate) stereotype. The popular comic strip "Garfield" occasionally features Jon Arbuckle's farmer parents who come to visit wearing overalls and not knowing how to use indoor plumbing and other modern conveniences.

Problems facing the profession of agriculture have typically been underreported in the news, probably because complex issues like the farm debt crisis are difficult to encapsulate into a brief TV or newspaper story. Also, the people involved with producing media in the United States are virtually 100% urban, usually from New York City or Los Angeles, with no roots in the farm community. It is not surprising that they, and the viewers they serve, had great difficulty understanding the U.S. farm crisis of the 1980s.

BOX 3.7: SINGLE ADULTS

The single adult in the world of television is stereotyped in several ways. Some of them are love- and/or sex-starved (e.g., Sam Malone on "Cheers," Ken Malansky on "Perry Mason," Arnie Becker on "L.A. Law," Joe and Brian on "Wings," Blanche Devereaux on "Golden Palace," Hawkeye on "M*A*S*H," Dan Fielding on "Night Court," Mona Robinson on "Who's the Boss?"), either having an active life of love and romance or desperately trying to find it. Others are social misfits who no one would care to marry (e.g., Lowell on "Wings," Les Nessman and Johnny Fever on "WKRP in Cincinnati," Cliff on "Cheers").

Unlike some other groups, single adults are not really underrepresented on television. In fact, they may actually be overrepresented, especially on ensemble shows centering on the workplace. Shows like "The Mary Tyler Moore Show," "Wings," "L.A. Law," "M*A*S*H," "Murphy Brown," "Cheers," "Night Court," and "Hill Street Blues" contain a disproportionate number of single characters, probably because the producers are reluctant to have background spouses whose characters cannot be developed extensively. There is also the prevailing industry wisdom that single characters allow more options for story lines, especially romantic angles and occupations that take them away from home for extended periods.

Lead characters in action-adventure, police, and detective shows are usually unmarried and unattached (e.g., "Murder, She Wrote," "MacGyver," "Quantum Leap," "Perry Mason"). Single life often appears to be one of considerable glamour and excitement, judging from watching such shows. In fact, many such single characters, especially in the more realistic drama shows, are workaholics who are tremendously wrapped up in their careers (e.g., the lawyers on "L.A. Law"; Murphy Brown on "Murphy Brown"; Perry Mason, and MacGyver) and probably would have no time for families if they had them.

---

we close here with mention of a controlled experiment by Slater (1990). Slater presented people with information about some social group. The information was attributed to fiction (from a novel) or nonfiction (from a news magazine) and was about a group that was either familiar or unfamiliar to the subjects. If the group was unfamiliar, the fictional portrayal actually was more influential in forming beliefs than the nonfictional portrayal, whereas the reverse was true for the familiar group. This suggests the great power of fictional portrayals on knowledge and attitude formation if life experience with the group in question is lacking.

For most of the groups described in this chapter, television is a very large, perhaps the predominant, source of information for most of us. However, it is usually not the only source; there is almost always at least some reality to temper the television picture. Thus, the perceived reality that our minds construct will not be totally taken from the media, although it may be very heavily in-

BOX 3.8: LESBIANS AND GAY MEN IN MEDIA

Although by the mid-1980s it had become acceptable to mention homosexuality on U.S. television and to even have an occasional gay man or (less often) a lesbian character, networks are still very cautious about introducing regular homosexual characters. With the exception of "Dynasty's" bisexual Steven Carrington, only an occasional guest character on dramatic shows is not heterosexual. Like all television programming decisions, this reluctance is basically economic, not moralistic. As recently as 1991, sponsors successively pressured ABC not to rerun an episode of "thirtysomething" that had one brief scene of two minor, nonregular gay male characters sitting in bed with each other (only talking). Controversy is not limited to electronic media. When the comic strip "For Better or for Worse" had a friend of teenager Michael declare his homosexuality, some papers refused to run the strip.

In the early 1980s a sitcom called "Love, Sidney" starred Tony Randall as a middle-aged bachelor living with a young single mother and her daughter. Based on a stage play where Sidney was clearly gay, the TV show hedged a bit due to sponsors' queasiness, only suggesting Sidney's homosexuality but never unequivocally stating it. To the show's credit, it dealt with realistic situations and only occasionally took laughs with sexual orientation jokes. However, it did not survive its first season.

Another short-lived sitcom, "Sara" (1985), featured an ensemble of young lawyers in a San Francisco legal clinic. One of the group was openly gay, and every line addressed to him seemed to comment on that fact in one way or another. Although not a stereotyped limp-wristed character himself, he was consistently responded to by others in a highly stereotyped fashion.

There have been several TV movies dealing with homosexuality and/or AIDS. Some of these have had moderate commercial successes. Still, TV and studio films have encountered an unusual difficulty in casting such films. Actors are reluctant to accept gay parts, because they perceive that such roles preclude their being considered for straight roles later. Actor Harry Hamlin felt that his gay role in "Making Love" (1982) sent his career into a nose dive that only recovered with the success of "L.A. Law" in 1986. Actors playing gay roles frequently report greater difficulty landing subsequent jobs, whereas producers report difficulty casting gay parts. One recent film was unable to cast a gay leading role, in spite of the producer taking out full-page ads targeted at actors listing 92 "big names" who had played gay or lesbian roles (Clarke, 1988).

BOX 3.9: THE DISABLED IN THE MEDIA

Another group that is very concerned about media stereotyping is the physically disabled (Cumberbatch & Negrine, 1991). Although largely absent from television through most of the medium's history, they have occasionally appeared in the "bitter crip" or "supercrip" stereotypes. In the former, the disabled person is depressed and bitter due to his or her disability and other people's failure to accept him or her as a full person. Often such story lines revolve around some character challenging the disabled person to accept him or herself. Often, miraculously, the disabled character finds this leads to a physical cure, perhaps subtly suggesting that happiness comes only from being physically whole. The "supercrip" image, on the other hand, is the superhuman and selfless paraplegic who wheels hundreds of miles to raise money for cancer research or the blind girl who solves the baffling crime by remembering a crucial sound or smell that sighted people had missed. A covert message of both of these portrayals is that individual adjustment is the key to disabled people's lives; if they only have the right attitude, they will be fine. Factors like prejudice and social and physical barriers of the broader society are underplayed (Kalter, 1986a; Longmore, 1985).

One of the fullest media portrayals of a physically disabled person came in the 1986 movie "Children of a Lesser God," where actress Marlee Matlin won the best actress Oscar for her role as a young deaf woman in love with a teacher at a school for the deaf. Down syndrome character Corky (played by Down syndrome actor Chris Burke) on "Life Goes On" struck new ground for the mentally handicapped. The wheelchair-bound teacher in the Canadian comic strip "For Better or For Worse" is a positive example of a character who just happened to have a disability. Such portrayals can have substantial impact. When a popular Brazilian soap opera introduced a character who was ruggedly handsome and very sexy but also deaf, interest in learning sign language soared nationwide.

---

fluenced by it. Occasionally, however, media may be the only source of information. Consider the example of prostitutes.

Practically all adults know what prostitutes are and could give some information about them. Few readers of this book, however, have probably ever known a real prostitute or knowingly had any contact with a person with any first-hand experience. Where does our perceived reality about prostitutes come from? In most cases it comes not mostly, or partly, but entirely from television and movies. The overdressed TV hooker standing on the street corner in the short, short skirt, high heels, and too much makeup is probably the reality of prostitutes, as far as most of us know. We might describe someone we see dressed this way as "looking like a hooker." But is this what hookers really dress like, or is it just the way TV portrays them? Even as the author of this book, I honestly do not know the answer. All I know is what I see on TV.

If I were to meet a woman tomorrow who was identified as a hooker, my TV stereotype would come into my mind to process information about this woman. It would not matter if that image was accurate or not. It would be the perceived reality for me. This is what is happening with children growing up learning about groups of people from television. Many children have had no more personal contact with Arabs, African Americans, lawyers, homosexuals, or even single adults than their exposure in the media. This is why stereotypes matter.

4

ADVERTISING: DO THE MESSAGES GO BY OR DO WE GO BUY?

Q: How much advertising are we exposed to in the mass media?

A: An average of about 300 ads and commercials per day on television, radio, and print media in the United States, over 100,000 per year, several million in a lifetime (Pratkanis & Aronson, 1992).

Q: What did Boris Yeltsin and his democratic resisters to the August 1991, attempted hard-line coup in Moscow do for meals when they were besieged inside the Russian Parliament building?

A: Ordered out for pizza from the nearby Pizza Hut.

We live in a sea of advertising. The average person in Western society sees over 100 TV commercials per day (almost 38,000 per year!), and another 100–300 ads from radio and print media. Every year, each of these people also receives 216 pieces of direct mail advertising ("junk mail"), 50 telemarketing phone calls, and sees countless billboards. Media advertising is a $45 billion-a-year business in the United States, which consumes 57% of the world's advertising (Pratkanis & Aronson, 1992). With the exception of public television and radio, most network and local broadcasting and much cable television are virtually 100% dependent on ad revenues for financial support. Even print media, newspapers, for example, typically derive around 70% of their revenue from advertising. Everything else except the ad costs money, whereas advertising brings in all the money. This simple fact explains much of the content of the media. Ultimately it is the advertiser, not the audience, who must be pleased.

In spite of the tremendous costs paid for network TV spots, up to $800,000 for a 30-second spot on the Super Bowl (Lever & Wheeler, 1993), such ads are still a remarkably efficient way to reach the buying public. Because of the huge size of the audience for highly rated shows, the cost per viewer is often in the neighborhood of a quarter to a half a cent per ad. These, of course, only include the purchase of air time; production costs are extra. On a smaller scale, local newspaper and radio ads are far more reasonable in cost but quite effectively reach the target area of interest to the advertiser.

Advertising makes very heavy use of psychology, and study of this usage could easily fill an entire book. This chapter examines certain aspects of the perceived reality from advertising but is by no means a thorough examination of its effects. After some initial introductory and historical material, we consider some psychological appeals in advertising, followed by a more specifically cognitive examination of ads, focusing on the issue of deceptive advertising, where the perceived reality is at particular odds with objective reality. Next we examine how children understand ads and finally how sexual appeals are used to build a reality of positive feelings and associations about a product. We also consider the issue of allegedly "subliminal" advertising.

HISTORICAL BACKGROUND

The earliest known written advertisement was a classified ad from around 1000 BC and was discovered by archaeologists at Thebes, Greece; it offered a "whole gold coin" for the return of a runaway slave. Advertisements in the true sense of mass communication did not really exist before Gutenberg's invention of movable type in the mid-15th century, however. Newspapers started carrying ads regularly in the mid-1600s. The rapid commercial growth associated with the Industrial Revolution in the 19th century gave great impetus to advertising, as did the rise of magazines during this same period, when transportation infrastructure, especially railroads, allowed distribution of national publications for the first time in a large country. The rise of radio after 1920, television after 1945, and cable TV in the 1980s provided tremendous new outlets for advertising dollars and creativity.

Although there were early experiments with radio by Marconi in Italy in the 1890s and DeForest in the United States in 1906, according to most experts, the first experimental radio station was set up in 1919 in a Pittsburgh garage by some Westinghouse engineers. Station KDKA broadcast the 1920 Presidential election results. There were 30 stations on the air by the end of 1920 and 400 by 1922. Ensuing concerns and debate about how to finance this new medium culminated in the Radio Act of 1927 for licensing and control of radio stations. This piece of legislation endorsed the free enterprise model to pay for radio (i.e., total revenue from the sale of advertising time with no government subsidy). At about the same time, Great Britain made a very different decision in establishing the government-supported British Broadcasting Corporation (BBC). Both of these economic models were carried over from radio to television in the late 1940s and still frame much broadcasting in their respective societies, although the United States now has some public broadcasting and British TV has become highly commercialized. One or the other of these two models of broadcasting has been adopted by most of the countries of the world.

TYPES OF ADS

Advertising is one type of communication designed to persuade (i.e., have some effect on the hearer or reader). This effect may be behavioral (buy the product), attitudinal (like the product), and/or cognitive (recognize the product). Although we tend to think of ads as trying to persuade us to buy particular brands of products, ads may also be for services, such as banks, plumbers, or electricians.

Frequently the most direct purpose of an ad is not selling as such but rather image building or good will. For example, when a multinational corporation spends 30 seconds on TV telling us how it provides fellowships for foreign study, it is trying to encourage viewers to think of it as a fine, upstanding corporate citizen. This is done by associating the company with very positive images and dissociating it from negative ones. Image-building advertising is especially prevalent following a time when a corporation or industry has received a public relations black eye, such as Exxon after the Valdez, Alaska oil spill in 1989. It also is common when a corporation tries to become involved in consciousness raising on some issue of importance and public interest, such as when a distillery runs an ad encouraging people not to drive drunk. They clearly seem to believe that the good will they achieve by being perceived as taking such a responsible public position will more than offset any decline in sales arising from people buying less of their product due to concern about driving under the influence.

A different kind of persuasive media message is the public service announcement (PSA), usually sponsored by some government agency or the Advertising Council. "Ads" by the American Cancer Society or the United Way are examples of PSAs. Historically, the Federal Communications Commission (FCC) has usually mandated that stations must offer a certain amount of time free for PSAs but does not usually specify when that time must be aired; thus PSAs frequently air heavily at off-peak hours like late night or weekdays. With the deregulation and weakening of U.S. regulatory agencies in the 1980s, PSAs suffered even more.

A final kind of advertising is political advertising, usually designed to persuade the viewers to support some candidate, party, or issue. In many ways political advertising is very similar to commercial advertising, although there are some important differences. Political advertising is considered in detail in chapter 8 and thus is not further discussed here.

Whatever the type of ad, it is trying to affect the reality perceived by the consumer (i.e., give us a new image of a product, candidate, or company or make us feel we have a need or desire for some product that we may not have been particularly wanting before). Such processes involve attempts to change our *attitudes*. Our attitudes about products or anything else actually have three components. The *belief* or *cognition* is the informational content of the attitude. For example, Jim prefers Toyota cars because of features a, b, c, and d. The *affective* (emotional) content of the attitude is the *feeling* toward that product. Jim prefers Toyotas because he trusts them, he likes them, he feels safer with them. Finally, the *action* is the attitude's translation into behavior. In the case of ads, the advertiser typically hopes the final step in the chain to be a purchase. Some ads are designed primarily to influence our beliefs and others are designed to influence our affect. See McGuire (1985a) and Pratkanis and Aronson (1992) for reviews of psychological research on attitude change and persuasion. Next we examine how advertising shapes our attitudes to help us construct a reality.

PSYCHOLOGICAL APPEALS IN ADVERTISING

Any type of media advertising, whether print or broadcast, uses a variety of psychological appeals to reach the viewer. In one way or another, ads attempt to tie the product or service to our deepest and most basic psychological needs. Implicitly, then, buying the product will do more than give us something useful or pleasant; it can help us be better people as well.

Informational Appeals

Although not the most common type, some ads primarily provide information in an attempt to influence the belief component of our attitudes. A good example of this type would be an ad for a new product; such an ad may explain what that product does and what its features are. As a medium, newspapers are particularly well suited to conveying information in ads (Abernethy, 1992).

Some of the most common belief appeals are exhortations to save money or receive a superior product or service. The feeling that we are getting a good bargain is a powerful motivator in deciding to purchase something. It is so powerful that often official list prices are set artificially high so that products may be advertised as costing considerably less, when in fact they may have never been intended to sell at the full list price. Some products like stereos and furniture are notoriously often "discounted" in such ways.

Emotional Appeals

Very often ads appeal to the affective component of our attitudes. Influencing emotions is often the best first step to influencing beliefs and, ultimately, behavior. For example, there are many ads that appeal to our love of friends, family, and good times and the good feelings that these bring us. We are asked to call people long distance to affirm our love, buy diamonds and flowers to show how much we care, and drink beer or pop with friends as part of sharing a good time. Such slogans as "Reach out and touch someone" or "Friends are worth Smirnoff" illustrate such appeals. Products are an integral part of showing our love and caring for others. The more closely the advertiser can link the product with those natural and positive emotions, the more successful the ad.

Closely related to family and love appeals is the linking of the product with fun. This is especially clear in ads for soft drinks and beer. Photography and copy that intertwine good times at the beach, in the ski lodge, or just relaxing at home with friends using the product encourage people to think about that product whenever they have or anticipate such good times. The product becomes an integral part of that activity, and, more importantly, the feelings associated with that activity. Watching a sports event on TV with friends may naturally cause us to seek such a product, which has become part of the event.

Certain cultural symbols have come to evoke warm feelings in viewers, which advertisers hope will transfer to warm feelings about the product. A boy and his dog, Grandma baking an apple pie, the flag, or a family homecoming are examples. Such symbols appear frequently in advertising for all sorts of products and services. Connecting one's product with the positive feelings people have for such symbols can associate a lot of positive affect with that product.

Frequently the major selling pitch focuses on how the product will affect your psychological well-being and deep-seated personal needs. For example, a camera ad may say, "Look how good you can be" with their product, not simply "Look what good pictures you can take." The product goes beyond providing you with a good product; it actually makes you a better person. A baby food company once advertised that it helps babies learn to chew. Such an appeal links the product with a very basic developmental event in the baby's life, thus giving it a much more central role in the child's growth than any mere product, even an excellent product, would have. A car advertises itself as "part of the family," not merely offering something to the family but actually being part of it.

Often an appeal is centered around the uniqueness of the product or consumer. Interestingly enough, this type of appeal is especially common from the largest corporations, trying to fight an image of large, impersonal, and uncaring corporate institutions. For example, McDonald's "we do it all for you" campaign and Wendy's ads against "assembly-line burgers" illustrate this approach, as does General Motors' "Can we build one for you?" campaign. This is even more apparent in Saturn automobile advertising, which stresses the importance of the individual consumer and in fact never even mentions that Saturn is a General Motors product! Personal attention and showing interest in the individual is almost always appealing.

Patriotic Appeals.   Appeals to consumers' national pride are common in ads. They are very abundant during the quadrennial Olympic game season and other events like the French Bicentennial in 1989 or the Columbus quincentennial in 1992. The nationality of the manufacturer is of minor importance. Toyota is just as likely as General Motors to use an American patriotic appeal to sell cars in the United States. Volkswagen in New York salutes the U.S. Olympic hockey victories and McDonald's in Dublin helps raise money for the Irish Olympic team. In terms of advertising themes, patriotism is where the market, not the home office, is.

Sometimes particular international events have their repercussions in advertising. Shortly after the Soviet invasion of Afghanistan in late 1979, a strong wave of anti-Soviet sentiment swelled up in the United States. One Turkish vodka manufacturer began a campaign of "Revolutionary vodka without the revolution" (i.e., "buy our vodka and still get imported quality without supporting those dirty communists"). Still, when nationalism crosses the line to tasteless jingoism, it may become commercially counterproductive, as when a small-town U.S. restaurant in 1980 published an "Iranian coupon—good for nothing," or some advertisers took heavy-handed "Japan-bashing" approaches during times of high feeling against Japanese trade practices. Public outcry against excessively mean-spirited patriotic appeals backfires on the advertiser in ways that tend to discourage such campaigns, at least in their most blatant form.

Fear Appeals.   These involve some kind of threat of what may happen if one does not buy the product (e.g., a scenario of a child trying unsuccessfully to phone parents when in danger because the parents don't have Call Waiting). Selling home computers by asking parents "You don't want your child to be left behind in math because you wouldn't buy him a computer, do you?" is a subtle but powerful emotional appeal to guilt and fear. Somewhat less subtle are appeals of safety of one's children, such as when one car manufacturer showed an apparent sonogram of a fetus in utero as "the most important reason to buy" its car. Such appeals to parents, playing on their love and responsibility toward their children, are common and probably highly effective (see Sutton, 1982, for a review of research on fear-arousing communications).

Psychological research on persuasion shows that fear appeals have varying effects. The conventional wisdom in both social psychology and advertising for many years has been that there is an optimal level of fear for persuasion to be the strongest. A weaker appeal will be less effective, but, if the fear induced becomes too strong, the ad may turn people off and make them defensive, in which case they tune out the message. As Rotfeld (1988) pointed out in a careful review paper on fear appeals and persuasion, however, there is no consistency in the research on this point (see also King & Reid, 1990, for fear appeals in PSAs). It is hard to draw firm conclusions because what each researcher has used for a strong, moderate, and low fear appeal has varied widely, and there typically has been little assurance that the subjects in the studies have viewed the appeals similarly to the researchers. Fear appeals in ads are effective, but exactly which ones are most effective is not yet entirely clear.

Achievement, Success, and Power Appeals

Another popular theme in ads is striving to win, whether the prize be money, status, power, or simply having something before the Joneses do. A candy ad may blatantly say "Winning is everything," picturing a chocolate Olympic-style medal, or it may more subtly suggest that only the people who use the particular product have "really arrived." The idea that using some product enables us to "be a winner" is a powerful appeal, whatever the prize. Even an appeal to pure altruism in a PSA can use such an appeal, by calling on us to "achieve a moral victory."

Humorous Appeals

Humor is often used as an effective selling tool in ads. The audio-visual possibilities of television offer a particularly rich set of possibilities for humor, although there is much humor in print and radio advertising as well. Indeed, some humorous ad campaigns have become classics of popular culture (e.g., Alka-Seltzer's "I can't believe I ate the whole thing" campaign of the 1960s or Wendy's "Where's the beef?" of the 1980s). Radio's "see it on the radio" campaign drew on people's ability to use visual imagery to imagine a humorous situation described only through sound (Cantor & Venus, 1980; Madden & Weinberger, 1982, 1984; Sternthal & Craig, 1973).

One caution regarding the use of humor concerns its distractibility potential. Some humor clearly attracts attention and increases motivation and general positive feeling about the product or service. A very funny spot, however, may be so entertaining that it detracts from the advertiser's message. Viewers may remember the gimmick but forget what product it was selling (Gelb & Zinkhan, 1985).

A related concern in regard to humorous ads is the wear-out factor. Any ad campaign depends on repeated presentations to reinforce its message. However, if an ad appears too often in too short a time, its effect may wear out and even become counterproductive by turning people off due to overexposure. Humorous ads have a shorter wear-out time. They seem older, more tired, and more obnoxious faster than other ads. See Pechmann and Stewart (1988) for a thorough review and critique of research on wear-out and related factors.

Testimonials

In the *testimonial* type of ad, some identified person, typically a well-known personality, offers a personal pitch for some product or service. This person may clearly be an expert in the particular field, such as Lee Iacocca selling

Chryslers, or no more informed than the average person, such as Joe Namath selling pantyhose or Bob Hope selling gasoline. Social psychological research on persuasion shows that we are more likely to be persuaded by a prestigious and respected figure, even if that person has no particular expertise in the area of the product being sold (Hass, 1981; Heath, Mothersbaugh, & McCarthy, 1993; Kahle & Homer, 1985). We tend to trust that person more, and the positive associations and feelings we have about him or her may be transferred in part to the product.

Thus far we have primarily focused on the general psychological appeals in ads. Now we focus on the cognitive perspective and its application to advertising.

ADS AS INFORMATION TO BE PROCESSED

The cognitive approach to advertising considers an ad as information to be processed (Shimp & Gresham, 1983; Thorson, 1990). A broadcast commercial or print ad is a very complex stimulus, involving language (presented orally or in writing) and, for print and TV, pictorial stimuli as well. Television is a particularly complex medium, because it contains both the visual and auditory modalities (Shanteau, 1988). Typically there is a close relationship between the audio and video portion of a TV commercial, but this is not always the case (e.g., when a disclaimer is presented only in writing across the bottom of the screen [Kolbe & Muehling, 1992]). The question of how the consumer processes and integrates information from the verbal and visual components of TV commercials is a complex and important issue in itself (Alesandrini, 1983; Cook, 1992; Gardner & Houston, 1986; Percy & Rossiter, 1983; Shanteau, 1988).

Stages of Processing

When we perceive and comprehend an ad, there are eight stages of processing involved in understanding it and acting upon it (Shimp & Gresham, 1983). First of all, we must be *exposed* to the ad. Second, we choose to *attend* to it, perhaps selectively perceiving some parts more than others. Third, we *comprehend* the message. Fourth, we *evaluate* the message in some way (e.g., agree or disagree with it). Fifth, we try to *encode* the information into our long-term memory for future use. Sixth, some time later we try to *retrieve* that information. Seventh, we try to *decide* among available options, such as which brand of cereal to buy. Finally, we *take action* based on that decision (e.g., buying the product).

These eight stages are involved in our processing of every aspect of the ad. Even something as simple as the choice of a name or slogan for a product can have important ramifications for processing, depending on the nature of that name or slogan. For example, the memorability of a name may vary depending on various characteristics. A name that lends itself to an interactive logo or mental image may be remembered due to its amenability to organizational working memory strategies called *chunking*, which lead to a greater number of possible avenues of retrieval from long-term memory (Alesandrini, 1983). For example, a basement waterproofing sealant named "Water Seal" once used a logo of a seal (animal) splashing in water in the middle of a seal (emblem). This choice of a name allowed information about the product name (Water Seal), its use (sealing), and its sound (/sil/) to be unified into one mental image that is easy to remember.

If one or more of the stages is disrupted in some way, overall comprehension of the ad may be affected. For example, the phenomenon of *time compression* involves compressing a 36-second ad into 30 seconds by playing the ad at 120% of normal speed, an acceleration small enough that it is not readily detected and does not produce a higher pitch or other noticeable distortion. Studies of the reactions to such ads (e.g., Hausknecht & Moore, 1986; Moore, Hausknecht, & Thamodaran, 1986) show different effects at different stages of processing (e.g., reduced attention and evaluation, two processes that ultimately influence persuasion).

A Schema Theory Approach to Understanding Advertising

The cognitive principle known as *construction* argues that people do not literally store and retrieve information they read or hear but rather modify it in accordance with their beliefs and the environment in which it is perceived. The encoding and later retrieval of information about the product is guided by knowledge structures called schemas, and a major theoretical development of the last 10 years has been the growth of schema theory (see chapter 2, this volume; Brewer & Nakamura, 1984; Rumelhart, 1980; Thorndyke, 1984).

A schema is a knowledge structure or framework that organizes an individual's memory of information about people and events. It accepts all forms of information, irrespective of the mode—visual or auditory, linguistic or nonlinguistic. The individual is likely to go beyond the information available to draw inferences about people or events that are congruent with previously formed schemas (Graesser & Bower, 1990; Harris, 1981; Harris, Sturm, Klassen, & Bechtold, 1986; Kardes, 1992; Stayman & Kardes, 1992).

For example, a commercial for Lucky Soda might depict a group of dripping, smiling young adults running on a beach and opening a cooler filled with pop. In bold letters at the bottom of the screen are the words "Get Lucky." The slogan, along with the picture, evokes a schema from memory, a schema containing information about such events, based on the viewer's experience. This schema helps the viewer draw inferences to fill in information about the scene, as well as ascribe meaning to it beyond what is specified directly in the ad.

In this example, the readers' "beach party schema" lends a sense of coherence and meaning to a scene that is otherwise incomplete in letting them know exactly what is happening, has happened, or is about to happen. The viewer uses the schema to infer information not specifically stated in the ad, such as (a) the people have been swimming, (b) the temperature is hot, (c) the people are thirsty, and, most importantly, (d) drinking Lucky makes the people happy and playful.

DECEPTIVE ADVERTISING

One of the issues in advertising of greatest concern to the general public is the issue of deceptive advertising. This relates directly to the theme of perceived reality of media and is at heart a cognitive question. The comprehension of an ad may be tested to determine whether the consumer constructs a meaning at variance with the facts (i.e., is "deceived" [Burke, DeSarbo, Oliver, & Robertson, 1988; Harris, Dubitsky, & Bruno, 1983; Richards, 1990]). Ads may deceive either by increasing a false belief held by a consumer or by exploiting a true belief in ways designed to sell the product (Russo, Metcalf, & Stevens, 1981). This issue is examined in some depth in the following section as an example of an advertising issue eminently amenable to a cognitive analysis. There are, however, many other such issues as well.

Miscomprehension Versus Deceptiveness

Preston and Richards (1986) made a helpful distinction between *miscomprehension* and *deceptiveness*. Miscomprehension occurs when the meaning conveyed to the hearer (perceived reality) is different from the literal content of the message. Deceptiveness, on the other hand, occurs if the conveyed meaning is inconsistent with the facts about the product, regardless of what the ad states. From a cognitive perspective, the question is much more complex than merely determining the literal truth or falsity of the ad itself. Studies examining comprehension and miscomprehension of ads and other information from media have shown high rates of miscomprehension, typically 20%–30% of the material misunderstood in some way (Jacoby & Hoyer, 1987).

   If both the literal and conveyed message are true, then there is neither miscomprehension nor deceptiveness. If the literal message is false and is conveyed the same way, there is deceptiveness but no miscomprehension. That is, the hearer constructs a meaning not consistent with reality, but not because he or she misunderstands the ad. For example, if an ad states an incorrect price for a product and we believe it, we have been deceived but have not miscomprehended the ad. Such advertising is clearly both illegal and bad business and is thus fairly unusual. One type that does seem to occur fairly frequently is advertising, as in Example 1, for weight-loss products and diets; perhaps these advertisers bank on the gamble that dissatisfied customers will be too embarrassed or ashamed to want to admit being duped by such a claim.

Ex. 1: You will lose 30 pounds of ugly cellulite in a week.

It is also possible to miscomprehend without being deceived. An ad may state a claim that is literally false, but we comprehend it in some nonliteral way that is consistent with reality and thus we are not deceived. For example, claims like those in Examples 2–4 are unlikely to be comprehended literally; thus a "miscomprehension" leads to *not* being deceived. Generally the U.S. Federal Trade Commission (FTC) and the courts have allowed advertisers to assume some degree of intelligence in the consumer (see Box 4.1). Parenthetically, this issue involves an interesting psychological, and occasionally legal, question of how much intelligence may reasonably by assumed; according to a 1983 policy statement, interpreting earlier legislation, advertisers may assume that the consumer is "acting reasonably"(see Ford & Calfee, 1986). See Box 4.2 for a discussion of another type of clearly false but not so clearly deceptive advertising convention.

BOX 4.1: ADVERTISING REGULATION, THE FCC, AND THE FTC

In the United States, the watchdog agency overseeing advertising is the Federal Trade Commission (FTC). The FTC was established in the early 20th century in the "trust-busting" era of increasing concern over abusive monopolistic practices of large corporations. Its sister organization, the Federal Communications Commission (FCC) oversees radio and television and was set up primarily to deal with such issues as assigning frequencies and channels and insuring access and fair practices.

There have usually been stricter regulations and laws regarding children's advertising than commercials aimed at adults. For example, drug advertising aimed at children has usually been prohibited. In the 1970s the FTC was probably at its most aggressive as a proconsumerist organization, in such issues as deceptive advertising and children's ads. This changed in the early 1980s with increasing deregulation and the probusiness philosophy of the Reagan administration. For example, in 1983 the FCC abolished its children's TV guidelines and in 1984 lifted the limits on allowed commercial time per hour. In the 1980s the FTC became far less aggressive in pursuing claims of misleading advertising based on implication of a false claim. In the 1990s many began calling again for stricter regulation and enforcement.

BOX 4.2: MOCK-UPS

Ivan Preston (1975) discussed the photographic conventions called mock-ups, whereby a product is photographed for TV or print ads using something other than the "real thing." For instance, ice cream may be mashed potatoes covered with chocolate sauce, because ice cream melts too fast under hot studio lights. The head on beer is often shampoo or soap suds, because real heads do not last long enough for photography. These have been allowed on the grounds that the literal falseness actually presents the product less deceptively and more honestly than literal truth (e.g., real ice cream would look like creamed soup, not ice cream, whereas mashed potatoes look like ice cream).

Some other uses of mock-ups, however, have been more questionable and sometimes have been disallowed by the FTC or the courts. For example, how many marbles should be allowed in the bottom of a soup bowl to buoy up the solid ingredients before it should be considered deceptively suggesting more solid ingredients than are really there? How about the shaving cream commercial where the sandpaper being shaved was actually loose sand grains on clear plastic? The razor would in fact shave sandpaper, but only fine sandpaper, not coarse. Because fine sandpaper looked like regular paper on TV, the advertiser used the sand grains on plastic. This particular case was argued in the courts for several years.

Ex. 2: Our cookies are made by elves in a tree.

Ex. 3: A green giant packs every can of our vegetables.

Ex. 4: At this price these cars will fly out the door.

Sometimes the distinction is made between factual and evaluative advertising. *Factual* advertising involves objective claims that are clearly verifiable by reference to the external world (e.g., statements about the price or physical attributes of a product). In contrast to this is *evaluative* advertising, which involves subjective judgments of an unverifiable and unfalsifiable nature. One particularly common type of evaluative advertising is puffery, the superlative "puffing up" of one's product (e.g., "the best," "the greatest" [Preston, 1975]).

Assuming that an ad does contain factual, rather than evaluative, information, determining whether an ad is either deceptive or miscomprehended is not the same as assessing its literal truth value. Truth may be considered a legal or linguistic question, which may be resolved by examining external reality. Miscomprehension, however, is a function of the understanding of the consumer and is thus basically a question of information processing. As such, it is covert and unobservable and must be inferred from an assessment of someone's understanding of an ad. One may be deceived by an ad that is either true or false in some objective sense; the deception may or may not result from miscomprehension.

True-but-Deceptive Ads (Induced Miscomprehension)

The type of advertising claim that is potentially the most damaging is the statement that is literally true, but miscomprehended, thus deceiving consumers by inducing them to construct a meaning of the ad that is inconsistent with reality. Such statements may be either evaluative or factual statements that imply something beyond themselves. This class of ads is the one on which we focus. We have long recognized the inferential nature of information processing, and studies on inference strongly suggest that, in order to derive the meaning of a statement, people typically interpret beyond what is explicitly stated in the ad. When applied to advertising, the consumer may be led to believe things about a product that were never explicitly stated (e.g., an ad states that a mouthwash fights germs and the reader infers that it destroys germs).

There are several different types of linguistic constructions that may deceive the consumer without actually lying. Such claims may invite the consumer to infer beyond the information stated and thus construct a stronger interpretation. This inference-drawing tendency draws on our knowledge in the form of mental schemas discussed earlier and is a natural component of our information-processing system.

Hedges. One common class of true-but-potentially-deceptive claims is the hedge words or expressions (e.g., *may, could help*), that considerably weaken the force of a claim without totally denying it (see Examples 5–7).

Ex. 5: Scrubble Shampoo *may help* get rid of dandruff *symptoms*.

Ex. 6: Rainbow Toothpaste *fights* plaque.

Ex. 7: *Although I can't promise to make you a millionaire by tomorrow*, order my kit and you too *may* become rich.

Elliptical Comparatives. Another common type of linguistic construction that may imply false information is the elliptical comparative (see Examples 8–10). Comparative adjectives or adverbs necessarily involve some sort of standard that something is being compared to. When a product merely says it gives *more*, the statement is largely vacuous without knowing the basis of comparison ("more than what?"). As long as anything true could be used to complete the comparative, the statement cannot clearly be considered false. However, our minds tend to construct the most plausible basis of comparison, not necessarily the most accurate.

Ex. 8: The Neptune Hatchback gives you *more*.

Ex. 9: Fibermunchies have *more* vitamin C.

Ex. 10: Powderpower laundry detergent cleans *better*.

Implied Causation.   Often a causative relationship may be implied when no more than a correlational one in fact exists. This invitation to make a further inference beyond what is stated directly is one way that active cognitive processing by the consumer may be increased, which in turn may improve memory. One particular technique that does so is the juxtaposition of two imperatives (see Examples 11–12).

> Ex. 11: Help your child excel in school. Buy an Apricot home computer.
>
> Ex. 12: Shed those extra pounds. Buy the Blubberbuster massage belt.

In neither Example 11 nor Example 12 does the ad state that buying the product will have the stated effect, but the causative inference is very easy to draw.

Such a cause-and-effect relationship may also be implied in a more general sense. For example, consider a radio commercial for diet pop where a young woman talks about using and liking the product. Then at the end of the ad we hear a male voice saying, "And I like the way it looks on her too." Listeners may infer that drinking that product will cause female listeners to be more attractive to men, although the ad never states that directly.

An implicit conditional logical argument may be drawn on in a similar fashion (see Examples 13–15). Example 13 may be interpreted the same way as Example 14, a conditional statement. Conditional reasoning research (Evans, 1982; Griggs, 1983; Wason & Johnson-Laird, 1972) has shown that people often fallaciously infer a biconditional ("if and only if") relationship from statements like Example 14 so that consumers may infer Example 15 as well as Example 14 from Example 13.

> Ex. 13: Euphoria Capsules make you healthy.
>
> Ex. 14: If you take Euphoria Capsules, you will be healthy.
>
> Ex. 15: If you don't take Euphoria Capsules, you won't be healthy.

Implied Slur on Competition.   Something unfavorable may be implied about a competitor's products or services (see Examples 16–17). Although direct false statements about the competition are usually not tolerated, false implications are less clearly proscribed. For example, consumers may infer from Example 16 or Example 17 that competing companies do not provide the same service, whereas most in fact do so.

> Ex. 16: If we do your taxes and you are audited by the IRS, we will accompany you to the audit.
>
> Ex. 17: Our company gives refunds quickly if your traveler's checks are lost or stolen.

Pseudoscience.   Reporting of scientific evidence in incomplete fashion may also imply considerably more than what is stated (see Examples 18–20). In reporting results of surveys, for example, mentioning a percentage or absolute number responding without the sample size (Example 19) or the number sampled without the number responding (Example 20) is seriously incomplete and potentially misleading. Example 18 would not be false if only four people were questioned.

Ex. 18: Three out of four doctors recommended Snayer Aspirin.

Ex. 19: 2000 dentists recommended brushing with Laser Fluoride.

Ex. 20: In a survey of 10,000 car owners, most preferred Zip.

Comparative advertising may employ very selective attribute comparisons to imply a much more global impression. Example 21 may imply that the car has a more spacious interior on most or all dimensions than any of the competitors, which is not necessarily a warranted inference from the statement.

Ex. 21: The Egret Pistol has more front-seat legroom than a Ford Taurus, more rear-seat headroom than a Nissan Stanza, and a larger trunk than a Toyota Camry.

Studying Deception Scientifically

In experimental studies, people do in fact make the invited inferences described and remember the inferred information as having been stated in the ad (e.g., remembering that a toothpaste prevents cavities when the ad only said it "fights" cavities). This is a stable finding that occurs with a variety of dependent measures (Burke, DeSarbo, Oliver, & Robertson, 1988; Gardner & Leonard, 1990; Harris, Pounds, Maiorelle, & Mermis, 1993; Harris, Trusty, Bechtold, & Wasinger, 1989; Richards, 1990; Russo, Metcalf, & Stevens, 1981). Burke et al. (1988) even developed a computer-based measurement technique for assessing the deceptive effects of advertising claims.

Training people not to make such inferences is very difficult, because the tendency to infer beyond the given information is so strong. However, a training session that has participants individually analyze ads, identify unwarranted inferences that may be drawn, and rewrite ads to imply something more or less strongly, does have some significant effect in teaching them to put a brake on this natural inference-drawing activity (Bruno & Harris, 1980). Such research has direct application to the preparation of consumer-education materials, including some media literacy programs. See chapter 12 for a brief discussion of such programs and Brown (1991) for a detailed description and evaluation.

Sometimes changing the wording of an ad may induce highly different interpretations, although it may not neatly fit the deception model. For example, consider a meat advertised as "75% lean" versus "25% fat." Consumers evaluate the former more favorably than the semantically identical latter wording (Levin & Gaeth, 1988). The positive frame leads us to construct a more positive image of the product. One type of currently popular advertising where one must carefully watch the wording is ads that appeal to environmental consciousness (see Box 4.3).

The rest of this chapter examines two specific types of advertising that raise especially important and controversial psychological issues in regard to the perceived reality about advertised products. First we examine advertising targeted at children and then we turn to sex in advertising, including the issue of subliminal advertising.

CHILDREN'S ADVERTISING

An important concern in advertising is television commercials aimed specifically at children, primarily on Saturday morning programs and, to a lesser extent, after school shows (McNeal, 1987; Raju & Lonial, 1990). We must keep in mind, however, that children's programming, the so-called "kidvid ghetto," constitutes only a minority of the hours of TV that children watch, although the amount of that time spent in commercials increased in the United States during the 1980s (Condry, Bence, & Scheibe, 1988). Kidvid represented only 24% of the viewing time for 6-year-olds and a mere 5% for 11-year-olds. The rest of the many

---

BOX 4.3: GREEN ADVERTISING

One of the most recent kind of social responsibility appeals in advertising has been to the environment. Advertising one's product as being biodegradable, organic, or otherwise conserving the earth's resources is a popular concern and would seem initially to be a socially responsible position.

Although it may often be just that, sometimes the reality is more complex than what is presented in the ad. For example, one popular kind of trash bag advertised that it was made of "biodegradable plastic." Although this sounds good, once a sealed bag of contaminants is in a landfill, it may actually be better for the environment if it is not biodegradable, rather than slowly decomposing over several years, gradually releasing toxic content into the groundwater system. Some such products rely on the sun to initiate the decomposition process, and it is not at all clear how much sun the typical bag buried deep in a landfill would receive.

Other examples of green advertising include biodegradable disposable diapers for parents who want convenience without the guilt of befouling the earth.

thousands of ads that each child sees every year are seen on general programming (i.e., prime-time and daytime offerings such as game shows, soap operas, and syndicated sitcom reruns). Increasingly a sizable market, children between 4 and 12 years of age control about $9 billion of their own money, in addition to whatever influences they have on their parents' purchases (McNeal, 1990). In addition, they have considerable influence on many of their parents' purchases (Robertson, Ward, Gatignon, & Klees, 1989).

Turning now to kidvid ads specifically, over 90% of them advertise products in a mere four categories: toys, cereal, candy and snacks, and fast-food restaurants. One study shows that 82% of all children's ads were for some type of food, usually heavily sugared (Barcus, 1980). The toy ads are many, but are primarily concentrated during the pre-Christmas season, with numbers much lower during the rest of the year.

Children's ads are technical marvels, full of color, movement, and animation, most emphasizing how much fun children can have with the product. Special visual and sound effects are common and captivating. The pace is fast. There is even less "hard information" presented than in adult ads and more of a global association of the product and fun times. There is lots of alliteration (e.g., "Crazy Cow," "Kit Kat") and word plays (e.g., "fruitiful," a character yodelling "Cheerio-ios"). Commercials aimed at kids are made to be far more fun than adult ads. Behind all the fun, however, lie some serious concerns about the effects of these ads; let us turn to those now.

Differentiating Ads and Programs

One major concern about children and commercials is that very young children do not discriminate between commercials and program content and do not understand the persuasive intent of ads or the economics of television. Although children can identify commercials at a very early age, this identification seems to be based on superficial audio and video aspects rather than on an understanding of the difference between programs and commercials (Raju & Lonial, 1990). Studies show that preschool children have little understanding that commercials are meant to sell products. Depending on how such understanding is tested, elementary school children show various stages of development of the understanding of the purpose of ads (Bever, Smith, Bengen, & Johnson, 1975; Dorr, 1980; Robertson & Rossiter, 1974; Sheikh, Prasad, & Rao, 1974; Stephens & Stutts, 1982; Stutts, Vance, & Hudelson, 1981; Ward, Wackman, & Wartella, 1977). It also appears that the insertion of video and audio "separators" to mark the transition between program and commercials has not made this discrimination easier (Hoy, Young, & Mowen, 1986; Stutts et al., 1981). Discriminating ads and programs is especially difficult if a primary character in the show is also the spokesperson in the ad, the situation called "host-selling" (Hoy et al., 1986; Kunkel, 1988).

Children show increasing distrust of ads as they grow older. Most 5- to 7-year-olds say that ads "tell the truth," whereas older children are less likely to be so trusting (Blatt, Spencer, & Ward, 1972; Robertson & Rossiter, 1974; Ward et al., 1977). Typical explanations of middle elementary children center around the truth (or lack thereof) of the material; however, not until late elementary school is the distrust based on perceived intent and an understanding of the advertiser's motivation to sell the product. Among demographic groups, African Americans and lower socioeconomic class children tend to be the most trusting and least critical of ads (Wartella, 1980; Young, 1991).

Disclaimers

A particularly interesting issue in children's advertising is the question of disclaimers, those little qualifying statements like "partial assembly required," "batteries not included," "action figures sold separately," or "part of a nutritious breakfast" (Geis, 1982). For obvious reasons these are hardly the central focus of the commercial. In fact, the disclaimers often occur in vocabulary far beyond the age of the target viewer and often occur only in writing superimposed at the bottom of the screen. This is completely lost on a prereading child and probably on an older child as well, because the colorful activity in the background is so much more enticing and interesting. In a content analysis of 1,000 children's ads, Stern and Harmon (1984) found that 36% had some sort of disclaimer, most of these appearing only at the end of the ad and most in audio-only (60%) or visual-only (30%) format. Unlike the rest of the ad, almost all of the disclaimers used adult terminology. Most preschoolers do not understand such terminology (Stutts & Hunnicutt, 1987), although some disclaimers were less difficult than others.

Incidentally, disclaimers and other "fine print" information flashed at the bottom of the TV screen are by no means limited to children's ads. A content analysis of prime-time TV ads found two thirds to contain some sort of footnote (Kolbe & Muehling, 1992).

Drug Advertising

A particularly emotional issue in regard to children and advertising concerns their reactions to ads for drugs. The criticism argues that advertising implicitly assumes a chemical cure for every physical, psychological, or social ill, and that children grow up learning from television that the answers to all of their problems may be found in the medicine cabinet. Although this is a difficult question to carefully study scientifically, the research that has been done has generally failed to show a relationship between the amount of TV viewing and use of either over-the-counter (OTC) or illicit drugs or the instances of accidental child poisoning from ingesting overdoses of household drugs (Robertson, Rossiter, & Gleason, 1979).

One area of particularly acrimonious controversy can be found in the area of tobacco advertising, especially advertising that is allegedly aimed at nonsmoking youth. There is evidence of a causal relationship of advertising and consumption (Tye, Warner, & Glantz, 1987) and huge profits from sales of tobacco to minors and to those who became addicted to tobacco as minors (DiFranza & Tye, 1990). Tremendous criticism has been leveled at the "Joe Camel" character used to sell Camel cigarettes. He was as readily recognizable as Mickey Mouse to 6-year-olds but far less known to adults. This occurred at the same time that sales of Camels to minors were skyrocketing to one quarter of the brand's total sales ("Camels for Kids," 1991).

Programs as Commercials and the Toy–Program Connection

Although not the first such instance, in 1983 Mattel's popular He-Man toy made the move to television ("He-Man and the Masters of the Universe") and within a year became the second best-selling toy in the country (Diamond, 1987). This successful marketing approach has been massively copied since then and has raised a new issue in regard to children's TV ads, namely, the commercial-as-show phenomenon. By 1987, over 40 television shows were linked to toys in some way. Some of the most popular were "The Transformers," "She-Ra: Princess of Power," "G.I. Joe," "Teenage Mutant Ninja Turtles," "He-Man and the Masters of the Universe," "ThunderCats," "Smurfs," "The Care Bear Family," and "All New Pound Puppies." Toy companies routinely seek TV shows to promote their toys, as when Hasbro, Inc. subsidized the production of "G.I. Joe," "Jem," and "The Transformers," from its $217 million marketing budget. Thus the toy industry and television have been wedded almost as significantly and profoundly as have been sports and TV.

This marriage raises several concerns. Critics have argued that children's programming is driven too much by the marketability of associated toys rather than by the quality of the shows (Carlsson-Paige & Levin, 1990; Kline, 1992). Toy and broadcasting executives defend the policy by arguing that creative animated shows are preferable to tired syndicated reruns of "Gilligan's Island" or "Leave It to Beaver," often the most attractive alternative for after school or Saturday morning. Still, producers of nontoy-related children's programming report difficulty funding and selling their products. Programming is increasingly initiated around an existing (or soon to be marketed) toy. Although merchandising toys from successful shows has long been around ("Mickey Mouse Club," "Sesame Street"), until recently the show has come first, not the toy. That is no longer the case.

It has also been suggested that the toy–television connection has led to increased marketing segmentation by gender (Carlsson-Paige & Levin, 1990). The violent shows and accompanying toy weapons and action figures (they are never called "dolls" if marketed to boys) are sold to boys, whereas girls are offered the extremely soft, cuddly shows and toys like "The Smurfs," "My Little Pony," and "Rainbow Bright." Successful "boy toys" may be repackaged and sold to girls, as in the Adorable Transformables that change, for example, from a dog into lipstick instead of from a car into a robot.

Violence

A final concern is violence. Many of the toy-related shows, especially those targeted at boys, are highly violent in nature. This in itself is not new; children's cartoons have always been the most violent shows on TV, in terms of numbers of violent incidents (see chapter 9). A particular concern with the newer shows, however, is that the availability of toys makes it easier to act out the violence modelled by the cartoon characters. Whereas children have always played war games of sorts, in the past they have usually had to employ their imagination to make a stick into a sword or a cardboard cutout into a gun. In so doing, they also develop their creative capacities.

A plastic Uzi machine gun, however, can only be used to play killing people and thus requires no particular imagination. The more highly defined the violent purpose of the toy, the more it directs the child's play in a violent direction, even in a child who might not otherwise be inclined toward violent play. It also encourages the child to look on the real thing as "just a toy" (Carlsson-Paige & Levin, 1990). There are many serious consequences of the failure to distinguish toy weapons from the real thing; children using toy guns have been killed by police officers who thought they were being fired upon with real weapons. For this reason, in some jurisdictions such realistic-looking toy guns (but, curiously, seldom the real ones) have been banned.

Although there are still other issues in the study of children's advertising (e.g., effects on parents' purchase behavior, persuadability of children, memory for ad content), we turn now to a very common type of ad that we have not yet considered—the sexy ad.

SEX IN ADVERTISING

One of the most common type of appeals in advertising is the sexual one. Although some products such as perfume and cologne are sold almost exclusively through sexual appeals, practically any product can be marketed through associating it with a beautiful woman or man. The sexual association and allure, and even more so, the overall good feelings engendered, then become a part of the perceived reality of that product for many consumers.

Classical Conditioning

A psychological process called classical conditioning sheds some light on how sex in advertising can affect us. Classical conditioning is the process discovered by Ivan Pavlov, who studied the physiology of hunger in dogs in the early years of the 20th century. In his studies he noticed a curious fact; his dogs would often start to salivate merely at the sight of an empty food dish. Given that there is no natural connection between plastic dishes and drooling, why did they do it? Pavlov eventually decided that they had been "classically conditioned." This process became one of the cornerstones of experimental (especially behaviorist) psychology and is equally important for consumers of ads as it was for Pavlov's dogs.

An *unconditioned stimulus* (UCS) naturally, without learning, elicits an *unconditioned response* (UCR). For example, meat (UCS) naturally produces salivation (UCR) in a dog. Similarly, the sight of a gorgeous woman (UCS) naturally elicits mild sexual arousal or at least some positive feelings (UCR) in most heterosexual males. At this point in the process, there is no conditioning. The conditioning occurs when the UCS is *paired* (associated) with the *conditioned stimulus* (CS), which does not normally elicit the UCR. For example, Pavlov's dog dish (CS) was associated with meat (UCS), just as the attractive model (UCS) is associated with a product (CS) in a commercial. There may be some natural and obvious connection of the model and the product, such as a perfume ad that suggests a woman will attract sexy men if she wears that fragrance, or there may be no intrinsic connection at all, such as the beautiful woman next to the steel-belted radials.

After enough association of the UCS and the CS, the CS by itself comes to elicit the *conditioned response* (CR), which is very similar to the UCR. Just as Pavlov's dogs eventually began to salivate (CR) to the empty food dish (CS), so may we have positive feelings (CR) about the tire (CS) when we see it without the gorgeous model. This basic classical conditioning paradigm is the psychological process being employed by most ads using sexual stimuli.

Ironically, sometimes advertisers themselves may be loath to be associated with certain stimuli that they feel evoke strong negative responses in the majority of the population (see Box 4.4).

Subliminal Advertising

Although we could look at classical conditioning as a subliminal effect in the broadest sense, people are more likely to think of subliminal persuasion, especially as applied to advertising. In the late 1950s several popular press articles reported a study by advertising expert James Vicary whereby he reported increasing the sales of Coke and popcorn in a New Jersey theater by flashing the messages "eat popcorn" and "drink Coke" at one third of a millisecond every

---

BOX 4.4: ADVERTISING TO GAYS AND LESBIANS

In spite of the overriding principle of economic reality driving the advertising dollar, one sizable market has been largely ignored by national advertisers. The prospect of increasing sales to readers of gay publications seems to be more than offset by the fear of losing heterosexual buyers as a result of having one's product associated with the gay audience. Although gay magazines and newspapers successfully recruited some major advertisers in the late 1970s and early 1980s, the AIDS panic of the late 1980s apparently scared away most of those advertisers. Gay and lesbian publications have been struggling financially, with most mainstream national companies (with the exception of liquor companies and movie studios) pulling out in recent years. Even condom manufacturers fear association of their product with gays. Ironically, this drying up of ad money has caused many publications to rely increasingly on ads for sexual videos and paraphernalia and sexually explicit personal classifieds, exactly the sort of material that national advertisers shudder to be associated with. Whether advertisers' homophobic fears of guilt by association are justified remain untested. In the meantime, a sizable minority market that has significantly more than the average disposable income remains largely ignored (Alsop, 1988).

---

5 seconds during a movie. Although the research was never published and in fact was admitted by Vicary in 1962 to have been a complete fabrication only intended to increase his advertising agency's business (Pratkanis, 1992), the public became very alarmed, and the FCC and NAB outlawed the practice. Large numbers of people continue to uncritically accept the existence of subliminal persuasion, in spite of there being no credible scientific evidence for its existence.

Subliminal means below the threshold of conscious perception; we are not normally aware of something that is subliminal. Such stimuli may be a subaudible sound message in a store ("Don't shoplift"), a very brief message in a movie or TV show ("buy popcorn"), or a visual sexual stimulus airbrushed into an ad photograph ("S-E-X" spelled in the crackers or sex organs drawn in the ice cubes). What are the alleged effects of such stimuli? Do they in fact work to sell products?

An important distinction to bear in mind in considering this problem is the difference between establishing the *existence* of some subliminal stimulus and demonstrating that such a stimulus has some *effect*. Books like Wilson Bryan Key's *Subliminal Seduction* (1974), *The Clam-plate Orgy* (1981), *Media Sexploitation* (1976), and *The Age of Manipulation* (1989) focus on demonstrating the existence of subliminal messages and sexual implants, but they give few arguments to demonstrate any effects that such stimuli have. Implicitly such authors often assume that showing its existence also entails that it has an effect. Such is not the case at all, however. Although there is some reputed evidence (Cuperfain & Clarke, 1985; Kilbourne, Painton, & Ridley, 1985) of an effect, much of the so-called evidence is anecdotal or open to other interpretations. In fact there is little evidence that it affects people very much (see Merikle & Cheesman, 1987; Moore, 1982, 1988; Pratkanis, 1992; Pratkanis & Greenwald, 1988; and Saegert, 1987, for reviews of this topic).

Moore (1982) identified three possible problem areas: subliminal visual perception, subaudible speech, and embedded sexual stimuli, and carefully examined research evidence on possible effects in all three areas. Moore concluded that there is only a little evidence, although it is far from compelling and not directly related to advertising anyway, that subliminal stimuli may in some cases have a weak positive effect of a general affective nature (i.e., they make us feel a little better about the product, perhaps due to classical conditioning). However, there is virtually no evidence for any effects of subliminal stimuli on *behavior*. Saegert (1987) looked at the very few studies that seem to suggest effects and argued that other interpretations are possible. The conclusion at this point seems to be that subliminal stimuli may exist on occasion but that their effects are minimal, if not totally nonexistent. Subliminal advertising seems to be a perceived reality in the mind of much of the public, but not an actual reality that stands up to scientific scrutiny. The same is true for subliminal learning tapes (Greenwald, Spangenberg, Pratkanis, & Eskenazi, 1991; Merikle, 1988; Merikle & Skanes, 1992).

Similar issues are involved in heated controversies over subliminal messages in rock music. In 1990 the family of two teenage suicide victims in Nevada brought suit against the group Judas Priest and CBS Records, on the grounds that subliminal messages on their albums had directed the boys to take their own lives; the judge ruled against the family. Another concern has been allegedly "satanic" messages recorded backwards into certain rock music recordings. See Box 4.5 for details of a careful research program designed to test for effects of such stimuli.

CONCLUSION

This chapter is in no way a comprehensive review of the psychological effects of advertising or even of all issues relevant to the perceived reality of advertising. Rather, the emphasis is on looking at a few areas where advertising attempts to create a reality within our minds that is conducive to purchasing a product. We are "taught" positive emotional associations about the product through classical conditioning or association of the product with positive experiences in our past. Natural information-processing tendencies like drawing inferences and invoking knowledge schemas to interpret ads around are used by advertisers to encourage us to draw certain inferences and interpretations. Knowledge of the way that the mind processes information allows the advertiser to construct ads designed to encourage us to construct a meaning favorable to the advertiser's

---

BOX 4.5: SATANIC MESSAGES IN ROCK MUSIC?

Periodically one hears the claim that some rock music contains embedded messages recorded backward. Although no one claims that these messages can be consciously perceived easily when the record is played forward, concern had been expressed that there may be some unconscious effect unbeknownst to the listener. Furthermore, some conservative Christians have been concerned that such messages may be satanic and have caused legislation to be introduced in several states that would call for warning labels about such messages to appear on album jackets.

Vokey and Read (1985) of the University of Lethbridge were contacted by a radio announcer for information about this phenomena. They first made the point that the *presence* of such embedded messages does not presuppose any *effect* of such messages on the listener. The evidence presented by concerned members of the public is highly anecdotal and often debatable but nearly always speaks to the presence issue, not the effects issue.

These psychologists conducted a careful series of studies designed to test the effects of such messages (Vokey & Read, 1985), even assuming for the moment that they exist (an assumption that is not at all established, but we will leave that for now). When verbal messages on tape were played backward for subjects, they showed no understanding of the meaning; identifying the sex or voice of the speaker was about all that they could perceive. Next, they tested for *unconscious* effects by giving subjects a spelling test where some of the words were homophones (*read, reed*). A biasing context sentence (*A saxophone is a reed instrument*) was played backward but subjects were no more likely than a control group to write *reed* instead of *read*. When backward messages were played and subjects were merely asked to assign the statement to the category "Christian," "satanic," "pornographic," or "advertising," based on its content, they could not do so at greater than chance level. The only time that subjects ever perceived and reported anything at greater than chance level was in one study where the experimenter picked out words in advance and asked the subjects to listen for them. Only under conditions of such strong suggestibility could subjects comprehend anything from the backward messages.

Vokey and Read's studies clearly demonstrate that, even if backward messages do exist in albums, it is highly unlikely that they could be having any effect on the hearers. This conclusion is all the more striking considering that in their studies there was no competing forward message like the music in rock albums. In at least a couple of cases, proposed record-labeling legislation was withdrawn based on results of this research.

---

ends. On the other hand, knowledge of such processes also allows consumers to take steps to be less "manipulated." Advertising is not going to go away, nor would most of us seriously wish that it would. Our defense against its excesses comes through education in media literacy. This topic is explored further in the concluding chapter of this book.

CHAPTER

5

VALUES: RIGHTS AND WRONGS
IN THE MEDIA

Q: How many scenes of suggested sexual intercourse or innuendo are shown on TV per year in the United States?
A: 9,200 on prime time.
Q: How many of these are between persons not married to each other?
A: Five out of six in prime time (Liebert & Sprafkin, 1988), 24 out of 25 in soap operas (Lowry & Towles, 1989), 32 out of 33 in R-rated movies (Greenberg, Brown, & Buerkel-Rothfuss, 1993).
Q: What percentage of Americans claim a religious affiliation?
A: 89%.
Q: What percentage of fictional TV characters have an identifiable religious affiliation?
A: 5% (Skill, Lyons, & Larson, 1991)

One of the major concerns raised about the role of mass media in society is their role as teachers of values, "passing the social heritage from one generation to the next" (Lasswell, cited in Tuchman, 1987, p. 195). What the content of this social heritage is continues to be debated, however. Although relatively few print media stories or radio or TV broadcasts have the explicit purpose of teaching values, values are being taught implicitly, particularly by television. In this chapter we consider values as being very broadly defined as attitudes dealing with any subject where there is a readily perceived "right" and "wrong" position. Whether there is a right or wrong in an absolute sense need not concern us; values come in wherever people perceive rights and wrongs.

On the one hand, the media may be seen as mirroring the values of the society in which they occur. If sexual values are promiscuous in a society, this will be reflected in its media; if certain religious values predominate in a society, they will also prevail in its media. On the other hand, the media may be seen as a catalyst for value change in a society. Values in the media may not exactly reflect those prevailing in society but may serve, probably not intentionally so, as a catalyst for moving society's values in the new direction. This is, of course, exactly the concern of media critics who argue that U.S. television most strongly reflects the values of the New York and Los Angeles communities where most programming originates, but that it tends to cultivate those values in the rest of the otherwise more conservative country. Taking a different approach, critics sometimes argue that media have a responsibility to lead society in a direction of more prosocial values; for example, after the Los Angeles riots of 1992, there were calls for media to promote racial harmony and not inflame raw nerves by emphasizing racial violence.

We often hear laments that television is so much more permissive today than it used to be ("Oh, if we could just have back the good old days of 'Ozzie and Harriet,' 'The Donna Reed Show,' 'The Brady Bunch,' and 'Leave It to Beaver' when family values were solid"). Clearly, in many respects TV is more permissive today than it used to be, although it is far from "anything goes." However, this is not the whole picture; there are also ways in which TV is less permissive and more strict today than it was 30 years ago (see Box 5.1). See Selnow (1990) for a content analysis of TV values.

BOX 5.1: INCREASINGLY CONSERVATIVE MEDIA VALUES

Although there has been a greater permissiveness of representing divergent values in media since the 1950s, not everything is loosening up. In some ways, standards on U.S. television are much more restrictive than they used to be. Perhaps most prominent among the restrictive trends is any content or language that could be considered racist or sexist. The early TV hit sitcom "Amos and Andy" was considered too racist even to show in reruns as early as the mid-1950s; today it would be extremely offensive and inappropriate, if not downright grotesque. Racist jokes simply are not acceptable in U.S. prime-time media, except possibly from a very bad character in a drama. Different cultures, of course, vary in their sensitivity to such issues. Until recently, a brand of toothpaste called Darkie, with an Al Jolson-like minstrel character on the tube, was marketed in Hong Kong.

Any real or implied violence against women, unless it is, for example, critically examined on a TV movie, is another very touchy area. Ralph Kramden's gag line in "The Honeymooners" of shaking his fist in his wife's face and angrily saying, "One of these days, Alice, pow, right in the kisser!" was hilarious in 1955. Today it strikes modern viewers as offensive and inappropriate, much as Ozzie Nelson swearing profusely or having a homosexual experience would have seemed in 1955.

Because most of the concern and study of values has focused on the medium of television, this is the major focus of the chapter. However, print media and radio are by no means uninvolved in value issues, and some of their particular concerns are addressed. Newspaper editors are continually faced with questions of how much information to print about crime victims. Radio stations always worry about listener response to song lyrics that go too blatantly against prevailing social values (e.g., strong negative responses to rap star Ice-T's song "Cop Killer").

In this chapter we look at specific value issues and how media are involved in teaching or reinforcing those values. The three major general areas of values are family values, economic values, and religion. These areas are offered as examples and are not meant to be considered an exhaustive list of values with which media are involved. Most of the comments primarily reflect media in the United States and may or may not be accurate in other nations.

FAMILY VALUES

Family values is an often-heard phrase in social and political discourse in the 1990s. However, it has different meanings to different people, because there are many value issues that relate to the family and the relationships among its members. For reviews of research on the effects of television on family values, see Brown and Bryant (1990), Gunter and Svennevig (1987), and Robinson (1990). Modern television, at least in the United States, is a curious amalgam of considerable permissiveness and strong reaffirmation of traditional conservative values. We illustrate this by examining a few specific issues.

Models of Family

We see many more diverse models of families on TV today than were shown in the 1950s and 1960s, although this has only been the case since about the mid-1970s, in the case of sitcoms. The debut of "One Day at a Time" in 1975, featuring a divorced mother and her two teenage daughters, was the first sitcom to show a fully rounded and realistic divorced adult as a featured character. Not all TV children today are in nuclear families with mother, father, and 2.3 children. In recent years U.S. TV series have offered a variety of family situations, including children living with two divorced mothers ("Kate and Allie"); two single men ("My Two Dads"); widowed mother and her widowed father-in-law ("Our House"); widowed father and divorced aunt ("The Hogan Family"); widowed father, single uncle, and single male friend ("Full House"); widowed father, divorced female employer, and employer's child and mother ("Who's the Boss?"); adoptive single father ("Different Strokes"); and older brother, sister-in-law, and uncle ("One Big Family").

Still, however, the prototypical pattern is the traditional nuclear family ("The Cosby Show," "The Simpsons," "The Wonder Years," "Evening Shade," "Roseanne," "Major Dad," "Coach," "Home Improvement," "Brooklyn Bridge," "Life Goes On," "Fresh Prince of Bel Air," and "Married with Children"). A content analysis of TV family-interaction patterns showed more harmonious and conflict-resolution behaviors in traditional than in nontraditional families (Skill, Wallace, & Cassata, 1990).

These traditional nuclear families have changed, however. Most often, both parents have careers outside of the home ("Roseanne," "The Cosby Show"), or one parent brings his or her career into the home ("Growing Pains," where the psychiatrist dad has his office in the home). Indeed, one of the major concerns today is that modern TV families appear to be managing career and family so successfully that the difficulties inherent in managing two-career families are glossed over, if not totally ignored (Maynard, 1987). The presentation of family values on TV and the socializing role of TV vis-à-vis societal values is a continuing object of concern (Gumpert, 1987; Gunter & Svennevig, 1987; Morley, 1986).

Even in the context of traditional families, some of the patterns of interaction have greatly changed from the more authoritarian days of "Father Knows Best" and "Leave It to Beaver." Psychiatrist Alvin Poussaint, a consultant to "The Cosby Show," said that today's TV parents seem to have no needs apart from their children and "are more like pals . . . overly permissive, always understanding . . . never get angry . . . no boundaries or limits set" (Kalter, 1988c, p. 10). See Box 5.2 for an example from a popular sitcom episode, illustrating just how much family values have changed.

Family Solidarity

Probably the most pervasive of the family values on TV is family solidarity (i.e., loyalty, support, and love for one's family). This is most clearly seen in the family sitcom. The basic message here, as true for "Home Improvement" and "Roseanne" in the 1990s as it was for "Leave It to Beaver" or "Father Knows Best" 30 years ago, is that one's family is more important than money, power, greed, status, or professional advancement. Even the most irreverent family shows teach a family cohesiveness that tends in the end to strongly affirm traditional values; for example, when "The Simpsons" dad Homer lost his job, the whole family pitched in to help save money.

One may ask if such family solidarity is a realistic reflection of our society. It clearly is so with many families and just as clearly is not for many others, whose troubled family dynamics would more typically be characterized by vicious backstabbing, betrayal, and generally putting oneself above other members. Still, even those families might agree that the sitcom characterization is

---

BOX 5.2: CASE STUDY OF MODERN FAMILY SINS

An episode of the sitcom "Family Ties" in the mid-1980s presented a story in which high school senior Alex Keaton anticipates his 18th birthday by withdrawing from family responsibilities and interaction. The final blow comes when he goes with some friends to a bar, defying his parents and despite plans for a family birthday dinner. His mother Elyse drives some distance to retrieve an embarrassed Alex from this peer gathering. After they arrive home, both are seething with anger. After Alex sarcastically yells at his mother about his right to do as he likes now that he is an "adult," she responds in only slightly more controlled fashion, "you have complained to me, grunted at me, lectured to me, and presented me with ultimatums [but never] even come close to talking with me." She accuses him of cancelling out on family dinner plans "without a moment's thought to *my* concern." Growing contrite, Alex eventually acknowledges, "I'm sorry I wasn't more sensitive," and both acknowledge that they have made mistakes in dealing with each other. When Alex asks "How do we figure out who's right and who's wrong?" Elyse responds that there is no absolute right or wrong and then offers a startling statement about contemporary parent–child relations: "It's my job as a parent to set boundaries and it's your job to negotiate the changes."

In this scene, fairly typical of contemporary family shows, the morally serious transgression of the child is not disobedience but *insensitivity*. If there are troubles in the family, the parents have probably made mistakes as well as the children. Parent–child interactions are to be negotiations, not decrees and obedience. Even though traditional family solidarity and family values are in many ways affirmed today as they have always been on TV, the specific nature has changed somewhat.

---

a worthy ideal to hold up as a model, even if it is not totally realistic. Maybe this is a socially helpful model to portray.

Many sitcoms and dramatic shows are set in the workplace, which essentially becomes a surrogate family (e.g., "Wings," "Star Trek: The Next Generation," "The New WKRP in Cincinnati," "M*A*S*H," "L.A. Law," "Murphy Brown," "Designing Women," "Cheers," "Night Court," "Hill St. Blues"). The strong message in these shows is "always love your co-worker" (even if you do not) and "put his or her needs above your own." This, even more than traditional family solidarity, is very questionably tied to reality.

One area of workplace solidarity is probably a direct consequence of the TV series format. This is the way that co-workers are so intimately involved in the personal lives of fellow workers, employers, and employees. Although real-life co-workers may sometimes be close friends, this is typically not the case, and it is almost unheard-of in the real world for all of the workers in a unit to be close personal friends. Yet this is the typical case in television land. For example, when WKRP station manager Arthur Carlson's wife delivered her baby, the entire staff of the radio station was at the hospital. In real life this would not

only be unlikely, but most probably obtrusively inappropriate and unappreciat-
ed, even if for some reason it did occur.

Perhaps even more of a deviation from reality is the way that this workplace
solidarity is extended to the clients of a professional. For example, Dr. Gonzo
Gates on "Trapper John, M.D." regularly went running off hundreds of miles
to find a lost family member of a patient or to smooth out a domestic quarrel
that he felt was interfering with the recovery of his patient. In real life surgeons
do not do this sort of thing and would doubtlessly be derelict of their duty at
the hospital if they did. Still, such an image of a professional is appealing because that is what we want to think our doctor would be like. Even if I have
never been a patient in a hospital, it comforts me to feel that a doctor I might
have would be as caring as Gonzo.

Another area where workplace solidarity seriously distorts reality comes in
co-worker response to one employee receiving a job offer elsewhere. With the
exception of an actor's death or departure from a series, a prime-time employee
cannot truly resign. Still, as in the real world, TV workers do receive other opportunities for employment. Unlike in the real world, however, the employee's
co-workers will go to unbelievable lengths to keep the lucky co-worker from
leaving, even to the point of trickery and other underhanded practices sure to
engender furor if tried in the real world. For example, the whole WKRP staff
on "WKRP in Cincinnati" resorted to an elaborate ruse to coerce Johnny Fever
to turn down a clear professional advancement. Even more incredibly, people
offer great sacrifices to keep a clearly obnoxious and incompetent employee
like Ted Baxter on "The Mary Tyler Moore Show," Dan Fielding on "Night Court,"
or Herb Tarlek on "WKRP in Cincinnati" from leaving. In the real marketplace,
the graceful departure of an incompetent or obnoxious co-worker is greeted
with discreet relief, not elaborate self-sacrificial ruses to prevent its occurrence.
When one makes real job-changing decisions, they tend to be based on one's
own personal and family considerations and professional advancement, not the
reactions of co-workers.

All of this is understandable, however, with the realization that such shows
really portray the workplace members as family. The characters on "Night Court"
or "Cheers" or "L.A. Law" are essentially members of a family, not employees
at a court or a bar or a law firm. It is not accidental that an unusually high proportion of the characters on such shows are single, childless, in troubled marriages,
or in other situations where they might be more likely to turn to the workplace
for family-type support.

Before leaving the subject of family solidarity, we should consider one important class of apparent exceptions to this theme, namely soap operas and similar TV movies and miniseries. The Ewing family on "Dallas" clearly differs from
the Huxtables or the Cleavers in not showing much obvious solidarity. Indeed,
their mean-spirited and self-serving backstabbing and other conniving would
seem to be the opposite extreme. In this light, it is interesting to note the great

popularity of nighttime soaps that arose very fast as a genre with the onset and subsequent success of "Dallas" in the early 1980s. Was the prime-time audience wearying of solidarity? By 10 years later the nighttime soap genre had faded badly, although the family dramas and sitcoms were as strong as ever. Daytime soaps remain popular, however, including an increasing male audience, due to the time-shifting capabilities offered by the VCR. Also, in much of the world, soap opera-type shows remain the most popular type of program (e.g., the telenovelas of Latin America). See Pingree and Thompson (1990) for a discussion of the nature of the family in daytime soaps and Liebes and Livingstone (1992) for a comparison of British and U.S. soap operas.

Although nighttime soaps may provide a useful balance to the solidarity shows, it is interesting and somewhat troubling to note that "Dallas" and "Dynasty," more often than "Home Improvement" or "Roseanne," are most typically exported around the world as representatives of the United States, even years after their demise as prime-time shows. It is worth considering whether television is presenting realistic portrayals of families and the workplace and what the effects of these portrayals are. When "Dynasty" was the most popular television show in Zambia, what was it teaching about U.S. family values?

Sexuality

One of the most value-laden and emotional aspects of the family values debates involves sexuality, yet it is one of the most frequent themes on television, advertising, and many magazines. Although chapter 10 later deals with effects of sex in the media, we look now at some value-oriented issues in this area. Although we clearly have come a long way from the days where Lucy and Ricky Ricardo on "I Love Lucy" had to have twin beds and refer to her expectant state as "having a baby" but never as "pregnant," there are still firm standards that no network or mainstream cable TV shows dare cross, such as frontal nudity or explicit sexual intercourse.

Standards for television are much more conservative than for radio, which is in turn more conservative than the recording (album/tape/CD) industry. These differences are especially clear in terms of rock and rap lyrics. When Mick Jagger and the Rolling Stones appeared on "The Ed Sullivan Show" in the 1960s, they had to change the line "Let's spend the night together" to "Let's spend some time together." When Jagger performed this line, he did so with exaggerated gesture and body language to communicate his feeling about the censoring. Concern has continued ever since, such as when a song moves from the more permissive radio to the more conservative television, as in the case of MTV. Some of the strongest rap and song lyrics never even make it to radio, but are widely available to youth on compact disc.

We now turn to four specific value issues in regard to sexuality in media.

How Much Do We Need to Know?   How explicit should the media be in reporting news of sex-crime trials? When is the public's right to know overshadowed by its right to standards of good taste? Consider some examples.

A small city is the scene of a child sexual abuse case involving a prominent businessman and two 13-year-old boys. Each day's court proceedings are reported in great detail in front-page stories in the local newspaper, always identifying the accused but never the boys. Sexually oriented entertainment involving pornography and alcohol in the man's home was described in detail, along with extensive direct quotes from the testimony: "he rubbed our butts in the showers," "He called me to where he was sitting and told me to play with his penis," "He also made me [and the other boy] lay on the floor and have oral sex with each other while he watched." Other episodes such as the man asking the boys to reach inside his underwear and squeeze his penis hard were also explicitly described.

Predictably, this coverage provoked some community comment, although even the most outraged nevertheless always managed to read the articles. Although no one defended the events that had occurred, some argued that young readers should not be exposed to such explicit descriptions in the newspaper. Others countered, however, by saying that such events are horrible and need to be reported in detail to show everyone how horrible they are and to increase commitment to insure that they do not happen again. Each side took a strong value-oriented position about publication of this information.

In the early 1990s there were two celebrated date-rape trials of men of some notoriety. In the first, William Kennedy Smith was accused of raping a single mother at the Kennedy estate in Palm Beach, Florida. In the second trial, boxing heavyweight champion Mike Tyson was accused of raping a Miss Black America contestant whom he had met and invited to his hotel room. Both trials were broadcast on cable (with faces of victims blanked out) and were heavily covered in all news media. In both trials the basic legal question was whether there was consent. Viewers heard questions like "Did you ejaculate into her mouth?" "Did you have an erection?"; the answers to these questions were heard as well.

Although such sexually explicit language would never be accepted on prime-time entertainment programming, because these trials were news, their use was less controversial. Still, however, it caused concern, especially insofar as many apparently watched the rape trials and read the newspaper reports for entertainment purposes.

Premarital Sex.   Issues like premarital sex are openly discussed on TV news and entertainment shows today, at least superficially. Even in such cases, however, it is often traditional values that are affirmed in the end, especially in sitcoms. For example, a teenager may openly consider having sex with a boy friend or girl friend and discuss it openly with family and friends. In the end, however, more often than not the teenager decides that he or she is not ready and chooses to abstain. Even when the decision is affirmative, however, there is considerable moralizing. When Brenda on "Beverly Hills 90210" slept with her boy friend Dylan, she quickly regretted it. Moreover, actress Shannen Doherty, who plays Brenda, had openly expressed concern about the story line, fearing a bad moral example set for viewers. Doogie Howser ("Doogie Howser, M.D.") had his first sexual experience only after a tremendous amount of soul searching.

Very often, however, such issues are avoided altogether. On serious dramatic shows the issue may be avoided by presupposing a norm of early sexual activity on the part of dating adult couples. Often premarital sex is presented as accepted and noncontroversial with little indication of either party struggling with the decision. Only in story lines with adolescents does it seem to be considered a moral issue. Premarital sex is thus treated very conservatively in regard to teens and very permissively in regard to adults. See Box 5.3 for a case where a sitcom story line involving the consequences of premarital sex caused a national political furor.

Adultery. In television and movies, adultery is a frequent topic; the 9,200 scenes of suggested sexual intercourse shown each year on TV occur five to 32 times as often outside of marriage as inside of it (Greenberg et al., 1993; Liebert & Sprafkin, 1988). Depending on the situation, it may be treated farcically or seriously. If treated seriously, it may carry the implicit message that adultery is okay, or at least that it does not have terribly serious consequences, or it may convey the message that adultery has serious repercussions for all concerned.

The first shows that come to mind are the soap operas, both the daytime and nighttime variety. Adultery is a frequent theme, even an accepted way of life for many of the characters (Hardaway, 1979). In terms of values, both approval and condemnation come through at different times. A sympathetic character like Sue Ellen Ewing on "Dallas" who is "trapped" in an unhappy marriage uses an affair as a relatively healthy outlet for her needs. On the other hand, sometimes the resulting pain and hurt of adultery are dealt with in the plot line as well.

What is the perceived reality constructed from viewing such shows? In a study of cultivation effects of soap opera viewing by college students, Buerkel-Rothfuss and Mayes (1981) found that heavy viewing of soap operas was positively correlated with higher estimates of the percentages of people having affairs, divorces, abortions, and illegitimate children, although it was unrelated to their perception of how many people were happily married. Later research using a uses and gratifications approach showed that the motives and purposes of viewing must also be considered (Carveth & Alexander, 1985; Greenberg et al., 1982; Perse, 1986). The perceived reality constructed from such shows apparently depends not only on the program content, but also on the viewer's motives and uses.

BOX 5.3: VICE PRESIDENT QUAYLE
VERSUS *MURPHY BROWN*

On May 18, 1992, the sitcom "Murphy Brown" aired what turned out to be a more-memorable-than-expected season-final episode featuring the birth of the baby of divorced female news anchor Murphy Brown. The day after the TV birth, then U.S. Vice President Dan Quayle made a political speech lamenting the "poverty of values." In this speech he referred to the "bad example" set by character Murphy Brown in having a child alone, "mocking the importance of fathers, by bearing a child alone, and calling it just another 'lifestyle choice' " ("Dan Quayle," 1992, p. 20). Aside from the irony of coming from a leader very outspoken against legal abortion, the comment was interesting in highlighting the depth of emotion evoked by a sitcom portrayal. President George Bush, network executives, and many political leaders and columnists (and of course many humorists) commented extensively on the issue in the subsequent weeks. What was it about Murphy Brown having a baby that inspired so much feeling? Why didn't these people complain about all of the sex on soap operas or, for that matter, all of the real children born out of wedlock every day to parents far less capable than Murphy Brown?

Although Quayle's detractors chided him for making such a big deal out of a sitcom plot, they too may have missed the point. So what if Murphy Brown is not a real person, and no one ever had actual sex to produce that fictitious baby? A TV character has a reality and an impact on real people that most real people do not. In some sense both the vice president and his critics were affirming the thesis of this book.

Nor did the story end there. On the fall 1992 premiere of "Murphy Brown," the plot revolved around new fictitious mom Murphy seeing a real news report of Dan Quayle criticizing her moral example. Her office is besieged with reporters asking for reactions. Although staying secluded for awhile, Murphy eventually makes an on-air editorial response to the vice president. Subsequent news reports told of the fictional program's response to the real criticism by Quayle. Quayle even sent a real baby gift of a stuffed (Republican) elephant to the fictitious baby. Fantasy and reality had never become so blurred.

AIDS Education and Birth Control.   Although we accept great amounts of implied or semi-explicit sex on TV, even during the AIDS scare of the 1980s and 1990s, birth control ads were, for a long time, seen as too controversial for most U.S. television, although such ads had appeared regularly in magazines for years. It is as if the action of having sexual intercourse is acceptable if done in a passionate moment, but that planning for it is somehow unseemly; this is a potentially dangerous reality that may be communicated. The teen pregnancy rate is far higher in the United States than in any other industrialized country, and such rates elsewhere fell dramatically after media campaigns that included televised birth control ads (Kalter, 1987a). It is an interesting paradox that all sorts of nonmarital sex, much of which would clearly be against the personal values of most Americans, was not seen as inappropriate for story content, but that birth control devices, which are consistent in value and practice with most Americans, were seen to be too controversial for advertising.

The spread of AIDS has heightened the discussion of such issues. As AIDS spread beyond the gay and drug cultures in the late 1980s, the general population in many countries became concerned and alarmed. The common introduction of AIDS education in the schools suggests that fear of AIDS (and death) was gradually becoming stronger than fear of exposing children to sexual information. In terms of media, the advertising of condoms became a hot issue. In terms of entertainment programming, there was also a concern, namely that story lines contained too casual an attitude toward sex, especially among adults. Too often, sexual encounters did not seem to be preceded by concern about AIDS or the use of protection (so-called "safe sex").

The Influence of Television on Family Life

Does television add to or detract from the quality of family life? The conventional wisdom is that TV is a negative influence, but that conclusion is by no means certain or simple. In some instances family TV viewing can be a positive time of family discussion and interaction, including commenting on the programs or laughing and crying together. In other instances it can be very negative, for example, if it induces quarreling among family members over what program to watch or whether to turn off the set. Particular conflicts may occur around certain events such as mealtimes, bedtimes, or children's disagreement with parental prohibitions of certain programs.

A uses and gratifications approach to studying family TV use looks at people's motivations for watching, which may vary greatly depending on the program or the individuals' moods. For example, Kubey (1986) found that divorced and separated people watch TV more when they feel down and alone than married or other single people do, perhaps due to their use of TV for solace and comfort to replace the lost relationship.

Men and women may view television watching differently. When Morley (1988) studied working-class British families, he found that men and boys overwhelmingly were the ones who chose what the family would watch on TV or on videotape, especially if they had a remote control, which was generally controlled and operated by males. Women saw TV viewing as more of a social activity and were also more likely to be doing other activities (e.g., housework) concurrently, whereas men were more likely to devote full attention to the program. Men saw TV watching as "earned recreation," whereas women saw it as a "guilty pleasure," a distraction from homemaking duties.

Working within one's home to have television viewing enhance, rather than detract from, family life is a major challenge for media literacy programs (see chapter 12 of this volume and Brown, 1991).

The question of whether television could or should teach values often revolves around such controversial issues as family values or sex, but these are not the only values. Less often examined are more subtle values regularly promulgated by TV and other media.

ECONOMIC VALUES

Affluence as the Norm

A concern is often heard that television encourages excessive consumption and a desire to acquire money and the trappings of wealth (e.g., Greenfield, 1985; Hardaway, 1979). According to this criticism, television's fascination with affluence, even opulence, sends subtle messages to middle-class and poor viewers. This is most blatantly seen in voyeuristic shows like "Lifestyles of the Rich and Famous," "A Current Affair," and the continuing fascination with entertainment personalities in the tabloids and mainstream media. Seeing the glitz and glamor of daytime soap operas and prime-time shows like "Beverly Hills 90210" may lead viewers to accept such lifestyles as commonplace and as appropriate aspirations for themselves. Even sitcom families, although certainly not super-rich, typically live in very large, well-decorated homes in surprising splendor, given the great amount of time that the wage-earners spend at home.

Even the more-or-less typical sitcom families are relatively affluent. "The Cosby Show" (1984–1992), for years at the top of the ratings, presented a very affluent family, although clearly financial gain was not their dominant value. Even though a content analysis of U.S. family shows between 1978 and 1980 found that the primary value disseminated was that money does not buy happiness, and that the poorest families were the happiest (Thomas & Callahan, 1982), by the mid-1980s there were no popular prime-time family shows of people struggling financially, like "The Honeymooners," "Taxi," "The Waltons," "All in the Family," "Sanford and Son," or "I Love Lucy" of earlier days. After the end of the decade the pendulum began to swing back, with the popularity of such shows as "Roseanne," "The Wonder Years," "Married with Children," and "The Simpsons."

Why are affluent people so interesting to watch and poor people apparently so uninteresting? There is some evidence that hard economic times bring on more escapist stories of the perils of great wealth, as seen in the many movies of wealthy people that were popular during the Great Depression, in contrast to the "poor" movies and TV shows popular during the affluent 1950s. People like to watch rich people and their fine trappings like sports cars and fancy clothes but also like to be reminded that these people have serious problems too, often even more serious than the viewers'. Maybe this is reassuring.

Still another factor is that the producers of television and films tend to be rather affluent, mostly from southern California. Impressive arguments can be made that the media grossly overrepresent the world of those who produce the programming and tacitly present this world as far more typical of overall American life than is in fact the case (Stein, 1979, 1987). Even the settings of shows reflect this; many shows are set in Los Angeles or New York, few in Arkansas or South Dakota. A similar argument is considered in chapter 3 as a reason for the underrepresentation of women and minorities on television. Are drugs a part of this affluent lifestyle? See Box 5.4 for a look at one of the very sensitive value issues in U.S. media.

The Glitz Travels Overseas

One disturbing aspect of international program sales is that the most popular U.S. television shows exported are very often the shows with the most affluent characters and settings; for example, the 1980s nighttime soap operas "Dallas," "Knots Landing," and "Dynasty." For many, especially in Third World countries, such programs become the reality of what the United States is like. International visitors to the United States frequently express surprise that most people are not wealthy. Some research suggests that exported programs like "Dynasty" and "Dallas" may be cultivating negative images of Americans in viewers elsewhere (Massing, 1987; Tan, Li, & Simpson, 1986). Popular TV programs dwelling on the rich are by no means a uniquely North American phenomenon; however, many developing countries' domestic shows also present such affluent lifestyles. For example, the telenovelas of Mexico and Brazil present characters with income levels and lifestyles wildly beyond the reach of most of their nation's viewers. Sometimes patriotism values of the home country appear in the programming (see Box 5.5).

Sometimes the affluence in the context of one particular culture may be highly inappropriate, if not downright grotesque, when seen elsewhere. For example, the Bolivian government distributed 5,000 television sets in a poor tin-mining community in 1974. One Indian woman in that community described her child's reaction to the (largely imported) programming:

> My son watched a program on our neighbor's television that showed him a marvelous world full of beautiful castles and parks and mice that spoke. He came home and said to me, "Mommy, I'm going to be a good boy. Why don't you send me to Disneyland? I want to play with the little bear and the little mouse and the little train!" For weeks he didn't want to go out in the street and play with his toys anymore—his sardine cans and milk cans. He dreamed about Disneyland. (Will, 1987, p. 44)

BOX 5.4: ARE DRUGS PART OF THE GOOD LIFE?

In 1933 the song "Reefer Man" was cut from versions of the Cab Calloway film *International House* because of its reference to marijuana. Many years later the Beatles' "Lucy in the Sky with Diamonds" and the Byrds' "Eight Miles High" were also controversial for similar reasons. Even the innocent "Rocky Mountain High" by John Denver was the target of some censors who did not realize that the song referred to invigoration from mountains, not chemicals.

Some very deeply held values center around substance use and abuse. Perhaps the greatest change in this area since the early days of TV is in the attitudes and behavior about smoking. Like many early TV characters, Lucy and Ricky Ricardo smoked cigarettes regularly in the old "I Love Lucy" show of the 1950s, sometimes at the specific request of the tobacco company sponsor. With very few exceptions, however, regular characters on TV series have not smoked since the 1960s, clearly out of health concern over a possible negative effect on youth seeing admired TV characters smoking. Although this certainly reflects the great decline in the percentage of adult smokers since 1960, it may have also contributed to that decline. Even among teens, smoking is much "less cool" than it used to be, and television may be part of the reason for that. Curiously, however, the same trend is not apparent in movies, where characters smoke far more frequently; this is probably due in part to product-placement agreements with tobacco companies to feature those products.

In regard to alcohol, the most widely abused drug, the United States saw decreasing acceptance of alcohol abuse during the 1980s. Although social drinking remains at high, although modestly reduced, levels and alcoholism as a disease and a social problem is still rampant, attitudes against excessive drinking are much less tolerant in the U.S. than previously. The drunk is not so much an object of humor as of pity or disgust. Portrayals of drinking on TV have had to, at least implicitly, take note of this. Whether TV has been a factor in producing this societal change in values or merely reflecting what has been caused by other social forces is unclear at this point.

Finally, TV shows today are careful not to model illicit drug use by respected characters. Adults or teens may occasionally be shown using drugs, but it is nearly always presented as a "mistake." This mindset even carries over into news; when conservative U.S. Supreme Court nominee Douglas Ginsburg admitted in 1987 to past marijuana use, the media treated this as a very serious issue, ultimately culminating in his withdrawal from the nomination, even though polls showed that most Americans thought marijuana use should not disqualify one from the Supreme Court. As the "baby boom" generation, who came of age in the 1960s, began to move into leadership positions, however, reactions started changing. In 1992 Democratic Presidential nominee Bill Clinton admitted to trying marijuana once as a graduate student in 1969. This was greatly covered in the media (especially a rather curious statement that he "didn't inhale").[1] However, the public did not hold this transgression against Clinton; he won the election.

[1]When questioned later about the apparently self-serving "I didn't inhale" comment, Clinton explained that, having never smoked, he did not know how to inhale. This explanation, however, received very little coverage in the copious news coverage of this issue.

BOX 5.5: PATRIOTISM VALUES

Values of patriotism change with current events. In the 1950s, patriotic values in the United States were assumed and almost universally accepted and applauded. In the Vietnam War era (1963–1973), patriotism and even its symbols like the flag became co-opted by the political right; for some years it was difficult to express both patriotism and opposition to the Vietnam War. Remember Archie Bunker's patriotic expressions to his son-in-law Mike Stivic in "All in the Family." By the 1980s, patriotic values again became very fashionable and somewhat less politicized.

Television is a part of the overall political socialization of a society, whether it be in the heavy-handed propaganda of an authoritarian state or the more subtle values in U.S. sitcoms. U.S. TV children and real kids are taught that political freedoms, as exemplified in the Bill of Rights, are of the highest priority. Children in other places may learn that economic freedoms (e.g., freedom to have a job, health care, and affordable housing) are higher priorities.

Although patriotic values are generally cheered, they can draw criticism if presented too stridently or chauvinistically. As an appeal, it has the danger of backfiring if perceived to be tacky or in poor taste, especially in regard to advertising. Using the Statue of Liberty as a symbol to sell beer is probably perceived as acceptable, but having an animated Statue of Liberty drink a draft may well be considered exploitive and disrespectful (Simon, 1985).

This dream was sharply in contrast to the reality of living with his parents and six brothers in a two-room house with no running water, bathroom, or kitchen. What kind of aspirations is television implanting?

Advertising

One of the most controversial international media campaigns in Third World countries has centered around the selling of infant formula as an alternative to breast milk. Although it was sold as being healthier than mother's milk, the fact that it was often mixed with unsafe water and/or in dirty containers actually led to greater danger of disease, to say nothing of the added expense to already desperately poor families. Concern over the alleged social irresponsibility of such media campaigns led to a worldwide boycott of Nestle products (Fore, 1987).

The nearly ubiquitous presence of television around the world has led to numerous advertising campaigns that have come under fire on grounds of social responsibility. Poor children often spend what little money they have on expensive junk food and soft drinks rather than on wholesome school lunches, thanks in part to the influence of advertising. Even though 40% of Mexico's population has no access to milk, poor people are increasingly starting the day with a soft drink and a Ganso (a sort of Mexican Twinkie), in part due to massive TV ad campaigns of Coca-Cola and Pepsico, who sell more products in Mexico than in any other country outside of the United States (Ross, 1992). American tobacco companies are increasingly turning to developing countries as markets, finding less knowledge of health risks, fewer limits on smoking, and less stringent advertising restrictions.

How the commercial demands of television and other media confront the real world of desperate poverty leads to many questions of media transmission of values. Is it the media's responsibility to promulgate a more culturally sensitive set of values?

RELIGION

Perhaps no topic is so intimately tied up with values as is religion, the final general topic considered in this chapter. Gallup polls show the United States to be the most religious industrialized country in the world (90% of Americans believe in God; 41% attend religious services weekly), yet religion has often been a more taboo topic than sex, in regard to media. When John Lennon said offhandedly in 1966 that the Beatles were more popular than Jesus, many were highly offended. Even subsequent "clarifications" or apologies of a sort failed to mollify everyone. In fear of controversy, religion often becomes invisible on television, or rather invisible except for the overtly religious programming, which is most typically viewed by those already of that faith. Let us examine several aspects of religion in the media.

Religion in TV Series

Religion apparently plays no part at all in the lives of entertainment series characters. Even very traditional families hardly ever mention going to church or believing in God. They also, however, rarely mention that they do not go to church or that they do not believe in God. It appears that producers are loathe to offend anyone by identifying their favorite TV family with a particular faith or with saying that they have none. At least one prominent theologian has suggested that religious themes could be integrated into sitcoms in tasteful and nonoffensive ways (Marty, 1983). Action-adventure shows have virtually no mention of religion, with an occasional exception of having a crazed religious fanatic character as a villain.

This absence of religious themes probably reflects (a) TV producers' and writers' relative lack of involvement with religion themselves, compared to most Americans, and (b) an implicit recognition that it is a very touchy subject and one where people are easily offended. Perhaps they fear that Protestants and Jews will stop watching "Roseanne" if the Connors are identified as Catholic or that atheists and agnostics will lose interest in "Murder, She Wrote" if Jessica Fletcher were a Presbyterian.

In a content analysis of 100 episodes of U.S. prime-time network entertainment TV, Skill, Lyons, and Larson (1991) found only 5% of the characters with an identifiable religious affiliation, compared to 89% of the U.S. population. Over half of those identified characters were Roman Catholic, with the rest Protestant, cult members, or New Age adherents. There were no Jews, Muslims, or other religions represented. A large proportion of those that did occur appeared on a few episodes of shows like "Father Dowling Mysteries" or "Amen."

As Skill et al. (1991) found, adherents to religions other than Christianity are, as a whole, seldom seen on TV. When they are present, they are often stereotyped. Jews may be stereotyped by name, occupation, and perhaps by speaking a particularly grating New York dialect. In the news they seem to appear especially in stories about the Holocaust, particularly as protesting against something that they view as disrespectful to Holocaust victims, or in reaction to U.S. or Israeli government Middle East policy. Muslims appear as bomb-throwing terrorists or arrogant oil sheiks, with limousines and harems in tow (see chapter 3). Members of some Eastern religions appear as airhead airport panhandlers or ascetic navel gazers.

Religious Professionals

Except for the explicitly religious programming like the "Billy Graham Crusades," "The 700 Club," or programs on the Christian Broadcasting Network, religious professionals are greatly underrepresented on U.S. television. When they do occur, they are often, at best, rather saintly but very shallow, even insipid, characters, and, at worst, vicious hypocrites hiding behind their clerical collars. Perhaps the most rounded and developed religious character of long-running U.S. prime-time TV history is Father Mulcahy on "M*A*S*H." Compared to the cardboard clergy who make occasional cameo appearances on other shows, Mulcahy is interesting and complex, yet compared to practically every other character on the later "M*A*S*H," he is rather shallow. In many Westerns, there is a "man of the cloth" who often is a significant supporting, although seldom a lead, character.

A more insidious religious type is the fanatical cult preacher. These characters are very extreme and very evil. Such characters have to be very perverted so as not to evoke any sympathy or any criticisms about the program saying negative things about a real "Man of God." Such characters became especially popular after news stories like fanatic cult leader Jim Jones causing the poisoning death of dozens of his own followers in Guyana in 1978 or would-be messiah David Koresh leading the Branch Davidian cult to a fiery death in 1993 in Waco, Texas.

Religious News

Although, in general, religious news has traditionally been underreported in the United States, relative to its importance, looking at what *is* reported reveals some interesting trends.

What Is Covered. Religious news that is centered around an individual person receives relatively heavy coverage, following the "star" model of political news coverage (see chapter 7). Travels and pronouncements of the Pope, for example, are rather easy and predictable to cover, much more so than comparably important Protestant or Jewish happenings that are less focused on a particular person. One exception to this is a flamboyant TV preacher, particularly one with extreme views. Fundamentalist sects and especially bizarre cults like the Branch Davidians receive more coverage than mainstream religion, because they are more often focused on a charismatic individual with controversial views.

When religious events are covered by TV news, they tend most often to focus either on Roman Catholicism, whose colorful pageantry and identifiable newsmakers (especially the Pope) make good photogenic copy, or on Protestant fundamentalism, whose dogmatic theology and contentious political activism make good controversy-ridden stories, especially when centered around a colorful individual like Jimmy Swaggart or Jerry Falwell. Groups of mainline Protestants politely discussing multiple points of view on social welfare, or Jews examining different degrees of support for Israel may be just as important but less photogenically newsworthy.

The Televangelism Scandals. Some changes in religious news coverage started in 1987 with several key events. Early that year Oral Roberts announced that God had told him He would "call Oral home" if several million dollars were not donated to his Tulsa ministry and hospital before a certain date. The subsequent revelation that popular TV evangelist Jim Bakker had had a sexual liaison with a secretary several years before was sharply at odds with the pious image that he and other televangelists sought to portray. This was followed by discoveries of financial mishandling of Bakker's PTL Ministries funds and of the extravagant lifestyle of Bakker and his wife Tammy. Such items as an airconditioned doghouse were auctioned at a public sale to raise money to pay off PTL debts. Subsequent public name-calling among evangelists Bakker, Jerry Falwell, Jimmy Swaggart, and others had more the character of soap opera family feuds than what people had come to expect from the electronic pulpits.

The subsequent nabbing of Jimmy Swaggart with a prostitute hardly cleaned up the image. Unlike many earlier religious stories, these were widely reported in the media and widely ridiculed by comedians. "The Tonight Show," "Saturday Night Live," and most other comedy programs for months spewed forth Jimmy Swaggart sex jokes and Tammy Bakker mascara jokes.

The media apparently decided in this case that comedy about religion, even scathing and derisive comedy, was acceptable to the public. Such public criticism of religious leaders was almost unprecedented in the United States, however. When evangelist Jimmy Swaggart's sexual escapades were revealed in 1988, he underwent heavy, even smug, criticism from the press. The classic theme of the fall of the sanctimonious and mighty was an appealing one, so appealing that even very unsympathetic critics of televangelism like Father Andrew Greeley wondered if they were being treated unfairly by the media (e.g., Greeley, 1988).

The Role of Religion in Secular News Stories.   Although religion is sometimes superficially and simplistically presented as the divisive basis of what is actually a much more complex social problem, as in the uprisings in Northern Ireland, Palestine, or Lebanon, so in other cases is the importance of religion missed altogether. A prime example of this is the role of religion in the revolutions that brought down the communist regimes of eastern Europe in 1989–1991.

For example, in Poland the Roman Catholic church had been the only legal forum for political discussion for years and, as such, had been the focus of dissent. In Romania the revolt against the brutal regime of Nicolae Ceaucescu began with a protest after a Reformed church service in Timisoara, a western city near the border of less-censored, already-democratizing Hungary. The protesters were all gunned down but an outraged Romanian nation responded with a force that ended in the Christmas Day 1989 televised execution of the hated dictator and his wife. Rebellious Lithuania, the only former Soviet republic with a majority Roman Catholic population, was the first and most cantankerous to challenge Moscow and demand its independence.

Probably most dramatic, however, was the situation in the old German Democratic Republic (GDR; East Germany), where 40% of the officially atheistic country were practicing Lutherans, ironically a much larger percentage than in free West Germany. The weekly protests in Leipzig that led to the fall of the GDR government and its hated symbol, the Berlin Wall, in November 1989 actually began the previous summer with a weekly Monday night prayer meeting at a Lutheran church. Its numbers grew weekly from a handful of members who quietly picketed after the prayer meeting to a mass protest of thousands filling the streets. The church was given so much credit for the peaceful revolution that the Leipzig city government later hung a huge banner that read, "WIR DANKEN DIR, KIRCHE" (We thank you, church).

In the U.S. media, very little was said of the role of religion in these democratic revolutions. Why not? Probably it was not a conspiracy of silence, but rather simply an overlooking by people for whom religion was not too important in their own lives. Perhaps also they were not used to seeing politics and religion interact in this very different way than they did in the United States. Another possible factor was some uneasiness regarding how to present the role of religion to a society used to having the religious sphere completely separate from the secular sphere.

In a somewhat different type of situation, religious dimensions of the news are sometimes ignored or underplayed when they become politically awkward. For example, when the U.S. media were patriotically drumming up support for the Persian Gulf War against Iraq in 1991 (see chapter 7 for further discussion of this), much was made of Iraqi leader Saddam Hussein's brutal dictatorship but few stories mentioned that he did allow freedom of religion and that Iraq was one of the few Arab nations with a sizable Christian minority, the Chaldeans. Moreover, U.S. allies Kuwait and Saudi Arabia forbade the practice of any religion but Islam, even to the extent of not allowing Christian and Jewish U.S. soldiers stationed there during the war to privately practice their faith.

Religious Television

In the United States, although not in many other places, explicitly religious programming is a multimillion-dollar business (Bruce, 1990; Hoover, 1988; Peck, 1992). It is, however, produced and distributed totally separately from other television programming. This is consistent with the separation of religion from other aspects of American life. Religious books are sold in separate bookstores from secular books, religious music is typically recorded by different artists and marketed separately from other music, and religious television is produced by religious networks. Although largely a U.S. phenomenon, there is some international growth of TV evangelism, especially in Latin America, particularly in Guatemala, now the first majority Protestant country in Latin America (Assman, 1987a, 1987b).

Although there was some Christian broadcasting in the early days of radio and television, the modern "electronic church" really began with Billy Graham's TV specials starting in 1957. These were later followed by Rex Humbard, Oral Roberts, Jerry Falwell, Robert Schuller, Jimmy Swaggart, and Pat Robertson's "700 Club," and Jim and Tammy Bakker's "PTL Club." These took a variety of formats and emphases, including Robertson and Bakker's talk-show format, Falwell's emphasis on politics, and Roberts' focus on spiritual healing. All except Schuller were theologically evangelical to fundamentalist, with a heavy emphasis on evangelism (Hoover, 1988). At their peak, Nielsen ratings of these programs showed about 250,000 to 1,250,000 households viewing (Fore, 1987). In spite of its evangelistic emphasis, Christian TV attracts few nonbelievers and, in fact, serves mainly to reinforce the existing beliefs of its viewers (Fore, 1987).

The TV evangelism scandals of 1987–1988 became watershed events in the history of religious broadcasting. It seemed to confirm what critics of televangelism had been saying for some time, but now allowed them to say it much more publicly. Fundraising for all TV ministries, even those uninvolved in scandal, became more difficult. The media reality of the tainted preacher, long suspected by many skeptics, became the perceived reality for many. Ironically, the net effect in terms of evangelism may have been a negative one.

Effects of Television on Religion

It may be that the mere presence of television as a medium has altered all religion in subtle but profound ways, so much that the perceived reality about religion will never be the same again. In a provocative book, *Amusing Ourselves to Death*, Neil Postman (1985) argued that television has radically reshaped practically everything about our lives. One domain that has been greatly changed is religion, in ways that go far beyond the Sunday broadcasts and the TV evangelists. Postman argued that, because TV is, at heart, entertainment, then the preacher is the star performer, and "God comes out as second banana" (p. 117). Although Christianity has always been a "demanding and serious religion" (p. 121), its TV version can acquire its needed share of the audience "only by offering people something they want" (p. 121), which is hardly historical Biblical Christianity. Furthermore, Postman argues, TV is such a predominately secular medium that religious TV uses many of the same symbols and formats (e.g., "The 700 Club" modeled after "Entertainment Tonight").

Thus TV preachers are "stars" who are attractive and affluent just like movie stars. Worship on TV is not participatory; the audience can sit at home and absorb but cannot have the corporate worship experience of group singing, praying, or liturgy. Although a church may be considered "holy ground" where people act with more reverence, there is no comparable sacred space when watching church on TV at home, where one can sit in dirty underwear drinking beer and eating pizza during the sermon. The church, the stadium, and the jungle setting from a Vietnam War movie are all the same place—and all are no place (Meyrowitz, 1985).

Postman argued that, as more and more religious services are broadcast on TV and as pastors are more acquainted with the television medium, the "danger is not that religion has become the content of television shows but that television shows may become the content of religion" (p. 124). Pastors become concerned about providing the kind of worship conducive to television, even if the service is not being televised. Congregations subtly expect to be "entertained," even "amused." Places of worship have no particular sacred character, because one can worship through TV while at home. One congregation worships regularly in a former roller rink, another in an old laundromat, whereas yet another rents space Sunday mornings in a large university classroom. There is no sense

of the sacred as was found most strikingly in the magnificent Gothic and Renais-
sance cathedrals of Europe. Has television contributed to this change?

CONCLUSION

This chapter examined several issues in regard to values and the media. Questions of what is right and what is wrong provide different answers over time,
but those questions are always there. As influential as television is in our lives,
it becomes an obvious source to turn to for guidance on moral and ethical issues. How do our role models act? What are we taught is "right?" What are
possible consequences of moral positions taken? How can television socialize
values? In the case of U.S. media, we see a curious hybrid picture of considerable permissiveness in some areas, almost puritanical restriction in others, and
a sort of moderate mainstream value socialization in others. Neither the glib
protestations of the political left nor those of the right do the reality justice.

Returning to the question addressed early in this chapter, do media merely
reflect the values of society, or do they serve as a catalyst for changing those
values? Clearly, they do in some sense mirror somebody's values, but that somebody may hardly be a typical media consumer. More importantly, they can and
do serve as a catalyst for change. How this change occurs is of great importance but is far more difficult to study. The same processes discussed in earlier
chapters, by which we respond to media and construct a world based on its
teachings, also apply to values.

The cultivation theory approach of Gerbner and his colleagues (see chapter
2) may be particularly useful here (e.g., Gerbner et al., 1986, in press; Signorielli & Morgan, 1990). Television and other media cultivate a system of values
through the interaction of the viewer and the content presented. The social reality presented in media gradually becomes the reality for the public.

Mechanisms of reinforcement, modelling, disinhibition, and classical conditioning are also at work. For example, some values held by the viewer are reinforced more than others. Certain values and those holding them are associated
with very positive or negative stimuli and thus may be classically conditioned.
Watching a trusted model hold certain values but act against them may disinhibit contradictory values held by the viewer. More and better research on the
ways that media teach values is desperately needed to further elucidate these
issues.

6

SPORTS AND MEDIA: MARRIAGE OR CONQUEST?

Q: What event captures the largest TV audience in the world?

A: World Cup Soccer competition, with up to 2 billion viewers, almost one third of the entire planet, watching some part of the multigame series (Real, 1989)! The most-watched single show in U.S. TV history was the 1993 Super Bowl, seen by an estimated 133.4 million viewers, about half the nation's population (AP wire service release).

Q: How much did CBS and ESPN pay for national broadcasting rights of major league baseball in 1989?

A: One and a half billion dollars! As of 1992, they had lost half a billion on the deal (McCarroll, 1992).

Media sports are a part of the consciousness of everyone today, even those who have no interest in sports themselves. Events like the Super Bowl and the Olympics become cultural phenomena that touch the lives of people far beyond regular sports fans. The media, particularly television, are the way we learn about sports. Our perceived reality about particular sports is heavily a media creation. In the case of sports not played locally, media may be the only source of information. The marriage of sports and television is so commonplace and taken for granted today that it is easy to overlook the enormous influence that television and other media have had on the games themselves.

This chapter begins with a bit of historical perspective on media and sports. Next we look at the influence of media, especially television, on the games themselves. Finally, we examine several psychological issues related to sport (e.g., competition, violence, gender, hero worship) and see how media have become formative influences in our perceived reality about sports and playing sports.

HISTORY OF SPORTS IN MEDIA

To fully understand the perceived reality of sports and the role media play in the construction of that reality, some familiarity with the history of sports and media is helpful (see McChesney, 1989, for a review). This relationship is not a new one, but it is one that has evolved in sometimes strange and unexpected ways.

Sports in Print

In spite of the recent profound effect of television on sports, the marriage of athletics and the media is not a new relationship. The first sports story in an American newspaper appeared in 1733, when the *Boston Gazette* reprinted a British press story on a boxing match in England. The first British sports publication appeared in 1801, followed by the first U.S. sports periodical in 1819. Oddly titled *The American Farmer*, it included primarily results of hunting, fishing, shooting, and bicycling matches, plus some essays on the philosophy of sport. *The Spirit of the Times* began publishing in 1831 and featured a sort of classified ad program, whereby one sportsman could contact others to issue public challenges for boxing or racing. U.S. newspapers began regular reporting of sporting events in the 1850s, especially cricket and horse racing, followed by baseball in the 1860s, when Henry Chadwick invented the box score and the batting average, thus allowing fans to compare present and past performance much more easily (Rader, 1984). Reports of early horse and yacht races were sent over the telegraph.

By 1890 most major daily newspapers had established sports departments. The first play-by-play reporting appeared in 1889, when the *New York Sun* devoted three columns to coverage of the Harvard–Princeton football game (Loy, McPherson, & Kenyon, 1978). In the 1920s, large dailies began to sponsor sports promotions like the Chicago *Tribune*'s Golden Gloves boxing program. There was even a poetic period in the early 20th century, particularly exemplified by Grantland Rice, who wrote of Notre Dame's 1924 defeat of Army, "Outlined against a blue-grey October sky, the Four Horsemen rode again . . ." (Rader, 1984, p. 21). Other sportswriters of the period were busy inventing colorful nicknames for heroes like "The Sultan of Swat" for Babe Ruth. Sports myths were even being developed, such as the baseball origin myth (see Box 6.1). Sports journalism has continued to occupy a strategic place in print media. The sports pages are the most widely read section of newspapers.

Magazines were a late entry to print sport media, but they quickly became a very important one. *Sports Illustrated*, with a circulation of 3 million (Lever & Wheeler, 1993), has been a top-circulation magazine for decades since its 1954 inception. Many newer and more specialized magazines fulfill interest in partic-

---

BOX 6.1: THE ORIGIN OF BASEBALL: CREATION OF A NATIONAL MYTH

In 1889 a former pitcher and sporting goods manufacturer organized a world tour of baseball players to sell the "American National Game," to say nothing of his sporting goods, abroad. In the fervor to celebrate baseball as uniquely American, the New York *Clipper* declared that the vicious rumor that baseball evolved from the English game of rounders was "forever squelched." There was even a special commission appointed to study the origins of baseball. Their report in 1907 was based on no research except an inquiry letter to some ex-ballplayers; responses to this letter were lost in a fire. The report concluded that the Civil War hero General Abner Doubleday invented the game of baseball in Cooperstown, New York in 1839; evidence for this consisted solely of the recollections of one man almost 70 years later. The contrary evidence of (a) no mention of the game in Doubleday's memoirs and (b) documented accounts of its play earlier than 1839 deterred no one from celebrating the "centennial" of the game in 1939 at the dedication of the Baseball Hall of Fame in Cooperstown. Although thoroughly discredited today, the Doubleday myth survives to meet our need to think of baseball as uniquely American. Here the myth served a purpose that the facts could not (Rader, 1984).

---

ular sports, including some covering sports that receive relatively little coverage in newspapers or television (*Dirt Bike, Cycle News, National Dragster*). On the whole, readership of sports magazines tends to be heavily male, 87% for *Sports Illustrated* (Guttman, 1986), and disproportionately middle class and well educated, although this varies greatly according to the sport.

Sports on Radio and TV

With the advent of broadcasting, new horizons were opened to sports reporting. Baseball games were broadcast on radio almost from its inception. The Dempsey–Carpentier fight was broadcast from Jersey City in July 1921. One month later, pioneer Pittsburgh radio station KDKA broadcast a Pirates–Phillies game live. The first regular play-by-play season programming of baseball and football was in place by 1925, although for some years it was primarily the World Series that was carried play-by-play. Some apparently live play-by-play broadcasts as late as the 1950s were in fact "re-creations" by a local sportscaster reading Morse code transcriptions over the telegraph and ad-libbing a commentary about a far-off game, such as Des Moines station WHO's Ronald "Dutch" Reagan's re-creations of the Chicago Cubs' games.

The first sporting event to be televised was the Berlin Olympics of 1936, which was broadcast only to the area immediately around Berlin. The first TV sports in the United States came in 1939, with the broadcast in the New York area of a Columbia–Princeton baseball game and the Lou Nova–Max Baer boxing match, sent live to the approximately 200 TV sets in greater New York (Guttman, 1986). Widespread TV ownership had to wait, however, until after World War II (1939–1945). Early television technology was such that only sports with a small and fixed arena of action worked well on the screen. Boxing and wrestling thrived on 1940's and 1950's TV, whereas baseball and football became far more popular later with the advent of technology allowing multiple cameras, zooming, panning, and instant replays.

Regular television broadcast of sports has grown steadily since the 1950s, until sports occupied around 15% of the total programming on commercial television by the mid-1980s. Audiences for major sporting events are among the largest for any programming, and television has become an integral part of the financing of most professional sports as well as amateur sports such as the Olympics, regularly seen by over a billion people (20% of the population of the entire planet). Although such U.S. classics as the World Series and the Super Bowl are seen by millions of people, even these events are eclipsed by the 1–2 billion people that see the quadrennial World Cup soccer championships.

Although sports have been seen on television almost since its inception, TV was relatively unimportant to sports before the late 1950s, when professional teams began to see television as a potentially lucrative source of revenue. This revenue source was considerably more stable, with greater potential for increase than ticket sales and other more traditional sources offered. Usually broadcast on weekend afternoons, TV sports offered a chance to greatly increase the audience at traditionally low-viewing times. However, the great popularity of sports has led to prime-time broadcasting of games as well, most notably ABC's "Monday Night Football," the many evening baseball games, and the Olympics. The advent of popular all-sports cable channels like ESPN has further increased the amount of TV sports available. Over the years, the television audience has become considerably more important than the stadium spectators, and sports have changed much more to adapt to the needs and desires of TV and its viewers than to the fans in the stadium. For economic reasons the perceived reality of the TV audience has come to be more important than the reality perceived by the fans in the stadium.

In spite of the rampant growth of sports and television, there does seem to be a saturation point. This is perhaps most dramatically illustrated by the spectacular failure of the United States Football League in the early 1980s, formed in part in response to the apparently limitless reservoir of fans for the NFL. There are also signs of tedium and lower-than-expected ratings as division playoffs and tournaments seem to extend the season of different sports longer and longer. People often tire of baseball by late October or NBA (basketball) and Stanley Cup (hockey) playoffs still going on in June. The so-called "Triplecast" offering of 24-hour coverage of the 1992 Summer Olympics on three pay-per-view cable channels had disappointingly few takers; it may have been the steep $125 price tag or perhaps just that few had that much time to watch the saturation coverage!

Social Changes Affecting Sports and Media

Exodus to the Suburbs. Although television greatly affected sports in its early years, there were other profound social changes occurring during that time that played into sports–media growth. In the post-World War II years, unparalleled economic prosperity fueled a building boom and a massive migration from the inner cities to the new suburban areas. The suburbs were far more dependent on the automobile, signaling the shift from primary dependence on public transportation to private cars. Soon this led to the construction of better highways and freeways and the decline and even loss of public transportation.

With all of these changes came a privatization of leisure. As more people owned their own homes, with more space inside and lovely yards outside, their recreation and leisure time was increasingly centered around the home, or, at most, the neighborhood. One major activity of this home-based leisure was watching television. No longer did one have to ride the trolley to the theater to watch a movie; similar entertainment was available for free and more conveniently from television. The same was true for watching sports. The fact that most of the ballparks of the time were ancient edifices in decaying and dangerous parts of town with little parking and few modern conveniences did nothing to help stem this tide of change. The rise of auto racing as a local spectator sport and softball as a participant sport also competed with baseball.

Class Differences. There are noticeable class differences in the popularity of TV sports. Certain sports like wrestling or boxing are notoriously low class, whereas others, like bowling, may be low class to watch but not necessarily to play. More subtle differences include football fans being slightly higher class overall than baseball fans. Such differences take on great importance when it comes to marketing the products in the commercials. A higher income audience allows the producer to command higher ad fees than for a comparable-size audience of lower income. Professional football telecasts offer the highest percentage of middle- to upper middle-class males in the audience. This has obvious significant advertising ramifications.

Now let us look at how media, primarily television, have changed the nature of the games themselves. They will never be the same again.

HOW TV HAS CHANGED SPORTS

Probably the biggest change in sports thanks to TV is simply the fact that many more people participate in many more sports than they used to, following exposure to these sports on TV. Team owners' early fears that radio (and later

TV) would keep people from attending games in person proved, at worst, a temporary problem. The potential financial bonanza from selling TV rights only gradually came to be appreciated (Guttman, 1986; Lever & Wheeler, 1993; Powers, 1984; Rader, 1984; Whannel, 1992).

The New Look of Games

Television has changed sports in a myriad of ways. There is much more color in sports than there used to be. Before TV, tennis balls were always white; the so-called "optic yellow" really should be called "TV yellow." For centuries a sport of the elite, tennis was brought to the masses by television coverage of major tournaments. Before TV, football stadiums less often had colorful sections in the end zones. Female cheerleaders, even chorus lines of precision marchers, replaced the pre-World War II male "yell captains" at college football games. The increasing number of domed stadiums has lessened the number of boring rain delays that interfere with TV programming. Computer graphics technology has allowed for lively and colorful scoreboards. Hockey changed the center line from a solid to a broken line to show up better on television.

In several cases there have been rule and practice changes to accommodate television. Golf changed from match to medal or stroke play to help insure big name golfers in the final stages (i.e., the most televised and watched time) of PGA tournaments. Tennis introduced the sudden-death tiebreaker in the early 1970s to avoid long, nontelegenic deuce games. The NFL reduced its half time on some games to allow a better fit into a 2½-hour slot.

Continuing technical advances in broadcasting have affected sports. One of the most dramatic is the instant replay, first seen in 1963. The same play can be seen over and over at different speeds, from different camera angles. In the mid-1980s some pro leagues experimented with allowing instant replays to possibly change referees' decisions. Technical advances allow the editing and delayed broadcast of lengthy events with interpretation added and uninteresting sections deleted; such techniques have been used especially effectively with TV coverage of the Olympics. The growth of cable and satellite technology has greatly increased the available hours of sports programming, most notably, although not exclusively, through the founding of the USA network in 1975 and ESPN in 1979, although both networks later expanded to include other types of programming, with the USA network eventually becoming mostly nonsports. Signs in the early 1990s that pay-per-view television was beginning to catch on surely heralded additional changes to come.

Some sports are much better suited to commercial television than others. Baseball, with its many half-inning divisions, is a natural for commercial breaks. Football and basketball have fewer structured breaks, but the frequent time-outs and foul calls help somewhat. The continuous action and low scoring of hockey and soccer make them relatively poor TV sports. Some have suggested this to be why soccer, by far the most popular spectator sport worldwide, has never caught on in a large way in the United States. Soccer lacks a focus of attention like the pitcher to home plate area in baseball or the opposing lines in football. The ball often flies off in unexpected fashion, making TV close-ups worthless. Still, however, this lack of "TV friendliness" is not an entirely satisfactory explanation, because soccer (often called football) is seen on TV daily in dozens of countries. The quadrennial World Cup series is the most-watched professional sporting event worldwide, with between an estimated 600 million to 2 billion viewers (Real, 1989). Sometimes a bit of the action is lost due to commercial breaks, but there are also increasing experiments with alternatives like windowing, where we see, for example, the game in the middle of the screen and an ad around the edges or across the bottom, or the ad on most of the screen with the game in a window in an upper corner.

Very minor aspects of games may have telegenic importance. Even the size of the ball makes a difference. In this sense, basketball is excellent for TV with its large ball, whereas golf balls, the hockey puck, and even the baseball are relatively hard to see. Other kinds of "props" like baseball bats, basketball nets, and hockey sticks also add to the visual interest. Certain nonplaying characters like the Dallas Cowboy Cheerleaders, the San Diego Chicken, and various personified collegiate mascots add further color to the telegenic interest.

In spite of what one might think, some of the most popular sports in terms of attendance are not that popular on television. Two of the top American sports in gate receipts are auto racing and horse racing, yet they are seldom seen by large audiences on TV, except for the very top contests like the Indianapolis 500 and the Big 3 of thoroughbred racing (Kentucky Derby, Preakness, and Belmont Stakes). There are also considerable regional differences in sports interest (see Box 6.2).

Institutional Changes

There have been some structural changes in the institution of sport. One of the most dramatic examples is baseball. The 59 minor leagues of several different classes in the late 1940s were down to about 15 leagues 30 years later. The chance to see major league baseball on television all over the country has largely destroyed the appeal (and thus financial viability) of the minor leagues. A parallel development occurred with the soccer leagues in Great Britain after the onset of TV. Even the attendance at American pro football and major league baseball was at first cut by regular TV broadcasting ("blacking out" in home areas moderated this trend somewhat), but the huge financial bonanza of selling TV rights ultimately far more than compensated, eventually even increasing stadium attendance through the interest generated from seeing the games on television. The old American Football League (AFL) was saved from bankruptcy in 1964 by NBC's offer of $42 million for a 5-year TV contract (Guttman, 1986).

BOX 6.2: GEOGRAPHICAL DIFFERENCES IN SPORT

There are huge international differences in what sports are popular, both in terms of participation and TV watching. The two most popular TV sports in the United States do not command much worldwide interest. Baseball is big in some of East Asia (especially Japan and Taiwan), the Caribbean, and northern Latin America as far south as Venezuela, but it is largely unknown in Europe, Africa, and most of Asia and South America. There are a few occasional exceptions, most notably the professional Italian league, and there are some indications that interest in baseball is spreading into Europe and southwest from Japan into east Asia. Football is big in the United States and Canada but practically nowhere else, although the name *football* is often used for soccer (*American football* for the U.S. variety). Some current efforts to export it to Western Europe are having modest success. Bicycling as a major sport is immensely popular in France and Italy; the fact that an American (Greg LeMond) won the Tour de France in 1986 was completely unprecedented and helped to increase the interest in the event and the sport in the United States. In Britain and some Commonwealth countries (but nowhere else) cricket is popular. Bullfighting is popular on the Iberian peninsula and Northern Latin America but nonexistent elsewhere.

Even within the United States and Canada there are considerable regional differences in sports preferences. Throughout Canada and the extreme northern United States, hockey is often the major sport, far eclipsing football and basketball in quality and popularity at schools like the University of Maine and the University of North Dakota. Although college football is popular all over the United States, it is even more so in the Midwest and South; in Canada it is nonexistent. Basketball is most popular on the U.S. mid-Atlantic coast and especially in the state of Indiana, which begins interscholastic competition in elementary school and draws college recruiters from all over the country. Women's field hockey is popular in the Northeast, as is jai alai in south Florida. Obviously, winter sports like ice skating and snow skiing are more popular in colder climates.

There is some tendency for television to lessen these differences, as people become exposed to sports not currently played in their community. The increasing popularity of soccer in the United States, especially among youth, and American football in Europe testify to this.

Now let us look at several specific sports to further examine the effects of television coverage on the sport itself.

College Football

In college football, the NCAA severely restricted the TV broadcast of games in the 1950s, in spite of occasional disgruntled schools and legal challenges on antitrust grounds. With the advent of very "big bucks" contracts in the early 1960s, far more games appeared on television, although this primarily enriched the few very strong teams and conferences and weakened many others. This trend was accentuated by the postseason Bowl games, which sold TV rights for multimillion-dollar deals as early as the 1960s. By 1983 the Rose Bowl sold TV rights for $7 million, whereas rights to even "minor" bowls like Gator, Bluebonnet, and Liberty went for half a million or so each (Rader, 1984). Power conferences like the Big Ten, Big Eight, Southeastern, and Pacific Ten increasingly depended on Bowl appearances to recruit strong talent and bowl receipts to finance their programs.

The style of play also changed. A new, more wide-open offense and an increasing number of plays per game (more passes, scoring, rushing, and receiving in the 1960s than any time previously) made the game more exciting to watch on TV. More complicated strategies like the "I" and triple-option formations or Oklahoma's famed wishbone added to the fan appeal, especially as technical advances allowed the camera to follow them adequately. Although TV has brought big-time college football into the lives of many who never would have attended a game, it has been at the cost of heavily, even crassly, commercializing the football programs of the major schools, effectively leaving them amateurs in name only. It has also drawn a large TV audience in part at the expense of small college and high school football, whose supporters often prefer to watch Notre Dame versus Penn State on TV instead of attending a local game in person.

Pro Football

Although college football had been around and popular since the 19th century, pro football was only an athletic footnote on the U.S. sports scene before the age of television. The NFL was formed in 1920 by a group of mostly Ohio teams meeting in a Hupmobile auto showroom in Canton, Ohio. When Pete Rozelle became NFL commissioner in 1960, the entire staff consisted of "two guys and an eighty-year-old Kelly girl" (Rader, 1984, p. 83); by 1984 the same headquarters occupied five entire floors of a Park Avenue skyscraper. Pro football learned how to deal with television more adeptly and in a more unified fashion than did baseball. NFL commissioners Bert Bell and his successor Pete Rozelle negotiated craftily and with the support of the owners, using local blackouts often enough to preserve stadium audiences but not so often as to engender fan resentment. The close-up focus of television, coupled with interpretation by the sportscaster, served to make a previously opaque and uninteresting game fascinating to large numbers of new fans, who now were able to follow what was happening with the ball.

However, television has increasingly been calling the shots in changes in the sport. The increase of TV time-outs and other factors increased the average game length from 2 hours 57 minutes in 1978 to 3 hours 11 minutes in 1990 (Zoglin,

1990b). The length of the season was increased by 2 weeks in 1992–1993. Five more 30-second commercials appeared in 1992 than had appeared in 1989.

One of the most brilliantly marketed ongoing media events has been the Super Bowl, beginning in January 1967 after the merger of the NFL and the AFL the year before. By the early 1970s the Super Bowl had overtaken the World Series and the Kentucky Derby in TV audience size. Unlike these other events, the Super Bowl was a creation of television, not a pre-existent institution adapted to the new medium. "Super Bowl Sunday" practically became an annual January holiday, complete with ebullient media hoopla weeks in advance. The games themselves were frequently watched in over half of the U.S. households, in spite of a string of very uneven and unexciting games for many of those years. The broadcast in itself became the event; what happened in the game was almost irrelevant. By the 1980s, major advertisers, paying top dollar for ad time, launched new ad campaigns with commercials presented for the first time during the game; this "new advertising season" became a significant spin-off media event. Networks alternated the privilege of broadcasting the game. A whole serious of satellite events sprang up, such as numerous televised parties and pre- and postgame specials. This large audience is sometimes used for other purposes; in 1993 there was considerable publicity about the rise of wife-battering during and after the Super Bowl. Wenner (1989) even argued that the Super Bowl pregame show is a vehicle for subtle political socialization.

The Olympics

Two immensely important sporting events, in terms of their TV impact, are the quadrennial summer and winter Olympics. Although these games have occurred in modern times since 1896, the interest in them has soared exponentially since their broadcast on television worldwide. Although the initial World Cup TV rights were given away in Bern, Switzerland in order to get free publicity, Olympic committees have been selling broadcast rights ever since the 1960 Rome games, with ABC paying a record $309 million for the rights to televise the winter Olympics from Calgary in 1988 (up from $92 million for Sarajevo in 1984). This was an overextension, however, as ABC lost $65 million on the project. The 1992 Winter Olympics TV rights went to CBS for a mere $243 million, without even an opposing bid from ABC ("Television: For Gold," 1988)! The Olympics have become totally dependent on television financially, a status that gives them a "professional" character that they never had before (Seifart, 1984).

Due to the traditionally amateur status of the Olympics, however, TV has popularized sports that have not otherwise been sources of large revenues. Most notable here have been all women's sports, which have received a tremendous boost from Olympic coverage. Certain sports that have little audience elsewhere are very popular in the Olympics (e.g., gymnastics and ice skating). In such "minor sports" television serves an important education function; people learn about new sports from watching the Olympics. Sometimes this translates into their own participation in these activities. The Olympics have produced many heroes, including Mark Spitz, Olga Korbut, Nadia Comaneci, Kristi Yamaguchi, Carl Lewis, Brian Boitano, Bruce Jenner, and Mary Lou Retton. Olympic stars, through the catalyst of TV, can be catapulted to athletic or show business stardom, to say nothing of economic well-being.

Sometimes the commercial pressure to pay back the enormous cost of the broadcasting rights may lead to less than quality television. For instance, according to one count, the 1988 Winter Olympics ran about 20 minutes of commercials per hour (Stewart, 1988). Not only was the total ad time unusually high but the placement was often poor. Hockey goals were scored during commercials. The announcement of the scores for medal-winning figure skaters Gordeeva and Grinkov occurred during an ad aired immediately after their performance. Rights to televise the Olympics are a valued plum for a network but one that viewers expect to be done in a high quality fashion.

The Calgary Olympic Organizing Committee in 1988 made significant scheduling concessions to ABC for televising purposes (Klatell & Marcus, 1988). It altered the schedule to assure that there was a hockey game each day and fixed the schedule so that the United States hockey team would not have to play the top-rated Soviet Union or Czechoslovakia until the finals. In addition, Calgary in 1988 and Barcelona in 1992 lengthened the games to include three weekends, prime sports broadcasting time.

Olympic coverage may be used to further the host country's political or economic goals. South Korea used the 1988 summer games to showcase its economic progress. Viewers learned during the 1992 summer games that residents of host city Barcelona speak Catalan, not Spanish, and identify more with their autonomous region of Catalonia than with the nation of Spain. The way that sports such as the Olympics are broadcast may also reflect the national and cultural values of a nation. See Box 6.3 for an interesting contrast of U.S. and Brazilian Olympics coverage.

Synthetic Sports

Another product of the marriage of television and sports was what has come to be called "synthetic sports" or "trashsports." One type, frequently broadcast on ABC's "Wide World of Sports," runs the gamut from cliff diving at Acapulco or national logrolling championships to a rattlesnake hunt in Keane, Oklahoma or national wrist-wrestling championships in Petaluma, California. Audiences enjoyed the "World Buffalo Chip-Tossing Contest" and the "Joe Garagiola/Bazooka Big League Gum Blowing Championships." These unusual, even bizarre, activities were not necessarily invented for television but were easily and cheaply photographed in advance for use whenever the network needed them. Of course, they varied widely in their audience appeal.

BOX 6.3: SPORTS MEDIA COVERAGE
AND CULTURAL VALUES: A CASE STUDY

How do national social and cultural values affect media coverage of sports and sports heroes? The answer may be more substantial than we realize. Consider the following example from Kottak (1990) of the comparison of U.S. and Brazilian media coverage of their respective medal winners in the 1984 Olympics.

First of all, although Brazilian media overall gave less Olympic coverage to its own competitors than did the United States, there was also a much greater emphasis on team sports and victories by Brazilian media, whereas the U.S. media spent much time on individual human interest stories of participants (e.g., skater Dan Jansen's sister dying just before his competition). In contrast, Brazilian swimming medalist Ricardo Prado was lauded by his media for his stellar performance but only in the context of much criticism of the team's overall poor showing. Brazilian athletes were blamed by their media for poorer than expected performance, whereas U.S. athletes were praised for fine attempts and empathized with for disappointing showings. The theme of the underdog triumphing was prominent in U.S. media, whoever the winner. Brazilian media gave scant coverage to their own runner Joaquim Cruz' surprise gold medal, although U.S. media ran a human interest story on his rise from a humble upbringing in the slums to stardom. Pratfalls and slips were covered heavily in Brazilian media, typically in a humorous vein, not the "heartbreak" angle more common in U.S. Olympic coverage. Brazilian Olympic athletes reported being extremely worried about how the audience back home would judge their performance.

Why the difference? Kottak argued that, even though the United States in many ways embodies more competitive values than does Brazil, U.S. sports coverage is rife with the American cultural theme of the striving and success of the individual. The individual person and his or her efforts are celebrated and seldom criticized, even if the results are disappointing. Everyone has a chance, and even the lowliest individual can rise high through valiant individual effort. Brazilian media, on the other hand, reflect a more stratified and less mobile society where no one is expected to rise in the social hierarchy. Thus, people do not see hard work as being efficacious in raising one's social status, and it may even be seen as a threat.

A second kind of trashsport is celebrity contests, usually created entirely as television events. Such programs feature famous athletes or show business personalities participating in some competition outside their own area of expertise, from celebrity golf tournaments to track and field events featuring teams of present or former cast members of different TV shows (e.g., "The Brady Bunch" vs. "Days of Our Lives" stars). Because of the parasocial interaction we have with our TV "friends," we watch them participate in events that we would find totally uninteresting in other circumstances. Not unlike watching our own child in a ball game, we are there because of our relationship with the participants, not necessarily because of intrinsic interest in the sport itself.

Now we have looked at how the media have affected and changed various sports themselves and the reality about them that we perceive. Next we examine several psychological factors that are directly affected by the perceived reality of media sports.

PSYCHOLOGICAL ISSUES IN SPORTS AND MEDIA

Why do people seek sports media consumption, and what is the nature of that experience psychologically? In some ways it is like other media consumption, but in other ways it is unique. On TV, only sports (and, to some extent, news) is live and unrehearsed with the outcome unknown. This is very different than the rather predictable formulaic nature of most entertainment programming and advertising. In this section we examine several aspects of the sports media consumption experience, with the major emphasis being on the medium of television.

Sports Media Consumption as a Social Event

More often than other TV viewing, part of the reality of the experience of sports media consumption involves the presence of others (Rothenbuhler, 1988). Friends gather at someone's home or patrons congregate in a bar to watch a big game. Often the game seems more enjoyable in a group than it would be watching alone, with the presence of others somehow seeming more important than it would be watching a movie, a sitcom, or the news (Wenner & Gantz, 1989). The expression of emotion, discussed later, may be part of the reason. Also, watching with a group partially re-creates the stadium situation of watching the event in a crowd.

Food and Drink. One interesting aspect of the social reality of sports TV viewing is the eating and drinking that accompany the viewing. People eat and drink more watching sports than watching other events on TV, especially when viewing in groups, but the range of what they consume is fairly narrow. What we consume and how much depends on the sport; for example, pro football fans drink more just before watching the game (Wenner & Gantz, 1989). The food is most often junk food, snacks, or perhaps hot dogs, and the drink is typically soft drinks or beer. In short, we eat and drink the same sort of substances at home that we might consume if we were in attendance at the stadium. It seems somehow odd to have coffee and croissants while watching the Chicago Bears and the Green Bay Packers or to savor a fine red wine while watching the heavyweight boxing championship fight.

Competitiveness and Achievement

Obviously one of the major psychological components of sports is the competition and the achievement of victory. Part of the perceived reality of TV sports also involves this desire to win, which is learned early by the fans through the media. Part of the natural socialization process of child development often involves an identification and support for certain sports teams and individuals. Who this will be is often, although not necessarily, determined by geographical considerations. We most often root for the local team, the team of our school, or the team our family has rooted for, perhaps for generations. Still, major teams have fans all over. The hapless Chicago Cubs have supporters who have never been near Wrigley Field, whereas Roman Catholics throughout North America cheer for the University of Notre Dame's football team.

Patriotism comes into play in international competition. The U.S. hockey upset victory over the Soviet Union in the 1980 Winter Olympics was especially savored in a nation angry and frustrated by the Soviet invasion of Afghanistan a few weeks before. The World Cup, with one team per nation, becomes a national competition, during which the business life of certain soccer-happy countries in Western Europe and South America takes a de facto holiday. When the Toronto Blue Jays made the baseball World Series in 1992, all Canada celebrated, in spite of the fact that there were no Canadians on the team. The first-time entry of independent former Soviet and Yugoslav nations like Lithuania, Estonia, Croatia, and Slovenia into the 1992 Olympics was a moment of intense national pride.

There is some evidence of negative behavioral effects of watching aggressive sports. In research studies, fans leaving an Army–Navy football game (Goldstein & Arms, 1971) or wrestling or hockey events (Arms, Russell, & Sandilands, 1979) scored higher in hostility and aggressiveness than control subjects who had watched a swimming meet. It did not matter if one's team won or lost or if the aggression was stylized (wrestling) or spontaneous (hockey). Although these studies have not been replicated with fans who are television spectators, the results are provocative and suggest that the presence of aggressiveness may be more important than merely the element of competition.

Sometimes sports competition has some extreme and tragic consequences. In 1969, Honduras and El Salvador fought the so-called "soccer war," precipitated by a particularly bitter soccer game. In 1985, 39 people in Brussels died, and 450 were injured, in a deadly brawl among fans watching a championship soccer game between Liverpool, England, and an Italian team. Such incidents have caused fans to be screened with metal detectors, nations to exchange information on the most violent fans, and heavily armed soldiers to stand guard between the seating for fans of the opposing teams. These security measures have come to be part of the reality of sport, although those watching on TV need not be so inconvenienced.

The reward in sports is generally for winning, with very few kudos, endorsements, or dollars for coming in second, much less third or tenth. With its carrying of so many more sports into so many more lives, television has certainly, at least indirectly, encouraged competitiveness. With the star mindset that focuses on individuals, television lavishes attention and acclaim on the winner, whereas it often virtually ignores everyone else. This helps to construct a reality in viewers that coming in first is what is important. Athletes are not interviewed after the game for "doing their best" or being good sports. Sports metaphors carry over into our speech and thinking in many other areas of life, such as relationships. A fellow goes on a date and "scores" or "strikes out." A woman complains that men see women as "conquests" or "trophies." Parents feel like "losers" if their child is not accepted to a prestigious college.

A very different, and subtler, way that competitiveness can manifest itself in the sports viewer is in the accumulation and exhibiting of copious, seemingly endless, sports trivia and statistics. Sportscasters encourage this through their endless recitation of such information during radio and TV broadcasts, in part probably to fill the time where there is no play or commercial to fill what would otherwise be dead air. The computer has only made it easier to amass and retrieve such figures. Such statistics have become part of the reality of media sports. Even young children seemingly unable to remember much in school may recite voluminous facts about RBIs, passes completed, and shooting percentages.

Teamwork and Cooperation

Probably the major positive value cited for participation in sports is the learning of teamwork and cooperation. Parents most often give such reasons for encouraging their children to become involved in school and community sports. Team sports are indeed an excellent way to learn how to work with others as a team where each member must depend on fellow team members. How do televised sports teach teamwork?

The Star Versus the Team. Some disturbing indications suggest that, in terms of television, less noble values may overshadow the loftier ones. Often the "star mentality" of television and the entertainment business in general affects the presentation of sports in the media. The superstars are exalted and glorified far more than, for example, a show of fine teamwork on the field. Stories about sports tend to focus on the outstanding athlete, much as stories about religion tend to focus on the pope or Jerry Falwell or stories about government tend to focus on the president. This extolling of the individual may subtly undermine the importance of teamwork and cooperation for the viewer, especially the young viewer.

The Thrill of the Fight.   Even more serious is the way that media, especially television, tend to heavily focus on, perhaps even glorify, the occasional brawl or fight on the field. In a sense this is an auxiliary competition to the primary one being played. Although no sportscaster celebrates or even condones a serious tragedy like the Belgian soccer fan deaths, the camera and media attention immediately shift routinely to any fight that breaks out either in the stands or on the field. When results of that game are reported later on the evening news, it is more likely to be the brawl, not the play of the game, that is shown on the screen. Even if fighting is clearly condemned by the sportscaster, the heavy coverage given to the fight conveys a subtle message of its own. The perceived reality to the viewer, especially a young one, may be that the winner in the brawl is to be admired as much as the winner in the game itself. "Television has promoted the McEnroe model of competition, because temper tantrums, rudeness, and racket-hurling are more photogenic and lively than self-control and playing by the rules" (Tavris, 1988, p. 193).

Do people really enjoy watching sports violence? In a study of response to sports aggression, Bryant (1989) found that avid sports fans do enjoy watching rough and even violent sporting events, especially under certain conditions. Inherently more violent people enjoy sports violence more. The more one dislikes the victim of the violence, the more that violence is enjoyed. Bryant reported a study where highly prejudiced Whites greatly enjoyed seeing a race car crash where a Black driver was killed. Violence that is morally "sanctioned," that is, presented as acceptable or even necessary, is liked more than violence that is presented as unfair or out of line. Such moral sanctioning may come from several sources, including the rules and customs of the game, the tone of the commentary of the sportscaster or sportswriter, and even the reactions of other fans. The more of these conditions that are present, the more the viewer enjoys the violence.

Emotional Benefits

Although there are clear benefits from participating in sports, those benefits are somewhat less clear when it comes to consuming sports through media. Obviously, physical health and fitness are not enhanced by watching ball games on TV and may even be hindered if watching takes time that the viewers would otherwise be exercising themselves. Emotionally, the picture is a little less clear. The tension reduction or emotional release called *catharsis* may result from physical exercise where we release stress through muscular and aerobic exercise. Some psychologists dating back to Sigmund Freud argue that catharsis may also be achieved through substitute activities. Although research has not supported the value of a cathartic release of aggressive feeling through watching sports, there is widespread belief among the general public in such a process (Tavris, 1988).

There clearly is often a lot of emotion felt while consuming media sports. Zillmann, Bryant, and Sapolsky (1979) proposed a "disposition theory of sports-fanship" to describe such feelings. The enjoyment we experience emotionally from witnessing the success or victory of a competing party (individual or team) increases with the degree of positive sentiments and decreases with the degree of negative sentiments we feel toward that party. The reverse is true for what we experience when we witness a failure or defeat. The more we care about a team's success, the more emotional satisfaction we feel when they do well and the worse we feel when they do badly. Thus it is hard to become emotionally involved, or sometimes even interested at all, in watching a game between two teams that we do not know and care little about.

Still, feelings about the competitors are not the only determinants of emotional response to sports. As with any drama, the degree of perceived conflict is crucial. A game that is close in score and hard-fought in character evokes more emotional reaction, regardless of team loyalty, than one where the final victor is never in doubt or one where the participants appear not to be trying very hard. As with other kinds of drama, the unpredictability and suspense are important (Zillmann, 1980, 1991c). A close basketball game settled at the final buzzer carries the viewer along emotionally throughout its course. A game whose outcome is known is less likely to be of interest to watch in its entirety. How many ball games are ever rerun on television? How many people watch a video-taped ball game to which they already know the final score? However, a few people may actually prefer the predictable to the uncertain; see Box 6.4.

Sex Roles and Gender Bias

Men's and Women's Sports. It is an undisputed fact that the media cover male sports much more heavily than female sports, with estimates as high as 95% of coverage being of men (Coakley, 1986; see also Sabo & Jensen, 1992; Sabo & Runfola, 1990). It is also true that attendance at men's events is higher than at women's events. The nature of the relationship between the two is interesting and complex, however. Is the heavier media coverage of men's sports merely reflecting the reality of greater fan interest in men's sports, for whatever reason, or is the greater media coverage a cause of greater fan interest in men's sports?

Some major media sports, most notably football and baseball, are male only, without parallel female teams for the media to cover. In other sports, such as pro golf and tennis and college basketball, there are parallel women's teams and competition. Only in professional tennis and the Olympics does the media coverage of women's competition even approach the attention given to the men, however, and both of these cases are fairly unusual in that competition for both sexes occurs in the same structured event (e.g., Wimbledon includes both men's and women's matches, whereas the PGA and LPGA are separate events). Only

---

BOX 6.4: PERFECTIONISM, PROBABILISM, AND SPORTS FANATICISM

Why are some people rabid sports fans, whereas others could not care less? It does not seem to be particularly related to their personality, because even meek and nonassertive people can be extremely competitive watching sports. The author's personal theory, completely untested, offers a possibility.

Like statistics, sports is a very probabilistic venture. One can make all kinds of odds on who will win the game or the race, but they are only that—odds. If Team A is better on most relevant criteria than Team B, it will probably win. Probably but not necessarily. Once in a great while even the most invincible team is knocked off by a lowly challenger.

On the one hand, this uncertainty is part of what makes sports exciting to watch. On the other hand, uncertainty is handled very poorly by some people, particularly perfectionists. Perfectionists think in all-or-none terms; either they win (succeed) or they are a total failure. Perfectionists like predictability; if one side is objectively better on all relevant criteria, they should win—always. Unlike most people, perfectionist sports fans may prefer a 55–0 shellacking by their football team to a close victory.

More often, perhaps, perfectionists are not that drawn to watching sports at all. It is too unpredictable and it hurts too much when their side does not win. It may not be that they do not care who wins. They may care too much.

---

in these few cases like tennis and the Olympics is the perceived reality of sport gender balanced. Even in the reporting about female athletes that does occur, studies have found the coverage to be asymmetrical, with women being described in less powerful and success-oriented language (Duncan, Messner, & Williams, 1990; Messner, Duncan, & Jensen, 1993). They are more likely than men to be called by their first names and have their strengths described ambivalently (e.g., "small but so effective," "big girl," "her little jump hook" [Duncan, 1992]).

The Olympics are an instructive and somewhat exceptional instance. Generally, the summer and winter games are completely covered by television, often with both live coverage and extended edited excerpts broadcast a few hours later, often at more convenient local times. For example, the 1984 winter Olympics at Sarajevo were seen by most North Americans as delayed summarized coverage, instead of live in the middle of the night U.S. time. Because of the nature of this coverage, women's events received nearly, if not entirely, as much coverage as men's events. Interest in women's Olympic sports often has been very high, and many women superstar athletes such as Mary Lou Retton, Nadia Comaneci, or Dorothy Hamill have become genuine heroes and every bit as popular as the men.

Sportscasting and sports reporting is probably the last and most stubborn bastion of male supremacy in the journalism industry. Although female news anchors and reporters, meteorologists, and even editors are increasingly common and accepted, the female sportscaster or sports reporter (covering men's sports) is still highly exceptional. Whether this absence reflects the public's true dislike or distrust of women reporting men's sports or merely an industry fear that such a reaction would occur is unclear. Clearly the issue touches deeper chords than over-publicized pseudo-issues such as the problem of sending female sportscasters into men's locker rooms for postgame interviews.

Gender-Role Socialization. Although not nearly as dichotomous as in the past, boys are still encouraged to participate in sports of all kinds more than girls are. Less obviously, the same asymmetry applies to media consumption of sports. Boys are encouraged by their parents (usually their fathers) to watch games on TV as well as play ball and shoot baskets in the yard. Not only the playing of sports but also the watching of sports on TV has become a part of the socialization of being a man in our society. The boy who is not particularly interested in spending his time this way, but whose father is, often receives subtle or not-so-subtle messages that such lack of interest does not measure up and perhaps even undermines or calls into question his masculinity. Consuming media sports together has become a part of the reality of many father–son relationships, and some father–daughter ones. The boy who does not fit the idealized athletic, heterosexual male stereotype does not have role models in media sports.

One advantage of watching sports for men is that it is probably the one arena where they are most free to express emotion. Men watching a ball game together, somewhat like the players themselves, may relatively freely express feelings and even touch one another. In mainstream Anglo North American society this is practically the only time when most men feel comfortable embracing. Many heterosexual men probably never hug another man outside their family or perhaps inside it as well, except in the context of playing or watching sports.

In the past, girls were often given messages, especially after reaching puberty, that participation in sports was tomboyish and unfeminine and could be a serious liability in attracting a man. With the women's movement, this has changed considerably, and girls and women are now allowed to be both athletic and sexy at the same time. Less and less is it considered surprising or inappropriate for women to watch ball games or to know more about sports than their men, although TV audiences for most sporting events are still, by a large majority, male.

Racial Bias

Although a majority of players in the NFL (60%) and NBA (70%), as well as lesser but substantial numbers in other sports and the Olympics, are African American, their numbers are far smaller in administration (e.g., 7% of front office personnel in the NFL and NBA, one out of 28 NFL head coaches, 6 out of 27 NBA head coaches; Lapchick & Rodriguez, 1990).

A few content analysis studies of play-by-play broadcasting suggest that racist stereotypes are being at least subtly reinforced by sportscasting. For example, in a content analysis of 12 NFL games in 1976, Rainville and McCormick (1977) found that White players, as compared to African Americans, were more often described in terms of positive physical characteristics, as causal agents, and in terms of past positive accomplishments. Jackson (1989) looked both at NFL and NCAA college basketball commentary. He found that 65% of comments about African-American football players pertained to physical size or ability, compared to 17% for White players. On the other hand, 77% of comments about White football players stressed their intelligence, leadership, or motivation, whereas only 23% of comments about African-American players did (63% vs. 15% for basketball players).

In light of such figures, it is interesting and disturbing that sports is apparently widely perceived by young African-American men as a route out of poverty and the ghetto (Edwards, 1987), although research has shown no relationship between participation in sports and subsequent educational or occupational mobility for African-American males (Howell, Miracle, & Ross, 1984).

Hero Worship

Media coverage of sports has enhanced, or at least altered, the perceived reality of the hero. Sports stars have long been heroes emulated by youth, but the age of television, and to a lesser extent other media, has changed this role somewhat. On the one hand, Mary Lou Retton or Jose Canseco may be seen by many more people on television than was previously possible. On the other hand, the close scrutiny of television shows the faults as well as the nobler aspects of a potential hero.

Children emulate their TV sports heroes in some very traditional ways, but also in some new ways. A child may imitate not only John McEnroe's backhand but also his temper tantrums. Nor is emulation of athletes limited to children. Long-time golfers report that play on golf courses slowed noticeably after the start of televising of major golf tournaments. This occurred primarily because amateur golfers started lining up their putts and other behaviors they saw the pros do on TV, no matter that the amateur may not have understood what he or she was doing or looking for when lining up that putt.

One particular area of concern in regard to hero worship has been the use of drugs by sports stars and the resulting effects on youth (Donohew, Helm, & Haas, 1989). The widespread cocaine use by baseball and basketball stars in the 1980s seemed somehow worse than such use by other citizens, even by other public figures, because sports figures are heroes to youth. This has caused persons and institutions like the commissioner of baseball, the National Collegiate

Athletic Association (NCAA), and the NBA to be tougher on drug users among their athletes than they might otherwise be. The hero status is often used more directly to discourage drug use, as when Earvin "Magic" Johnson was hired to do an antidrug testimonial PSA, several years before he tested positive for HIV and became a spokesperson for AIDS awareness and safer sex (see Box 6.5).

BOX 6.5: SPORTS HEROES WITH THE AIDS VIRUS

In the early 1990s, there were increasing numbers of revelations of sports heroes who tested positive for HIV, the AIDS virus. Perhaps the most celebrated case was pro basketball's superhero Earvin "Magic" Johnson, who resigned from the Los Angeles Lakers at the height of his career in late 1991, announcing that he had tested positive for HIV. A widely recognized athlete of tremendous talent, as well as a positive role model for youth, Johnson's announcement was greeted with a massive outpouring of public sympathy. Moreover, he was appointed by former President George Bush to an advisory committee on AIDS policy (Johnson later resigned in disgust at a lack of government commitment to AIDS) and embarked on a heavy schedule of speaking engagements to youth about the importance of safe sex and traditional values. Receiving heavy media coverage for several weeks, Johnson admitted that he had been quite promiscuous as a single man before his recent marriage, and it was this activity that had presumably infected him. Interestingly, this violation of traditional morals did not seem to significantly affect his superhero status (including lucrative commercial endorsements), as an admission of homosexual relations surely would have.

In the wake of Magic Johnson's revelations, the media carried a number of stories about the sexually promiscuous lifestyles of some male professional athletes, and many athletes became vocally concerned about possible physical contact with HIV-infected opponents during a football or basketball game. Still, there seemed to be considerable moral ambiguity about such behavior; during this same period former basketball great Wilt Chamberlain publicly boasted of having had sex with 20,000 different women. Although clearly practicing exceptionally "unsafe sex" as well as behavior laden with moral questions, Chamberlain did not lose his hero status. Even a celibate but gay superstar athlete probably would not have been treated half so well.

A very different situation occurred around the early 1992 revelation by retired tennis great Arthur Ashe that he was HIV positive, as a result of a blood transfusion with tainted blood during heart surgery in the early 1980s. Although Ashe had known of his infection for over 3 years, he only chose to reveal the fact publicly after a USA Today reporter had discovered the information and told Ashe that he intended to make it public. Unlike Johnson, Ashe was retired and no longer a public figure and had acquired the HIV virus through means above moral reproach. Although public response to Ashe's announcement and his death in early 1993 was uniformly sad and sympathetic, the question remains about whether the privacy of Ashe and his wife and daughter had been violated, or was the public's right to know greater?

Another fringe benefit of hero status is lucrative product endorsement contracts for the major stars. For Olympic athletes this is often the critical part of their financial support, allowing them to pursue their "amateur" career. For wealthy professional athletes it is more of the icing on the already rich cake. These endorsement campaigns lead to an even greater media presence, as that person becomes familiar as a spokesperson in advertising for that product. Sometimes a single individual may endorse several different products in different classes. In the months following the 1984 Olympics, comedians had a field day with jokes about the omnipresent smile of Mary Lou Retton endorsing a large number of products. Overexposure was a definite concern. A certain wholesome status is required, however. When Romanian Olympic gymnast Nadia Comaneci emigrated to the United States, the fact that she was openly and unapologetically living with a married man apparently rendered her worthless to advertisers for endorsements.

Another aspect of emulating athletic heroes is seen in the area of fashion. Thanks to the influence of television, we not only want to act like the stars but we want to dress like them, also. Dress of different sports becomes chic at different times and places. Jogging clothes became high fashion, not only for nonjogging adults, but even for infants who cannot even walk! Clothing manufacturers make large sums selling high fashion clothes for tennis, skiing, or bicycling to folks who have never played those sports and who have no intention of ever doing so. Some people wanting to learn to ski may first buy the latest ski fashions and only later buy skis and poles.

In spite of television's enhancement of sports heroes, some (e.g., Coakley, 1986; Rader, 1984) have argued that today's sports heroes are not on the pedestal of past stars like Willie Mays, Johnny Unitas, Jesse Owens, or Stan Musial. The huge salaries and fast-track living seem to separate such persons from ourselves and stress their narcissistic and hedonistic tendencies rather than the righteous and humble characteristics that we at least used to think our heroes possessed. The intrusive eye of television focuses on a ballplayer not only when he makes that glorious play, but also when he is petulantly fuming on the sidelines or selfishly proclaiming that he cannot make ends meet on $1.5 million a year. No matter that all of us have our selfish and petulant moments; we like to think that true heroes do not, and the age of television makes it harder to maintain that fiction.

CONCLUSION

Media reporting sports events are doing more than reflecting the reality of that game. Television has changed the very sports themselves. Television has also changed the way that our minds consider these sports. TV sports is a world all its own, a world only imperfectly related to the world of real sports in the stadiums or the racetracks. These days when people think of sports, they are most likely to first think of watching television. The perceived reality of sports acquired through television is thus what sports are, for most people. Just as media are our knowledge source about groups of people, social values, or products for sale, so do they tell us about sports and what we should learn from sports.

7

NEWS: MORE THAN
REPORTING

Q: What was the average length of a TV news story about a U.S. presidential election campaign in 1968?

A: 43 seconds.

Q: What was the average length in 1988?

A: 9 seconds (Hallin, 1992)!

Q: Why did the city of Dresden, in the former East Germany, experience a crisis in the labor supply in the years before German reunification in 1990?

A: People were moving to other regions of East Germany, because the area around Dresden was the only part of the country that did not receive West German television (Cantor & Cantor, 1986).

If there is one area of media that people are most likely to uncritically accept as reflecting reality rather than creating it, that area is probably the news. People watch television news or read the newspaper to find out what happened in the world that day. However, the perceived reality often diverges quite dramatically from the "real world," where much more happened than can be reported in the day's news. Even if they earnestly try to accurately and fairly represent the day's events, producers and editors must select which items to cover, how prominently to cover them, and in what manner to cover them.

These choices necessarily involve some *agenda setting* (see chapter 2); that is, telling us what is important (Berelson, 1942; McCombs, 1981; McCombs & Shaw, 1993; Rogers & Dearing, 1988; Watt, Mazza, & Snyder, 1993). Agenda setting tells us what to think about, what is important. It does not necessarily tell us what to think about that topic. See Brosius and Kepplinger (1990); Demers,

Craff, Choi, and Pessin (1989); and Edelstein (1993) for different measures of agenda setting in regard to news. When the months-long U.S. presidential primary elections are given massive media coverage, the public receives the implicit but very clear message that they are important. Likewise, when stories receive little coverage, a message is communicated that they are not important. Those in power know this well. For example, when the White South African government in the mid-1980s prohibited any coverage of unrest in Black townships, it was trying to create a perceived reality where such activity was unimportant.

News programming is put in an especially tricky position by the economic realities of the mass communications industry. Even though news divisions are separate from entertainment divisions at the U.S. television networks and news clearly has the primary function to inform rather than entertain, the "success" of news is determined by ratings, just as the success of a sitcom is, and that increases the pressure to entertain. Similarly, a newspaper must try to maximize its advertising dollars, usually closely related to the number of subscriptions. In deciding what news to include in a publication or broadcast, pressures clearly exist to tell people what they want to hear and what will entertain them, in order to keep them coming back and keep advertisers happy. If the public does not want to hear that its leaders are conducting an unjust war or if major advertisers do not care to see news coverage that their product is harmful, those pressures are unlikely to be ignored.

Although there is much to be gained from a careful study of the *text* of the news messages themselves (e.g., Van Dijk, 1985a, 1988), a full understanding of the psychology of media news requires an examination of the nature of the medium itself, as it transmits news. This is particularly important in regard to television. After some background on television news, this chapter examines what news is, in a psychological sense, and how the perceived reality about world events is constructed from reading or watching news reports. The rest of the chapter examines effects of consuming news, including effects on memory, decision making, behavior, and even foreign and domestic policy.

THE RISE OF TV NEWS

Although print news journalism has been with us for many years, television news as a medium has its roots in the movie newsreel of the early to mid-20th century. With such news shorts, shown in theaters before feature films, the audience experienced an immediacy with distant world events, even if delayed several weeks, that had never been possible before. This use of moving visuals to convey the news brought a new power to the media, that of *montage*, the juxtaposition of images for dramatic effect. To a large extent reporters and editors must "reassemble the ingredients of the reality" (Bogart, 1980, p. 225) to best express what they perceive as the reality. Montage allows the telling of a news story using many of the dramatic techniques from drama and fiction writing to make the event more compelling and entertaining. This of course opens the door for other elements of fiction to enter as well.

Although news has been on television from its early days, the TV coverage of John F. Kennedy's assassination and subsequent events in 1963 gave a tremendous impetus to TV news with its immediate live coverage. In the next 5 years, the U.S. TV news audience jumped 50%, the sharpest increase ever. By 1977, 62% of all adult Americans watched at least one newscast per weekday, making television the major source of news in the United States. This 62% broke down to 12% network only, 30% local only, and 20% both. These figures point to the great popularity of local news, including weather and sports. Local news shows are also extremely crucial for local stations to establish their unique identity in the community, because the large majority of programming is either network initiated or syndicated, both of which are identical regardless of the station. See Box 7.1 for further discussion of weather reports and reporters.

TV news reporters, especially network news anchors, become trusted "friends" in our lives. More than other TV personalities, they are a part of our mealtimes, especially on the morning news shows at breakfast and the evening news at dinner. It is almost like having Dan Rather, Peter Jennings, or Tom Brokaw as a regular dinner guest. We invite them into our homes through our choice to turn on the TV to the particular channel. It is not unusual for people to audibly respond to a greeting, such as responding "Hi, Tom," back to Brokaw as he signs on with "Good evening." They become substitute friends in a sort of "parasocial interaction" (Rubin, Perse, & Powell, 1985), as discussed in chapter 2. There is a sense of solidarity with them. As one person explained such a relationship, "I grew up watching him . . . I guess I expect him to be there when I turn on the news. We've been through a lot together" (Levy, 1982, p. 180). That feeling of "being through a lot together" captures very well why news anchors are far more important people in our lives than merely folks who read us the day's events. There is no equivalent relationship with newspaper editors or writers.

Network anchors command high salaries but also high respect. When longtime CBS anchor Walter Cronkite was asked in 1980 if he would be available for a vice-presidential nomination, he made a joking reply. However, his teasing was seen as serious equivocation and he later had to issue a categorical denial of any political ambitions. Although it apparently had never occurred to Cronkite that any answer of his to such a question would be taken seriously, by many it was. A few years earlier Cronkite had been deemed the "most trusted man in America" by the polls, ahead of the president, the Pope, and movie stars.

BOX 7.1: TV WEATHER FORECASTS:
MORE THAN TELLING IF IT WILL RAIN

Local news anchors, sportscasters, and weathercasters are extremely important to local TV stations in establishing their "signature" and identity in their market. Although a large majority of programming on commercial television is either network or syndication, local news is one of the few programs where a local station has control of all aspects of the programming. A popular team of local broadcasters can bring an extremely helpful ratings boost that greatly raises the visibility of that station in the target market.

A seemingly indispensable part of all local news shows, as well as some national ones, is the weather forecaster. There is even an entire cable channel devoted to weather. Although all U.S. weathercasters use essentially the same data, those gathered by the National Weather Service, clearly not all weathercasts are equal. Some weathercasters, but not all, actually have training in meteorology, and those who do are usually prominently identified. Some are more performers than reporters; NBC's Willard Scott has done the weather dressed in various costumes and always with pizzazz. Early TV events like a Chicago weatherman giving his Thanksgiving forecast to a turkey or the Milwaukee weathercaster puppet named Albert the Alleycat delivering the forecast are probably unlikely in the 1990s. The high quality computer graphics now allow even small local stations to give a weathercast of high technical quality, a far cry from 1950s weatherman Bill Carlsen who squirted his map with shaving cream to show snow! (Garelik, 1985).

Although weathercasts are often seen as the "frivolous" or "soft" side of the news (the first on-the-air newswomen were the "weathergirls" of the late 1950s and early 1960s), often the subject is deadly serious. Forecasts and warnings of tornadoes, hurricanes, and floods can mean the difference between life and death. Although the National Weather Service issues the watches, warnings, and advisories, often the local weathercaster does additional interpretation as to how strongly to advise precaution. A wrong judgment call in such a situation could have tragic consequences.

WHAT IS NEWS?

Jamieson and Campbell (1992, p. 31) defined *hard news* as any "report of an event that happened or was disclosed within the previous 24 hours and treats an issue of ongoing concern." The event itself need not be recent (although usually it is) but it must involve some new revelation or previously unknown connection. Revelations of Abraham Lincoln's suffering from Marfan syndrome, Franklin Roosevelt's previously unknown extramarital affair, or the discovery of the shroud allegedly used to wrap Christ's body when taken down from the cross have all been news in recent years.

In contrast to hard news are "human interest" stories, which touch universal concerns and are less tied to place and time. These features are most prevalent on so-called "slow news days" and may include anything from a farmer in west Texas who planted 1959 Cadillacs tail-fin-upward in his field, a bizarre feat celebrated in Bruce Springsteen's song "Cadillac Ranch," to the heartwarming story of a poor Mississippi sharecropper whose nine children have all graduated from college (most with advanced degrees), to the mildly titillating story of a brothel madam with a master's degree.

Qualities of a Newsworthy Event

Jamieson and Campbell (1992) identified five qualities of a newsworthy event. They may not all be present in every story, but no doubt several of them will be for each hard news story. The more of these characteristics a story has naturally, the more likely it is to be heavily covered in the news.

First, the story is personalized, about individuals. This allows audience identification with the person and may make a dauntingly complex event easier to comprehend. It lends itself well to photography and the interview format (e.g., Heritage, 1985), which works well on TV, but it may be at the cost of oversimplifying (and possibly distorting) complex events and overemphasizing "stars" such as the president, other political leaders, the Pope, or some extremist spokesperson.

Second, a newsworthy event is dramatic and conflict filled, even violent. We are used to entertainment TV as being dramatic (Zillmann, 1980). Shots of Israeli police beating intifada protesters makes "better copy" for TV news than a debate on Palestinian rights among politicians of different views. With its emphasis on conflict, this tendency helps to insure coverage of opposing views but, on the negative side, may overemphasize the conflict and violent nature of the story. Very infrequent violent events may be assumed by viewers to be the norm. Nonviolent events may be neglected and very important issues not conducive to drama, conflict, or personalization may be grossly underreported. For example, complex economic stories like the Third World debt crisis or changing interest rates in the United States are often covered on TV news only through specific events that reflect those problems.

Third, a newsworthy event contains action and some observable occurrence. This often becomes the "hook" on which to hang what is essentially a more abstract story. For example, trends in inflation may be covered by interviews with specific consumers shopping and expressing their views on rising prices. Important stories that do not have such a convenient "hook" or discrete encapsulating event receive less attention. For example, the dramatic shift in the Third World over the last 30 years from domestic-food producing to export agriculture is a profound change, but it is seldom mentioned in the news because it is not easily symbolized by discrete events.

These three characteristics of personalization, drama, and observable event are all involved in the need, especially crucial for television, for a story to be packaged in small pieces ("sound bites"). Broadcast news stories are almost always very brief, as are a vast majority of print stories. A story that fits this packaging demand is much more likely to receive coverage than one that does not. The size of these bites is decreasing: the average length of a TV news story about a U.S. presidential election campaign declined from 43 seconds in 1968 to 9 seconds in 1988 (Hallin, 1992)!

The fourth characteristic of hard news is that an event is more newsworthy if it is novel or deviant. Contrary to popular views, most news is not particularly surprising. For example, much political and economic news is covered by the normal beat reporters who know in advance that certain speeches will be made, votes taken, or meetings held. Events outside this predictable range of news will stand a better chance of being covered if they are novel, with chances of coverage increasing as the events get more strange and bizarre. A junkie being shot to death in New York City is not big news, but a Sunday school teacher killed in a Satanic ritual in rural North Dakota is. Once in a while, merely being bizarre is enough to insure news coverage (e.g., the Cadillac ranch), but in most cases it needs to be related to some prevailing theme, the next characteristic of newsworthy events.

Finally, events are more likely to be covered in news if they are linked to issues of ongoing current interest in the media. Some of these themes are deep seated, almost archetypal, at least within a society. For example in the United States, the first theme, that of appearance versus reality, has always been a common theme in literature and drama. News stories about deception and hypocrisy make good copy; the Watergate scandal of 1972–1974, which eventually led to the resignation of President Richard Nixon, was one of the hottest news stories in the nation's history. The television evangelism scandals of 1987–1988 received heavy media coverage because their reality was revealed to not fit the appearance. Second, "big versus little" is a powerful theme, nicely captured by some of the crusading stories on "Sixty Minutes" or "20/20." Closely related is the good versus evil theme, a moral framework often imposed on news stories (e.g., the brave consumer vs. the evil polluting corporation). The fourth theme is efficiency versus inefficiency, commonly used in stories such as exposés of government or corporate waste or mismanagement. Finally, the unique versus the routine highlights the unusual.

Besides these underlying, archetypal themes we also have cyclical themes such as the quadrennial presidential elections in the United States and seasonal, holiday, and weather themes. For example, we know we will see the Pope saying midnight mass on Christmas, the groundhog looking for his shadow every February 2, and local news reporters in the spring telling us how to protect ourselves from tornadoes. Such events appear in the news because they fit the cyclical themes, in spite of having few of the other characteristics of newsworthy events.

Besides these five basic characteristics of newsworthy events, it helps if a story is *inoffensive* or at least not blatantly offensive. For example, the press was very slow to pick up on reporting on the AIDS epidemic in the early 1980s, in part because they balked at mentioning the most common way to acquire the disease, namely, anal intercourse (Meyer, 1990). Also, a serious story must be perceived as *credible*. An occurrence so bizarre that readers or viewers would not believe it is less likely to be reported, at least by the mainstream press (Meyer, 1990). Although this may sometimes have the salutary effect of "weeding out" fringe oddities such as Elvis sightings at K-Mart, it may have a less benign effect, as when news media self-censor a story that they do not believe their public would accept or want to hear, such as a report that a very popular and respected leader has been involved in corruption.

The surest way to obtain coverage of one's activities is to imbue them with these newsworthy characteristics. The more of these an event has, the more likely the media will show interest. Possessing these characteristics does not necessarily ensure that the event is important or unimportant, but it does ensure that the perceived reality will be a newsworthy event. For example, the brutal videotaped beating of motorist Rodney King by Los Angeles police officers in 1991 had all of these characteristics. It focused on a person, it was violent, and it was full of action and conflict. It was at least perceived by White Americans as unusual, and it was centrally related to many of the cultural themes (big vs. little, right vs. wrong, appearance vs. reality). The urban riots triggered by the "not guilty" verdict in the criminal trial of the officers involved in April 1992 also were full of newsworthy characteristics. See Box 7.2 for a study of the coverage of an important set of events that did not have so many of these characteristics.

The Local Hook

A final consideration determining newsworthiness is the "local hook," the connection of the story to the community of the reader, viewers, or listeners. At the local level, a newspaper or TV/radio station will be much more likely to cover a national or international event if it has a local angle (e.g., a local resident caught in an uprising in Angola; the closing of a local plant because of Mexican economic policy). On a national level, the hook in the United States may be a current policy debate in Washington. For example, civil wars in Nicaragua or El Salvador received attention in the 1980s primarily when there was an upcoming vote in Congress about aid to one of the governments or opposition movements. Coverage is given when U.S. troops invade (or are "invited" into) a country.

Sometimes the need for a local or national hook can seriously distort reality. For example, any intermittent harassment, censoring, or closing of the independent newspaper *La Prensa* by the leftist Sandinista government in Nicaragua

BOX 7.2: NEWS COVERAGE OF NUCLEAR WAR

Although a terribly important story, nuclear war is a constant and iterative threat that does not have many of the characteristics of a newsworthy story on a day-to-day basis.

Rubin and Cummings (1989) performed a content analysis of network news coverage of three stories in 1983 related to the nuclear threat. The first was the proposal of the new scientific theory of nuclear winter, which proposed that a nuclear war would trigger enough fires to send up enough smoke, dust, and soot to block 95% of the sun's light in the mid-latitudes of the northern hemisphere. This would be followed by a huge disruption of the ecosystem and growing season and the possible destruction of humanity. The second event was the televising of the ABC movie "The Day After" on November 20, 1983. Reaching 38.5 million homes, it became the highest rated TV movie to that time. Embraced by the "antinuke" movement and attacked by conservatives, its impact was less than either group predicted (Scholfield & Pavelchak, 1985). The third story was the continuing discussion by members of the Reagan administration about the possibility of fighting and winning a limited nuclear war.

Compared to what one might expect about their importance, Rubin and Cummings (1989) found coverage of these three stories minimal and offered four hypotheses about TV news' response to nuclear war issues. It may be that TV journalism had accepted that life could not survive a nuclear exchange; thus additional evidence of this was uncritically embraced and thus ignored. The nuclear winter story and the message of "The Day After" was "not so much displaced . . . as smothered by uncritical acceptance." A second more paternalistic possibility is that TV journalism had decided that viewers were too threatened and unable to emotionally handle any more discussion of this issue. Third, it is possible that TV journalism had decided that nuclear weapons were here to stay and thus should not be politicized. In support of such a view is the fact that the network cut a line from "The Day After," which stated that the justification for the Soviet attack was the U.S. movement of Pershing missiles, and also the fact that there was very little questioning of the Reagan administration assumptions about nuclear war. Finally, the paltry coverage may have been due to the fact that TV has only acquired a limited inventory of images for communicating the horror of nuclear war, such as computer graphics, writer landscapes, file footage of Hiroshima and Nagasaki, Pentagon film of missile tests, or scenes of everyday life with a voiceover intoning the consequences of nuclear war.

In conclusion, the "coverage of these events in 1983 was fatalistic, overly respectful of government, visually unimaginative, and politically neutralized. The strongest impression of the image of nuclear war on television news in the Reagan years was of no image at all" (Rubin & Cummings, 1989, p. 56).

generally received heavy media coverage in the mid-1980s in the United States, whereas the violent and permanent closing of *El Cronico del Pueblo* and *El Independiente* in U.S. ally El Salvador in 1980 and the 65 journalists killed in the next 8 years went basically unreported in the United States. Was this due to a pro-Reagan administration bias in the press? Perhaps, but it more likely resulted naturally from a greater focus on Nicaragua, where U.S. policy on aid to the opposition contras was frequently, and contentiously, up for discussion and voting by the U.S. Congress. Whatever the intent or the cause, the perceived reality for many was clearly that Sandinista Nicaragua was censoring the press. Although this was true at times to differing degrees, the failure to report even worse conditions of the press in U.S. ally El Salvador allowed many to uncritically perceive as reality the Reagan administration's painting of that country as a free democracy.

Now that we have seen what makes a newsworthy event, we examine how the media form and communicate the news.

NEWS MEDIA AS CREATING A PERCEIVED REALITY

The term *media* suggests that mass communication "mediates" between the audience and some objective reality that actually exists somewhere "out there" in the world. In Western culture, at least, we had often assumed that such an external reality exists. More than with any other domain of media content, people tend to assume that news conveys objective reality to us in clear and unbiased form. However, news writers and producers communicate their interpretation of that world reality both through their choice of topics and amount of coverage (agenda setting). News is a "frame that delineates a world" (Tuchman, 1978; see also Altheide, 1976; Schlesinger, 1978, 1987).

> Reality does not come neatly packaged in two- or three-minute lengths; raw history is filled with perversities, contradictions, ragged edges . . . TV is a storytelling medium. It abhors ambiguities, ragged edges, and unresolved issues. . . . The effect all too frequently is to impose upon an event or situation a preconceived form that alters reality, heightening one aspect at the expense of another for the sake of a more compelling story, blocking out complications that get in the way of the narrative. (Abel, 1984, p. 68)

Although choices of media coverage are usually motivated from a sincere desire to present news stories to the public in the most complete and accurate way possible, there are occasional instances when the construction of reality goes beyond the bounds of what most would consider acceptable (see Box 7.3).

BOX 7.3: NEWS REPORTER OR NEWSMAKER?

In their desire to make "an invisible truth visible, dramatic, and entertaining" (Bogart, 1980, p. 235), television occasionally goes too far. In 1966, CBS helped to finance an armed invasion of Haiti in exchange for exclusive TV rights of the event; the invasion was aborted by U.S. Customs. The next year a U.S. soldier cut off the ear of a dead Vietcong soldier; it later came out in his court martial that he did it after being offered a knife on a dare by a TV news cameraman (Lewy, 1978). There were numerous accounts of TV news crews in the 1960s arranging for demonstrations or drug parties to be staged again for the cameras if the "original" event did not happen to be timed right for the camera.

Other times, news journalists may become newsmakers in more positive ways. For example, Egyptian President Anwar Sadat's historic trip to Israel in 1977 was arranged not by the United Nations or U.S. State Department diplomats, but by CBS News anchorman Walter Cronkite. It was Cronkite who persistently called Sadat and Israeli Prime Minister Menachem Begin to arrange their eventual meeting (Weymouth, 1981).

Manipulation of News

Sometimes forces inside and outside of government also impinge on journalists in ways that affect the reality of news they create.

Direct Censorship. In countries with prior censorship, where material must be submitted to government censors for advance approval before being aired, or where the government owns and controls all news media, a very selective piece of reality may be offered, so much so that history may be substantially rewritten. For example, Russian citizens' view of the United States were for many years very heavily colored by news stories about crime, racism, homelessness, and imperialism that appeared in the Soviet press. Even if very little there was actually false, one's overall perception is grossly distorted if, for example, crime is believed to be the rule rather than the exception.

Blocking Access. Certain news stories may be effectively censored purely through blocking the access of the media to the scene of the story. For example, during the apartheid era in South Africa, journalists were at times forbidden to enter the Black townships. Similar policies by the Israeli government have sometimes kept the press out of the West Bank during times of Palestinian unrest. In both cases the governments involved clearly hoped that public attention to the problem would wane if compelling images could no longer be obtained for publication or broadcast.

Probably the clearest and most controversial examples of blocking press access have come in the coverage of recent regional wars. Working on the conventional (although dubious) wisdom that press coverage "lost" the Vietnam War for the United States, Britain in 1982 and the United States in 1983 forbade the press from accompanying troops in the island wars in the Falklands/Malvinas and Grenada, respectively (Servaes, 1991). The same policy was followed by the United States in the 1989 invasion of Panama to oust dictator Manuel Noriega. Only much later did the public learn that casualties were far more than originally reported, including the nearly total destruction of a large poor neighborhood in Panama City. The most widespread, even notorious, case of censorship through blocking access was exercised by the United States, Saudi Arabia, and their coalition allies in the 6-week Persian Gulf War against Iraq in 1991. Coverage of this war is examined in more depth as a case study later in the chapter.

Subtle Censorship.   In some nations, it is an official crime to broadcast material that is in any way against the interests of the state. Such vague legislation is available for use according to the political whims of the current rulers. At other times, the government and large business interests are so close that politically suspect TV stations and newspapers cannot get the advertising that they need to survive. Even in democratic countries, the government issues licenses for TV and radio stations. Sometimes these are withheld or delayed for political reasons. Some countries require journalists to be licensed, a practice consistently condemned by the International Press Institute as threatening freedom of the press. In other cases the supply and distribution of newsprint is controlled by the government and may be allotted according to political considerations.

Subtle Manipulation.   Even in a thriving democracy with constitutional guarantees of a free press, there are limits on news. Release of classified information damaging to national security is not permitted, although just how broad this doctrine should be has been the subject of many court challenges. In many ways, the government manipulates, although does not control, the press. For example, U.S. President Richard Nixon's firing of Watergate special prosecutor Archibald Cox in October 1973 was announced on a Saturday evening; the next year Nixon's successor Gerald Ford's pardon of Nixon for any Watergate-related crimes was announced on a Sunday morning. In 1992, former President George Bush pardoned Iran-contra defendants on Christmas Day. All of these unpopular policies were announced at times that were sure to receive the least possible coverage and attention. Often, government sources strategically leak stories about upcoming policy to gauge public reaction ("trial balloon"). If that reaction is negative, the policy need never be officially announced and the government will not be blamed for proposing it.

Media Self-Censorship. Sometimes censorship is self-imposed by the media. The three largest U.S. commercial TV networks gave very short attention to major corporate changes involving themselves (e.g., General Electric's takeover of NBC; Diamond & Noglows, 1987). Often newspapers or the TV networks are in possession of information that they choose not to reveal for some reason. For example, the networks knew about the transfer of some American hostages in Teheran in 1980 but said nothing to avoid jeopardizing the hostages' safety.

Other times the press concludes (rightly or wrongly) that the public just does not care to hear certain highly negative news about their country or government. For example, when the Soviet Union shot down a Korean commercial airliner (KAL 007) in 1983, the Kremlin made the predictable charge that it was an American spy plane. This claim was widely reported in the United States but practically never taken seriously. In a careful analysis of the coverage of this issue by *Time, Newsweek,* and *U.S. News & World Report,* Corcoran (1986) concluded that all three publications, with an estimated combined readership of around 50 million (Gans, 1979), followed a virtually identical Reagan administration party line of anti-Soviet diatribe and paranoia (see also Entman, 1991). Outside of the United States (e.g., in reputable British publications like the *Guardian*) available evidence supporting the theory that KAL 007 was on a spy mission was fully examined and seen to be a credible explanation. Why was this perspective not heard in the United States? It was not due to government censorship but perhaps was due to the press sensing that the U.S. public did not want to seriously consider (or perhaps would not believe) such a claim.

In the Watergate scandal of the early 1970s, the press chose to call President Nixon and other high U.S. government officials liars only after a considerable period of time and after compelling evidence had been presented. In the mid-1980s, the press was very hesitant to directly expose the very popular President Reagan's apparent misinformation about Soviet involvement in Nicaragua. Only after the revelation in late 1986 that the Reagan administration had been sending arms to Iran with the profits being diverted to the Nicaraguan contra rebels did the press seem to give itself permission to seriously criticize the president. Finally, the Washington press corps long knew of the Reagan administration's disinformation campaign in attributing the Berlin disco bombing in 1985 to Libya's Muammar Gaddafi but said nothing.

Consolidation of News-Gathering Organizations

Although not exactly manipulation of news as such, another concern in determining the perceived reality of world events is the increasing consolidation of news-gathering organizations. Skyrocketing costs, plus the undeniable logic of efficiency, mandates a pooling of resources. Clearly, not every newspaper, news magazine, and TV and radio station can afford to have its own reporter in every potential news spot in the world.

The consolidation, however, has reduced news sources to a very small club. In terms of newspapers, most news copy in most newspapers comes from a very few sources, especially the wire services of Associated Press (AP), Reuters, Agence France Presse (AFP), and, until its demise in 1992, United Press International (UPI). Only a very few large dailies have their own wire service (*New York Times*, *Los Angeles Times*). In terms of television, the "Big Three" U.S. commercial networks of ABC, NBC, and CBS, plus the newer Cable News Network (CNN), have enormous influence worldwide. A few other major networks, such as the BBC and ITN in the United Kingdom and Brazil's TV Globo, take large pieces of the remaining pie. These few sources have enormous impact on our perceived reality of distant events. For example, even in as stridently an ideological anti-American publication as the mid-1980s *Barricada*, the Sandinista daily in Nicaragua, over half of the news copy came from the AP wire service.

A small number of sources is not in and of itself cause for alarm. Large organizations like the AP or CNN take great pains to present a diversity and a balance of viewpoints, and it is strongly in their interest to be perceived as fair and unbiased. Still, however, the potential impact of any of these sources on people's knowledge worldwide is sobering.

Now that we have looked at how the media mediate the reality of the news to the reports we receive, we examine such processes in operation in an extended case study of the reporting of the 1991 Persian Gulf War.

The Persian Gulf War News Coverage: Case Study

For 6 weeks beginning January 16, 1991, much of the world was at war for the stated purpose of ousting Saddam Hussein's Iraq from its occupation of neighboring oil-rich Kuwait. Until the war's last week, the primary activity was an almost continuous U.S.-led air assault on Iraq and its forces in occupied Kuwait. This air war and 1 week of ground assault succeeded in ousting Iraq from Kuwait, although that country and much of Iraq lay in ruins. Widespread belief existed that uncontrolled press coverage of the Vietnam War (1964–1975) had contributed to the loss of (a) the war itself, the only war ever lost by the United States; and (b) public support for the war. This prevailing but unsupported conventional wisdom led to the press in the Gulf being kept on a very tight leash, as part of a campaign "managed like an American political campaign . . . imagery was a dominant concern" (Zoglin, 1991, p. 57). Referring to the sympathetic media coverage, former Reagan White House staff member Michael Deaver commented: "If you were going to hire a public relations firm to do the media relations for an international event, it couldn't be done any better than this is being done" (Lee & Solomon, 1991, p. xv).

How the News Was Managed by the U.S. Military.   To start with, reporters were put in pools. The numbers of persons in these pools grew during the war, up to around 200 during the ground campaign in the last week. The stated purpose of these pools was to protect journalists and prevent allied forces from being overwhelmed by reporters. Stories were subject to censorship, ostensibly to prevent the leakage of troop movement information helpful to Iraq. However, sometimes stories were held up for days; in some instances the Pentagon actually announced the story first at its briefings.

There were total blackouts at the start of the air and ground campaigns, as well as a ban on photos of coffins of killed U.S. soldiers arriving home at Dover Air Force Base. Far from hiding from the press, military spokespersons held daily briefings in Riyadh, Saudi Arabia at central command and at the Pentagon. These briefings were filled with facts and figures, such as the number of missions or the number of Iraqi Scud missile sites destroyed. The talks were illustrated with colorful maps and other visuals. Those holding the briefings were friendly and cooperative and appeared to provide much information. They were, however, very cautious in their estimates of Iraqi damage, apparently to avoid excessive optimism and thus hold expectations to a point that could be very easily exceeded.

Beyond their informative function, the media were used by the military to help the coalition cause and to confuse the Iraqis. For example, reporters were frequently taken to the area near the southern Kuwaiti border with Saudi Arabia but not to the western border area where the real build-up for the ground invasion was occurring. Pools were taken to cover practice maneuvers for an apparent sea assault on Kuwait, an assault that never came but was rather used to divert attention from the planned ground thrust from the west. The CIA planted a false story of 60 Iraqi tanks defecting early in the war, with the hope of encouraging actual Iraqi defections.

Cheerleading by the Media.   Although they occasionally complained, the media (especially in the United States) were remarkably compliant, even obsequious, in their acquiescence to the military censorship guidelines. They continually marveled over the technological prowess of new weapons, not bothering to question the accuracy of claims of very high percentages of hits on military targets with few civilian casualties (collateral damage, as it was euphemistically called). Long after the war, accuracy was revealed to have been much less than reported at the time.

Experts interviewed on TV news programs almost always were supporters of Bush administration policy. Voices of dissent were only heard in minimal coverage of antiwar protests, typically portrayed as lunatic fringe elements. The experts interviewed were almost entirely White men, whereas polls showed minorities and women having lesser support for the war. Saddam Hussein was continually demonized and compared to Hitler and nonhuman species, whereas prior U.S. support for him in the Iran–Iraq War (1980–1988), as well as serious human rights abuses of coalition partners Saudi Arabia, Syria, and Kuwait, were not emphasized. The U.S. military's use of fuel-air bombs and white phosphorus was almost never mentioned (Lee & Solomon, 1991).

Why was the press, in many ways so diverse and independent, so unquestioning of the military and of the Bush Administration? Partly, of course, it was because they were denied access to the real story. That cannot explain the high degree of cheerleading and uncritical support, however. Journalists were probably themselves highly supportive of the coalition effort; even the most strident critics of U.S. policy had no sympathy or support for the brutal Saddam Hussein. Just as the military and political powers were planning policy in reaction to the Vietnam War conventional wisdom of the press having had too free a hand, the media themselves were determined not to allow themselves to be criticized as they had been in Vietnam. They were not going to be made the scapegoats for a war if it was less than a rousing success. They were not going to allow themselves to be called unpatriotic. This concern may not have been unrealistic; the little independent coverage that did occur sometimes elicited angry cries of "traitor."

Independent Coverage. In spite of efforts to discourage it, there was some independent (i.e., nonpool) coverage of the war. Most visible was CNN's Peter Arnett, the only Western journalist left in Baghdad after the start of the air war. Arnett transmitted daily stories and photos to Western media. These were subject to Iraqi censorship and were always identified as such. This led to some Western charges of Saddam using Arnett for his own ends and of his being duped by Iraqi propaganda. Arnett's reports did, in fact, show numerous photos of destruction caused by Allied bombings, the only photos then available of such damage. Some called this unfair and unpatriotic, even going so far as to picket CNN's headquarters in Atlanta or writing angry letters to the editor in newspapers.

There was other independent coverage, however. For example, Patrick Cockburn of the British *Independent* reported at the time how the air strikes were less successful than announced (Lee & Solomon, 1991). The massive oil slick unleashed by the Iraqis occupying Kuwait was covered by the independent British ITN crew a full 2 days before the pool reporters got to it (Zoglin, 1991). As the war went on during its 6 weeks, there were increasing attempts by journalists to go out on their own. In one case a CBS crew set was actually captured and held by the Iraqis for a few days. If the war had lasted longer, there probably would have been greater numbers of independent reports.

Media coverage of the Gulf War will continue to be debated and analyzed for many years (e.g., Iyengar & Simon, 1993). Aside from the obvious controversy around the whole censorship issue, other concerns arose. CNN became recognized as the preeminent news source and received kudos from widespread segments of electronic and print journalism. World leaders watched CNN, including George Bush and Saddam Hussein, to learn what was happening. Other TV networks carried CNN footage. To whatever extent that CNN may have boosted the fortunes of those promoting the war, the reverse may have been even more true with longer lasting effects (Zelizer, 1992). See Greenberg and Gantz (1993) and Mowlana, Gerbner, and Schiller (1993) for sets of readings on press coverage of the Persian Gulf War.

EFFECTS OF NEWS

Long after the events reported in the news, what is remembered is the coverage. "The reality that lives on is the reality etched in the memories of the millions who watched rather than the few who were actually there" (Lang & Lang, 1984, p. 213). Now let us turn to examining the impact and effects of consuming news coverage. First we look at memory for the news and its effects on decision making and other behaviors. Then we examine the effect of news reporting on foreign policy. Before we begin to look at effects, directly, however, we need to examine how our point of view can affect our interpretation of news.

The Impact of Different Points of View

Part of the reason that people in different nations tend to perceive the same situations so differently is that the reality they construct in response to news is so different. Not only the reporting of such events in the media varies in different places, but even more basically, the interpretation of the same events differs, depending on the knowledge and experience of those who hear or see the news. To illustrate, we look at a few case studies.

In late 1991, the beating of African-American motorist Rodney King by some White Los Angeles police officers happened to be captured on videotape by an onlooker. The ensuing criminal trial of the officers resulted in a verdict of "not guilty" on most charges of police brutality in April 1992. The country was generally outraged at the verdict that seemed to go so against what appeared to be obvious from the video shown numerous times on the news. Resulting civil disturbances and riots in Los Angeles and elsewhere brought to the forefront issues of race relations and urban decay. For our purposes, however, what is interesting is the different views of African Americans and White Americans about the verdict. They did not differ in their general appraisal (most found it shocking and unfair). They did differ, however, in how typical they saw such a verdict. Most Whites saw it as an exceptional, although disturbing, miscarriage of justice. Most African Americans, used to receiving the short end of institutional justice and services, saw the outrageous verdict as more typical; thus their response was far more impassioned. The same news story and the same video sequence had a very different meaning for the two groups.

Many of the most intractable and chronic world conflicts have at their heart a gigantic divergence in point of view, a chasm that causes the two sides to interpret the same events totally differently. They also consistently fail to appreciate how differently the other group views the events. For example, during the Cold War (1945–1990), the Soviet Union and Western nations viewed each other through their own bias (Hirschberg, 1993). Israelis and Palestinians, Serbs and Croats, and Northern Irish Catholics and Protestants see themselves besieged and oppressed by the other. See Box 7.4 for a more extended example of the divergent points of view of Islam and the West on political, social, and religious issues.

Memory for the News

News offers an interesting case to test people's memory in a real-world setting, with obvious applied as well as important cognitive theoretical import (Graber, 1989; Reeves, 1989). News stories are typically fairly short, self-contained pieces, unlike longer, more involved TV programs or in-depth magazine articles. As with any verbal material, memory is highly dependent on the quality of initial comprehension (Findahl & Hoijer, 1981, 1982). This comprehension can be studied. For example, Larsen (1983) applied the text processing model of Kintsch and van Dijk (1978; see also van Dijk, 1985a, 1988) to radio news stories to study how people integrate new knowledge to information already in memory. Schneider and Laurion (1993) studied metamemory for radio news, finding that people's assessment of what they had remembered from news was fairly accurate.

In the case of television, however, the information involves more than the verbal content. The simultaneous presence of both the visual and auditory information provides the potential of their either complementing or interfering with each other in the processing and memory for TV news content. In general, memory for visual themes is better than memory for verbal themes (Graber, 1990), and overall memory is better if there is a close fit between the video and the audio component, such as when the video illustrates exactly what was being described by the reporter. When the relationship is less clear or when the video and audio portion evokes different previous information from the viewer's memory, comprehension and memory for the new information suffers (Grimes, 1990, 1991; Gunter, Berry, & Clifford, 1982; Mundorf, Drew, Zillmann, & Weaver, 1990). See Graber (1988) and Gunter (1987) for discussions of memory for broadcast news.

How the visual and auditory portions might interact and possibly interfere with each other is both an important theoretical and practical issue. A particu-

---

BOX 7.4: THE POINT-OF-VIEW GULF BETWEEN ISLAM AND THE WEST (EASTERBROOK, 1989)

Islam as a religion is very poorly understood in the West, a fact especially troubling to Muslims, given the historical connection of their faith to Christianity and Judaism. People making light of Islam particularly hurts when no effort has been taken to understand it. It is very much against their faith to criticize Judaism or Christianity as a faith. Considerable criticism of Western politics is permitted but not of its religions (Judaism and Christianity), which are seen as part of the foundations of Islam.

There is also a fundamental difference between Islam and the West in the relation of church and state. Most Muslim countries accept some degree of theocracy, although the degree varies. Thus an insult of Mohammed is an insult of all Muslim nations and all Muslims, even those not practicing their faith. This is somewhat like nonreligious Jews' abhorrence to anti-Semitism, although there is no real parallel in Christianity, which has much less nonreligious cultural identity than does either Judaism or Islam.

One of the most basic beliefs in western Europe and especially in the United States is the separation of church and state, a belief whose deep ideological character and ramifications are not well understood by Muslims. In the West, it is unacceptable for someone's religious beliefs to infringe on another person's political freedom. Although it is a political belief, this tenet is highly ideological and almost religious in character, especially in the United States. Furthermore, the Western democratic tradition of free speech is also practically like a religion to most people in the United States and the European Community. The treatment of women is seen more in the West as a political right, not a religious decision, although most Western religions support equality of the sexes as well.

Although it is acceptable for Christians to make gentle jokes about Jesus, in Islam there exist strong proscriptions against discussing the personal life of Mohammed or even of having any pictorial representations of him. Intellectual debate and disagreement about his actions is quite acceptable but anything personal or "disrespectful" is not. Finally, Islam is not all monolithic, any more than all Christianity is like the faith of Jimmy Swaggart. Muslims are very offended when the media portray the Ayatollah Khomeini or radical terrorists as typical Muslims.

---

larly interesting type of case occurs with an emotionally intense visual shot of the sort that frequently is available for news stories about wars, accidents, famines, or riots. Its effect on memory turns out to be complex. An intense emotional image, such as a shot of a bloody disfigured body of an accident or war victim, actually inhibits memory for verbal information presented just prior to that picture (Christianson & Loftus, 1987; Loftus & Burns, 1982; Newhagen & Reeves, 1992). However, material presented during or after the intense image is remembered shortly afterward as well as or, in the case of material presented after the image, sometimes even better than, material not accompanied by an intense image. It also makes a difference exactly how memory is measured (Brosius, 1993).

In a careful experimental study manipulating the presentation of televised news stories with or without an accompanying visually intense image, Newhagen and Reeves (1992) found that, 6 weeks after exposure, memory for factual information and topics was better for stories without the compelling visual image, but that memory for the visual images themselves was better in cases where they had been emotionally compelling. Apparently what happens cognitively is that the intense emotional image disrupts the rehearsal in working memory of the immediately preceding information, much as a moderate head injury can produce retroactive amnesia for events just preceding the impact. However, the intense picture is itself highly memorable and may enhance memory for following related information by serving as an organizational schema for construction of a memory representation. Thus a TV news editor deciding whether and when to show a bloody shot of accident victims should recognize that the decision has ramifications for viewers' memory for material in that story.

Effects of News on Decision Making

Our comprehension of the news has implications beyond those involving memory, however. For example, what is the effect of media publicity on juror decision making? There are two general concerns here. One regards specific pretrial publicity about that case. Jurors' exposure to information about a particular case affects verdicts (see Carroll et al., 1986, for a review). For example, lurid pretrial information about a rape or murder case increases the likelihood of a conviction vote. This is not affected by a judge's direction to disregard the information. A second concern involves general pretrial publicity and jurors' exposure to information about other cases involving similar issues.

To test this second type of effect, Greene and Wade (1987) asked students to read a newsmagazine story about either (a) a heinous crime, a rape of elderly women; (b) a miscarriage of justice, a wrongful conviction of a man for a rape to which someone else later confessed; or (c) no pretrial publicity. In a second phase of the study, which participants were told was an unrelated experiment, the research subjects acted as jurors, reading an excerpt from a different court case and deciding on a verdict.

Reading about the prior case did affect their verdicts. Compared to the control group, twice as many (20% vs. 10%) who had read of the unrelated heinous crime said that the defendant in the second case was "definitely guilty." Although 57% of those reading about the prior miscarriage of justice called the new defendant "probably not guilty," only 25% did so after reading about the heinous crime, probably due to having that very available instance in their memory (cf. Tversky & Kahneman, 1973). In the real world, jurors' prior exposure to such examples is all but impossible to control, because such cases receive wide media coverage.

Suicides: Triggered by News?

A very different approach to studying the effects of news stories was taken by sociologist David Phillips (Bollen & Phillips, 1982; Phillips, 1977, 1984; Phillips & Carstensen, 1986), in his studies of the role of media news in triggering suicides. This research examines the hypothesis that news coverage of suicides encourages others to take their own lives.

Phillips' basic method is to examine correlations of media reports of suicides with changes in the rates of actual suicides. For example, Phillips and Carstensen (1986) examined 7 years (1973–1979) of such relations by looking at 12,585 actual teenage suicides in relation to TV news reports and feature stories about suicide. They found that there was a significant increase in suicides 0–7 days after such a news story. This increase was correlated ($r = .52$) with the number of news programs carrying the story. This correlation was significant only for teen, not adult, suicides, and was stronger for girls than for boys. The experimenters concluded that the news stories (either general feature stories or reports of actual suicides) do in fact trigger teen suicides. In their article, Phillips and Carstensen discussed and refuted several possible alternative explanations of their findings, although the findings necessarily remain correlational.

How Media Affect Foreign Policy

A few of the consumers of print and broadcast news are the policymakers themselves. Larson (1986) identified several ways that news media, especially television, can have substantial effects on foreign policy and foreign relations.

The transnational character of media news gathering necessarily involves it in policymaking issues. The sharing of wire service stories and TV footage is common. Reporters, especially for television, in a foreign locale depend on local facilities to transmit news stories home, and often must cope with local censorship of such coverage. Governments sometimes try to manipulate our perceived reality by limiting the coverage of that reality. For example, when Saudi Arabia prevented Western reporters from covering repression in its society during the Persian Gulf War of 1991, it was attempting to prevent this reality from entering the world's consciousness.

The presence of the press makes private or secret negotiations between governments more difficult. Diplomats negotiating sensitive issues must also consider the implicit third party in the negotiations (i.e., public opinion). With television it is especially hard to keep secret talks secret. Veteran Israeli diplomat Abba Eban (1983, p. 345) spoke of "the collapse of reticence and privacy in negotiation." Although such public scrutiny has probably placed some highly desirable curbs on corruption and extra-legal chicanery, it has also made legitimate secret negotiations in the public interest much harder to keep secret, such as talks to secure the release of hostages.

The availability of relevant and appropriate video material affects the choice of stories. This clearly leads to overcoverage of some photogenic issues and undercoverage of others that are less so, thus covertly setting the agenda toward some issues. It also favors coverage from places where networks or wire services have correspondents on site, which usually (for U.S. media) means primarily Western Europe, with many other places covered first hand only if there is a current crisis (Larson, 1984).

A particularly compelling visual image can galvanize world opinion. The picture of a lone person standing in front of a line of tanks in the Tiananmen Square massacre in Beijing in 1989 helped to increase the world's condemnation of the Chinese government's ruthless squelching of the spring 1989 pro-democracy movement. In the late 1960s, vivid photos of a Vietcong prisoner being shot in the head and a naked little girl running from U. S. bombing in Vietnam helped to turn U.S. public opinion against the continuation of that war. More recently, one can argue that the policy of the United Nations sending military forces to oversee relief efforts in Somalia in 1992–1993 was directly a product of reactions to the omnipresent grotesque images of starving children broadcast worldwide. Unlike victims of other famines elsewhere (e.g., Mozambique, Sudan), these faces became too widely seen to be ignored by government leaders.

The power of media, especially television, to convey emotions and a sense of intimacy can be a factor in foreign policy. Coverage of hostage stories is encouraged by the ease with which TV conveys the wrenching emotion associated with such captivity, especially seen in interviews with captives and their waiting families. One reason for the U.S. government's agreement to sell arms to Iran in exchange for hostages in 1986 may have been such coverage, which seemed to make arranging release of the captives a higher priority than other considerations.

Larson (1984) argued that television networks and major wire services usually follow or reinforce government policy. This occurs not due to slavish conscious adherence to official policy by media, but rather because so many of the sources for most stories come from inside governments. Also, the focus is so much on individuals that policymakers and spokespersons tend to be followed by reporters more than trends and background are. For example, summit meetings between world leaders are massively covered in the press, even when it is known in advance that little substance will emerge.

Media sometimes even participate in foreign policy by serving as a direct channel of communications between government officials or policy elites in different nations. CBS news anchor Walter Cronkite's role in bringing Israel's Begin and Egypt's Sadat together (see Box 7.3) was pivotal. In some crisis situations, media may actually know more than governments and may thus reverse the usual government-to-media flow of news. For example, early in the crisis of the hijacking of the TWA airliner in June 1985, CBS had more information about what was happening than the U.S. government did (Joyce, 1986). On occasion the press actually briefs the government! During the 1991 Persian Gulf War, both President Bush and Iraqi leader Saddam Hussein regularly watched CNN to learn what was happening in the war!

Policy problems may be created or exacerbated by lack of media attention to basic processes of social and cultural change in developing nations. The bias in international news coverage by U.S. sources toward heavier coverage of developed nations and those of obvious present geopolitical importance has long been known (Larson, 1984). Western Europe, Japan, and Russia receive heavy coverage in the United States, whereas Africa, Latin America, and much of Asia are largely invisible (Larson, McAnany, & Storey, 1986; McAnany, 1983). Only in a crisis or when events thrust the United States into immediate involvement does the focus shift to such places, as was seen in Iran in 1979, Iraq in 1990, Somalia in 1992, or Bosnia in 1993. Thus the perceived reality is heavily ahistorical with no background for understanding the puzzling present events.

Media can change public perceptions about foreign affairs, particularly when they convey new visual information and when such information is repeatedly presented over a long period of time. The dramatic change in U.S. public opinion about the Vietnam War from 1965 to 1969 is perhaps the most dramatic example, but there are others. As well as being the first war lost by the United States, the Vietnam conflict was the first television war. This aspect is sometimes cited as a major reason why it lost support among the American people to an extent never before seen in the United States. Although there were many other reasons for the lack of public support for the Vietnam War, the fact that the public could see the horrors of war every night while they ate dinner brought home the reality of how violent and deadly it truly was. The romantic ideals that some soldiers traditionally have taken to war and some family members back home have clung to simply could not continue to be embraced. This war (like all others) was hell, but this time everybody could see it first hand. The effects of bringing such wars into our living rooms has been a hotly debated topic; see Arien (1969), Cumings (1992); and articles by Wattenberg, Thimmesch, and Goodman in Hiebert and Reuss (1985).

Protracted and detailed coverage of the Iran hostage crisis of 1979–1981 contributed to an intense national frustration with the situation itself and with then-President Jimmy Carter, who had failed to have them released. Although it is not clear what he or any other president could have done to bring home the hostages, Carter became a scapegoat in the November 1980 election, which swept Ronald Reagan into office in a landslide. See Box 7.5 for a look at U.S. press coverage of Iran before, during, and after this period.

BOX 7.5: COVERAGE OF THE IRAN HOSTAGE CRISIS (LARSON, 1986)

The apparent surprise of Iran's 1979 Islamic revolution to many Americans was in part attributable to the nature of news coverage prior to then. From January 1972 to October 1977, U.S. network news coverage of Iran was only about 1% of all international news stories. Of those stories that did occur, only 10% originated from Iran itself, the others being wire service stories or overseas reports from another country about Iran. The two dominant themes of those stories were oil and arms sales, exactly the focus of U.S. government relations with Iran during that period. Although there were occasional hints of discontent, such as demonstrations against the Shah (the autocratic Iranian ruler and U.S. ally), no consistent attention was paid to the developing unrest. Professional writings by foreign policy experts during this period showed little understanding of grassroots discontent in Iran either (Mowlana, 1984).

From November 1977 to January 1979, U.S. reporting on Iran changed considerably. The Shah's visit to Washington in November 1977 evoked an anti-Shah demonstration, which was quelled by tear gas that floated across to President Carter's South Lawn reception for the Shah at the White House. After this "newsworthy" event, attention began to be paid to flaws in the Shah and his regime. In 1978 all three TV networks placed correspondents in Teheran, which resulted in over half of the stories on Iran originating from there and focusing on antigovernment demonstrations, strikes, and marches. After the departure of the besieged Shah in January 1979, TV served as the major communication between the exiled Islamic leader Ayatollah Khomeini in Paris and the fragile caretaker government in Teheran. After the return of Khomeini to Iran in February, U.S. TV focused on Iran, especially its implications for the United States. From April to October, however, coverage of Iran on U.S. TV dropped off sharply.

After the Iranian seizure of the U.S. hostages at the U.S. embassy in Teheran on November 4, 1979, however, coverage increased dramatically, comprising nearly one third of all international news stories in 1980. Television, and to a lesser extent, newspapers, became major channels of communication between the two governments, as all diplomatic and commercial channels had been broken. Iran allowed an NBC interview with hostage William Gallegos and even took out a full-page ad in the *New York Times* to print the text of a Khomeini speech to the U.S. people. U.S. media also covered the hostage families and early release of some hostages, as well as the continuing activities and eventual death of the Shah in Egypt in July 1980, and the effect of the Iran hostage crisis on the 1980 U.S. presidential election. The release of the hostages on Ronald Reagan's Inauguration Day in January 1981 received heavy coverage, but subsequent stories on Iran that year originated elsewhere or occasionally from correspondents of other nations in Iran. For an analysis of the Iranian media before, during, and after the revolution, see Beeman (1984).

Although a terrorist incident is often a highly newsworthy story in terms of the characteristics discussed earlier in this chapter (Weimann & Brosius, 1991), terrorism stories place a difficult set of pressures on the media. Wittebols (1991; see also Herman & Chomsky, 1988; Herman & O'Sullivan, 1989) distinguished between *institutional* and *grievance* terrorism. Grievance terrorism challenges the powers that be and actively seeks media to advance its cause and publicize its side of the story. For example, fundamentalist Muslim groups who captured Western hostages in Lebanon in the late 1980s and Irish Republican Army terrorists placing bombs in London or Belfast are grievance terrorists. On the other hand, institutional terrorism has the purpose of maintaining the status quo and generally shuns media coverage, even actively threatening those who try to cover it. For example, paramilitary death squads in El Salvador in the 1980s, the assassination of Brazilian environmentalist Chico Mendes in the late 1980s, or Bosnian Serb paramilitary groups attacking Muslim and Croat homes in the Balkan war of the early 1990s represent institutional terrorism.

The most likely trap media fall into with grievance terrorism is excessive coverage that risks legitimatizing or glamorizing the terrorists, a frequent criticism of coverage of terrorism in the 1970s and 1980s. On the other hand, the risk with institutional terrorism is failing to cover it at all, or failing to identify those really responsible for it, assuming that such responsibility can even be determined. See Alali and Eke (1991), Paletz and Schmid (1992), and Picard (1993) for further examinations of media coverage of terrorism.

CONCLUSION: FICTION BECOMES REALITY

Television as a medium has become news in itself. The weekly top-10 Nielsen ratings are reported on TV news and in newspaper wire services and feature stories. Certain blockbuster TV entertainment shows become news events in themselves, receiving coverage throughout print and broadcast media. For example, the last new episode of "M*A*S*H" in February 1983, the last new "Cheers" in May 1993, and the last Johnny Carson "Tonight Show" in May 1992, were major news stories.

The Docudrama: Fact or Fiction?

Sometimes the line between the genres of media news and fiction becomes blurred. A particularly controversial form is the docudrama, a fictional story based on real events. Although it is certainly not new to take some historic events and build a story around them, embellishing where facts are unavailable or undramatic (Shakespeare did it all the time), there is greater concern with such recent TV dramas and miniseries based on spectacular crimes, political and international figures, and other stories. Such programming is popular with the networks. On one weekend in January 1993, CBS, NBC, and ABC all aired premiere TV docudrama movies based on the story of Amy Fisher, the "Long Island Lolita" teen prostitute who only months earlier was accused of trying to kill her alleged lover's wife. All three movies did at least reasonably well in the ratings.

Often these dramas are taken as truth by the viewing public. For example, the 1985 TV movie "The Atlanta Child Murders" aired just 3 years after the real-life conviction of Wayne Williams for two of those crimes. The program's strong suggestion of Williams' innocence and the city's overzealous desire to obtain a conviction at any cost may have been good drama but was not fair and unbiased presentation of the evidence. Still, more viewers saw the docudrama than any lengthy news story of those events.

Docudramas are growing ever more "timely" and difficult to distinguish from news. In one week in late May 1993, networks aired TV movies about the World Trade Center bombing (February 1993), Hurricane Andrew (August 1992), and the siege of the Branch Davidian cult in Waco, Texas. The latter script was written and came to the screen in record time. From the initial shootings of federal agents in late February to the final FBI assault on the compound on April 19, the country waited for news of how the siege would be played out. All the while, the TV movie was in production, the script being written and rewritten in response to the day's news. The movie aired on May 23, 34 days after the real death of its lead character David Koresh and dozens of his followers. For millions of people, that script's interpretation of the Waco events became reality.

Producers are hungry for such deals and have few compunctions about changing the facts to suit entertainment needs. For example, when North American peace worker Jennifer Casolo was approached about a movie contract about her experiences working in El Salvador and being falsely arrested for being a revolutionary, the producers wanted her permission to make two changes in the story. They wanted her to be actually guilty instead of innocent, and they wanted her to fall in love with one of her captors. Unimpressed, Ms. Casolo turned down the lucrative offer.

One of the most controversial American docudramas was Oliver Stone's 1991 film release *JFK*. This story of the investigation of the Kennedy assassination in 1963 strongly suggests a conspiracy involving Lyndon Johnson, the CIA, and the defense industry. Just as Shakespeare's *Richard III* became the perceived historical king for many people, so did Oliver Stone's conspiracy theory become reality for many viewers, especially those too young to have lived through or remembered the event. Is art imitating life, life imitating art, or are they both the same? See Box 7.6 for a detailed comparison of fiction and reality in another docudrama.

BOX 7.6: CASE STUDY OF THE DOCUDRAMA: *MISSISSIPPI BURNING*

In late 1988, the movie *Mississippi Burning* was released. This film is a fictionalized story based on the investigation of the murders of three civil rights workers, two Northern Whites, and one local African American in Philadelphia, Mississippi in 1964 (Corliss, 1989).

What the Movie Said

In the film, the FBI, the righteous protector of African-American rights, floods the area with agents after the disappearance of the three young men. Most of the movie centers on the conflict between two White leaders of the investigation, the by-the-book Ward, and the "good ole boy" Anderson. When Ward's traditional methods come to no avail, and only make things worse for people they try to talk to, he finally and reluctantly asks Anderson to do it "his way." The case is finally broken when Anderson sweet talks the deputy sheriff's wife into revealing where the bodies are. The situation is thus saved by honest homespun Southern virtue that knows, after all, what is "really right." The FBI hires a local African-American man to kidnap the mayor, bind and gag him, and threaten to castrate him to reveal names of the conspirators. Furthermore, the FBI knowingly falsely arrests several suspects, telling them that their buddies have betrayed them. Anderson himself puts a knife to the throat of a major suspect and threatens him unless he confesses. The story ends with several arrests and convictions on violating civil rights, because they know that they could not get a conviction on a murder charge, given the racist nature of the state courts.

What Really Happened

The FBI had been dragging its feet on helping the civil rights movement and in fact had spent most of its time going after Martin Luther King, Jr., whom FBI director J. Edgar Hoover obsessively disliked. The Philadelphia case was the first to force the FBI to become involved in protecting civil rights of African Americans; it only did so then due to the national outrage in response to the killings. The case was actually broken by a $30,000 payment to a greedy Ku Klux Klan informant, not by a virtuous person "doing the right thing." The real heroes of the civil rights movement were African American, not White, but the African Americans portrayed in the movie were all rather passive supporting players. The director of the film said: "Our film is not about the civil rights movement. It's about why there was a need for a civil rights movement. . . . The two heroes had to be white. That is a reflection of our society as much as of the film industry" (Corliss, 1989, p. 58).

Which interpretation became the perceived reality of the Philadelphia murders for the generation of moviegoers not yet born when the events occurred? Does this involve a rewriting of history?

Limits of Media Influence

We must be careful not to attribute a larger role in the perceived reality of our world to TV news than is appropriate. In an article based on interviews with several researchers on the subject, Kalter (1987a) attempted to debunk what she called "media myths" about the role of TV news. Although two thirds of the respondents in a Roper poll asking where they "usually get most of their news" reported that they did so from TV (twice as many as reporting doing so from newspapers), more people responded that they read a newspaper than watch TV news in a typical day (67% vs. 52%). Of those who watched TV news, many watched only local news and a large majority did not attend fully to the newscast. Thus TV is a very important source of news but by no means the only one. Some research (e.g., Gunter, 1987; Robinson & Davis, 1990) even suggests that television is not a very effective way of acquiring news information.

Kalter (1987a) also presented her opinion and evidence that newspapers set more of the agenda on news, and that television adopts that agenda. Using the Vietnam War as an example, she argued that critical media coverage, starting around 1967, followed public opinion, rather than preceded it. The change in public opinion away from supporting the war occurred similarly for both the Korean (1950–1953) and Vietnam wars and was more due to increases in U.S. casualties than to the nature of news coverage. Although the worry that news coverage is influencing neutral people away from someone's desired attitude is widespread, such change may happen less often than we believe (Perloff, 1989).

Even if television news is not quite the pre-eminent influence it is sometimes heralded to be, TV news occupies a major place in the popular imagination. The television coverage of news has itself become news, sometimes bigger news than the event being covered. On the eve of the Iowa presidential caucuses in early 1984, a voter in the studio was asked if she planned to attend the caucus and thus participate in the selection of a nominee for president. Her reply was to look around the studio and say, "Oh, I guess so, but I hate to miss all the excitement here." In other words, the act of reporting had become the newsworthy event, eclipsing the event being reported. This example suggests the continuation of this discussion in the context of the specific area of politics, the subject of chapter 8.

8

POLITICS: USING NEWS AND ADVERTISING TO WIN ELECTIONS

Q: In general what is the most common type of television news content across different cultures?

A: Politics. It comprised between 25% and 40% of all news stories of each nation in a cross-cultural study of television news in the United States, Japan, Germany, Soviet Union, Italy, India, Colombia, and China. This was more than economic, social, cultural, military, or crime stories (Straubhaar et al., 1992).

Q: In these days of expensive media campaigns, how much money would a U.S. senator need to raise per week during his or her 6-year tenure to have enough to pay the costs of the average election campaign?

A: Ten thousand dollars a week through a 6-year term, for about $3 million total (Magnuson, 1988)!

Politics and the media have long been intimately involved with each other. As the opening questions and answers just given make clear, media are telling us that politics is very important. Although television has made some drastic changes in the nature of that relationship, the connection itself is not new. Print media have long covered political campaigns, and the level of political rhetoric has sometimes been far more vicious than is typical today. For example, the U.S. presidential campaign of 1884 saw Democrat Grover Cleveland's alleged fathering of an illegitimate child as a major campaign issue ("Hey, man, where's my pa?" "Gone to the White House, ha, ha, ha!"). See Box 8.1 for more on the political use of the media by abolitionists in the pre-Civil War United States.

Still, from the first tentative and fragmented radio reporting of Warren Harding's presidential victory in 1920 to today's framing of whole campaigns around

---

BOX 8.1: ABOLITIONIST MEDIA CAMPAIGNS IN THE 19TH CENTURY

One of the major political and philosophical issues in 19th-century America was the slavery issue, a controversy so divisive that it played a major role in leading to the calamitous American Civil War (1861–1865). Historical novelist John Jakes (1985) identified several ways that the Abolitionists successfully used pre-electronic media to help reshape the nation's thinking against slavery. Abolitionism was a rather extreme position in its early days of popularity in the 1820s, in that it advocated the end of all slavery, on moral grounds, not merely proscribing its extension to the new Western territories. The Abolitionists ran their own newspapers and had supporters in the editors' chairs at many publications. Probably the most famous was William Lloyd Garrison's *Liberator*, begun in 1831. There was also Frederick Douglass' *North Star* (1847), Horace Greeley's New York *Tribune*, and even a children's newspaper called *The Slave's Friend*.

Also tremendously influential were several books. Narratives of escaped slaves became popular in the 1840s, with the preeminent example being Frederick Douglass' autobiography. Far eclipsing all other books, however, was Harriet Beecher Stowe's *Uncle Tom's Cabin* (1852), written more out of religiously motivated concern for treatment of slaves than of any political conviction or true egalitarian sentiment (Stowe favored sending freed slaves back to Africa). In fact the novel was based on only one short visit to a Kentucky plantation and contained very condescending portraits of African Americans. Still, it had substantial political impact.

Highly newsworthy events that received wide coverage and polarized already strong opinions helped lead the nation to war. Public meetings led by white clergymen or escaped slaves drew increasing crowds. Protests over the Fugitive Slave Law allowing Southern slaveowners to hunt and retrieve runaway slaves in the North occasionally led to dramatic, even violent, reaction, as when a mob of 20,000 people unsuccessfully tried to stop seizure of runaway slave Anthony Burns. Shortly afterward Garrison burned a copy of the U.S. Constitution, calling it "a covenant with death and an agreement with hell." In 1859 Abolitionist extremist John Brown and 21 followers tried unsuccessfully to seize arms from the federal arsenal in Harpers Ferry to arm a slave rebellion. He was caught, tried, and hanged, but coverage of the trial split the country more sharply than ever.

---

the use of television news and advertising, broadcast media have transformed political campaigns beyond recognition from Grover Cleveland's days. Franklin D. Roosevelt was perhaps the quintessential radio president (1933–1945); his lofty mellow tones electrified listeners in ways that watching his body in a wheelchair could never do. In recent decades candidates have had to deal with the visual aspect of television. Although it is no longer necessary to be a great orator and physical presence like William Jennings Bryan or even Jesse Jackson, astute use of television is essential.

Joshua Meyrowitz (1985) argued that television coverage has forever changed politics by decreasing the distance between the politician and the voter. Although it is no longer necessary to cross the wide gulf between oneself and the voters by being an imposing physical presence in a crowd or an accomplished orator, it is now imperative to know how to use the more intimate medium of television to one's advantage. Analysts of different political persuasions have acknowledged that Ronald Reagan and Bill Clinton were highly effective television politicians, as was John F. Kennedy in an earlier period. Other recent presidents and candidates, such as George Bush, Gerald Ford, Richard Nixon, Michael Dukakis, Jimmy Carter, and Walter Mondale, have been criticized for less-than-effective use of television.

Because of TV, political audiences are not as segmented as they used to be. A candidate cannot deliver one speech to an audience of factory workers and a contradictory address to a group of lawyers, because both may be reported on the evening news, particularly if reporters perceive any inconsistency. A single unfortunate statement or behavior in one location may have a lasting contaminating effect through the magic of television transferring that one place to all places. For example, Democratic presidential candidate Edmund Muskie was the front-runner for his party's nomination in 1972 until he was seen on TV shedding a tear in New Hampshire in response to an editor's unfounded attack on his wife. This reaction, however noble and loyal, was interpreted as weakness and may have cost him the presidential nomination. Nixon Agriculture Secretary Earl Butz' private racist joke, which became public, and Reagan Interior Secretary James Watt's comment about a group containing "a Black, a Jew, and a cripple" had costly career effects.

Richard Nixon may have never fully realized why the Watergate tapes of White House conversations were so damning and ultimately forced him to resign from the U.S. presidency in 1974 in the face of certain impeachment. Meyrowitz (1985) suggested that Nixon was evaluating those tapes as private conversations rather than as public statements. In private most people say things that they would not deem appropriate for a public forum. Limited to the private event world, such conversations may not be inappropriate. As public discourse, however, they appeared highly inappropriate and even shocking. Taping and television technology has broken down that public–private barrier by bringing formerly private discourse into the public world.

In this chapter we begin by looking at the media news coverage of political campaigns. Then we examine how politicians can manipulate the news coverage that their campaign receives. Next we take a careful look at political advertising, when candidates pay to say exactly what they want. Finally, we briefly look at the argument from cultivation theory that television cultivates a political moderation in frequent viewers. Politicians consistently hope to use media to create a favorable reality about themselves in the public mind. The examples discussed are primarily from the United States, because that is the area known best to the author and the one most studied by scholars examining politics and the media. Most of the principles discussed, however, are also applicable elsewhere.

COVERAGE OF POLITICAL CAMPAIGNS

In the United States and many other nations, the media set the agenda in such a way that politics is prominently featured. Overall, political campaigns, especially at the national level, receive heavy coverage. Looking at this coverage more closely, however, reveals that some aspects receive more coverage than others.

What Is Heavily Covered

Certain aspects of political campaigns are inordinately heavily covered and others lightly covered, in large measure depending on how newsworthy they are, in the sense discussed in chapter 7. First, major pronouncements receive press attention, especially formal announcements of intent to run for office or to withdraw from a race. Other types of strong statements, like a strident attack on an opponent, also have high visibility.

Second, any type of major blunder, even if substantially inconsequential in the long run, receives wide attention. Gary Hart's apparent overnight tryst with model Donna Rice received heavy media coverage and led to his temporary withdrawal from the Democratic presidential race in the spring of 1987. When he later re-entered the race, his campaign never really caught on. One of the most notorious blunders was President Gerald Ford's statement in the 1976 presidential debates about Poland being a "free country." Although this was clearly in error, and so acknowledged shortly after by Ford, the press did not let the country forget. Ronald Reagan's "teflon presidency" was sometimes held up as an exception to this, in that his many misstatements did not receive as wide press coverage or public concern as those of others. For a case study of a very outrageous and offensive set of campaign misstatements, see Box 8.2.

Third, any kind of colorful response to a political speech or event captures coverage. Cheering masses or angry demonstrations draw cameras. In many countries, rulers of questionable legitimacy regularly pay people to attend a speech and "spontaneously" cheer. Likewise, protests against a leader are carefully orchestrated primarily for the TV cameras, not for the speaker. Many felt that the Philippine revolution of 1986 could never have happened without the press on hand to cover protests against Ferdinand Marcos' apparent stealing of the election (Kolatch, 1986a, 1986b). This revolution was broadcast around the world and the lesson was duly noted. In the summer of 1987, widespread

---

BOX 8.2: WOMAN-BASHING IN CAMPAIGN DISCOURSE: AN OUTRAGEOUS CASE STUDY

Although politics in most countries has been long dominated by men, women are entering in record numbers, having recently held the top elected positions in Great Britain, Norway, Pakistan, India, Israel, Iceland, Argentina, Bolivia, Nicaragua, the Philippines, and elsewhere. Still, in many places being a woman candidate is still a liability. In 1990, Texas Republican gubernatorial candidate and political novice Clayton Williams seemed to bring insensitivity to new depths in his campaign against Democratic state treasurer Ann Richards. First he vowed to bring back the days when "a man was a man" and "a woman knew her place was not at the top of the Democratic ticket." Later at a cattle roundup he commented that bad weather was like rape, "If it's inevitable, just relax and enjoy it," a comment that drew shocked widespread condemnation from people concerned about violence against women. Slow to learn, Williams went on to insult Hispanics and Mexicans by saying that during his youth, crossing into Mexico and "being serviced by prostitutes" was part of a healthy male's coming of age. Aides of Williams called Richards an "honorary lesbian" for supporting gay rights (Carlson, 1990). Do such tactics work? Although Williams began over 10 points ahead of Richards, he became an acute embarrassment to Texas Republicans and lost the election.

---

and broad-based popular protests in South Korea were televised over the world and soon forced President Chun Doo Hwan to agree to popular elections for President and a stated return to democracy. Televised images of anti-Soviet protests in the Baltic nations and elsewhere in 1990 and 1991 helped to hasten those states' independence from the crumbling Soviet Union. At least since the 1979 Islamic revolution in Iran, protesters worldwide routinely have sets of posters and banners in several languages to display as appropriate, depending on which nation's camera crew is present.

Fourth, meetings of a candidate with important people receive press coverage. This is particularly important for candidates without wide experience in some areas. For example, U.S. presidential aspirants with little foreign affairs background often make visits to foreign leaders, in order to be seen on the evening news shaking their hand and conferring. Once in a great while one is able to pull off a major media coup of some substance as well on such a visit, as when candidate Jesse Jackson met with Syrian President Assad to successfully negotiate the release of a captured U.S. flyer. This tactic, of course, involves some risk; if Jackson had failed, he would have been widely accused of inappropriate self-serving meddling in affairs of state.

Finally, and probably most importantly, any aspect of a campaign that emphasizes the "horse race" receives coverage. Poll results are reported widely and promptly, as are predictions by experts and any event that "upsets" the relative standings of the "players." Relatively unknown candidates suddenly perceived as serious contenders or frontrunners receive a rapid and substantial increase in coverage. They do not necessarily even have to win; simply a "better-than-expected" showing is often enough for a media victory. After doing well in the 1992 New Hampshire Democratic primary, Paul Tsongas suddenly was everywhere in the news, after several months of desperately seeking coverage of his lackluster campaign. Dark horse peace candidate Gene McCarthy's surprisingly good showing in the New Hampshire Democratic primary in 1968 was instrumental in President Lyndon Johnson's surprise decision not to seek renomination himself. Right wing Patrick Buchanan's surprising (although not winning) showing in the 1992 New Hampshire Republican primary catapulted him from a fringe extremist to someone that the media apparently perceived as a serious challenger to incumbent President George Bush.

The race aspect that is covered the most heavily of all is, of course, the result of the actual election. There is a lot of concern that knowledge of the results, or predicted results, in the case of network projections of winners, may actually affect the outcome of the election by influencing voters who have not yet gone to the polls. See Box 8.3 for a discussion of this issue.

What Is Lightly Covered

Just as some aspects of political campaigns are heavily covered, so others are relatively lightly covered. Candidates' qualifications in intangible, but highly important, ways are relatively difficult for the press to cover. What has someone gained from being governor of Arkansas or senator from Kansas, for example, that would help him or her as president? Very abstract issues such as character are in one sense extremely important but in another sense very difficult to assess. Coverage that does occur tends to focus on superficial, but not necessarily irrelevant, indicators of integrity (or more often lack thereof), like marital infidelity or shady business dealings. Although there was much talk early in the 1992 presidential campaign of Democrat Bill Clinton's apparent extramarital affair some years before, the exact relevance or irrelevance of this to his possible performance as president was never clarified (and perhaps could not be).

Also relatively lightly covered are positions on issues, especially complex ones. Television news especially is ill-suited to detailed presentations of positions on complex issues like the economy. Print media can do much better, as in publication of a candidate's lengthy position paper on some issue. However, few people read such papers; they listen to television's 30-second interpretation of it, which may focus on peripheral aspects that are more "newsworthy." Some candidates and incumbents have written scholarly books or papers carefully outlining comprehensive positions on complex issues; such positions may be vitally important to predicting their performance in office, yet they are difficult to cover adequately in the media, especially on television. A 200-page treatise on eco-

BOX 8.3: PUBLIC OPINION POLLING
AND ELECTION RESULTS

Started by newspapers in the 1800s but greatly refined recently, public opinion polls are an integral part of political life most everywhere. The famed Gallup Poll began in the 1930s and held a margin of error of 4% in the period of 1936–1950, but this had fallen to .3% by 1984. This is larger if there are three, instead of two, candidates, as in 1980 when the Carter–Reagan–Anderson contest produced a margin of error of 4.7%.

One of the most notable errors in polling occurred in the *Literary Digest* presidential poll in 1936. Mailed to auto and phone owners in the heart of the Great Depression, the poll came back favoring Republican Alf Landon, who in fact lost to incumbent Franklin Roosevelt by the largest landslide in U.S. history. The poll, so inaccurate due to a skewed sample of more affluent than average voters, was such a point of disgrace that it helped lead to the demise of the magazine.

One particularly controversial issue concerns the broadcasting of election results and projection of winners before the polls have closed in all states. In the days of paper ballots, no substantive results could be obtained for several hours anyway, but that is no longer the case. Four studies done many years ago assessed West Coast voters' exposure to election results and projections before they voted (Fuchs, 1966; Lang & Lang, 1968; Mendelsohn, 1966; Tuchman & Coffin, 1971). These studies show only modest exposure to the projections and very small proportions indicating changing their vote or deciding not to vote (1%–3%). Still, however, many elections are decided by such margins.

Since these studies were done, sampling techniques have improved and networks today take "exit polls" by asking voters as they leave the polling places which candidate they voted for. Assuming appropriate sampling and truthful responses, exit poll results and thus projected winners can be obtained before the polls close. Networks, in a race to scoop the competition, routinely have declared projected winners in races with only a tiny percentage of the votes counted (less than 10%). Although this may be scientifically sound, based on the statistics of representative sampling, it may convey a very different message to viewers. If results can be obtained with only 5% of the votes in, it may not seem to an individual voter that a single ballot can make much difference. The United States has consistently had one of the lowest voter turnout rates in the world, not infrequently less than half of the qualified voters. There is not much incentive to vote after you have already heard the results on television.

nomic issues simply does not translate well to a 20-second news story. Most TV campaign coverage is much shorter than that; the length of an average TV political news story fell from 43 to 9 seconds from 1968 to 1988 (Hallin, 1992).

When such issues are covered, they tend to be seriously distorted. For example, early in the 1992 Democratic presidential primary campaign, major rivals Bill Clinton and Paul Tsongas had both written extensive, detailed, and well thought out economic programs for the country. What one heard about these from the media was that Clinton favored a modest income tax reduction for middle income Americans, whereas Tsongas did not, calling the proposal a "gimmick." What one did not hear, however, was that almost the entire economic programs of Tsongas and Clinton, except that relatively minor point, were very similar and each offered a reasoned viable alternative to the programs of Republican incumbent George Bush. Because of the media's highlighting of differences (conflict is more newsworthy), the truth suffered.

The U.S. Presidential Debates

An exception to television not dealing well with complex candidate positions would seem to be the presidential candidate debates, first in 1960 (Kennedy vs. Nixon), and regularly since 1976 (Ford–Carter), 1980 (Carter–Reagan), 1984 (Reagan–Mondale), 1988 (Bush–Dukakis), and 1992 (Bush–Clinton–Perot). See Hinck (1992) and Kraus (1962, 1977, and especially 1988) for analyses of these debates. Here the candidates have a chance to put forward their positions in more detail than usual for television and, most importantly, in perhaps the only forum where partisans of the other candidate will actually listen to them.

Still, however, the debates are typically analyzed by both media commentators and the public in terms of superficial appearances and performances. No one remembers what Nixon spoke about in 1960, but every commentator writes of how he "lost" because of poor makeup and looking tired and wan. Gerald Ford "lost" the 1976 debates because of his Poland remark. Reagan "won" the 1980 and 1984 debates because he seemed friendly and trustworthy and stuck to generalities; the one exception was the 1984 debate that he "lost" because he became too bogged down in facts where he was not comfortable, eloquent, or accurate. Bill Clinton "won" the third 1992 debate, which involved talking directly to audience members, a format at which he excelled. Third-party candidate Ross Perot impressed viewers in the first debate with his pithy, down-to-earth, no nonsense replies; by the third debate, however, these aphorisms seemed to many as shallow, hackneyed, and lacking in substance.

Debate Coverage. The media mediate between the debate itself and the viewers' interpretation of it. There has consistently been much criticism of presidential debate coverage as being too superficial. However, Kraus (1988) argued that such critics often fail to accept the reality of debates and campaigns. In spite of their stated intent, people expect the debates to produce winners and losers. They are an integral part of a candidate's campaign designed to produce a winner. The debates are part of a society that loves a contest and expects to be constantly entertained by television. The specific format of a particular debate is whatever the candidates themselves decide, because they must agree and will only agree to what they think will help them.

Most of this is not really new. The Lincoln–Douglas debates of 1858 in Illinois are often seen as a prototype of pure debate, but in fact they actually were much more like today's presidential debates than we often realize. Candidate Abraham Lincoln manipulated the press and used the occasion to launch his national platform and campaign for the presidency in 1860. At least today technology allows the accurate recording of a debate; Lincoln–Douglas relied on the biased memories of each side.

The "horse-race" type of debate coverage has always predominated. In a study of the 1980 debates, Robinson and Sheehan (1983) found that CBS and UPI both devoted more space to horse race aspects than to any other, and 55%–60% of the coverage failed to contain even one sentence about an issue. This type of coverage of debates is in fact very natural and predictable and totally consistent with other political coverage and what makes an event newsworthy (see chapter 7).

Effects on Viewers. What are the effects of the debates on the public? To begin with, at least the presidential debates draw large audiences. They are regularly followed by polls about the candidates' debate performance. Campaigns know this and carefully plan to try to make a strong impact first. One very important, although fairly intangible, function is to activate the electorate. "Televised presidential debates may be unparalleled in modern campaigning as an innovation that engages citizens in the political process by building large audiences, creating interest and discussion among voters, and influencing voter decisions" (Kraus, 1988, p. 123). The research is inconsistent in regard to the effects of debates on actual voting. They certainly reinforce and crystallize existing attitudes and may actually influence votes. One 1983 study cited by Kraus showed that 58% of people said that the debates were more helpful in deciding their vote than were TV news reports or TV political ads.

There is one additional thorny problem of the televised debates, and that is how to handle minor candidates. Presumably one would not want any and all fringe candidates, most of whom typically have minuscule popular support. In the case of a viable third-party candidacy, however, it becomes awkward. For example, in 1980 Centrist Independent John Anderson showed strong support in early polls. However, to be included in the televised debates, both other major candidates would have to accept his participation. Because one did not, it was not a three-way debate. Anderson's fortunes fell sharply after this event. A very different solution was reached in 1992, with populist billionaire, third-party candidate H. Ross Perot. Perot had a substantial minority of the electorate supporting him, and Democrat Bill Clinton and Republican George Bush apparently both thought that the damage to them from Perot's debate presence would be less than the public relations damage if they were to exclude him, so Perot participated in a set of three-way debates.

Following the precedent of the presidential debates, increasing numbers of local candidates are organizing debates and televising them. Now let us turn to looking at how candidates can use the media news coverage to their advantage. Later in the chapter we look specifically at political advertising and its effects.

CANDIDATES' USE OF NEWS MEDIA

Campaign strategists devote considerable energy to examining how to most effectively use news coverage to create a positive and electable image of their candidate. This is both much cheaper and often more believable than using advertising. Use of the news for political gain can be done in many different ways, some of which are an integral part of the daily life of newsmakers. For example, an elected official may have more or fewer news conferences, depending on the eagerness for coverage. An incumbent has considerable advantage over the challenger in such matters. For example, while Democratic presidential candidates were squabbling among themselves in early summer 1972, Republican candidate (and incumbent president) Richard Nixon captured media attention with his historic trip to China. His landmark voyage opened up the world's largest country to the West and contrasted sharply to the petty bickering of his Democratic opponents who attacked each other in their primary campaigns. Similarly, Ronald Reagan tried to divert media attention from the unfolding Iran-contra scandal in early 1987 by becoming more active and outspoken in seeking an arms control agreement with the Soviet Union. His historic trip to Moscow in spring 1988 contrasted to the Democratic primary squabbles going on at the time.

In any political system, but especially in totalitarian ones, it is not uncommon for a leader to whip up support and mute discontent by emphasizing or even provoking a foreign "enemy." Iraq, under Saddam Hussein, and Iran, under the Ayatollah Khomeini, periodically invoked the American "bogey man" to distract from dissatisfaction with failing domestic policies, whereas Argentina's military government in part provoked the Falklands/Malvinas War with Britain in 1982 to unite the country and mute criticisms of the economy and human rights abuses. In the Cold War period, right-wing dictatorships used to blame all of their problems on communism, whereas communist states blamed the CIA or international capitalism.

Candidates help to set an agenda by telling us what issues are important in the campaign. Ronald Reagan in 1980 and 1984 told us that it was important to "feel good" about America, and that struck a responsive chord in a nation weary of inflation, Watergate, and international terrorism. The same appeal by George Bush in recession-weary 1992 failed to resonate with voters who did not "feel good" about their economic distress. In 1984 Walter Mondale tried unsuccessfully to argue that honesty was an important issue, even to the point of saying that he might have to raise taxes. It is a reality that, in setting the agenda in terms of issues, candidates must consider not only what they believe is important, but also what they believe the public wants to hear.

Credible "pseudo-events" may be created to capture media coverage and, in effect, produce hours and hours of free advertising. For example, when Bob Graham ran for governor of Florida in 1978, he began as an unknown state legislator with a name recognition of 3% and 0% of the vote among six candidates. How he overcame this was largely due to his "work days" project. During the campaign he worked for 100 days doing different jobs around the state, apparently to learn the demands and needs of different sectors of the electorate. These were heavily covered by the media and worked greatly to Graham's advantage, in spite of the obvious political motivation behind them. He defused some of the predictable criticism of self-serving gimmickry by dressing appropriately and actually working a full 8 hours on each job. The first 9 days were done before the media were invited in, so Graham fine-tuned his procedure. Photos from the workdays were of course used in his campaign advertising, but they were also widely covered as news. In his speeches he made references to insights he had gained from these days, and he continued them intermittently after becoming governor, all in all confirming the impression that he had actually learned from them and was not merely dealing in transparent political grandstanding. All in all, it was a brilliant example of the use of news media for one's own political gain; no amount of paid advertising could have done what he had for free in the news.

New opportunities for pseudo-events appeared in 1992 with the advent of "talk-show politics." Candidates Clinton, Bush, and Perot all took to being interviewed on MTV, "Larry King Live" and other entertainment talk shows. In fact these programs opened new avenues for the candidates to present themselves as "real people" who were very approachable. Lasting images remained from some of these appearances. When amateur musician Clinton donned sunglasses and played the saxophone with the band on "The Arsenio Hall Show," the contrast of the energetic and hip young baby-boomer candidate with the aging and cautious Bush and the stodgy and curmudgeonly Perot was striking.

Earlier, in the Democratic primary campaign, candidate Clinton had been accused of an extramarital affair that allegedly occurred years before. The forum he chose to respond to this was a "60 Minutes" interview where he and wife Hilary admitted that there had been "problems" in their marriage but said that those had been worked through and were thoroughly reconciled. It was a masterful combination of confession and avoidance of admitting critical information. Clinton's story of having his daughter Chelsea hug him after hearing of the accusations melted people's hearts ready to forgive what they saw on TV as sincere repentance and love for family. Shortly after the interview, the alleged affair ceased to be a campaign issue. It is hard to see how it could have been so effectively refuted and defused in a traditional press conference or political beat reporting format.

Creating pseudo-events may backfire, however. In 1988, modest-sized Michael Dukakis sitting in a tank to try to project a "strong on defense" symbol instead looked more like a turtle sticking his head out of a shell. Likewise, Ivy Leaguer George Bush's occasional attempts to don cowboy boots and eat pork rinds to appear like a "true Texan" did not always ring true.

One of the most frustrating aspects of the quadrennial U.S. presidential sweepstakes is the attempt of lesser-known candidates to have the media take them seriously. If the public does not perceive them to have a realistic chance of winning, the public acceptance or rejection of their stand on issues or themselves as persons is largely irrelevant. Although polls showed that large numbers of Americans favored the positions of moderate independent candidate John Anderson in the 1980 presidential race, less than 10% voted for him, largely because they felt that he had no chance to win. Similarly, in 1992, early summer polls showed Ross Perot's support substantial enough to conceive of his winning the presidency. However, his support gradually waned by November, although he still acquired a larger share of the vote (around 20%) than any other third-party candidate. Because no one besides a Republican or Democrat has been elected president in the United States since 1848, people perceive such an eventuality as highly unlikely, a social perception that can become a self-fulfilling prophecy.

How a political candidate responds to attacks from the opposition can be very important. Although an unchallenged attack may be accepted uncritically, an overly vicious or petty response may actually engender support for the opponent. An incumbent has less flexibility in handling attacks. In some cases it may be better to ignore or brush off an attack than to "dignify" it with a response (e.g., candidate Reagan's famous "Well, there you go again" comment to President Jimmy Carter in the 1980 debates). On the other hand, an incumbent's attack on a challenger is not always so easily dismissed by the latter. Candidate Reagan's criticism of President Carter in 1980 for the failure to bring home the Iranian hostages became a substantive one, in spite of the fact that neither he nor anyone else offered any idea of what Carter might have done to free the hostages.

There always exists the danger of a backlash of sympathy for the opponent if an attack is perceived as too unfair. This tends to keep in check some potential mudslinging. However, sometimes this fear may also suppress useful dialogue. For example, in the 1988 Democratic primary, other Democrats were somewhat reluctant to squarely attack Jesse Jackson, the only African-American candidate, for fear of being labeled racist. However, this caution also led to less public debate about his policies. If a candidate is not attacked by opponents, the perception is of a less-than-serious campaign. In fact, if a candidate is far ahead in the polls, he or she usually does refrain from attacking the opponent, because an attack only tends to legitimatize that opponent.

Now that we have considered the use of news for one's political advantage, let us now consider a more direct form of political media, namely political advertising. Although political advertising has much in common with advertising in general (see chapter 4), there are also some important differences (Thorson, Christ, & Caywood, 1991).

POLITICAL ADVERTISING

One of the major political issues of our time is the rapidly escalating costs involved in running for office, largely due to the increased purchase of television time and hiring of media consultants. Being independently wealthy has practically become a de facto prerequisite for running for national or even state office. In 1984 Reagan and Mondale each spent about $25 million on advertising (Devlin, 1987). The average U.S. senator spends around $3 million to hold that job, requiring fundraising at a level of $10,000 a week through a 6-year term (Magnuson, 1988)! Some Senate campaigns have spent over $1 million in ads alone. The political arguments of the campaign funding debate are outside of the major focus of this book, so it is not considered further. However, we want to examine the purposes and effects of political advertising, whose aim is to affect the perceived reality of that candidate in our minds.

Purposes

What are the purposes of political advertising? A primary one for lesser-known candidates and those campaigning outside of their previous constituency (e.g., a senator or governor running for president) is simply awareness and recognition of their name. Voters must have heard of a candidate before they can be expected to have any image or attitude toward that candidate. Name recognition is the perennial problem of "long-shot" candidates for presidential nominations or "unknown" challengers to a popular long-time incumbent for any office. In this sense the goal of political advertising is not unlike the goal for advertising a new product on the market.

Political advertising also sets the agenda on issues by conveying to us what issues we should feel are particularly important (Schleuder, McCombs, & Wanta, 1991). Obviously a candidate will try to highlight those issues where he or she is strongest. For example, an incumbent president with several foreign policy successes but economic problems at home is going to try to position foreign policy issues as being the major ones in the campaign, whereas the opposing candidate may try to set the agenda of the campaign toward domestic issues. Sometimes such decisions are not so clear-cut. For example, Democrats in 1980 had to decide whether to make age an issue in regard to Republican Ronald

Reagan, who would be the oldest president ever elected. On the one hand, they stood to gain if voters became concerned that 69 was too old to begin the job. On the other hand, they stood to lose if voters perceived them to be too mean spirited and unfairly attacking a nice older gentleman fully capable of competently functioning in office. For better or worse, Democrats chose not to make age an issue, a strategy adhered to in 1984 against then 73-year-old Reagan.

Schleuder et al. (1991) argued for a spreading activation memory model (e.g., Collins & Loftus, 1975) of agenda setting. For example, if a person is primed by exposure to a prior story about the economy, associations from that initial concept will travel in one's memory to activate related information on that topic to a higher level than other information, thereby setting the agenda that that is important when it comes to processing later information such as a political ad. In this model either a prior ad or a news story could serve a priming function and set the agenda for interpreting a subsequent ad. Thus, a candidate must be concerned about an ad appearing following a news story that sets a different agenda than he or she would like. For example, a candidate weak on economic issues would not want his or her ad to follow a news story about gloomy economic indicators.

Political advertising seeks to convey an image of a candidate, or perhaps reinforce, soften, or redefine an existing image. This construction of an image is done especially effectively by television. Clearly this is related to setting an agenda. The widespread use of media consultants testifies to the importance of image. Polls are taken by a candidate's campaign staff to determine what issues voters are concerned about and what aspects of their own and the opponent's campaigns attract or trouble them. Then the candidate's image is tailored accordingly.

Some studies of candidate image have focused on general affective traits (Patton, 1978; Powell, 1977) or personality or social attributes (Anderson & Kibler, 1978; Bowes & Strentz, 1978; Kendall & Yum, 1984; Nimmo & Savage, 1976) and compared the image a voter has with actual voting behavior. More situational approaches (Husson, Stephen, Harrison, & Fehr, 1988) have demonstrated a relationship between voters' ratings of candidate behaviors and voting preference. Another approach has been to use cognitive schema theory (see chapter 2) to study how voters use their schemas to form an image of a candidate, which subsequently affects their evaluation (Garramone, Steele, & Pinkleton, 1991). Lau (1986) argued that there are four general schemas that people use to process political information: candidate personality factors, issues, group relations, and party identification. Many individuals fairly consistently use one of these schemas more than others.

There are limits, of course, to what a media campaign can do; an urban candidate is not going to easily look comfortable and convincing astride a horse making a political ad for the rural West. Also, one cannot assume that all voters will understand an ad in the same way. The image that the members of the public construct in response to the same ads may be strikingly different because of their different experiences and political predilections. See Box 8.4 for an example.

Occasionally ads may even develop or explain a candidate's position on issues. Such ads are more conducive to print media, particularly direct mail ads, but there is the high probability that a large majority of voters will not read such material. Of course, due to the mass nature of media communication, even a minuscule percentage of the population reading a newspaper ad might be considered a success for the candidate. If the appeal is simple, even a TV spot can effectively communicate a candidate's position, perhaps even more successfully than a televised debate (Just, Crigler, & Wallach, 1990).

Finally, ads may be used to raise money. George McGovern in 1972 and John Anderson in 1980 successfully paid for their TV ads by including appeals for funds in them (Devlin, 1987). Thus, ads, which are a major expense, may also be used as a way of attracting money to meet those expenses.

BOX 8.4: NIXON AND McGOVERN SUPPORTERS' RESPONSES TO THE SAME ADS

Sometimes the reality that one voter may construct in response to a political ad may differ dramatically from what someone else might interpret from the same ad. As discussed in chapter 2, our different points of view give us cognitive schemas around which to interpret new stimuli (e.g., political ads) around. To illustrate this point, Patterson and McClure (1976, p. 114) offered several different responses to the same TV spots for George McGovern, Democratic presidential candidate in 1972. Pro-McGovern viewers said:

1. "McGovern had his coat off and his tie was hanging down. It was so relaxed, and he seemed to be really concerned with those workers."
2. "It was honest, down-to-earth. People were talking and he was listening."
3. "I have seen many ads where McGovern is talking to common people. You know, like workers and the elderly. He means what he says. He'll help them."

To the same TV spots, pro-Nixon viewers responded:

1. "He is trying hard to look like one of the boys. You know, roll up the shirt sleeves and loosen the tie. It's just too much for me to take."
2. "Those commercials are so phoney. He doesn't care."
3. "He's with all these groups of people. Always making promises. He's promising more than can be done. Can't do everything for everyone."

Appeals in Political Advertising

Political ads use most of the same types of appeals discussed in chapter 4 on advertising. Psychological appeals are very common. Basic appeals to security come out both in the "strong national defense" and "law and order" types of appeal. Fear appeals can be especially powerful in political advertising. For example, in George Bush's infamous "Willie Horton" ad of the 1988 presidential campaign, viewers were encouraged to fear that Democratic opponent Michael Dukakis would let dangerous criminals go free, citing the example of Massachusetts felon Willie Horton, who had been released on parole and then committed murder. The fact that Horton was an African American subtly played to White fears about Black crime and may have reinforced racist stereotypes of African-American men. Fear appeals in general are most often used by incumbents, playing on voters' fear of the unknown quality of what the challenger's work in office would be like.

Patriotic appeals are of course especially common in political advertising, with certain symbols like the American flag very commonly present in political advertising, even for state and local races. Certain other patriotic symbols like familiar public buildings in Washington, the Statue of Liberty, and national historical symbols are widely used.

Family and affiliation appeals are seen in the typical family campaign ad photo of a candidate with smiling supportive spouse and children, as if being married or a parent somehow qualified one to hold public office. It is interesting and ironic that an occupation virtually guaranteed to take enormous amounts of time away from family is so heavily "sold" with such family appeals. Using only pure logic, one might argue that an appeal from an unmarried, childless candidate who could say, "I have no family responsibilities; I'll spend all my time in office working for you" would be the most successful. In fact, such an appeal would probably be a dismal failure.

Testimonials are often used, sometimes by famous "endorsers" such as a senator or president plugging for the local candidate, or by the man or woman in the street saying how much they trust a candidate to look after their interests in Washington. A popular president or other office holder of one's party is eagerly sought for testimonial purposes; an unpopular one, such as the recently resigned Richard Nixon in 1974, may be an embarrassing liability for candidates of their party for other offices.

Negative Advertising

The issue of how stridently and directly to attack the opponent in one's advertising is a major question that all political campaigns must deal with. Attacks on the opposition may be highly effective if they are perceived as fair. Regardless of their merit, or lack of it, if they are perceived as mean-spirited "cheap shots," they can disastrously boomerang against the candidate (Garramone, 1984, 1985; Merritt, 1984). Fear of such a scenario sends shivers to all politicians and often causes them to not take chances in this area, as seen in the Democrats' decision not to make Ronald Reagan's age an issue in 1980 or 1984. Nevertheless, negative advertising did increase in the 1980s compared to the 1970s, to about one third of the TV ads in the presidential campaigns (Kaid & Johnston, 1991). Industry experts expect its use to continue (Hill, 1991).

Attacks may be strong without being direct or even mentioning the opponent by name. For example, in 1964 Lyndon Johnson ran a TV ad (shortly afterward withdrawn due to complaints) showing a little girl in a field of daisies. Suddenly an atomic bomb explodes and we hear Johnson's voiceover: "These are the stakes: to make a world in which all God's children can live, or go into the dark" (Devlin, 1987). Republican candidate Barry Goldwater was never mentioned, but the ad clearly played on viewers' fears of his hawkishness.

Does negative advertising work? The answer seems to be yes and no. Research suggests that negative ads are remembered well, even if not necessarily well-liked (Faber, 1992; Garramone, 1984; Garramone, Atkin, Pinkleton, & Cole, 1990). For example, in a study of responses to TV commercials used in the 1988 Bush–Dukakis presidential campaign, Newhagen and Reeves (1991) found that subjects judged negative ads more unfavorably than positive ads, yet they remembered them better. Such a finding is quite consistent with the widespread negative attitudes about negative political advertising and the perception that such ads apparently work (Kaid & Boydston, 1987). Negative emotional ads are remembered better than positive emotional ads, perhaps due to their greater use of automatic, as opposed to controlled, cognitive processing (Lang, 1991). It also seems to be important whether the negative message is embedded in a positive or negative context. Messages that contrast with their context are recalled better (Basil, Schooler, & Reeves, 1991).

Whether negative ads affect voting behavior is less clear (Faber, 1992). It may matter what the source of the negative message is, whether there is an issue or personal focus, what point in the campaign they are used, and what sort of response is made to the negative attack. A widespread public impatience with negative advertising was apparent in the U.S. presidential campaign in 1992. Whether this was due to the public's perception of Bush's 1988 Willie Horton ads as unfair or due to Bill Clinton's more deft handling of negative attacks than Michael Dukakis had done in 1988 is unclear.

Effects of Political Ads

The effects of political ads, as well as other forms of political communication in media, can be of several sorts (Biocca, 1991a; Chaffee & Choe, 1980; Comstock et al., 1978; Klapper, 1960). The study of such effects has come primarily from the perspective of political science, political advertising, social psychology, and communication.

In spite of the perception that the overriding intent of political ads would appear to be to cause attitude change in people, relatively few political ads actually change anyone's mind, in the sense of causing them to switch loyalties from one candidate to another (Blumler & McQuail, 1969; Comstock et al., 1978; Mendelsohn & O'Keefe, 1976; Trenaman & McQuail, 1961). This is not to say that they are ineffective, however. They frequently help crystallize existing attitudes by sharpening and elaborating them. For example, perhaps someone was slightly leaning toward Bill Clinton for president in 1992 because of his leadership as governor of Arkansas. Political advertising for Clinton may help "flesh out" that attitude, by providing more information about his positions and more intangible impressions about the candidate on which to base an emotional reaction.

In a related vein, political advertising may reinforce existing attitudes in voters to "keep in the fold" a voter who is leaning toward a candidate but not strongly committed. Such an attitude that is reinforced is more likely to translate into voting on Election Day and greater resistance to an opposing candidate's attempts to change that attitude. Political strategists are always concerned about reinforcing "soft" support from voters who are leaning toward their candidate but not strongly committed. Many ads are targeted at such people.

Sometimes political advertising may actually convert a voter from one candidate to the other, but this is quite rare and has not increased substantially since the advent of television (Campbell, Gurin, & Miller, 1954; Simon & Stern, 1955; cf. Lazarsfeld, Berelson, & Gaudet, 1948; Berelson, Lazarsfeld, & McPhee, 1954, for pre-TV studies). Of course, because many elections are decided by a tiny fraction of the vote, such people are not insignificant. See Boiney and Paletz (1991) and Comstock et al. (1978) for reviews of this work.

Reactions to political advertising may depend on the bond that the voter feels with the candidate (Alwitt, Deighton, & Grimm, 1991). Such an attitudinal bond may be based on objective ("I like his program for the economy") or subjective ("I feel good about him") criteria. Sometimes the two may be opposed, as in the case where there is objective bonding in terms of agreement with the candidate's positions on issues but passionate opposition on more emotional levels. Also, an image-oriented ad may have a different impact than an issue-oriented ad. For example, Geiger and Reeves (1991) found that candidates were evaluated more favorably after issue ads than image ads, but visual memory for the candidate was better following an image ad.

Increasing emphasis is being placed on the knowledge structures that people construct about candidates and other subjects of political discourse. For example, Biocca (1991b) offered a theory of semantic processing of media, drawing on both cognitive schema theory and semiotic theory. See Faber (1992) and Johnson-Cartee and Copeland (1991) for extensive reviews of political advertising and its effects.

TELEVISION AS CULTIVATOR
OF POLITICAL MODERATION

Before leaving the topic of politics entirely, let us examine the arguments of one group of researchers who feel that television, in a very general sense, is shaping our political attitudes in some less obvious ways than we generally consider. Our perceived reality about politics may be affected by TV viewing in a more general sense. Using cultivation theory, Gerbner, Gross, Morgan, and Signorielli (1982, 1984, 1986) examined the relationship between television viewing in general and political attitudes. Using data gathered for several years in the late 1970s and early 1980s by the National Opinion Research Center in their General Social Surveys (NORC/GSS), Gerbner et al. looked at the correlation of amount of TV viewing (and other media use) and political self-designation on a liberal–moderate–conservative dimension.

Frequent TV viewers were most likely to label themselves as moderate politically, whereas frequent newspaper readers labeled themselves conservative and heavy radio listeners labeled themselves liberal. This relationship was quite consistent within various demographic subgroups, especially so for the conservatives and the moderates. Among light viewers, there was consistently greater difference of opinion between liberals and conservatives on several different specific issues than there was between the liberal and conservative heavy viewers. Gerbner et al. (1982, 1984, 1988) argued that television, with its mass market appeal, avoids extreme positions that might offend people and thus by default it cultivates middle-of-the-road perspectives.

Nor are such effects limited to North American culture. Morgan and Shanahan (1991) found that Argentine adolescents who were heavy viewers were more likely to agree that people should submit to authority, approve of limits on freedom of speech, and believe that poor people are to blame for their own poverty. In a country having recently come through a repressive military dictatorship, it appears that television "cultivates views that provide legitimacy to authoritarian political practices" (Morgan & Shanahan, 1991, p. 101). See also Morgan (1989, 1990) for other applications of cultivation theory to international settings. For an interesting comparative of the 1988 presidential elections in France and the United States, see the readings in Kaid, Gerstle, and Sanders (1991).

Television may interact with political ideology in other ways to subtly support or undercut existing structures in a society. The social and commercial realities of television may sometimes produce politically strange bedfellows. See Box 8.5 for an interesting example.

CONCLUSION

Our perceived reality of the political world is largely a product of the media. The role of the media, especially television, in politics will continue to be hotly debated. The loudest critics will decry how TV has corrupted the democratic

---

BOX 8.5: TELEVISION AND IDEOLOGY: BRAZILIAN CASE STUDY

Does television serve to indoctrinate or perpetuate political and social ideologies? The answer is a complex one with no easily generalizable answer. A case study of the Brazilian "telenovela" (soap opera) is an instructive example. In developing countries television is typically controlled largely by the economic elites, often with close political ties to right-wing ideologies. This was true in military-ruled Brazil in the 1970s, when the huge Globo communications network thrived and rose to become the world's fourth largest TV network, after the "big three" in the United States. Globo came to be acclaimed for its high-quality programming, which is exported to dozens of countries around the world. The most popular shows, both domestically and for export, are the telenovelas, which typically air for 1 hour 6 nights a week for a period of several months. Somewhat like a very long miniseries, they do have a fixed ending, after which they are replaced by another novela.

During the 1980s, the content of some of the novelas came to reflect some politically left themes. For example, *Isaura the Slave* is set in colonial Brazil and strongly condemns racism and slavery. *Malu, Woman* shows the struggles of a divorced woman and has a strong feminist message. *Roque Santeiro* tells of a small town controlled by political bosses who stop at nothing to maintain power. *Wheel of Fire* tells of a business executive who repents of past corruption. It features characters who are torturers, rulers, and guerrillas during the years of military rule (1964–1985). Formerly shunning television as a tool of the capitalist elites, leftist artists like *Roque Santeiro*'s author Dias Gomes, a self-described Marxist, later realized the potential of television, particularly through a large and powerful corporation like TV Globo, to reach far more people than theater, films, or print media could ever hope to. On the other hand, Globo's corporate executives began realizing the immense profitability of television programs that deal with some of these progressive themes. Maybe there is a place for programming of artistic and technical quality that reflects a wide spectrum of political and social attitudes while still enjoying commercial success (Bacchetta, 1987).

---

process and reduced political discourse to banal superficialities. Its defenders will point out the technical marvels and improved dissemination of information that technology has allowed us to use in the political process. This sort of "TV-bashing" may in fact only be the most recent example of a trend of being most critical of the newest medium. "If one goes back through the history of press criticism, a distinct pattern emerges: the most modern medium is always regarded as the most issueless, the most frivolous—first in print, then daily press, then radio, then television . . . newest medium attracts the loudest complaints" (Robinson & Sheehan, 1983, cited in Kraus, 1988, p. 88).

What is certain, however, is that media do create a political world that is the basis of most of our perceived political knowledge and subsequent political behavior, such as voting. That role is not likely to change, so it behooves us to understand it better. "With these technological advances, both the sending and receiving of political information changed. Our thinking about political events changed. What constituted political reality for us was not the influence of a political event alone but the interpretation (often, the alteration) of the event by the mass media, especially television" (Kraus, 1988, p. 8).

9

VIOLENCE: DOES ALL THAT
MAYHEM MATTER?

Q: How many murders has the average child seen on TV by the time he or she finishes elementary school?

A: Eight thousand, plus 100,000 other acts of violence (Huston et al., 1992).

Q: What type of TV show has the most violence?

A: Children's cartoons have by far the greatest number of violent acts per hour (26, compared to 5 per hour on prime time) (Gerbner & Gross, 1980).

Although specific figures depend on our precise operational definition, any way we look at it, a major part of the perceived reality of media, especially television in the United States, involves violence. For example, between 70% and 93% of U.S. television programs contain some sort of violence (Signorielli, Gross, & Morgan, 1982). In 1984–1985 and 1985–1986 the figures were 82% and 79%, respectively, with more violence in early prime time (8–9 p.m. Eastern Time Zone, 7–8 p.m. Central Time Zone) than later (Gerbner, Gross, Signorielli, & Morgan, 1986). On U.S. television, there are 5 violent acts per prime-time hour and 18 violent acts per weekend daytime hour, the latter mostly due to cartoons, which are very high in violence—26 violent acts per hour (Gerbner & Gross, 1980; Huston et al., 1992). Considerable violence even occurs in programming we do not immediately associate with aggression, such as news and rock videos (Sherman & Dominick, 1986; Sherman & Etling, 1991). For every 10 males on prime time who commit violence, there are 11 male victims. For every 10 violent females, there are 16 female victims (Gerbner, Gross, Signorielli, & Morgan, 1986).

Consistent with the definition of most researchers, violence is here defined as intentional physical harm to another individual. Excluded from this definition are accidental injury, so-called "psychological" violence, and vandalism of property. Aggression is the internal motivation behind the violent behavior. Acts of violence may be observed directly; aggression may be inferred from those acts.

Violence on television has long been a hot political issue. Groups as diverse as the national PTA, the American Medical Association, the National Coalition of Television Violence (NCTV), and the consumer-oriented but now defunct Action for Children's Television (ACT) have taken up the cause of opposing TV violence. Periodically, the level of violent content goes down in response to particularly vigorous criticism, but it generally returns to the higher levels within a few years. The question of whether people actually like to watch violence is a complicated one. For example, Diener and DeFour (1978) found no correlation between the amount of violence and the Nielsen ratings of U.S. TV shows. A violence-edited version of a "Police Woman" episode was liked just as well as the uncut, more violent version, except that the highly aggressive men did prefer the more violent version. In a study of reactions to sports violence, Bryant (1989) found that enjoyment was heavily dependent on whether it was morally sanctioned and whether the victim was a hated foe or an admired hero.

There has probably been more psychological research on the topic of violence than on all other topics in this book put together, something like 3,000 studies (Cannon, 1989; Huston et al., 1992). This chapter makes no claim to comprehensively review all of that literature, as more thorough reviews and discussions are available elsewhere (e.g., Andison, 1977; Comstock et al., 1978; Eysenck & Nias, 1978; Freedman, 1984; Gunter, 1985, in press; Liebert & Sprafkin, 1988; Wood, Wong, & Chachere, 1991). Often the discussion of the scientific issues has been clouded and colored by the economic or philosophical perspectives of those involved, and much of the popular writing on the topic has taken the form of either polemical and often unfounded criticism or a besieged defense supported by economic self-interest but ignoring the research. In both cases, crucial distinctions among diverse types and contexts of violence and among different populations are often lacking.

In considering the role of television in encouraging violent behavior or attitudes supporting such behavior, we must not make the mistake of imagining TV to be the only factor, or even the major factor, contributing to violence in society. Negative social conditions like poverty, racism, crowding, drugs, easy availability of weapons, and the ghetto subculture doubtlessly contribute far more than television. Negative family and/or peer role models also have substantial effects. Still, however, because of the nature of mass communication, even a very small effect of media can be substantial in terms of numbers. To take a hypothetical example, suppose a violent movie could be shown to cause .001% of the viewers to act more violently. Although the percentage may be minuscule, .001% of an audience of 20 million is still 200 people!

We approach the study of media violence in this chapter by looking at the various effects of the violent view of the world presented on television. This study of the perceived reality of media violence focuses on the psychological processes involved and the weight of the evidence supporting the existence of those effects. Later in the chapter we look at longitudinal studies probing for long-term effects and finally address the question of what may be done to provide balance to this violent perceived reality and thus mitigate negative effects of media violence. One form of media violence of greatest concern is sexual violence; consideration of this issue is deferred to the next chapter, on sex and the media.

PSYCHOLOGICAL EFFECTS OF MEDIA VIOLENCE

Most of the public concern and scientific study of the perceived violent reality of television centers around the effects of viewing video violence. The effect that many think of first is modelling, when people imitate violent behavior that they see on television. However, this is only one of several psychological effects. The following section separately examines several different effects of media violence and the evidence supporting each of them.

Modelling

This construct comes out of social learning theory (Bandura, 1977), which applies principles of learning to social situations. See Tan (1986) for details on the application of social learning theory to media violence.

How Modelling Works.   People see a violent act in the media and later, as a result, behave more violently themselves than they otherwise would. For this to happen, first the relevant behavior of the model must be *attended to*. Second, it must be *retained*, somehow encoded into memory in some form, as it is being analyzed and interpreted through cognitive processing. Whether the learned behavior is actually later *produced* by the viewer will depend on many factors, such as motivation and the strength of prevailing inhibiting factors.

The process of modelling may actually teach new behaviors, much as one might learn a new athletic skill by watching a teacher demonstrate it. When teenagers killed themselves playing Russian roulette imitating the famous scene of crazed POWs in Vietnam in *The Deer Hunter* (Radecki, 1984), they may not have known or thought to behave that way before seeing the film. This is a particularly grisly example of the common phenomenon called *observational learning*. Another example is the notorious New Bedford gang rape case of the mid-1980s, where several men raped a woman on a pool table in a bar (later the basis of the movie *The Accused*). The rapists had recently seen a movie with a barroom gang rape scene in a nearby theater. See Box 9.1 for the story of

BOX 9.1: ARE MEDIA CRIMINALLY LIABLE FOR EFFECTS OF VIOLENT CONTENT?

From time to time lawyers defending perpetrators of violent crimes that appear to have been affected by television have used rather creative defenses, which inevitably come up against First Amendment freedom of speech issues. Two such cases were the Zamora and Niemi cases of the 1970s.

Ronald Zamora, 15, killed his 82-year-old neighbor in a robbery attempt after she discovered Zamora and threatened to call the police. What was particularly unusual was that the defense attorney argued for temporary insanity at the time of the crime, arguing that Zamora was "suffering from and acted under the influence of prolonged, intense, involuntary, subliminal television intoxication" (Liebert & Sprafkin, 1988, p. 127). He further argued that the shooting was a TV-learned "conditioned response" to the stimulus of the victim's threatening to call the police. Television was thus an accessory to the crime. In the end, however, the jury failed to accept this reasoning, and Zamora, whose hero was Kojak, was convicted on all counts and sentenced to life.

The second case involved the assault on a 9-year-old girl, Olivia Niemi, by three older girls and a boy. In the process she was raped with a bottle. Four days before, a TV movie, "Born Innocent," had been aired, showing a scene of a girl being raped with a plumber's helper. Olivia's mother then sued NBC for $11 million for alleged negligence in showing the movie in prime time. Her lawyer argued for "vicarious liability" and claimed that the movie had incited the children to criminal activity. The defense argued on First Amendment grounds and also called into question whether the assailants had in fact seen the movie. (They denied it but other witnesses reported their discussing it with them.) After a series of appeals and countersuits, the case was finally thrown out in 1978 when a judge ruled that the plaintiff had to prove that the network had to intend its viewers to imitate the violent sexual acts depicted. However, when NBC aired "Born Innocent" as a rerun, it aired at 11:30 p.m. and with most of the critical rape scene edited out (Liebert & Sprafkin, 1988).

Such cases are not unique to television. The magazine *Soldier of Fortune* ran the following classified ad:

FOR HIRE—U.S. Marine and Vietnam veterans. Weapons specialists with jungle expertise for high-risk assignments in the United States or overseas. Call ————.

Texan Robert Black hired a former marine through this ad, with the assignment of murdering his wife. Her surviving family brought suit against the magazine for negligence and was awarded $9.4 million in damages in a federal court case (Brockhoff, 1988). The legal basis of the judgment was that the magazine should have known that its offer included illegal acts such as murder. How much responsibility does a publisher (or broadcaster) have to anticipate such consequences of its messages?

some especially tragic cases where legal charges were filed to blame media for teaching violent behaviors.

More often, however, it is not the specific behavior itself that is learned from the media. A second process by which modelling can work is where watching media violence *disinhibits* one's tendency to commit some violent act that has already been learned. For example, watching a movie with scenes of street fighting might disinhibit one's tendency to fight. The viewer already knows how to fight; the medium cannot be blamed for teaching that behavior. However, TV may be faulted for disinhibiting the behavior (i.e., breaking down the normal inhibitions that we have against engaging in violence). Thus the violent behavior may occur in the future with a lesser provocation than would have been necessary to evoke it prior to the disinhibition. Disinhibition may also occur through the teaching of more accepting attitudes toward aggression. This change in attitude thus leads to the disinhibition that may subsequently and indirectly lead to violent behavior, although such a causal connection is very difficult to empirically demonstrate unequivocally.

Most of the concern with modelling effects of TV violence assumes that persons may be violent in their own behavior in a somewhat different way than the media model; that is, when the effect generalizes from the specific behavior demonstrated in the media. For example, watching a war movie may disinhibit violent behavior generally, and a viewer may subsequently punch or kick another person but not necessarily start shooting with an AK-47. This generalized type of modelling is far more common than the modelling of a very specific behavior.

There are other even more indirect ways that modelling may occur. Violence may alter the general affective responsiveness of the viewer, which could in turn lead to violent behavior. It could raise the overall arousal level, which could prime the person for (among other behaviors) violence. Now let us turn to looking at some of the research done to test the modelling hypothesis and identify the conditions under which modelling occurs.

Early "Classic" Research.   The best-known early research studying modelling of media violence was social psychologist Albert Bandura's Bobo doll studies (Bandura, 1965; Bandura, Ross, & Ross, 1963; Bandura & Walters, 1963; see also Hicks, 1965, 1968; Hanratty, O'Neal, & Sulzer, 1972; Savitsky, Rogers, Izard, & Liebert, 1971). In a typical Bobo doll study testing modelling, Bandura had young children watch someone else behave aggressively toward a large plastic inflatable doll/punching bag. The child's own behavior with the Bobo doll was subsequently observed. Studies of this type consistently demonstrated that children frequently imitated violent behavior previously observed in a live model. More important for our purposes, the same effect was found when the aggressive model was on film rather than "live" (Bandura, Ross, & Ross, 1961; Lovaas, 1961; Nelson, Gelfand, & Hartmann, 1969; Rosencrans & Hartup, 1967; Waters & Willows, 1968).

Although these studies were important, they were not without criticism. Primarily they were attacked for being too artificial and of questionable generalizability to the "real world." Later research moving away from the laboratory also found corroborative evidence for modelling, however (Centerwall, 1989a, 1989b; Huesmann, Lagerspetz, & Eron, 1984; Joy, Kimball, & Zabrack, 1986; Lefkowitz, Eron, Walder, & Huesmann, 1977; Leyens, Camino, Parke, & Berkowitz, 1975; Parke, Berkowitz, Leyens, West, & Sebastian, 1977). For example, Centerwall's and Joy et al.'s work found that the rates of violent crimes rose in societies following the introduction of television with its steady diet of violence. Thus it seems that modelling media violence is not purely an artificial laboratory phenomenon. Other recent research on the media modelling of violence has worked to identify other factors that affect how much the violent behavior will be modelled.

Important Interactive Factors. A violent model does not affect everyone the same way under all circumstances. There are several important variables that heighten or attenuate a modelling effect. First, several characteristics of the model are important. People are more likely to imitate or be disinhibited by the aggressive behavior of an attractive, respected, prestigious model than one who does not have such qualities. Also, the more we identify and empathize with a model, the more likely we are to imitate that person (Huesmann, Lagerspetz, & Eron, 1984). These points suggest that violence by the "good guys" (i.e., the characters we admire and like to identify with) may be a more serious problem and influence than violence by the "bad guys." This has important ramifications for assessing effects of action-adventure and police shows.

Whether or not the violence is reinforced (i.e., followed by some event which increases the probability of the violence recurring) is also an important factor. If acting violently appears to pay off for the violent character (in money, power, relationship, etc.), it is thus reinforced in the context of the story. Some evidence suggests that reinforced violence is more likely to be modelled than nonreinforced or punished violence (e.g., Bandura, 1965). In a typical TV story line, the violence of the hero is likely to ultimately pay off (i.e., to be reinforced) more than the violence of the villain, although the latter may have been reinforced for much of the show. This is a second reason that "good-guy" violence may have more deleterious effects than "bad-guy" violence.

Another important factor is whether the violence is seen as real or makebelieve (i.e., the degree of perceived reality; Van der Voort, 1986). There is some evidence of stronger effects of violence that is perceived as real than violence that is perceived as unreal. For example, by far the most violent genre of TV show is the children's cartoon, yet it is also the most stylized and unrealistic violence of all. Some studies (e.g., Feshbach, 1976) show cartoon violence to have less negative effect than more realistic violence.

In understanding the perceived reality of violent television, it is important to consider the child's cognitive understanding of television at any given time (e.g., Cantor & Sparks, 1984; Gunter, 1985; Sparks, 1986; Van der Voort, 1986). A very young child might think that a violent death on a police drama actually shows someone dying, rather than merely an actor pretending to die. Children who believe such staged violence to be real are often more disturbed by it than those who understand the convention of acting. Continuing this line of reasoning, the most difficult forms of TV violence for children to deal with might be news and documentaries, because violence on these programs is real and not staged.

It is also possible that a modelling effect may occur but only in people who are somewhat inclined toward violence to begin with (Heller & Polsky, 1975; Parke et al., 1977), although this result has not been found consistently (e.g., see Huesmann, Eron, Lefkowitz, & Walder, 1984). Unfortunately, studies suggesting such conclusions have often been used by others to argue that the lack of a *general* effect indicates no substantial effects of media violence. As suggested previously, however, a modelling effect on even a tiny percentage of the population may be cause for serious concern.

Another important factor in the reality of violence perceived by the viewer may be the thoughts that one has in response to viewing media violence (Berkowitz, 1984). Those thoughts may focus on the suffering of the victim, the triumph of the violent person, the relation of the violence to one's own experience, and so on. See Dorr and Kovaric (1980) and Tamborini (1991) for a discussion of individual differences in reactions to TV violence.

Finally, the variable of arousal level of the subject is important. A person who is already physiologically aroused for whatever reason is more likely to engage in violence in response to seeing a violent media model than a nonaroused person is (Tannenbaum, 1971, 1980). The arousal may come from the film itself, given that violent films tend to be emotionally arousing and exciting, or it may come from some prior and unrelated source, such as the manipulation in some experiments that makes one group of subjects angry before exposing them to a violent media model (e.g., Berkowitz, 1965; Hartmann, 1969; Zillmann, 1978). See Zillmann (1991a) for a recent review and discussion of the media and arousal issue. This issue of the interaction of arousal and a violent model becomes important later when sexual violence is examined in chapter 10.

Reinforcement

One of the central principles of operant conditioning, and indeed of all psychology, is reinforcement, which refers to any event that follows a response and increases the probability of that response occurring again. The connection (contingency) between the response and the reinforcement is learned; thus the response is made in anticipation of receiving the reinforcement. Rover learns to fetch a stick because he is reinforced with a dog biscuit when he performs the act. Ashley does her homework each night because she is reinforced by being allowed to watch TV after she is finished. After learning has occurred, responses continue to be made for some period of time without the reinforcement, until they gradually diminish and finally extinguish altogether. Although already discussed insofar as its interaction with modelling occurs, reinforcement is now examined further in its own right.

In regard to the effects of violence in the media and the nature of its perceived reality by viewers, reinforcement can work in one or more of four ways. First of all, violence in the media may reinforce violent tendencies already present in the viewer, although it is not the source of those tendencies (*preobservation reinforcement*). The more such tendencies are reinforced, the more likely they are to manifest themselves in behavior. This sense of reinforcement is similar to disinhibition, discussed earlier.

The second manner that reinforcement may occur in was also alluded to earlier, whereby violent behavior that is reinforced in the context of a story is more likely to be modelled than violent behavior that is punished or not reinforced in the story (*vicarious reinforcement*). For this reason many critics are more concerned about media violence where violence, particularly violent crime, appears to pay (i.e., is reinforced).

A third type of reinforcement is where media, rather than reinforcing behavior or tendencies to behave in certain ways, may reinforce certain values about the use of violence. For example, characters on action-adventure TV shows and movies frequently use violence to settle interpersonal disputes. As such, they are subtly reinforcing the value that such aggressive behavior is a realistic and morally acceptable manner of dealing with conflict, a value that may become part of the viewer's perceived reality.

Finally, violent behavior or tendencies to be violent may be reinforced purely by virtue of their occurrence in a context that is overall very reinforcing. For example, because viewers may choose to identify more with the affluent opulence of "Beverly Hills 90210" than the gritty seediness of "Commish," violence on the more glamorous show may have a greater effect, even if the actual violence is less in quantity or graphicness. However, this effect may be mitigated by the fact that the more realistic shows may have a greater impact than the less realistic ones due to their greater relationship to the viewers' own experience. Thus we see that many factors are at work in determining modelling effects.

Sensitization

Sensitization is a sort of reverse modelling effect, whereby viewers react so strongly to seeing some violence and have such a traumatized perceived reality that they are actually *less* likely to imitate it as a result. This is most likely to occur with very extreme, even sensationalized, violence, as might be the reaction of someone who has never seen anything stronger than a Disney movie to seeing one of the *Friday the Thirteenth* or *Lethal Weapon* films. The tendency away from violence might arise from the arousal of anxiety about the violence and/or the arousal of empathy for the victim of the violence. For example, Tamborini, Stiff, and Heidel (1990) used physiological and questionnaire measures to conclude that people who most dislike watching graphic violence (i.e., those who are most sensitized) are those who score high in the empathy dimensions of wandering imagination, fictional involvement, humanistic orientation, and emotional contagion. That is, these people can more easily imagine themselves in the position of the victim of the violence and vicariously experience the negative emotions that person would feel. Someone who cannot easily do this would also be aroused but would be more likely to enjoy the violence, because the negative emotions would not be so strongly felt.

It may be that some of the strongest sensitization effects could come from very graphic violence that is clearly understood as real (i.e., the news). Some-

---

BOX 9.2: EXTREMELY VIOLENT NEWS IMAGES

In January 1987, photographers covering what they thought was a routine news conference by Pennsylvania Treasurer C. Budd Dwyer captured an unexpected and unforgettable image on their tape. During the conference Dwyer killed himself by putting a pistol in his mouth and pulling the trigger. Stunned photographers recording the news conference had the whole episode on videotape. Network news, TV stations, and newspapers were then faced with the decision of whether to run the entire grisly sequence. Most TV stations chose not to show the tape or showed it only to the point of Dwyer placing the gun in his mouth. A few TV stations and newspapers carried pictures of what happened after that, saying it was an important historical event and should be covered.

In January 1993, Telemundo television crews in Florida were interviewing a woman on camera in a park in broad daylight when she was suddenly accosted and shot several times by her estranged husband, with her death duly recorded by the TV crew. Although the photos were certainly not planned and could serve as important legal evidence, the network was faced with the decision of whether or not to air the footage. Many (including CNN) did so. The public has a right to know, but how much does the public have a need or right to know *and see explicitly*?

The answer is obviously an ethical and policy question, but one study suggested a positive effect of learning at least some gory details. College students who read a newspaper report of a wife-battering incident rated it more serious and rated the batterer more negatively if the victim's injuries were described in detail, compared to a condition where they were not explicitly described (Pierce & Harris, 1993).

times producers face a difficult decision as to whether to air an extremely violent scene from a news story (see Box 9.2 for a couple of especially compelling examples). Once in a while they may be unable to prevent the image, especially if it comes in the form of a political ad, which may not be censored, due to Equal Time laws. Although product and political advertisers generally are loathe to offend, once in a great while a political candidate may desire to. In the fall 1992 U.S. election campaigns, several anti-abortion candidates for Congress and other offices chose to air photos of what they said was an aborted fetus. Their explicit goal was to offend viewers, or rather to show them "how offensive abortion really is." Such tactics are risky, however, because viewers might be even more offended by their decision to use such an image. Although sensitization effects are hard to study scientifically for ethical reasons, general sensitization effects are probably not too widespread and do not occur nearly as often as their opposite, desensitization. In general, any situation for which one can posit sensitization effects can also be interpreted in terms of desensitization. For example, people have argued that daily news broadcasts of the Vietnam War sensitized us to the horrors of war and eroded public support for that conflict, in contrast to previous wars. On the other hand, others have argued that the same news broadcasts desensitized us to war and thus we now are not as bothered seeing images of other conflicts (see chapter 7). See Box 9.3 for a history of the treatment of the Vietnam War in films.

Desensitization

Although we often limit our concern about effects of TV violence to worries over increases in violent behavior, there may be far more pervasive attitudinal effects, especially in the area of desensitization. The basic principle here is that viewing much violence in the media makes us less sensitive to it, more jaded, and less aroused and bothered by it. We become so used to seeing people wasted, blown apart, or impaled every night on TV that it no longer particularly troubles us. For example, after seeing a violent TV show, sixth graders were less sensitive to violent images in a subsequent film than were subjects who had seen a nonviolent film (Rabinovitch, McLean, Markham, & Talbott, 1972). Desensitization is typically measured experimentally through physiological and/or attitudinal measures.

Desensitization may be seen as a straightforward example of classical conditioning (see Fig. 9.1). The normal, unlearned responses to being physically hurt include pain, fear, and disgust. The first time one sees media violence, it probably evokes such negative emotional responses, due to its similarity to real violence (Fig. 9.1a). Such a single occurrence may actually produce sensitization.

What happens with repeated viewing of violence in comfortable surround-

BOX 9.3: HOLLYWOOD GOES TO VIETNAM

The 1966 pro-military film *The Green Berets* starred John Wayne in a stylized epic with good guys and bad guys. Its ending of the sun setting in the east fairly accurately reflected the level of realism of the entire film. By 2 or 3 years later such a simplistic approach to Vietnam rang very shallow and false and was not often seen again until a new generation became captivated by Sylvester Stallone's cinematic comic book *Rambo: First Blood Part II* in 1986.

A very few years after *The Green Berets*, sentiment in the United States had turned completely around and whatever glory there had ever been to the Vietnam War had long since disappeared. The 1974 Oscar-winning documentary *Hearts and Minds* by Peter Davis was very graphic and carried such a strong antiwar message that some newspapers refused to publish reviews of the film.

Although the last U.S. troops left Vietnam in 1973 and Saigon fell in 1975, there were practically no commercially successful film images of Vietnam before 1978, when *The Deer Hunter* and *Coming Home* picked up seven Oscars between them. Both of these (along with *Apocalypse Now*) carried a strong antiwar message and reflected the country's disgust with the war in Vietnam, a wound that had started to heal just enough to be able to handle these graphic and realistic films.

Still, these were not followed by others, as had the first World War II movies. The wound of Vietnam was still unhealed in 1986, when Oliver Stone's *Platoon* appeared and became a heavy experience for the whole nation, particularly the Vietnam vets themselves. First seen as a commercial gamble, *Platoon* took years to acquire the necessary funding. The Pentagon refused to help the producers, although it enthusiastically aided the makers of the heroic *Top Gun*, on the grounds that it wanted to ensure a "realistic portrayal" of the military! Stone then turned to a private consulting firm headed by a retired marine captain, who ignored the Pentagon's pleas not to help the producers of *Platoon*. Widely hailed as a critical success (including "Best Picture" Oscar for 1986), *Platoon* astounded everyone with its huge commercial success as well. As commercial successes generally are, it was then followed by a spate of "realistic" Vietnam films like *Gardens of Stone, Casualties of War, The Hanoi Hilton*, and *Full Metal Jacket*, none of which received close to *Platoon*'s critical or commercial success.

By 1988, the wounds of Vietnam had healed enough to allow the production and commercial success of the first Vietnam War TV series ("Tour of Duty") and big-screen comedy—*Good Morning, Vietnam*. A comedy about Vietnam would have been unthinkable much before that time. Not too long later followed another Oliver Stone film *Born on the Fourth of July*, the biographical story of gung-ho soldier turned antiwar protester Ron Kovic. After the short and victorious defeat of Iraq in the Persian Gulf War of early 1991, however, the difficult Vietnam War again disappeared from the screen. We now had a less painful and ambiguous war to remember and enjoy on the screen.

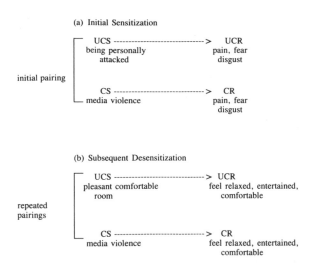

FIG. 9.1.   Desensitization as classical conditioning.

ings is quite different, however (Fig. 9.1b). Suppose, for example, that the normal, unlearned response to sitting at home in one's easy chair is feeling relaxed and happy. When this is repeatedly paired with violence on TV, vicarious violence in a pleasant home context gradually becomes associated with that situation and itself comes to be seen as entertaining, pleasant, and even relaxing. The natural association of the video violence and real-life violence has been weakened as the new association of video violence with recreation is strengthened. We repeatedly see violence without experiencing pain or hurt ourselves and thus the normal negative responses to it weaken. Given what we know about classical conditioning in psychology, it is unlikely that such frequent and repeated exposure to stimuli could not have a substantial effect. In the adolescent subculture, part of the male gender-role socialization has been for a boy to desensitize himself so that he can watch graphic violence and not appear to be bothered by it (Mundorf, Weaver, & Zillmann, 1989; Tamborini, 1991; Zillmann et al., 1986). Desensitization to violence thus becomes a way to impress a date. Suppose that people are desensitized to violence from the media. What are the implications of that? Becoming jaded to news of war and violence will cause such stories not to bother us so much anymore. Although we may never actually like violence or act violently ourselves, we may not dislike it nearly so much; it does not seem all that serious. This has important implications for behavior. For example, Drabman and Thomas (1974, 1976) had 8- to 10-year-old children watch a violent or nonviolent film and then watch younger children at play. When the younger children started to get rough, the older children who had watched the nonviolent film called an adult sooner than did the older children who had watched the violent film.

Another area of concern with desensitization has to do with tolerance of violence toward women. Male college students who viewed a series of "slasher" movies later showed less empathy and concern for victims of rape (Linz, Donnerstein, & Penrod, 1984). Sexual violence is one of the major current concerns among media researchers studying violence; we examine this aspect of violence in some detail in chapter 10.

Cultivation

Another type of effect on attitudes about violence, which then may indirectly affect behavior, is cultivation. As discussed in chapter 2, George Gerbner and his colleagues argued that, the more exposure a person has to television, the more that person's perception of social realities will match what is presented on TV (Gerbner, Gross, Morgan, & Signorielli, 1980, 1986, in press; Gerbner, Gross, Signorielli, Morgan, & Jackson-Beeck, 1979; Signorielli & Morgan, 1990; see also Pingree & Hawkins, 1981; Weaver & Wakshlag, 1986). Although cultivation researchers first tested their theory in regard to violence, the notion of cultivation is much broader. Gerbner et al. (1986) argued that cultivation is "part of a continual, dynamic, ongoing process of interaction among messages and contexts" (p. 24). In contrast to modelling and reinforcement, cultivation attributes a more active role to the viewer, who is interacting with the medium, not being passively manipulated by it. Nevertheless, there is a coming together of the viewer's outlook and that of the medium, whereby the person's perceived reality gradually approaches that of the TV world.

Cultivation theory is best known for its research on the cultivation of attitudes related to violence (Gerbner, Gross, Morgan, & Signorielli, 1980; Gerbner, Gross, Signorielli, & Morgan, 1986). Such studies show that frequent viewers believe the world to be a more dangerous and crime-ridden place than infrequent viewers. The world of TV shows 50% of TV characters involved in violence each week, compared to less than 1% of the population per year in real life. This cultivation effect could be due either to TV teaching that this is what the world is like or to the fact that more fearful people are drawn to watching more TV. If it is the former, and cultivation theorists believe it is, TV can induce a general mindset about the position of violence in the world, completely aside from any effects it might have in teaching violent behavior. Finally, cultivation theory speaks of TV teaching the role of victim. From watching a heavy diet of crime and action-adventure shows, viewers learn what it is like to be a victim of violence, and this role becomes very real to them, even if it is completely outside of their own experience.

We turn now to the final apparent psychological effect of violence—catharsis.

Catharsis

The notion of catharsis extends all the way back to Aristotle's *Poetics*, where he spoke of drama purging the emotions of the audience. In modern times, however, the notion was developed largely in psychoanalytic theory. According to Freud, the id, ego, and superego are locked in battle, with anxiety resulting from id impulses trying to express themselves and, in so doing, coming into conflict with the moralistic superego. The threatening unconscious impulses like sex and aggression are repressed from consciousness but may cause anxiety when they creep back into consciousness from time to time. These repressed impulses and the anxiety that they produce may be dealt with directly by overt sexual or aggressive behavior or indirectly through some sublimated substitute activity, such as watching others act sexually or violently on television.

The emotional release called *catharsis* comes from "venting" the impulse (i.e., expressing it, either directly or indirectly). This emotional purging has been a notoriously difficult concept to operationally define and test, but it has continued to have a lot of intuitive appeal and anecdotal support (e.g., people report feeling better after watching a scary movie). Catharsis theory does, however, make one very clear prediction about the effect of TV violence on behavior, a prediction that is exactly opposite to the prediction of modelling theory. Although modelling predicts an increase in aggressive behavior after watching media violence, catharsis theory predicts a reduction in violent behavior (Feshbach, 1955). If the substitute behavior of watching the violence provides the emotional release that would normally require actually being violent, then violent behavior should actually decrease after watching media violence. Thus the two models are clearly and competitively testable. When such tests have been done, modelling theory has usually been supported (e.g., Siegel, 1956), whereas catharsis theory seldom has. In spite of consistent failures to provide scientific evidence for catharsis (Geen & Quanty, 1977; Zillmann, 1978), it continues to occupy a prominent but undeserved place in the conventional wisdom about the effects of media violence.

Later refinements of catharsis theory were proposed (Feshbach & Singer, 1971). It may be that the media violence elicits fantasizing by the viewer, and that fantasizing, rather than the media violence per se, is what leads to catharsis. Another version of catharsis theory argues that watching media violence reduces the arousal level and thus the person is less prone to violence. There is evidence that a reduction of arousal level is associated with decreased violent behavior. Third, TV violence may elicit an inhibition response, which puts a "brake" on tendencies toward violent behavior. This is very similar to a sensitization hypothesis.

The effects of media violence just discussed are not presented as an exhaustive list but rather as general classes into which most proposed effects fall. Occasionally an effect falls outside of those classes, however; see Box 9.4 for some interesting evidence of violent media causing amnesia in viewers.

BOX 9.4: DO VIOLENT IMAGES CAUSE AMNESIA?

One curious effect of media violence not on the typical lists of effects is amnesia, but just such an effect has been proposed by Loftus and Burns (1982; see also Christianson & Loftus, 1987; Newhagen & Reeves, 1992). It has been known for some time that a physical injury to the brain can result in a loss of memory for events immediately preceding the impact. For example, the shock of one's head flying against the headrest in an auto collision may lead to amnesia for events immediately preceding the impact. It is as if the brain had not yet had time to transfer the event from short-term to long-term memory. Loftus and Burns demonstrated that such an effect may also occur solely from the mental shock of seeing graphic violence on the screen. Research participants saw a 2-minute film of a bank robbery, in either a violent or nonviolent version. In the violent version the fleeing robbers shot their pursuers and hit a young boy in the street in the face, after which he fell, clutching his bloody face. The nonviolent version was identical up to the point of the shooting, at which point the camera cut to the interior of the bank. Measured using both recall and recognition measures, people seeing the nonviolent version of the film remembered the number on the boy's t-shirt better than those seeing the violent film, although the shirt was shown the same amount of time in both. A second study ruled out that the effect could have been due to the unexpectedness or surprisingness of the shooting.

LONGITUDINAL STUDIES

Although hundreds of studies have shown some psychological effect of media violence, most of those have been short term and in the laboratory, often using the methodology of showing participants a film and subsequently measuring their behavior or attitudes in some way. Although these findings are important, they do not offer definitive answers about the long-term cumulative effects of watching hundreds of hours of violent television as recreation throughout one's childhood. There have been a few studies that have addressed this issue, most notably those from the laboratory of University of Illinois at Chicago by Huesmann and Eron.

Longitudinal studies over 10 years in the United States and Finland provided the first evidence of a causal relationship between real-world viewing of TV violence through childhood and aggressive behavior as a child and a young adult (Eron, Huesmann, Lefkowitz, & Walder, 1972; Lefkowitz, Eron, Walder, & Huesmann, 1977; Pitkanen-Pulkkinen, 1981). Through careful design and control for other variables, Eron et al. and Lefkowitz et al. concluded that they could rule out other plausible explanations (such as dispositional violence in people) as being the cause of both more violent TV viewing and more violent behavior.

In a later 3-year longitudinal study, Huesmann, Lagerspetz, and Eron (1984) further explored the role of several intervening variables on the relation of TV violence viewing and aggressive behavior in U.S. and Finnish children in elementary school. The study collected a mass of data between 1977 and 1980 from the children, their parents, the children's peers, and the school. Data gathered included measures of TV viewing, attitudes, behaviors, ratings of self and others, and family demographics. A few of the highlights are presented here.

As had been found in many other studies, there was a positive correlation of violent TV viewing and peer-rated aggression, stronger for boys than girls and for U.S. people than Finns; the overall level of violent behavior was higher in the U.S. children. One of the most striking results for both samples was the strong correlation of violent behavior and self-rated identification with the violent TV model, especially for boys. The best predictor of later aggressive behavior was the interactive product of violent viewing and identification with the violent character. There was no evidence that violent TV only affects children naturally more predisposed to violent behavior or that children who fantasize more were affected any differently. Neither were there particular effects of level of parental violent behavior or TV viewing on children's violence. This research is continuing with samples in Australia, the Netherlands, Poland, and Israel.

This positive relationship between violent TV viewing and subsequent aggressive behavior has been the general finding of recent longitudinal studies, with only a few exceptions (most notably Milavsky, Kessler, Stipp, & Rubens, 1982). Although many researchers have concluded that a convincing causal link between media aggression and violent behavior has been demonstrated (e.g., Friedrich-Cofer & Huston, 1986; Wood et al., 1991), others have urged caution in interpreting beyond correlational and suggestive causal results (e.g., Cumberbatch & Howitt, 1989; Freedman, 1986, 1988).

The clearest conclusion about the mass of research on the effects of media violence requires taking a convergent validation approach. Any study taken by itself is subject to some criticism in terms of methodology, interpretation, or ecological validity. When looking at the big picture, however, the weight of the evidence clearly falls on the side of violent media having several negative behavioral and attitudinal effects, especially modelling and desensitization. These effects typically are not general and frequently are interactive with other variables, but they do seem to be causal in nature. The no-effects or no-clear-picture-yet conclusion is simply not tenable.

HELPING CHILDREN DEAL WITH VIOLENT TELEVISION

Given the probable negative effects and influences of violent television, what can a parent do, short of prohibiting viewing altogether? Prohibition would not be totally successful, anyhow, because children see TV at friends' homes and may rent violent videos and movies.

Although mitigating the effects of TV violence has not been the major thrust of the research, there have been some interesting findings that speak to this issue. Huesmann, Eron, Klein, Brice, and Fischer (1983) developed a treatment designed to change children's attitudes about violent TV. One hundred sixty-nine first- and third-graders who watched a lot of violent TV were exposed to two treatment sessions over 2 years. The first session involved showing children TV film clips and having them discuss the violence and alternative nonviolent "realistic" ways that the problems could have been solved. Neither the treatment session nor a control group session discussing other aspects of TV had any effect on the subjects' own aggressiveness or their belief about the reality of TV violence.

However, a second intervention 9 months later with the same children had subjects develop arguments about the negative effects of TV violence, write a paragraph on the topic, and make a group video with everyone reading his or her essay. This treatment (but not the control) led to reduced aggressive behavior and a weaker relationship between aggression and violent TV viewing. In terms of attitudes, the treatment had a substantial effect on subjects' ratings on two questions ("Are television shows with a lot of hitting and shooting harmless for kids?" "How likely is it that watching a lot of television violence would make a kid meaner?"). The effect occurred most strongly in children who identified least with the violent characters, suggesting the important role of identification with the aggressive model.

A somewhat different approach by Barbara Wilson and Joanne Cantor and their colleagues used systematic desensitization techniques to reduce children's fear reactions to scary media presentations (Wilson, 1987, 1989; Wilson & Cantor, 1987; Wilson, Hoffner, & Cantor, 1987). For example, before watching a scary movie about lizards, children of ages 5–10 either (a) saw a live lizard, (b) saw the experimenter touch a live lizard, or (c) had no exposure to a live lizard. The group where the experimenter modeled touching the lizard led to the most reduction in negative emotional reactions and interpretations (Wilson, 1989).

The success of Huesmann and Wilson and their colleagues in mitigating the effects of TV violence through training is encouraging if for no other reason than it shows that learning is subject to alteration by new learning. This is especially encouraging, because violence as a dispositional behavior trait is known to be remarkably stable over time (Huesmann, Eron, Lefkowitz, & Walder, 1984; Olweus, 1979).

Another approach to mitigating negative effects of media violence is suggested by the individual differences research of Tamborini and his colleagues (Tamborini, 1991; Tamborini & Stiff, 1987; Tamborini, Stiff, & Heidel, 1990; Tamborini, Stiff, & Zillmann, 1987; see also Cantor, 1991). If certain types of personalities (e.g., highly empathic) find graphic violence distasteful and disturbing, and others (e.g., sensation seeking, Machiavellian) find it pleasantly arousing, cultivating those empathic qualities in one's children and discouraging

Machiavellianism and sensation-seeking presumably should help in ensuring that they will not find viewing violence to be pleasurable. Similarly, encouraging psychological identification with the victims and not the perpetrators of violence should decrease the enjoyment level of violent TV.

CONCLUSION

What, then, may we conclude from this mass of research on media violence inside and outside of the laboratory? Probably no single study in itself should be seen as thoroughly definitive in establishing a deleterious effect of TV violence on children. However, the evidence overall converges substantially on the conclusion that media violence does have harmful effects on children, both in the sense of increasing aggressive behavior and in altering attitudes and values, particularly through processes of desensitization and the cultivation of fear. The laboratory research generally has yielded stronger conclusions than the field studies, and different researchers interpret the same data very differently (e.g., Friedrich-Cofer & Huston, 1986; Huston et al., 1992; or Wood et al., 1991; vs Freedman, 1984, 1986, 1988; or Cumberbatch & Howitt, 1989). Even in the unlikely event that the effects turn out to be somewhat more restricted than some would argue today, considerable cause for concern is still present.

Although most of the longitudinal field studies have shown a significant positive correlation between viewing televised violence and subsequent aggressive behavior, such correlations have typically been small in magnitude (e.g., Pearson r correlations between .15 and .30, accounting for 2.25%–9% of the variance). The fact that this amount is small, however, should not be surprising. Social learning theory, for example, would predict such a modest effect, because television is, after all, only a small part of the matrix of influences in people's lives (Tan, 1986). It is, however, clearly one of those influences.

The effects of media violence, however, do not fall equally on all viewers. Some people are affected more than others, and some portrayals of violence and some shows have more effect than others. In proposing policy, either legislative regulation or network industry guidelines, such distinctions must be considered. All violence is not equally harmful.

The debate over the effects of media violence has been strident and heated and probably will continue at that level. Predictably, the networks and television industry in general have refuted the conclusions of much of the behavioral research (e.g., Cumberbatch & Howitt, 1989; Wurtzel & Lometti, 1987a, 1987b). The negative effects of TV may not be quite as widespread and serious as suggested by the strongest critics, but neither are they anywhere nearly as benign as suggested by the apologists (e.g., Freedman, 1984, 1986; Howitt, 1982).

An approach taken only infrequently in the research has been to examine what attracts viewers to violence and why some are attracted much more than others. Fenigstein and Heyduk (1985) found that aggressive thoughts and be-haviors increase one's preference for viewing violence and that the presence of sexual aggressive fantasies increases the desire to view violent pornography. Such a factor may be turned more positively. The induction of affiliation mo-tives by a 10-minute fantasy induction actually increased the preference for view-ing affiliation-oriented TV 40 minutes later (Fenigstein & Heyduk, 1985).

We have not yet seriously addressed one of the types of media violence caus-ing the greatest concern today (i.e., sexual violence). We examine this issue and research on the problem in detail in the next chapter after a look at sex in the media.

10

SEX IN MEDIA: WHAT ARE WE TURNING ON TO?

Q: What is the best-selling magazine single issue in the U.S.?

A: The *Sports Illustrated* swimsuit issue (Sabo & Jansen, 1992).

Q: Although violent men are sexually aroused by viewing an explicit rape or sexual assault scene, normal heterosexual men are generally not turned on by watching a rape scene UNLESS what occurs in the scene?

A: If the woman is portrayed as enjoying and being turned on by being raped, normal men are aroused by it (Malamuth, 1984; Malamuth & Check, 1983).

Some of our major sources of information about sex come from the media. Everything from the mildest innuendo on a network sitcom to the most explicit pornographic video can contribute to our perceived reality of what sex is all about. We are continually learning more about sex and modifying our constructed reality of its nature. How we act on that information may have serious consequences on our lives and the lives of others. After examining the nature of sex in the media in this chapter, we examine research on its effects, with particular focus on one of the most controversial varieties, sexual violence.

THE NATURE OF SEX IN MEDIA

Definitional Issues

Whenever we speak of sex in the media, we must clarify what we are examining. There is a class of media (at least in the United States) explicitly labeled "erotic," "pornographic," or "sexually explicit." These materials are typically marketed

205

separately from nonsexual media and are at least somewhat restricted from children, although just how restricted they are or should be remains a controversial issue. These media are generally recognized as being for sexual purposes only and without recognized literary or artistic merit. One possible exception to this is the relatively tame *Playboy*, which, practically alone among sex magazines, also has some recognized literary respectability. There is also a class of serious educational and semi-educational materials such as sex manuals like *The Joy of Sex*.

The 1986 Meese Commission (Final Report, 1986) identified five classes of what it called "pornography."

1. *Sexually violent materials* portray rape and other instances of physical harm to persons in a sexual context.
2. *Nonviolent materials depicting degradation, domination, subordination, or humiliation* constitute the largest class of commercially available materials. These generally portray women as "masochistic, subservient, and over-responsive to the male interest."
3. *Nonviolent and nondegrading materials* typically depict a couple having vaginal or oral intercourse with no indication of violence or coercion.
4. *Nudity* shows the naked human body with no obvious sexual behavior or intent.
5. *Child pornography* involves minors and, although illegal to produce in the United States, still circulates widely through foreign magazines and personal distribution.

Because not everyone would agree that all of these classes of materials are "pornographic," and because the term *pornographic* is highly value laden but scientifically imprecise, we instead generally refer to such materials as *sexually explicit* rather than *pornographic*.

Clearly, sex also occurs in the media in other than explicitly sexual materials. For example, it is rampant in advertising, particularly for products like perfume, cologne, and after-shave, but also for tires, automobiles, and the kitchen sink. Sex in media is not limited to explicit portrayals of intercourse or nudity, but rather may include any representation that portrays or implies sexual behavior, interest, or motivation. However, the major focus in this chapter is on the more explicit materials.

History of Sex in Media

Sexual themes in fiction have been around as long as fiction itself. Ancient Greek comedies were often highly sexual in content, such as Aristophanes' *Lysistrata*, an antiwar comedy about women who withhold sex from their husbands to coerce them to stop fighting wars. Literary classics like Chaucer's *Canterbury Tales* and Shakespeare's *The Taming of the Shrew* are filled with sexual double entendres and overtly sexual themes, some of which are missed today due to the archaic language and the "classic" aura around such works. Throughout history, the pendulum has swung back and forth in terms of how widespread and explicit sexual expression in literature can be.

Since the advent of electronic media, standards have usually been more conservative for radio and television than for print, because it is easier to keep sexually oriented print media from children than it is radio or TV. With the advent of widespread cable and videocassette technology, a sort of double standard has arisen, with greater permissiveness for videocassettes and premium cable channels like Playboy, Tuxedo, and American Exxxtasy than for network television, on the logic that premium cable and rented movies are "invited" into the home, whereas network programming is there uninvited whenever a TV set is present.

Media Sex Today

Content analyses (Fernandez-Collado & Greenberg, 1978; Greenberg, Brown, & Buerkel-Rothfuss, 1993; Greenberg & D'Alessio, 1985; Lowry & Towles, 1989; Sprafkin & Silverman, 1981) show that, although the sex on network television is not explicit, innuendoes are rampant, often occurring in a humorous context. References to premarital and extramarital sexual encounters far outnumbered references to sex between spouses, as high as 24:1 for unmarried versus married partners in 1987 soap operas (Lowry & Towles, 1989) and 32:1 in R-rated movies (Greenberg et al., 1993). Although more sexual references overall occurred in daytime soaps than on prime-time TV, evening programming contained more references to intercourse and sexual deviance (Greenberg, Abelman, & Neuendorf, 1981).

In a study examining the sources from which children and teenagers have acquired information about sex over the last few decades, Gebhard (1977) concluded that children are learning basic facts about sex earlier than was formerly the case. More interestingly, mass media have risen in importance as a source of such information (up to third in the 1975 sample, behind peers and mother).

Sex in media is one area where we clearly accept some limits on freedom of speech. The sharp differences of opinion surface in deciding just where those limits should be. Few are arguing that "Home Improvement" or "Northern Exposure" should be allowed to show frontal nudity or child prostitutes in chains, although of course it is highly unlikely that the producers would ever care to do so. One important issue in discussion of where the limits should be is the age of the viewer or reader. There is far more concern about the effects of sexual media on children than on adults. Even a highly libertarian person might not want their 6-year-old reading *Hustler*, whereas even a morally very conservative person would be less alarmed about adults viewing X-rated videos than about children seeing them.

Explicit sexual materials have traditionally been designed by men and for men. As such, they have a distinctly macho and hypermasculinized orientation. Although all varieties of heterosexual intercourse are shown, there is little emphasis on associated foreplay, afterplay, cuddling, or general tenderness. Women are seen eagerly desiring and participating in sex, often with hysterical euphoria. There is little concern with the consequences of sex or the relational matrix within which most people find it. Quite recently there has been some increase in sexual materials with more emphasis on relationship, pre- and postcoital behaviors, and the woman's point of view generally, developed primarily to be marketed to women. As yet, however, these comprise only a minuscule part of the $5 billion market worldwide (Day & Bloom, 1988; Hebditch & Anning, 1988; Weaver, 1991). Although men are much more active seekers and users of sexual material than are women, this cannot be assumed to be due to greater intrinsic male interest in sex; it may merely reflect the pornography industry's extreme slant to the traditional male perspective.

Media are clearly major sources of information about sex, information that we use to construct our reality of what sexuality and sexual behavior and values are all about (Dorr & Kunkel, 1990; Fabes & Strouse, 1984, 1987; Strouse & Fabes, 1985; Wartella, Heintz, Aidman, & Mazzarella, 1990). To better understand this perceived reality, let us turn to examining some effects of viewing sex in the media. How do we change after exposure to such material?

EFFECTS OF VIEWING MEDIA SEX

Although many people might wish it otherwise, sex apparently does sell, even very explicit sex. Sexually oriented media, both print and broadcast, are highly profitable commercially, and this fact has ramifications for all media. However, this economic effect is not the focus of this book; we turn now to the various psychological effects (see Linz & Malamuth, 1993; Lyons, Anderson, & Larson, 1993; and the papers in Zillmann and Bryant, 1989, for reviews of the literature on the effects of viewing sexual media).

Arousal

A fairly straightforward effect of sex in media is sexual arousal, the drive that energizes or intensifies sexual behavior. Sexually oriented media, especially explicit magazines and videos, do tend to arouse people sexually, both in terms of self-rating of arousal level and physiological measures such as penile tumescence (Eccles, Marshall, & Barbaree, 1988; Malamuth & Check, 1980; Schaefer & Colgan, 1977), vaginal changes (Sintchak & Geer, 1975), and thermography

(Abramson, Perry, Seeley, Seeley, & Rothblatt, 1981). Sexual violence is particularly arousing to sex offenders and much less so to normal men, unless the victim is portrayed as being aroused by the assault; these findings are discussed in more detail later in the chapter.

Sexual arousal to stimuli not naturally evoking such response may be learned through classical conditioning. For example, Rachman (1966) and Rachman and Hodgson (1968) classically conditioned heterosexual men to be sexually aroused by women's boots, by pairing the boots with nude photos, thus providing a model of how fetishes could be learned. More generally, this could account for the vast individual differences in what specific stimuli arouse people sexually. Through our different experiences, we have all been conditioned to different stimuli through their associations with those we love.

Contrary to what one might expect, the degree of arousal is not necessarily highly correlated with the degree of explicitness of the media. Sometimes one is actually more aroused by a less sexually explicit story than a more explicit one (e.g., Bancroft & Mathews, 1971). Censoring out a sex scene may actually make a film more arousing, because viewers can fill in their own completion. Sexual arousal is highly individual. When people are allowed to use their own imaginations to construct the ending of a romantic scene, they are more likely to construct a reality that is more arousing to them personally than if they view someone else's idea of what is arousing. There is some validity to the old truism that the major sex organ is the brain.

Attitudes and Values

Some Issues. A large class of effects of media sex have to do with effects on attitudes and values. One frequent concern is a desensitization to certain expressions of sexuality deemed by others to be "inappropriate." For example, parents may be concerned that sitcoms showing teenagers considering being sexually active may contradict and thus weaken family-taught values against premarital sex. Women may be concerned that car magazines selling shock absorbers by showing a bikini-clad woman held in mock bondage by a giant shock absorber may desensitize readers about violence toward women.

Sometimes the media may actually change one's value or attitude, rather than merely desensitizing or reinforcing an existing one. It may be that teenage girls watching Roseanne's daughter as she considers having sex with her boy friend may also come to adopt those values. This is especially likely to happen if the TV characters holding those values are respected characters with whom viewers identify. Sexual promiscuity by a prostitute character is less likely to influence the values of a viewer than promiscuity by a respected suburban wife and mother. This type of concern is reflected, for example, in former U.S. Vice President Dan Quayle's 1992 criticism of the single adult woman sitcom character Murphy Brown being a poor role model, because she had a baby (and presumably intercourse) outside of marriage (see chapter 5).

Another concern about the effects on values and attitudes is that sexually oriented media may encourage people not to take sexual issues as seriously as they should. When a sex magazine has a regular cartoon called "Chester the Molester" featuring a child molester, many argue that this is an inappropriately light treatment of an extremely serious subject. One article in a sex magazine aimed at male teenagers was entitled "Good Sex with Retarded Girls"; this too is open to such criticism. Although few would probably argue that sex should never be comedic, there are for most people some sexual subjects that do not seem appropriate for light treatment.

One type of value of particular concern is attitudes toward women. One of the major criticisms of sexually explicit material is that it is antiwomen in an ideological sense. It is usually women, not men, who are the playthings or victims of the opposite sex. Although this concern spans the gamut of sexual content in media, it is particularly leveled at sexual violence. What are teenage boys first learning about sex going to think that women want when they see a picture of a jackhammer in a woman's vagina as the opening photo to a story called "How to Cure Frigidity"? When *Hustler* magazine runs a photo spread of a gang rape turning into an orgy, showing the women appearing to be aroused by the assault, what is being taught about women and their reactions to forcible sex? Research examining this question is discussed in detail later in the chapter.

Finally, in regard to values and attitudes, people sometimes complain that media sex, especially the more explicit varieties, removes some of the mystique, some of the aura, from what is a very mysterious, almost sacred, activity. This argument holds that sex is very private and more meaningful and more fun if it is not so public. This is a hard concern even to articulate, even harder to refute or test empirically, but it is one often expressed.

Research Evidence.   Several studies have shown effects on attitudes and values about sex as a result of exposure to nonviolent sexually explicit materials. After seeing slides and movies of beautiful female nudes engaged in sexual activity, male subjects rated their own partners as being less physically endowed, although they reported undiminished sexual satisfaction (Weaver, Masland, & Zillmann, 1984). In another study, men reported loving their own mates less after seeing sexually explicit videos of highly attractive models (Kenrick, Gutierres, & Goldberg, 1989). Men who saw a pornographic video responded more sexually to a subsequent female interviewer than those seeing a control video, although this result only held for men holding traditional gender schemas (McKenzie-Mohr & Zanna, 1990). All of these studies show significant attitude changes after a very limited exposure to sexual media.

Using a paradigm of showing subjects weekly films and testing them 1–3 weeks later, Zillmann and Bryant (1982, 1984) found that subjects seeing the films overestimated the popularity of sexual practices like fellatio, cunnilingus, anal inter-course, sadomasochism, and bestiality, relatively to perceptions of a control group seeing nonsexually explicit films. This may reflect the cognitive heuristic of *availability*, whereby we judge the frequency of occurrence of various activi-ties by the ease with which we can generate examples (Taylor, 1982; Tversky & Kahneman, 1973, 1974). Recent vivid media instances thus lead to an overes-timation of such occurrences in the real world and a perceived reality substan-tially at odds with actual reality.

Using the same methodology that was used in their 1982 and 1984 studies, Zillmann and Bryant (1988a, 1988b) found effects of this perceived reality on attitudes about real people. Subjects seeing the explicit films reported, relative to a control group, less satisfaction with the affection, physical appearance, sexual curiosity, and sexual performance of their real-life partners. They also saw sex without emotional involvement as being relatively more important than the con-trol group did. They showed greater acceptance of premarital and extramarital sex and lesser evaluation of marriage and monogamy. They also showed less desire to have children and greater acceptance of male dominance and female submission. Results generally did not differ for males versus females or students versus nonstudents.

The medium may make a difference. Dermer and Pyszczynski's (1978) sub-jects were told to think about their mates before reading some explicit passages about a woman's sexual fantasies. They later rated their own partner as more sexually attractive. This inconsistency with the Zillmann and Bryant results may be due to specific procedural aspects of the research, particular materials used, or psychological differences in responses to print versus video material. Non-pictorial descriptions of sex in words in the print medium (e.g., the *Penthouse* Advisor column) may be more conducive to fantasizing about one's own part-ner, whereas photographic sex may encourage unfavorable comparison to that person.

Catharsis

Another alleged effect of media sex is catharsis, that emotional release so important to psychodynamic models of personality (e.g., Freud). Applied to sex, the catharsis argument says that consuming media sex relieves sexual urges, with the magazine or video acting (perhaps in conjunction with mas-turbation) as a sort of imperfect substitute for the real thing. A catharsis argu-ment is frequently used by libertarians to support appeals for lessening re-strictions on sexually explicit material (e.g., Kutchinsky, 1973, 1985). The research support for catharsis as a function of viewing media sex is meager if not totally nonexistent, however (Comstock, 1985; Final Report, 1986).

Behavioral Effects

Teaching New Behaviors.   Another large class of effects is effects on behavior. On the one hand, sexual media may actually teach new behaviors. As part of sex therapy, a couple may buy a sex manual in order to learn new sexual positions or behaviors that they had not tried before. New behaviors are not always so benign, however. One issue of *Penthouse* contained a series of photographs of Asian women bound with heavy rope, hung from trees, and sectioned into parts. Two months later an 8-year-old Chinese girl in Chapel Hill, North Carolina, was kidnapped, raped, murdered, and left hanging from a tree limb (*New York Times*, 1985, cited in Final Report, 1986, p. 208). Of course, such examples are not commonplace, and definitively demonstrating a causal relationship in such cases is difficult, but the juxtaposition is nonetheless disturbing.

Some of the rawest material shows extreme sexual violence that might be copied by a viewer. These include very violent and offensive images, including women apparently being killed ("snuff" films) through torturing them with power tools or even such bizarre and twisted images as sexual penetration of eye sockets after death ("skull-fucking"). For obvious ethical reasons, it is difficult to scientifically study effects of such extreme materials.

Disinhibition.   Erotic material may also disinhibit previously learned behavior, such as when watching TV's treatment of premarital sex disinhibits a viewer's inhibition against doing such behavior. Watching a rape scene where a woman is portrayed as enjoying being assaulted may disinhibit the constraint against some men's secret urge to commit such a crime. This is of particular concern given some evidence suggesting that a surprisingly large number of college men reported that they might rape if they were sure they would not be caught (Check, 1985; Malamuth, Haber, & Feshbach, 1980).

Sex Crimes.   One of the main concerns about a behavioral effect of viewing sexually explicit materials is that it may have a relationship with sex crimes. There have been many studies looking at rates of crimes like rape, exhibitionism, and child molestation, relative to changes in the availability of sexually explicit materials. In a careful review of such studies, Court (1984; see also Court, 1977, 1982, and Bachy, 1976) argued that there is in fact a correlation of availability of sexually explicit materials and certain sex crimes. Court claimed that earlier studies, especially Kutchinsky's (1973) study claiming a drop in reported sex crimes in Denmark after liberalization of pornography restrictions in the 1960s, are not really valid, due to an inappropriate lumping of rape with nonviolent acts of voyeurism, indecent exposure, and homosexual sex.

Most Western nations have experienced a large increase both in the availability of sexually explicit media and the rise in reported rapes in the last 20 years.

However, Court (1984) presented some data from the Australian states of Queensland and South Australia that show a sharp increase in rape reports in South Australia but not Queensland after state pornography laws were liberalized in South Australia in the early 1970s. A comparable downturn in reported rapes occurred temporarily in Hawaii between 1974 and 1976 during a temporary imposition of restraints on sexually explicit media. For an interesting apparent counterexample, see Box 10.1.

Firmly establishing a causal relationship between the availability of sexually explicit media and the frequency of rape is extremely difficult, due to the many other relevant factors, including the different varieties of sexual material, changes in social consciousness about reporting sexual assaults, and changing norms sanctioning such behavior. Some evidence (see Baron & Straus, 1985; Jaffee & Straus, 1986; Scott & Schwalm, 1985; all cited in Final Report, 1986) suggests a correlation of rape and circulation of sex magazines, particularly those containing sexual violence. For example, Baron and Straus found a correlation of +.64 for rape rates and circulation rates of eight sex magazines in 50 states. Although others have argued that there is no demonstrated relationship, very few (Kutchinsky, 1985) support a catharsis explanation that sexually explicit

---

BOX 10.1: PORNOGRAPHY IN JAPAN

As discussed by Abramson and Hayashi (1984), Japan is an interesting and unusual case study of a society with wide availability of sexual media but very low rape rates. Sexual themes in art and society go back centuries to ancient fertility religious objects and wood block prints called *ukiyo-e*. Although some restriction and censorship occurred after the Meiji Restoration in 1868 and even more under the U.S. occupation after World War II ended in 1945, sexuality continued to be a strong theme of Japanese society and one not associated with shame or guilt. Although there are specific restrictions on showing pictorial representations of pubic hair or adult genitalia anywhere in Japan, there is no restriction of sexual media to certain types of magazines, bookstores, or theaters, as occurs in the United States. Thus nudity, bondage, and rape occur regularly on commercial television and popular movies and magazines, including advertising. Although less explicit sexual scenes with no pubic hair or genitalia are shown in Japan, films often portray very vivid scenes of rape and bondage.

Why, then, is the incidence of reported rapes so much lower in Japan than elsewhere (2.4 per 100,000 vs. 34.5 in the United States, 10.1 in England, and 10.7 in Germany)? Abramson and Hayashi (1984) argued that the answer may lie in cultural differences. Japanese society emphasizes order, obligation, cooperation, and virtue, and one who violates social norms is the object of shame. Also, sex is not compartmentalized relative to other segments of society as it is in the United States. Others have suggested that rape in Japan is more likely to be group instigated, perpetrated by juveniles, and greatly underreported by victims (Goldstein & Ibaraki, 1983).

material allows open expression of sexual urges and thus decreases the rate of sex crimes.

Although no one has argued that rape is a victimless crime or should be permitted, pornography and obscenity laws are often attacked in part on the grounds that they proscribe victimless crimes that are not worth police and judicial effort to prosecute. See Box 10.2 for a different perspective on this question.

Prevailing Tone

The perceived reality of media sex and the responses to and effects of sex in the media are not entirely due to the nature of the material itself. They also depend on the context of the material and the context in which the person sees

---

BOX 10.2: PORNOGRAPHY: A VICTIMLESS CRIME?

One of the most frequent arguments against any legal restrictions on the production or sale of sexually explicit media is that, because people freely choose to model for it and consume it, it is not hurting anyone, so why bother prosecuting crimes that have no victims? Increasingly, however, some critics are arguing that there are in fact many victims of pornography. The Meese Commission (Final Report, 1986) heard lengthy testimony from such people. A few of the more extreme cases follow:

> A five-year-old girl told her foster mother, "We have movies at home. Daddy shows them when mother is gone. The people do not wear clothes, and Daddy and I take our clothes off and do the same thing the people in the movies do." (p. 200)

> A mother and father forced their four daughters, age ten to seventeen, to engage in family sex while pornographic pictures were being filmed. This mother also drove the girls to dates with men where she would watch while the girls had sex, then she would collect fees of thirty to fifty dollars. (p. 202)

> This guy had seen a movie where a woman was being made love to by dogs. He suggested that some of his friends had a dog and we should have a party and set the dog loose on the women. He wanted me . . . to put some sort of stuff on my vagina so that the dog would lick there. (p. 204)

> A Playmate of the Year . . . testified that a man attempted to rape her after he recognized her from the magazine. (p. 202)

> [My father would] hang me upside down in a closet and push objects like screwdrivers or table knives inside me. Sometimes he would heat them first. All the while he would have me perform oral sex on him. He would look at his porno pictures almost every day, using them to get ideas of what to do to me or my siblings. (p. 206)

> My husband had a large collection of S & M and bondage pornography . . . [he] tied me to our bed and sodomized me . . . after I refused to agree to be bound and tied as the models appeared in . . . magazines. (p. 207)

BOX 10.3: PROSOCIAL USES
OF SEXUALLY EXPLICIT MATERIALS

Most of the research on sex in the media tends to focus on and test for undesirable effects. However, sexually explicit media may also be used in positive ways. First, sexual dysfunctions such as excessive sexual anxiety or failure to achieve orgasm may be treated by, for example, videotaped models presented for observational learning, and systematic desensitization therapy for reducing anxiety. Such techniques have been successful in changing both attitudes and behavior (Caird & Wincze, 1977; Heiby & Becker, 1980; Heiman, LoPiccolo, & LoPiccolo, 1976).

Second, sexual materials are used in diagnosis and treatment of sex offenders. For example, testing one's arousal patterns to different photos might indicate an "inappropriate" pattern, such as sexual arousal in response to children. This arousal pattern may then be modified through behavior therapy. Such techniques have been successful, especially if combined with social skills training (Abel, Becker, & Skinner, 1980; Whitman & Quinsey, 1981). See Quinsey and Marshall (1983) for a review of such approaches.

---

it (Eysenck & Nias, 1978). This diverse collection of variables is called the *prevailing tone*. The nature of this prevailing tone can make enormous difference in the experience of consuming sexually explicit media.

One of the relevant variables of the prevailing tone is the degree of playfulness or seriousness of the material. Even a highly explicit and potentially controversial topic may not be particularly controversial when presented seriously. For example, a documentary on rape or a "tastefully" done TV movie on incest may be considered perfectly acceptable, whereas a far less explicit comedy with the same theme may be highly offensive and considered "too sexual." What is really the concern in such cases is not the sex as such, but rather the comedic treatment of it. Highly explicit videos, books, and magazines are used routinely and noncontroversially in sex therapy to treat sexual dysfunctions generally and sex offenders specifically (see Box 10.3).

A second factor in the prevailing tone is the artistic worth and intent. We react very differently to a sexually explicit drawing from Picasso versus *Hustler* magazine. Shakespeare, Chaucer, *The Song of Solomon* in the Bible, and serious sex manuals like *The Joy of Sex* are seen to have serious literary or didactic intentions and thus the sex therein is considered more acceptable and even healthy. One interesting issue in this regard is how to respond to something of clear artistic worth but written at a time when standards differed from what they are today. For example, should Rhett Butler's forcing his attentions on Scarlett O'Hara in *Gone with the Wind* be seen as rape or as the noncontroversial romantic moment that it appeared to be in 1939? A parallel concern has been raised in regard to racism, where some people want to remove *Huckleberry Finn* from high school libraries and curricula because the portrayal of the African-American slave Jim seems racist by modern standards.

The relation and integration of sex to the overall plot and intent of the piece is also a part of the prevailing tone. A sex scene, even a mild and nonexplicit one, may be offensive if it appears to be "thrown in" merely to spice up the story but having no connection to it. Something far more explicit may find greater acceptance if it is necessary and central to the plot. Sex scenes in a story about a prostitute may be much less gratuitous than comparable scenes in a story about a female corporate executive. Sex, of course, is not the only common gratuitous factor in media; for example, contemporary TV shows and movies frequently insert car chases and rock video segments completely unrelated to the plot.

Although it is not the overriding factor in predicting reactions to sexual media as many think it to be, the degree of explicitness of the sex is nevertheless a real factor. Sex may be shown explicitly or implied by innuendo. In the latter sense, some of the sexiest TV shows are sitcoms like the old "Three's Company" or the more recent "Married . . . with Children," which have constant remarks and double entendres dealing with sex, but never anything explicit. A study of women's reactions to sex in TV commercials (Johnson & Satow, 1978) found that older women were more offended by the more explicit material, whereas younger women were more offended by innuendo, especially commercials that could readily be considered sexist.

The context of the viewing also influences the experience and effect of sex in the media. Watching an erotic film may elicit different reactions, depending on whether you watch it with your parents, your grandparents, your children, by yourself, in a group of close same-sex friends, or with your spouse. It can be seen as more or less erotic or arousing and more or less appropriate or offensive.

The cultural context is also a factor. Some cultures do not consider female breasts to be particularly erotic or inappropriate for public display. We recognize these cultural differences and thus, at least after the age of 14, most readers do not consider topless women from some exotic culture in *National Geographic* photos to be the slightest bit erotic, sexual, or inappropriate. Even in Western culture, standards have changed. In much of the 19th century, knees and calves were thought to be erotic, and the sight of a bare-kneed woman would be as scandalous, perhaps even as sexually arousing, in most settings as a topless woman is today. As societies go, North America overall is a bit more conservative than many Northwest European or Latin American cultures but far more permissive than many Islamic and East Asian cultures.

Finally, the expectations we have affect our perception of the prevailing tone. Sex is less offensive and shocking if it is expected than if it appears as a surprise. Seeing a photo of a nude woman being fed through a meat grinder may be less shocking in *Hustler* magazine than if one were to suddenly encounter it in *Newsweek*. The stimulus may be the same, but the perceived experiential reality of the fact of seeing it would differ considerably in the two cases.

We now turn to examine that potent combination of sex and violence in the media—sexual violence.

SEXUAL VIOLENCE

Although neither sex nor violence in the media is anything new, the integral combination of the two has become far more prevalent in recent years. Cable and VCR technology has greatly expanded the capability of much of the public to privately and conveniently view sexually explicit material. Although many people are not willing to seek out and visit theaters that show such films, the chance to see such material safely and privately in one's own home make them much more accessible. Although sex magazines are not new, some particularly violent publications are relatively new, and even more "established" publications like *Penthouse* and *Playboy* show some evidence of increasing themes of sexual violence (Malamuth & Spinner, 1980). Dietz and Evans (1982) content analyzed the covers of 1,760 sex magazines from 1970 to 1980; they found a huge increase in bondage and domination imagery (up to 17.2% of the covers by 1981).

Finally, another old familiar genre, the horror film, has recently evolved into showing frequent and extensive scenes of violence against women in a sexual context (Palys, 1986; Yang & Linz, 1990). These films are heavily targeted at teenagers, in spite of the R ratings that many of them receive. With all of these, the major concern is not with the sex or violence in and of itself, but with the way the two appear together. The world constructed in the mind of the viewer of such materials can have some very serious consequences. Let us turn now to examining some of the effects of viewing sexual violence.

Erotica as Stimulator of Aggression

Links between sex and aggression have long been speculated upon, particularly in the sense of sexual arousal facilitating violent behavior. The research has been inconsistent, however, with some studies showing that erotic materials facilitate aggression (Baron, 1979; Donnerstein & Hallam, 1978) and others showing that they inhibit it (Donnerstein, Donnerstein, & Evans, 1975; White, 1979). The resolution of this issue apparently concerns the nature of the material. Sexual violence and unpleasant themes typically facilitate aggression, whereas nonviolent, more loving and pleasant "soft-core" explicit materials may inhibit it (Zillmann, Bryant, Comisky, & Medoff, 1981). Thus, in considering the effects of sexual media, it is necessary to separate sexual violence from consenting, loving sex and also to consider the affective nature of the material (Sapolsky, 1984).

Effects of Seeing Sexual Violence

Malamuth (1984) reported several studies that showed male subjects scenes of sexual violence and afterwards measured attitudes on several topics. Subjects seeing the films showed a more callous attitude toward rape and women in general, especially if the women victims in the film were portrayed as being aroused by the assault. In terms of sexual arousal, subjects were aroused by the sexual violence only if the victim was shown to be aroused but not if she was not so portrayed.

Individual Differences.   Other studies examined convicted rapists and found them to be aroused by both rape and consenting sex, whereas normal subjects were aroused only by the consenting sex (Abel, Barlow, Blanchard, & Guild, 1977; Barbaree, Marshall, & Lanthier, 1979). An important exception to this occurred if the victim was portrayed as enjoying the rape and coming to orgasm; in this case normal males (but not females) were equally or more aroused by the rape than by the consenting sex (Malamuth, Heim, & Feshbach, 1980).

In further examining this question in regard to individual differences in males, Malamuth (1981) identified one group of college males who were "force oriented," that is, prone to use force in their own lives. This group, and a group of nonforce-oriented men, were shown a film where a man stops his car on a deserted road to pick up a woman. Following this, they either have sex in his car with both clearly consenting or he rapes her, although she is depicted as finally enjoying the assault. Students were then asked to create their own sexual fantasies to achieve a high level of arousal. Although nonforce-oriented males were more aroused by the consenting scene than the sexual violence, the reverse was true for the force-oriented males!

A similar study (Malamuth & Check, 1983) had male subjects listen to a tape of a sexual encounter with (a) consenting sex, (b) nonconsenting sex where the woman showed arousal, or (c) nonconsenting sex where she showed disgust. Where the woman showed disgust, both force-oriented and nonforce-oriented males were more aroused (in terms of both self-report and penile tumescence) by the consenting than the nonconsenting (rape) scene. However, when the woman was portrayed as being aroused, the nonforce-oriented males were equally aroused by both consenting and nonconsenting versions, whereas the force-oriented subjects actually showed more arousal to the nonconsenting (rape) version.

Donnerstein (1980) showed male students either a nonviolent but sexually explicit film or a film where a woman was sexually abused and assaulted. Subjects seeing the latter but not the former film were more likely to administer electric shocks to a third party in a subsequent "experiment" on learning and punishment, especially so in subjects who had been previously angered. In a similar study (Donnerstein & Berkowitz, 1981), male subjects saw a sexually violent film where a woman is attacked, stripped, tied up, and raped. In one version of the film the woman was portrayed as enjoying the rape. Afterward, subjects were given a chance to administer electric shocks to a confederate of the experimenter, the same confederate who had earlier angered them. Subjects seeing the film where the woman enjoyed being raped administered more shocks to a female confederate, but not to a male. This suggests that the association of sex and violence in the film allows violent behavior to be transferred to the target confederate.

Most of this research has been conducted on men. However, a few studies examining women have obtained behavioral effects of aggression toward women (Baron, 1979) and desensitization effects of trivialization of rape and rape myths (Malamuth, Check, & Briere, 1986; Zillmann & Bryant, 1982).

Several conclusions emerge from this line of research. One is that a critical aspect of the perceived reality of sexual violence is whether the woman is seen as enjoying and being aroused by the assault. Far more undesirable effects occur in normal men if the woman is seen to be aroused than if she is seen to be terrorized. This media portrayal of women as being "turned on" by rape is apparently not only a distasteful deviation from reality, but also a potentially dangerous one. A second important conclusion is that sexually violent media often affect different men very differently, depending on their own propensity to use force in their own lives. Convicted rapists and other force-oriented men are more likely to become aroused or even incited to violence by sexually violent media, especially if the woman is portrayed as being aroused by the assault.

Slasher Movies.   Because the studies discussed so far used very sexually explicit materials, the kind that would be considered "hard-core pornography," many might consider them beyond the limits of what they themselves would be exposed to. However, sexual violence is by no means confined to "pornographic" materials restricted from minors. Hundreds of "mainstream" R-rated films are readily available to teenagers anywhere, in theaters and even more so in video stores. There are the highly successful series like *Halloween, Friday the Thirteenth*, and *Nightmare on Elm Street*, but also many lesser known films. Most are extremely violent with at least strong sexual overtones. For example, *Alien Prey* shows a blood-stained vampire sucking out a dead woman's entrails through a hole in her stomach. *Flesh Feast* shows maggots consuming live human beings, starting with the face and working down. *Make Them Die Slowly* promises "24 scenes of barbaric torture," such as a man slicing a woman in half ("Child's Play," 1987, p. 31). *The Offspring* shows a soldier choking a little-girl captive to death while kissing her. In some countries rape and other acts of violence against women are even more standard entertainment fare (see Box 10.4).

Although some of these films have R ratings in the United States, others are released unrated to avoid the "accompanied by parent" restriction of R-rated movies. Because no restrictions apply in video stores, the rating is not a major issue. The viewing of such films is widespread among youth. A survey in the early 1980s of 4,500 English and Welsh children found that almost 20% of the 13- to 14-year-old boys had seen the sexually violent *I Spit on Your Grave*, a film deemed legally obscene and liable to prosecution in the United Kingdom

---

BOX 10.4: RAPE TO SELL, INDIAN STYLE (PRATAP, 1990)

The nation producing the largest number of movies annually is India. Many of these use rape scenes as major audience draws. The great Indian epics *Mahabharat* and *Ramayana* have demure heroines who are nearly raped but are indeed rescued from their attackers by their own virtue. This pattern also appears in Indian movies featuring the same type of heroine. But the women characters who are portrayed as more independent, corrupt, immoral, or even morally ambiguous must suffer their fate, which is more typically blamed on their lifestyle rather than on the attacker. A 1989 film *Crime Time* advertised: "See first-time underwater rapes on Indian screen." One popular Indian actor, Ranjeet, has enacted over 350 rape scenes in 19 years of film acting.

There is some call for change from women's groups and others. Bharatendu Singhal, chairman of the Central Board of Film Certification, announced his intent in 1990 to force producers to remove much of the titillation from the rape scenes, although filmmakers lobbied for his removal from the post.

Does this state of affairs reflect society or help mold it? Over 8,000 rapes, half against poor and lower-caste women, are reported yearly in India, although that is probably a small fraction of those that occur. Occasionally a rape case even comes to trial. In 1989 policemen accused of raping 18 women were acquitted by a judge in Bihar, who felt that the women were so poor that they could have been bribed to file a false complaint!

(Hill, Davis, Holman, & Nelson, 1984)! A later U.S. study (Oliver, 1993) found that punitive attitudes toward sexuality and traditional attitudes toward women's sexuality were associated with high school students' greater enjoyment of previews of slasher films.

The major concern with such films is the juxtaposition of erotic sex and violence. For example, one scene from *Toolbox Murders* opens with a beautiful woman disrobing and getting into her bath, with the very romantic music "Pretty Baby" playing in the background. For several minutes she is shown fondling herself and masturbating in a very erotic manner. Suddenly the camera cuts to the scene of an intruder breaking into her apartment, with loud, fast-paced suspenseful music in the background. The camera and sound track cut back and forth several times between these two characters until he finally encounters the woman. He attacks her with electric tools, chasing her around the apartment, finally shooting her several times in the head with a nail gun. The scene closes after she bleeds profusely, finally lying on the bed to die with the sound track again playing the erotic "Pretty Baby."

Linz, Donnerstein, and Penrod (1984; see also Linz, 1985; Linz, Donnerstein, & Adams, 1989) examined the effects of such films. Their male college-student participants were initially screened to exclude those who had prior hostile tendencies or psychological problems. The remaining subjects in the experimental group were shown one standard Hollywood-released R-rated film per day over

1 week. All of the films were very violent and showed multiple instances of women being killed in slow, lingering, painful deaths in situations associated with much erotic content (e.g., the *Toolbox Murders* scene described earlier). Each day the subjects filled out some questionnaires evaluating that film and also completed some personality measures.

These ratings show that these men became less depressed, less annoyed, and less anxious in response to the films during the week. The films themselves were rated over time as more enjoyable, more humorous, more socially meaningful, less violent and offensive, and less degrading to women. Over the week's time, the violent episodes in general and rape episodes in particular were rated as less frequent. A similar study by Krafka (1985) tested women and did not find the same effects. Although these data provide clear evidence of desensitization in men, there is still the question of generalization from the films to other situations.

To answer this question, Linz, Donnerstein, and Penrod (1984) arranged to have the same people participate in a later study, where subjects were not aware of any connection to the movies. For this experiment, they observed a rape trial at the law school and evaluated it in several ways. Compared to a control group, men who had seen the slasher films rated the rape victim as less physically and emotionally injured. These results are consistent with those of Zillmann and Bryant (1984), who found that massive exposure to sexually explicit media resulted in shorter recommended prison sentences for a rapist. Such findings show that the world we construct in response to seeing such movies can be at variance with reality and can have dire consequences when actions are taken believing that such a world is reality.

Not surprisingly, this study and others by the authors along the same line (see Donnerstein, Linz, & Penrod, 1987, for a review) have caused considerable concern in the public. They have also caused considerable scientific concern. Some of the major effects have not been replicated in later work (Linz & Donnerstein, 1988), and there have been some methodological criticisms (see Weaver, 1991, in press, for discussions of these criticisms).

The sharp distinction that Donnerstein and Linz made between the effects of violent and nonviolent pornography has been called into question (Weaver, 1991; Zillmann & Bryant, 1988c). Research findings have been somewhat inconsistent in each area; Zillmann and Bryant argued that Linz and Donnerstein were too quick to cite failures to reject the null hypothesis as support for the harmlessness of nonviolent pornography, yet they all but ignore such results in arguing for serious deleterious effects of sexual violence. Check and Guloien (1989) found that men exposed to a steady diet of rape-myth sexual violence reported a higher likelihood of committing rape themselves, compared to a no-exposure control group, but the same result was found for a group exposed to nonviolent pornography. There is considerable controversy about the use and interpretation of data from particular studies. How this will be resolved is still unclear; we clearly need more research, especially on slasher-type movies.

Mitigating the Negative Effects of Sexual Violence

Whatever the exact nature of the effects of sexual violence, results from the studies just discussed tend to be disturbing, especially given the widespread viewing of slasher films by children and young teens and the overall increase in sexually violent media. Some studies have developed and evaluated extensive pre-exposure training procedures to attempt to lessen the desensitizing effects of sexual violence (Intons-Peterson & Roskos-Ewoldsen, 1989; Intons-Peterson, Roskos-Ewoldsen, Thomas, Shirley, & Blut, 1989; Linz, Donnerstein, Bross, & Chapin, 1986; Linz, Fuson, & Donnerstein, 1990). These studies have typically shown mitigating effects on some measures and not on others. Linz et al. (1990) found that men were most strongly affected by the information that women are not responsible for sexual assaults perpetrated upon them. There is also some evidence that desensitization can be reduced by introducing pertinent information about rape myths and the inaccuracy of media portrayals after people have seen some of the sexually violent media. At least some participants were more impressed with such arguments after they had felt themselves excited and aroused by the film and had seen very specific examples to illustrate the point of the debriefing/mitigation information. In the context of having seen such a film, the specific points of the sensitization training have greater impact. See Box 10.5 for further discussion of ethical issues in such research.

Using a different approach, measuring the effect of seeing a prosocial TV movie about rape, Wilson, Linz, Donnerstein, and Stipp (1992) found that, compared to a control group, people viewing the film generally showed heightened awareness and concern about rape. However, not all groups were so affected.

BOX 10.5: ETHICS OF SEXUAL VIOLENCE RESEARCH

The more potential harm is identified from viewing sexually explicit, especially sexually violent, materials, the more question is raised about the ethics of doing research by exposing people to such materials (Malamuth, Feshbach, & Heim, 1980; Sherif, 1980). Although we have clearly learned some valuable information, what will be the cost of this knowledge in terms of the lives of the research participants? This issue has been taken seriously by Malamuth, Heim, and Feshbach (1980) and others, who have offered an extensive debriefing, complete with information on the horrible reality of rape and the complete unreality of the victim enjoying it. Malamuth et al. even included a discussion of why the myth of enjoying being raped was so prevalent in sexually violent media. Some studies have included evaluations of such debriefing sessions and shown that, compared to a control group not in the experiment, debriefed people showed less acceptance of rape myths (Donnerstein & Berkowitz, 1981; Malamuth & Check, 1980b). It is, of course, unethical to have an "ideal" control group that views the sexual violence in the experiment but is not debriefed!

Unlike women and young and middle-aged men, older men (over 50) had their pre-existing attitudes reinforced and actually blamed women more for rape after seeing the film. This suggests that the attitudes and experiences of the target audience of interventions must be carefully considered.

We conclude this chapter with a brief look at the two U.S. pornography commissions, which provide a fascinating, albeit often unsatisfying, case study of the interaction of politics and social science research.

THE PORNOGRAPHY COMMISSIONS

U.S. Commission on Obscenity and Pornography

This commission was established by then U.S. President Lyndon Johnson in 1967 to analyze (a) pornography control laws, (b) the distribution of sexually explicit materials, and (c) the effects of consuming such materials, and to recommend appropriate legislative or administrative action. It funded more than 80 research studies on the topic, providing important impetus to the scientific study of sexually explicit material. The final report 3 years later (U.S. Commission on Obscenity and Pornography, 1970) recommended stronger controls on distribution to minors but an abolition of all limits on access by adults. The latter recommendation was based on the majority conclusion that there was "no evidence that exposure to or use of explicit sexual materials play a significant role in the causation of social or individual harms such as crime, delinquency, sexual or nonsexual deviancy or severe emotional disturbance" (U.S. Commission on Obscenity and Pornography, 1970, p. 58). The report also included a series of minority conclusions, which argued for some curbs on sexually explicit materials.

Although the composition of the commission has been criticized for being overloaded with anticensorship civil libertarians (Eysenck & Nias, 1978), its majority conclusions were rejected anyway by the new administration of Richard Nixon, who declared, "so long as I am in the White House there will be no relaxation of the national effort to control and eliminate smut from our national life" (Eysenck & Nias, 1978, p. 94). During the same period, the Longford (1972) and Williams (Report of the Committee on Obscenity and Film Censorship, 1979) commissions in Great Britain issued reports, followed a few years later by the Fraser commission in Canada (Report of the Special Committee on Pornography and Prostitution, 1985). The major conclusion of these commissions was that there is a lack of conclusiveness of the research to date. See Einsiedel (1988) for a discussion of these commissions and their social and political context and interpretations of research.

The "Meese Commission"

The nature of sexual media changed greatly from 1970 to 1985, particularly in the great increase of sado-masochistic themes and the linking of sex and violence, themes relatively rare in 1970, or at least not seriously addressed by the earlier U.S. commission. Additionally, technological advancements like cable and satellite TV and VCRs made sexually explicit material available in the home far more easily and privately than formerly had been the case. In 1985, 1,700 new sexually explicit videocassettes were released in the United States, accounting for about one-fifth of videotape rentals and sales (Final Report, 1986). These changes, plus certain social and political considerations, led to the formation of the new commission.

U.S. Attorney General Edwin Meese charged the newly formed commission in 1985 to assess the nature, extent, and impact of "pornography" on U.S. society, and to recommend more effective ways to contain the spread of pornography. Although there is a clear political position even in this charge, the part of the Final Report (1986) of most interest here concerns the issue of possible harmful effects of exposure to sexually explicit material. See Paletz (1988) for an examination of the political context and press coverage of the Commission.

One of the major conclusions of the commission dealt with the effect of sexual violence, "the available evidence strongly supports the hypothesis that substantial exposure to sexually violent materials . . . bears a causal relationship to antisocial acts of sexual violence, and for some subgroups, possibly the unlawful acts of sexual violence" (Final Report, 1986, p. 40).

Groups like the Meese Commission typically have both a scientific and a political agenda (Paletz, 1988; Wilcox, 1987). Sometimes, even if there is relative consensus on the scientific conclusions, there is often strong disagreement about the policy ramifications. For example, Linz, Donnerstein, and Penrod (1987) took exception with some of the conclusions drawn by the Meese Commission from those researchers' own work demonstrating deleterious effects of sexual violence (see previous discussion). Linz et al. (1987) argued that the commission's call for strengthening obscenity laws was not an appropriate policy change based on the research, because it ignored the strong presence of sexually violent themes in other media not covered by such laws. See Box 10.6.

CONCLUSION

What may we conclude from the research on the perceived reality and effects from viewing sexual media? For a careful review of results from 81 experimental studies on the effects of viewing sexually explicit media, see Lyons, Anderson, and Larson (1993). First, it is useful to make a distinction between violent and nonviolent sexual media, although this distinction may not be as important

---

BOX 10.6: THE PORNOGRAPHY VICTIMS'
COMPENSATION ACT

Just before his 1989 execution in Florida, convicted serial killer Ted Bundy granted an interview in which he blamed pornography for his brutally violent behavior.
Although this report was widely carried in the media, Linz and Donnerstein (1992)
argued that a careful reading of Bundy's statement actually blamed violent movies and television. A spokesperson for the FBI told a Surgeon General's panel in
1986 that violent detective magazines, not pornography, were usually found in
violent criminals' possession at their arrest.

However, in response to concern over people like Bundy, the U.S. Senate
Judiciary Committee approved a bill that would allow rape victims and families
of murder victims to sue producers of sexually explicit materials. However, the
bill would not cover R-rated "slasher" movies that research discussed in the text
suggests may be just as damaging (Linz & Donnerstein, 1992). Debate on this issue
illustrates the double standard in the United States of far greater acceptance of
violence than sex in the media. With research increasingly showing deleterious
effects of the combination of sex and violence, sorting out policy implications becomes even more complicated.

---

as Linz and Donnerstein argued. While there are some negative effects of nonviolent material, especially on attitudes toward women (Weaver, 1991; Zillmann
& Bryant, 1988a, 1988b), the research is even more compelling in the case of
sexual violence. Sexual violence is arousing to sex offenders, force-oriented men,
and sometimes even to "normal" young men if the woman is portrayed as being aroused by the attack.

Repeated exposure to sexual violence may lead to desensitization toward
violence against women in general and greater acceptance of rape myths. In
this sense the "no effects" conclusion of the 1970 commission must be revised.
Not only does this suggest that the combination of sex and violence together
is considerably worse than either one separately, but it also matters further what
the nature of the portrayal is. If the woman being assaulted is portrayed as being terrorized and brutalized, negative effects on normal male viewers are less
than if she is portrayed as being aroused and/or achieving orgasm through being attacked. Perhaps more than any other topic discussed in this book, this
is an extremely dangerous reality for the media to create and for us to accept
as real. There is nothing arousing or exciting about being raped, and messages
to the contrary do not help teenage boys understand the reality of how to relate to girls and women.

Not all the themes of sexual aggression against women are limited to specifically sexual material or even very violent movies. These images are found in
mainstream television. For example, in a content analysis study, Lowry, Love,
and Kirby (1981) found that, except for erotic touching among unmarried per-

sons, aggressive sexual contact was the most frequent type of sexual interaction in daytime soap operas. Some years ago a story line of "General Hospital" focused on the rape of one main character by another. Although the woman first appeared humiliated, she later fell in love with the rapist and married him. *Newsweek* ("Soap Operas," 1981) reported that producers and actors in soap operas believe the increase in sexual aggression in that genre has attracted more male viewers, who "started watching us because we no longer were wimps. When a woman was wrong, we'd slap her down" (p. 65).

Such images appear in other media as well. A content analysis of detective magazines found that 76% of the covers depicted domination of women, whereas 38% depicted women in bondage (Dietz, Harry, & Hazelwood, 1986), all of this in a publication never even considered sexual, much less pornographic! Studies of rock videos (Hansen & Hansen, 1990; Zillmann & Mundorf, 1987) show that sexual content is highly appealing but that violent content is not. Although sexual violence may have the negative effects just discussed, it may not even be enjoyed! The effect of parental warning labels about sexual content on CDs and tapes is not entirely clear, but in one study (Christenson, 1992) these labels seemed to decrease appeal to middle school students. However, these sexually violent themes are pervasive in much media and no "quick fix" of stricter pornography laws or warning labels will make them go away entirely.

The perceived reality of some of these media is that men dominate women and even brutalize them. The seriousness of this is lessened if the women are, after all, turned on by being raped or tortured. That is what much of the media is saying about how men treat women, but what is the cost of this message on those in the public who may not realize that this picture deviates so significantly from reality?

11

PROSOCIAL MEDIA: HELPING MEDIA, HELPING PEOPLE

Q: What is the most watched educational television program of all time?

A: "Sesame Street," on the air continuously since 1969.

Q: What was the most popular television program of all time in India?

A: "Hum Log," the feminist family drama produced for the explicit purpose of advancing the status of women (Brown & Cody, 1991).

Although it is obviously too simplistic to say that media are all good or all bad, much of this book has focused on rather negative types of perceived realities gleaned from the media—worlds of excessive violence, deception, stereotyping, and misleading distortion. However, media can clearly be used in more positive ways, some of which we have already examined in the context of looking at other issues. Sometimes, however, the overriding purpose of a major media enterprise is prosocial in nature (i.e., specifically intended to produce some socially positive outcome). The media have tremendous potential, much of it as yet untapped, for inducing and encouraging positive social change.

In this chapter we examine some such projects, where the media are explicitly used to attempt to create a better world than what would exist otherwise. Although some prosocial activity has been considered elsewhere in this book (e.g., using the media to teach positive values, mitigating effects of sexual violence), this chapter considers efforts with a central focus of teaching skills, attitudes, knowledge, and behaviors, as well as values. The three major areas of focus are educational television for children, prosocial media targeted at adults, and social marketing for health and safety concerns. All of these projects attempt to alter the perceived reality that we acquire from media in ways that have socially positive effects on individuals and society.

PROSOCIAL CHILDREN'S TELEVISION

Given children's massive exposure to media, primarily television, it is all but inconceivable that they are not learning anything from it (Berry & Asamen, 1993). Just what their perceived reality is and what they are learning requires careful examination of both the content of the programs and the cognitive processing that the child is capable of at different developmental stages. For a careful review of such issues, see Huston and Wright (1987). Here, however, we focus on some specific projects designed to teach through television.

Although there had been some specifically educational children's shows on the U.S. commercial networks since the 1950s (e.g., "Ding Dong School," "Romper Room," "Captain Kangaroo"), by the mid-1960s there was increased interest in developing some more children's television programming that would be explicitly educational and socially positive. In the United States, the Corporation for Public Broadcasting was founded in 1967, followed by the Public Broadcasting System (PBS) in 1970. Although there had been some educational TV stations since the early 1950s, the programming tended to be low budget and local and often of low artistic and technical quality. This situation changed drastically with the founding of the Children's Television Workshop (CTW) in 1968, initially supported by both public and private funds.

"Sesame Street"

The next year saw the debut of "Sesame Street," one of the most important television shows of all time. Although it was only the first of several such shows, "Sesame Street" is still by far the most successful and popular young children's show worldwide; it has been translated into many languages but is always locally produced and adapted to local culture. Its original stated purpose was to provide preschoolers with an enriched experience leading to prereading skills. The creators especially hoped to target so-called "disadvantaged" children who often enter school less prepared than their peers to learn to read. In fact, however, the show appealed to children across the social spectrum. Regular characters like Big Bird, the Cookie Monster, Oscar the Grouch, and Bert and Ernie have become part of almost everyone's childhood.

The technical quality of "Sesame Street" has been consistently very high, using much animation, humor, and movement. There is a pleasing mixture of live action, animation, and puppet/muppet characters. Recognizing that commercials appeal to children, "Sesame Street" draws on many technical characteristics of ads (e.g., "This program has been brought to you by the letter H and the number 6"). More recently the influence of music videos is apparent in the many segments that use that form. The segments are short, so as to not lose even the youngest viewers' interest. In fact, even some infants under 1 year old are regular watchers. Practically all people now reaching adulthood in many societies of the world have had some exposure to "Sesame Street," and many have had very heavy exposure. In many markets it is shown 3–4 hours per day on PBS affiliates. According to the 1981 Nielsens, 78% of 2- to 5-year-olds saw it at least weekly, making it by far the most watched educational TV program in history.

There is also much to amuse adults watching with their children or listening in the background. A rock band of insect muppets sings about nutrition in the song "Hey Food," which just happens to sound a lot like the Beatles' "Hey Jude." There is also spoofing of its own network, PBS. The frequent segment "Monsterpiece Theatre" features a smoking-jacket-attired Cookie Monster ("Good evening. I'm Alastair Cookie") introducing classics about numbers and letters, including "The Old Man and the C," "1 Flew over the Cuckoo's Nest," and "The Postman Always Rings Twice." In its own version of *Lethal Weapon 3*, Mel Gibson and Danny Glover duck a falling concrete 3. Children are introduced to operatic music at the "Nestropolitan Opera" with conductor Phil Harmonic and lead tenor Placido Flamingo. Popular adult stars frequently put in guest appearances; Jay Leno, Glenn Close, Candace Bergen, Paul Simon, Robin Williams, and even New York Mayor David Dinkins have visited "Sesame Street." Adults who had earlier watched the show as preschoolers frequently have the feeling seeing "Sesame Street" as adults that there are a lot of nuances that they had missed earlier!

The intentional use of a multiracial, multiethnic, multiclass, and increasingly gender-balanced cast ensemble has set a valued social model for children as well, a far more diverse and positive multicultural modelling than anything offered by commercial television. Among the human characters on the show, there have always been substantial numbers of women and minorities, who go about their business of being human, not particularly being minorities. Sometimes the teaching is more focused. For example, there is a heavy drawing from various Hispanic cultures, including Spanish and bilingual English–Spanish songs, such as "Somos Hermanos"/"We are Brothers." During a segment in the 1991–1992 season, the characters from "Sesame Street" took a trip to the Crow Indian Reservation in Montana to learn about that particular Native American culture. There have also been visits to Louisiana for exposure to Cajun culture and food and zydeco music.

Besides being the most watched young children's TV show of all time, "Sesame Street" has also been the most carefully evaluated show, in terms of research. We turn now to some of the effects of watching "Sesame Street" (Ball & Bogatz, 1970; Bogatz & Ball, 1972; Cook et al., 1975).

As most parents can tell, children's attention and interest level while watching "Sesame Street" is high; preschoolers really do like the show. In terms of more substantive effects on learning, the results are mixed. There is some solid evidence for short-term effects, both in the sense of acquisition of prereading skills and positive social skills and attitudes, such as showing evidence of nonracist attitudes and behavior. Longer term effects are less clear, and some studies have shown that the advantages of watching "Sesame Street," compared to a control group not watching it, disappear after a few months or years (Bogatz & Ball, 1972).

Some interesting qualifications of these effects have been found. The positive effects are stronger if combined with parental discussion and teaching (Cook et al., 1975). This suggests that, among other functions, the program can serve as a good catalyst for informal education within the family, a theme returned to in chapter 12. Another interesting finding is that "Sesame Street" helped higher socioeconomic status children more than lower socioeconomic status children (Ball & Bogatz, 1970). Thus the show had the ironic effect of actually increasing the reading readiness gap between the higher and lower socioeconomic status children, when its stated goal had been to decrease that gap. In another sense, however, this should not have been unexpected, because any kind of intervention generally helps those who are most capable to begin with and thus more able to take full advantage of what it has to offer.

There were also positive social effects. Minority children watching "Sesame Street" showed increased cultural pride, confidence, and interpersonal cooperation (Greenberg, 1982). Also, after 2 years of watching "Sesame Street," White children showed more positive attitudes toward children of other races (Bogatz & Ball, 1972; Christensen & Roberts, 1983).

"Sesame Street" is still going strong after more than 20 years. New material is continually being created, but there is also a heavy reusing of old material, and old and new segments appear together in the same show. Preschoolers are not bothered by reruns; in fact, the familiarity makes it more attractive. Although often at the forefront of dealing with social issues, there are some areas about which "Sesame Street" has remained silent. For example, there generally is no treatment of religion or religious holidays and there are no gay or lesbian characters.

Other CTW Projects

In the fall of 1971, CTW launched a second major programming effort with "The Electric Company" (TEC), which used much of the successful "Sesame Street's" format but was aimed at improving the reading skills of older children (around second grade). TEC was heavily used in the schools as well as at home. Evaluative research (Ball & Bogatz, 1973) found that viewing TEC led to improved scores on a reading test battery in children who had watched in school, but there was no improvement compared to a control group in those who had merely watched "The Electric Company" at home. This suggests that the show was helpful in teaching reading, but primarily so in conjunction with the experiences offered in the classroom by the teacher and curriculum. Never as popular as "Sesame Street," it later operated in reruns and was finally cancelled in 1986.

A third CTW project, "3-2-1 Contact," debuted in 1980 with the goal of teaching scientific thinking to 8- to 12-year olds. It attempted to help children experience the excitement of scientific discovery and encourage all children, particularly girls and minorities, to feel comfortable with science as an endeavor (Mielke & Chen, 1983).

There have been other CTW projects (e.g., "Feeling Good," "The Lion, the Witch, and the Wardrobe," and "Square One TV"), as well as independent prosocial programs like "Where in the World is Carmen Sandiego?," "Ghostwriter," "Barney and Friends," "Freestyle," "Vegetable Soup," and "Infinity Factory." A continuing concern is obtaining funding for such productions, especially in the era of decreased federal assistance and general budget cutting in the United States. Some have criticized especially the newer programs for being more entertainment than education, due to economic pressures to attract an audience. For reviews of these programs and their effects, see Bryant, Alexander, and Brown (1983) and Watkins, Huston-Stein, and Wright (1980).

Changing Sex-Role Attitudes

A series called "Freestyle" was produced for U.S. public television with the intention of changing sex role attitudes in 9- to 12-year-olds. The 30-minute show presented episodes showing boys and girls learning nontraditional sex-role behavior (e.g., boys expressing nurturance and emotion, girls being independent and athletic). Evaluative research shows that sex-role attitudes changed in a less traditional direction after watching the show, particularly when the show was viewed at school and followed up with class discussion and exercises (Greenfield, 1984; Johnston & Ettema, 1982, 1986). Such a project suggests the considerable and still largely untapped potential of prosocial television in changing social norms.

Commercial TV Contributions

Similar effects may occur in responses to regular commercial programming. Corder-Bolz (1980) showed 5- to 11-year-old children an episode of the old sitcom "All in the Family," which featured a neighbor family where the husband and wife performed many nontraditional sex-role activities. Children were interviewed about sex-role attitudes before and after viewing. Children more than 5 years old showed decreased sex-role stereotyping after viewing the show, especially if an adult viewing the show with the child made supportive comments about the nonstereotypical behavior. Even entertainment shows not aimed primarily at children may carry strongly prosocial messages; see Box 11.1 for a discussion of the nonviolent messages of the action-adventure series "MacGyver," formerly a network prime-time show and since 1992 in syndication.

BOX II.I: MESSAGES OF "MacGYVER"

In many ways the action-adventure show "MacGyver" was the ultimate formula show. The lone hero confronts villain after villain, besting them all to extricate himself and others from impossible situations, while working for numerous noble causes and principles. There is, however, one striking difference between "Mac-Gyver" and other action-adventure shows: MacGyver never uses a weapon. He survives by his wits and inventiveness, plus a lot of scientific knowledge. He uses this knowledge regularly to break out of all sorts of captivity. For example, he escapes from a locked wine cellar on one show by using cylinders of compressed nitrogen to turn a wine barrel into a jet-propelled missile with enough force to break through a brick wall (Zechmeister & Johnson, 1992). Not surprisingly, Mac-Gyver star Richard Dean Anderson has some personal commitment to these issues; he has filmed PSAs for the Center to Prevent Handgun Violence. In one he urged parents to keep handguns out of the reach of children, and in another he explained to children the difference between handgun violence on TV and real life. Can "MacGyver" and its star have some prosocial impact?

The commercial networks have a limited amount of prosocial programming for children, primarily for those older than the "Sesame Street" audience. CBS' "In the News" provides brief news features to children during their Saturday morning cartoon diet. Some such recent efforts, such as NBC's "Main Street," ABC's "After School Specials," and CBS' "Schoolbreak Specials" have received critical plaudits, even if not attracting huge audiences. Through group discussion or dramatic stories, lessons are taught on a variety of issues. For example, "Schoolbreak Specials" have presented stories on dealing with a high school classmate who is gay or who has AIDS.

Perhaps the most controversial effort at a sort of prosocial children's TV has been Whittle Communications' "Channel One," a service of daily news for high school students. Offered directly to schools since 1990 in an attempt to partially remedy the often-bemoaned ignorance of world affairs and geography among youth, "Channel One" has been highly controversial since its inception, primarily because of its inclusion of 2 minutes of commercials, whose sales support the 10 minutes of news in the program. Although commercials are hardly new to teenagers, the "captive audience" nature of the school experience causes particular concern. Initial evaluation research (Greenberg & Brand, 1993) suggests that students report a greater desire to buy the advertised products, relative to a control group. Interestingly, another concern seldom expressed about "Channel One" is the potential for abuse of some future producers who might choose to set a particular agenda or offer a very biased view of the news.

An International Perspective

Prosocial programming for children is hardly a uniquely American phenomenon, however. For example, the Russian "Spaconi Nochi Malashi" ("Good Night, Little Ones") is a "Mister Rogers' Neighborhood"-type show appearing for 15 minutes every night at 8:00. Hosted by the attractive young mother Tatiana Vedeneeva, the show uses a spartan studio set, plus lots of high-tech puppets and animation. A favorite theme is teaching nonviolent and constructive means to resolving personal conflicts, as when puppets Karusha the pig and Stepashka the rabbit learn to set aside their differences and help each other pick up their toys. Vedeneeva and Fred Rogers became a part of the thaw in United States–Soviet relations in late 1987 when "Good Night, Little Ones" and "Mister Rogers' Neighborhood" broadcast cooperative shows from Moscow and Pittsburgh (Townley, 1988).

Educational television is used as an integral part of literacy programs for both children and adults in many Third World countries, sometimes in part compensating for a lack of qualified teachers or the funds to pay them. For example, the Teleniger project in the West African country of Niger uses TV lessons and grade school-educated teachers with 3 months of special training in how to interact with the students to maximize their learning from television. Reports show impressive gains in reading (Egly, 1973; Pierre, 1973; Schramm, 1977). See also reports of projects in Mexico (Diaz-Guerrero, Reyes-Lagunes, Witzke, & Holtzman, 1976; Himmelweit, 1978) and El Salvador (Mayo, Hornik, & McAnany, 1976).

PROSOCIAL ADULT TELEVISION

The target of prosocial media is not always children, however, and the purpose is not always connected with reading or literacy. The media may be used for other socially positive purposes appealing to adults as well. This approach has been especially used in developing countries, which is our focus here. Let us now examine some of these.

In many developing countries, television has been seen as a tool for development and positive social change, rather than largely a vehicle for entertainment. One of the earliest concerted efforts in this direction came in 1975–1982 from the Mexican network Televisa, which produced several series of programs, many in the very popular genre of telenovela (soap opera). These were designed to promote gender equality, adult literacy, sexual responsibility, and family planning (Brown, Singhal, & Rogers, 1989; Lozano, 1992; Rogers & Singhal, 1990; Singhal & Rogers, 1989b). The shows were very popular and viewers did request the services promoted by the programs (Lozano, 1992).

Televisa's model of communicating prosocial messages through entertainment was emulated elsewhere. In 1987 Kenya aired the prosocial soap opera "Tushariane" ("Let's Discuss") designed to promote family planning; it became the most popular show in the history of Kenyan TV (Brown & Singhal, 1990). The Nigerian soap opera "Cock Crow at Dawn" encouraged the adoption of modern agricultural practices (Ume-Nwagbo, 1986). Televisa's "Sangre Joven" ("Young Blood") telenovela of the early 1990s dealt with family planning, AIDS, and drug abuse. Jamaica produced a family planning radio soap opera "Naseberry Street," which reached 40% of the Jamaican population from 1985 to 1989 (Rogers & Singhal, 1990).

One of the most impressive commercial successes was the Indian TV drama "Hum Log" ("We People"), which debuted in 1984. It became the most popular program in the history of Indian TV and also had substantial social impact (Brown & Cody, 1991; Singhal & Rogers, 1989a, 1989c). Although a commercial entertainment program, "Hum Log" also had the overt purpose of advancing the status of women, dealing with such issues as wife battering, the dowry system, and political and social equality of women and men. At the end of every episode, a famous Indian film actor gave a 30- to 50-second summary of the episode and appropriate guides to action. "Hum Log" encouraged women to work outside of the home and to make more of their own decisions.

Evaluation research (Brown & Cody, 1991) found the show's impact to be complex and not always what was predicted. For example, many women viewers identified with the "negative" role model Bhagwanti, the family matriarch and traditional woman, rather than her more independent daughters Badki and Chutki, at least in part because of discouragement over the difficulties that the younger women's more independent stance had brought to them. There is an interesting parallel between the effects of "Hum Log" and the U.S. show "All in the Family," where more traditional viewers identified with the bigoted Archie Bunker and found him to be a more positive figure than the producers had envisioned (Vidmar & Rokeach, 1974).

In considering the conclusions about the effectiveness of entertainment–education media in developing countries, Rogers and Singhal (1990; see also Rogers & Singhal, 1989, and Singhal & Rogers, 1989a) drew five conclusions:

1. Placing an educational message in an entertainment context can draw a mass audience and earn large profits, which thus support the prosocial campaign.
2. The educational message cannot be too blatant or hard sell or the audience will reject it.
3. The effect of the media message in such programs is enhanced by supplementary specific tips on behavior change.
4. The repetition of prosocial themes in a telenovela has a greater effect than a one-shot media PSA campaign.

5. Prosocial campaigns are most successful if the media, government, commercial sponsors, and public health organizations work together.

We now turn from prosocial media to looking at social marketing more broadly, with an eye to seeing how the use of mass media fit in as part of an overall social marketing campaign.

MEDIA USE IN SOCIAL MARKETING

A traditionally underemphasized but currently booming area of marketing is *social marketing*, which involves the "selling" of socially and personally positive behaviors like taking steps to insure or improve one's health or safety (Atkin & Arkin, 1990; Barach, 1984; Bloom & Novelli, 1981; Flay & Burton, 1990; Manrai & Gardner, 1992; Wallack, 1990). Many social critics, researchers, and practitioners long concerned with selling products are now turning their attention to how to sell healthy, safe, and socially positive behaviors. Clearly mass media are a major, although not the only, component of a social marketing campaign. The perceived reality of the medium is intended to be a catalyst for some behavior or attitude change.

Obstacles to Social Marketing

Although selling good health or safety is in many ways not unlike selling soap or automobiles, there are some difficulties that are particularly acute for social marketing. Social and product advertising differ in several important ways, most of which lead to greater obstacles facing public health and other social advertisers, compared to commercial advertisers (Fine, 1981; Manrai & Gardner, 1992; Schlinger, 1976).

First, social ideas tend to have a higher degree of both shared benefits and shared responsibilities than products. For example, some (perhaps most) of the benefits of recycling household waste will be to society, not to the individual. Those individuals may view society as also having much (or most) of the responsibility for the problem. Thus motivating ("selling") the social message will be more difficult than selling a product with individual benefits.

Second, the benefits that do exist with social marketing tend to be delayed and/or intangible. Often there is a great physical, or at least psychological, distance between the "consumer" and the "product." Selling toothpaste can stress how much sexier your breath will be for that big date tonight. Selling the idea of quitting smoking has a much less immediate payoff. Teenage smokers think much more about looking cool with their friends this weekend than dying from lung cancer or emphysema in 30–40 years. Young healthy adults do not typically feel much urgency to sign an organ donor card; the need is very distant psychologically. Often in social marketing, the consumer is not all that opposed to the message and may even support it; they simply do not feel the immediacy of it and thus are not particularly inclined to act on the message.

Third, the social marketing campaign may be very complex, compared to what is typically involved in commercial marketing. Particularly in regard to health, the beliefs, attitudes, and motives for unhealthy practices are deeply rooted and highly emotion laden and thus very resistant to change. For example, trying to convince women to self-examine their breasts for lumps flies against their enormous fear of cancer and the potential damage to one's sexual self-image by the contemplation of possible breast surgery. Convincing people to wear seatbelts when they have driven for 50 years without them is not easy. Encouraging people to sign an organ donor card forces at least a fleeting contemplation of one's mortality and thus becomes a very unpleasant request. People are particularly resistant to change if such anxieties occur also in the context of unrealistic fears (e.g., fear of being declared dead prematurely in order to acquire organs for transplantation; Hessing & Elffers, 1986; Shanteau & Harris, 1990).

Fourth, social marketing messages frequently face strong opposition, unlike product advertising. This opposition may be social, as in the adolescent peer group that encourages and glamorizes drug use, or it may be organized and institutional, as when tobacco companies threaten to withdraw advertising from magazines that carry articles about the dangers of smoking. Social marketing campaigns are typically not well-funded, often with opposing forces holding much of the economic and political power. For example, the Tobacco Institute, the oil industry, and National Rifle Association are tremendously powerful lobbies set to oppose media messages against smoking, alternative energy sources, or handgun purchase restrictions. Public service announcements (PSAs), whether print or broadcast, often are noticeably poorer in technical quality and appear less frequently than commercial ads, because of budget limitations. Although radio and TV stations air a certain number of unpaid PSAs, they generally do so at the hours when they are least able to profitably sell advertising. We see many PSAs during the "late late movie" and very few during the Super Bowl or "Murder She Wrote." Thus specific demographic groups cannot be targeted by PSAs as well as they can by commercial advertising.

Fifth, social marketers often set unrealistically high goals, such as changing the behavior of 50%–100% of the public. Although a commercial ad that affects 1%–10% of consumers is hugely successful, social marketers often have not fully appreciated that an ad that affects even a very small percentage of a mass audience is a substantial accomplishment. Persons preparing social marketing campaigns are often less thoroughly trained in advertising, media, and marketing than those conducting product ad campaigns.

Finally, social marketing appeals are often aimed at the 15% or so of the population that is least likely to change. These may be the least educated, most traditional, or most backward segment of the population, precisely the people least likely to stop smoking, start wearing seatbelts, or request medical check-ups. Just as political media strategists target advertising at the few undecided voters, so might social marketing better target those people most conducive to attitude and behavior change in the intended direction, rather than the group that is least likely to ever change at all.

Considering the Audience

Knowing the audience well and targeting it as specifically as possible is helpful. Targeting a reasonable audience, not the ones least likely to change, and setting realistic goals and targets are useful. Trying to see the issue from the audience's point of view will make a more convincing message. Frequently social marketers are fervently convinced of the rightness of their message and fail to see how anyone else could view the issue differently. Self-righteousness tends not to be convincing. The attitudes, desires, motivations, and reasonable beliefs of the audience may be used to drive the character of the message. A serious consideration of what kinds of psychological appeals will be the most effective in motivating the particular target audience will be helpful; see Box 11.2 for an unusual approach using shame as a motivator for a PSA. Sometimes the most apparently obvious motivations may not in fact be the most convincing; see Box 11.3 for an example of such a counterintuitive case.

Focusing on specific behaviors that the audience may change, one small step at a time, is often more useful than a general exhortation aimed at changing attitudes. Very often people know very well that they should stop smoking or start wearing seat belts. What they most need are more specific realistic behaviors that can be used to meet that end. Often existing motivation may be harnessed and channeled to build confidence in taking appropriate specific actions. Merely exhorting people to stop smoking may be of limited use. Showing a PSA of a young child smoking and talking about how cool he looks, "just like Daddy," might reach the smoking parent more effectively. For further discussion of the particular problems facing social marketing, see Barach (1984), Bloom and Novelli (1981), and Manrai and Gardner (1992).

Characteristics of Effective Campaigns

Flay and Burton (1990; see also Brown & Einsiedel, 1990) identified seven steps for a public health media campaign to be maximally effective:

1. Develop and use high quality messages, sources, and channels.
2. Disseminate effectively to the most appropriate target audience.
3. Gain and keep the attention of the audience.

BOX 11.2: SHAMING PEOPLE TO CLEAN UP AFTER THEIR DOGS

Although positive feel-good emotions and negative fear appeals are the most typical psychological appeals in advertising (see chapter 4), other sorts of negative motivators can on occasion be effective. Tony Schwartz wrote an advertisement employing a very strong shame appeal to exhort people not to let their dogs mess up the sidewalks:

> Let me ask you something. Have you ever seen someone allow his dog to go on the sidewalk? Sometimes right in front of a doorway, maybe your doorway? Did it make you feel angry? Well, don't get angry at the poor soul. Feel sorry for him. He's just a person who's not able to train his dog. He's just not capable of it. In fact, after he's had his dog for a short time, what happens? The dog trains him. So the next time you see a person like that on the street, take a good look at him, and while you're looking, feel sorry for him because you know he just can't help himself, even though he might like to. Some people are strong enough and smart enough to train their dogs to take a few steps off the sidewalk. Other people aren't. Makes you wonder, doesn't it, if the master is at the top of the leash or the bottom of the leash. (Schwartz, 1981, pp. 100–101)

Sometimes what people at first think would motivate someone does not in fact do so. Schwartz (1981) offered another example where New York City police wanted to encourage elderly crime victims to report crimes more faithfully. Appeals to deal with the presumed fear of retribution from the young hoodlums were largely ineffective, until someone discovered that the real reason for lack of reporting was a fear by the residents that reporting crimes would cause their own children to insist that they move from the neighborhood that they considered their home. Schwartz then suggested an appeal based on keeping the neighborhood safer and thus not having to move away.

---

4. Encourage favorable interpersonal communication about the issue after exposure to the message.
5. Work for behavior changes, as well as changes in awareness, knowledge, and attitudes.
6. Work for broader societal changes.
7. Obtain knowledge of campaign effectiveness through evaluation research.

Although theory-building in this area has not been extensive, Manrai and Gardner (1992) have developed a model to explain how the differences between social and product advertising predict a consumer's cognitive, social, and emotional reactions to social advertising.

BOX 11.3: SELF- AND OTHER-ORIENTED APPEALS
TO DONATE ORGANS

What type of appeal in a PSA would be the most effective in persuading someone to become a kidney donor? Barnett, Klassen, McMinimy, and Schwarz (1987) suggested a surprising answer. Research participants heard a PSA from the (fictitious) National Kidney Association, which stressed either self- or other-oriented reasons for donating a kidney. The other-oriented PSA included the following:

> Few decisions in your life will have such a dramatic effect on the lives of others. A donated kidney provides immeasurable benefit to those who receive the donation. It will help others overcome a debilitating and potentially life-threatening kidney disease. Just imagine how they will feel to be healthy and to live a normal life again with their family and friends. Please consider the decision to donate. Do it for them. (Barnett et al., 1987, pp. 335–336)

The self-oriented PSA was identical except for the following:

> Few decisions in your life will be as meaningful to you as this one. Donating can be extremely beneficial to you, the person who makes the positive decision to donate. It is an important personal decision that will make you feel better about yourself and says something very positive about you as an individual. People who learn of your decision will undoubtedly think of you as a good and caring person. Please consider the decision to donate. Do it for yourself. (Barnett et al., 1987, pp. 335–336)

In a subsequent questionnaire, college-student subjects rated the other-oriented PSA as presenting the reasons for donating more clearly but found the self-oriented PSA more convincing, in terms of reported inclination to donate one's own or a next-of-kin's kidneys upon death. This suggests that, even though people most often volunteer other-oriented, altruistic motives for organ donation (Fellner & Marshall, 1981; Hessing & Elffers, 1986; Prottas, 1983; Shanteau & Harris, 1990), they may in fact be more convinced by more self-centered appeals.

Positive Effects of Social Marketing

In spite of the obstacles, there are several clear positive effects that social marketing media campaigns have (Barach, 1984; Bloom & Novelli, 1981; Schlinger, 1976). The first effect is an altered perceived reality that includes a heightened awareness of the problem. Virtually everyone in North America is aware of the health dangers of smoking; this was not the case 40 years ago. Unlike 10–20 years ago, most people today are aware of the need for organ donors (Shanteau & Harris, 1990), largely due to media publicity. Also, sometimes a media campaign on some specific health issue can raise the level of awareness about health topics generally.

A second positive effect is making the problem more salient, thus increasing receptivity to other influences in the same direction later. Even though a particular PSA may not immediately send a person to the doctor to check a suspicious mole for possible melanoma, that person may pay more attention to a later message on that topic and may be a little more careful about excessive exposure to the sun. An eventual behavioral effect may actually be a cumulative effect from several influences. This, of course, makes it very difficult to scientifically measure such effects of media campaigns.

A third effect of media campaigns is the stimulation of later conversation with one's family, friends, or doctor. Publicity about the dangers of smoking may encourage supper table conversation between parents and teen-agers encouraged by peers to smoke. Although a decision not to smoke may result more from the personal interaction than directly from the message, the latter may have partially laid the groundwork for the discussion. By the early 1990s pediatricians were being warned against overdiagnosing Lyme disease. A high level of media publicity over the preceding few years was leading patients to ask about this illness and physicians to be quicker to diagnose it.

A fourth effect of social marketing campaigns is the generation of self-initiated information seeking. Someone may seek additional information on some topic as a result of their interest being piqued by media attention to that issue. They might ask the doctor about it on their next visit; they might read a newspaper article on the topic that they would not have noted before.

Finally, prosocial media campaigns can reinforce positive existing attitudes and behavior, such as encouraging the ex-smoker to try hard not to succumb or reinforcing someone's feeling that he or she really should see a doctor about some medical condition. Often people know what they should do but need a little encouragement to actually do it.

Now we examine one of the major domains of social marketing campaigns, public health.

Public Health Media Campaigns

Breslow (1978) identified three methods of risk-factor intervention in medicine. *Epidemiological* intervention involves identifying the characteristics correlated with increased frequency of the disease and taking steps to reduce those characteristics (e.g., identifying cardiovascular risk factors like smoking, obesity, cholesterol level, physical inactivity, and hypertension, followed by screening people with blood pressure and blood chemistry tests).

Environmental intervention involves taking steps to change the environment in a healthier direction. For example, legislation restricting smoking in public places or reducing industrial emissions into the air or water, and adding fluoride to drinking water, illustrate such interventions. Adding air bags to cars, substituting corn oil for coconut oil in fried foods, and selling lower fat milk also manipulate the environment.

The third type of intervention, *educational* programs, often involving the media, are of most concern for our purposes here. Such programs may aim to alter the perceived reality by changing knowledge (providing more information about risk factors) or providing an impetus for changing behavior (persuading people to stop smoking). Often changes in knowledge are easier to effect than changes in behavior. For example, even though most smokers are well aware that smoking is bad for their health, their own perceived reality, at least at an emotional level, is that they will not develop lung cancer. Sometimes the most important cognitive message of such a campaign is that treatment and cure is possible if the illness is diagnosed early enough. This is important in combatting irrational fears that a diagnosis of cancer is a death sentence and thus to be avoided at all costs.

All three types of interventions must keep in mind the culture of the target population (Ilola, 1990). For example, an AIDS-prevention campaign would (or at least should) take a very different form if targeted at North American gay men, IV drug users, health care workers, or promiscuous African heterosexuals. See Box 11.4 for a discussion of the effectiveness of AIDS PSAs aimed at different groups.

Stanford Heart Disease Project. A very clear and consistent finding from studies of public health social marketing campaigns is that mass media campaigns are most successful when used in conjunction with other types of intervention (see Solomon & Cardillo, 1985, for a discussion of the components of such campaigns). A good example of such a campaign is the extensive and relatively well-controlled project conducted by Stanford University to reduce the instance of coronary heart disease (Maccoby & Solomon, 1981). This project involved three towns with a population of 12,000–15,000 each in central California. Two of the towns received multimedia campaigns about coronary heart disease (CHD) over a 2-year period. One of those towns also received intensive interventions targeted at the high-risk population. These interventions involved both media messages and cooperation of the medical community. Health screenings were held, specific behavior-modification programs were set up, and people's attempted reduction of high-risk behaviors and characteristics was monitored.

Changes in both knowledge and behavior were monitored in both of the experimental towns and in the control town, which received no media campaign and no intervention. Results show that media campaigns by themselves produced some increases in knowledge but only very modest, if any, changes in behavior and/or decreases in the overall percentage of at-risk people. Media campaigns, coupled with specific behavioral interventions and health monitoring, produced substantial improvements and reduction of the numbers in the at-risk population.

BOX 11.4: AIDS PSAs: WHEN DO THEY WORK?

One of the most urgent recent health issues for PSA campaigns has been AIDS. Worldwide, different nations and organizations have taken a variety of media approaches in trying to increase general awareness and knowledge and to change risky behaviors, especially in target groups like gay men, intravenous drug users, and promiscuous heterosexuals.

What kind of appeal is most effective? A content analysis of 127 AIDS-awareness PSAs in the United States televised in 1988 shows that most were directed at general audiences, rather than target audiences at high risk. They tended to use rational rather than emotional appeals and emphasized the acquisition of information rather than change of behaviors (Friemuth, Hammond, Edgar, & Monahan, 1990). Taking an experimental approach, Flora and Maibach (1990) measured subjects' personal cognitive involvement with the AIDS issue and exposed them either to a rational or emotional PSA. Results show that emotional appeals were more memorable than rational ones, especially for low-involvement subjects. Emotional appeals were also more effective in stimulating a desire to learn more about AIDS. For a careful analysis of changing Australian media messages about AIDS, see Tulloch (1989), Tulloch and Chapman (1992), and Tulloch, Kippax, and Crawford (1993).

Sometimes certain high-risk groups react differently to AIDS spots than the general public does (Baggaley, 1988). In general, prevention programs targeted at White gay men have been the most successful in changing risky behaviors (Coates, 1990; Stall, Coates, & Hoff, 1988; Witte, 1992), whereas the more general appeals and those targeted at other groups have been less successful. Especially in the developing world, changes in longstanding and deep-rooted social customs are required to slow the spread of AIDS. For example, in parts of central Africa, where AIDS is spread primarily from men to women by heterosexual intercourse, polygamy and multiple sex partners for men are condoned, and women have little social power to resist men's sexual advances or insist on condom use. Such behaviors and attitudes may be extremely resistant to change, but will have to be altered before the spread of AIDS can be contained.

A similar program, the North Karelia project in rural Eastern Finland, which had one of the highest CHD rates in the world, had national and local government cooperation. Along with media campaigns and medical intervention, environmental interventions were instituted, including restrictions on smoking, selling more low-fat dairy foods, and substitution of mushrooms for fat in the local sausage. After 4½ years of the project, there were dramatic reductions in systolic blood pressure and stroke incidence (McAlister, Puska, & Solonen, 1982).

CONCLUSION

A recurring theme throughout this chapter, if not throughout the entire book, is that the effect that the media has depends on more than its content. What happens in the context of media consumption is also important in the perceived reality constructed by viewers, readers, or listeners as their minds interact with the TV, radio, or written message. Programs like "Sesame Street" have more positive impact if buttressed by related conversations and work in the home or school. It also helps if the prosocial message is in an entertaining context and of high artistic and technical quality, like "Sesame Street" or "Hum Log." Frightening or troubling aspects of television may be made less threatening by sensitive adult discussion with the viewing child. Media exhortations to live a healthier lifestyle are more effective if combined with behavioral interventions with specific tips on how to do so and support for efforts in that direction. See Wober (1988) for an examination of the systems available for maximizing the benefits of television.

This idea is not unlike research on how children and adults survive traumatic life experiences in general (e.g., Leavitt & Fox, in press). The ones who survive and grow, rather than suffer defeat and trauma, are those who have support in the rough times, those who can talk over the troubling events and have countervailing positive influences to partially balance the strong negative ones.

It is almost a truism that television and other media may be a force for ill or good. Much writing and research has focused on the ill wind of TV. Television and other media are with us to stay; we cannot isolate our children from these influences. We can, however, take steps to make that interaction a more positive, even rewarding, experience than it would be otherwise. This theme is continued in the next chapter.

12

LIVING CONSTRUCTIVELY
WITH MEDIA

Q: Television preacher and evangelist Jerry Falwell once sued *Penthouse* magazine for publishing a freelance interview with him, but he frequently appeared on TV talk shows on the same forum as those involved in the pornography business. Why?

A: According to Meyrowitz (1985, p. 84), "Finding Falwell in *Penthouse* is like finding him in a red-light district, but finding him on television is like meeting him in a metaphysical arena that is neither here nor there."

Q: What was Mexican soap opera star Veronica Castro doing in Moscow in September 1992?

A: Being entertained by President Boris Yeltsin and Russian Parliament members. Her triumphal tour was in celebration of the success of the Mexican telenovela "The Rich Also Cry" in Russia. It had recently drawn 200 million daily viewers, 70% of the nation's population, making it the most watched TV series in the history of the world (Kopkind, 1993).

In this book we have examined the way that the perceived reality that we create from the media often deviates substantially from the real world. Although media are not the only source of knowledge about the world, our perceived reality of what the world is like is often far more heavily influenced by the media than we realize. It greatly affects our attitudes and behavior when we implicitly assume that the world of the media faithfully reflects the real world. In much of this book we have discussed the media in a global fashion that may inadvertently suggest that the differences among television, radio, and print are nonexistent or irrelevant. Most of the research that has been done, as well as most of the public concern, focuses on television. Nonetheless, it is worthwhile to examine some of the differences between the types of media. In this final chapter, we examine some of those differences, as they relate to the perceived reality theme. Following that, we focus on behavioral responses that we can make to media, including media literacy campaigns in the school and home and political strategies designed to induce change in media. Finally, we look at the way that the reporting of news about the media in the press may affect the perceived reality constructed in the minds of the public.

COMPARISON OF DIFFERENT MEDIA

Although fiction occurs in both written and television format, children recognize at an earlier age that books are fiction (Kelly, 1981); television looks more like real life. Thus the perceived reality based on television is more easily confused with reality itself than is the printed construction of reality. The medium itself affects how the child can extract information from that medium and represent it in memory (Salomon, 1979, 1983, 1987). In general, television involves a lower amount of invested mental effort (AIME) than print media, although this varies with age and type of program (Bordeaux & Lange, 1991; Salomon, 1984). Lower socioeconomic status and minority children are even more likely to accept the television reality as accurate than are White middle-class children (Dorr, 1982).

Greenfield (1984) offered an insightful discussion of the historical development of media in regard to the psychological processes engaged by each medium. The onset of print media several centuries ago permitted the tangible storage of information for the first time. People who had acquired the skill of literacy thus had access to vast amounts of information previously unavailable except through oral tradition. Literacy also had a social implication, in that it was the first medium of communication that required solitude for its effective practice. Critics of television who fear that its advent has isolated children from social interaction are in fact concerned about an earlier effect of the onset of print media; television only continued the requirement of physical isolation, but did not initiate it. In fact, research has shown no relationship between amount of television watched and time spent in interpersonal activity (reviewed in Murray, 1980).

Information Extraction

In some ways radio and newspapers may have more in common cognitively with each other than either does with TV. Both radio and print are largely verbal media, whereas television involves the pictorial dimension as well. There is a positive correlation between the comprehension of a story read from a book and one heard on the radio, but less relationship between a story read and one seen on television (Pezdek & Hartman, 1983; Pezdek, Lehrer, & Simon, 1984; Pezdek & Stevens, 1984). This suggests that skills for extracting information from television are different from those used to extract information from the words of radio or print. Studies of television show that children derive more information from the visual component than from the verbal one (Hayes & Birnbaum, 1980), although the high degree of redundancy between the two generally aids comprehension. Overall, comprehension of information presented via television was better than the same story presented via radio to second- and sixth-grade children (Pezdek et al., 1984). Thus television is a very efficient way to transmit information to children, suggesting both greater potential and greater concern regarding this medium.

Beagles-Roos and Gat (1983) had children retell a story heard on the radio or seen on television. The style of the retold stories differed in an interesting fashion. Retold TV stories contained more vague references, such as the use of pronouns without identifying the referent, the use of definite articles ("the" boy . . .) without first introducing the referent, and other forms presupposing more shared information with the hearer. Retold radio stories provided more information, much as a radio sports play-by-play provides more information than a televised play-by-play. Having children write a story from either "TV" or "real life," Watkins (1988) found that the amount of television the child watched determined how elaborate and complex the "TV story" was. Greenfield (1984) suggested that one subtle effect of watching a lot of television could be to learn a verbal style that is relatively vague in reference, much like talking face-to-face. In both cases much shared knowledge may be assumed and thus less must be explicitly explained. With radio and print, however, the language must be more explicit to compensate for the lack of a pictorial component.

Baggett (1979) found that adults recalled information from either a silent movie (*The Red Balloon*) or a constructed spoken version equally well, whereas young children remembered the silent film version better. This visual advantage in memory may be part of the appeal of television. Although it decreases somewhat with age, it is a natural characteristic of our information-processing systems, rather than one that is subtly induced by television exposure. The visual continues to have some advantage even with adults, however. In delayed testing a week later, Baggett found that the adults also showed better memory for the visual than the verbal story.

One sometimes hears the claim that radio is the medium requiring the most imagination, due to the need to mentally fill in the missing visual aspect. A fascinating study reported in Greenfield (1984) had children complete interrupted stories told via radio or television. Results showed that radio stories evoked more novel elements in the imagined story endings than did the televised versions of the same stories. For a thorough review of the medium of radio and its effects, see MacFarland (1990).

Singer and Singer (1981) found that preschool children who watched more

TV were less likely to have an imaginary playmate and showed lower scores on imaginative play. It may depend on the nature of the program, however. "Sesame Street" and especially the slower paced "Mister Rogers' Neighborhood" have been shown to stimulate imaginative play (Singer & Singer, 1976; Tower, Singer, & Singer, 1979), whereas action-adventure shows are associated with the lowest imaginative play scores (Singer & Singer, 1981). Of course, television does teach visual information-processing skills and is overall a very efficient way to transmit information, especially to children. See also Meringoff (1980) and Meringoff et al. (1983) for a comparison of acquisition of stories from different media.

Taking a field study approach to comparing information transmission through different media, Spencer, Seydlitz, Laska, and Triche (1992) compared the public's responses to newspaper and television reports of an actual natural hazard, in this case the saltwater intrusion from the Gulf of Mexico into the lower Mississippi River in 1988. Results found that each medium was better in different ways in communicating information and eliciting responses to this hazard. Newspapers were better at presenting complex and potentially ambiguous information about possible consequences of the hazard, whereas television was better in communicating material that was relatively simple and in making direct behavior appeals (e.g., buying bottled water).

Does watching television interfere with the development of reading skills? It probably depends on what activity television is replacing. See Box 12.1, for a look at several hypotheses about the effects of television on reading. Under a few specialized conditions, watching television in itself actually involves extensive reading; see Box 12.2.

We look now at the practical concern of what may be done, in a general sense, to help children better deal with media, especially television, which they are inevitably going to be exposed to.

MEDIA LITERACY

There is increasing recognition of the need for a higher level of media literacy in modern society. There were consumer media-education movements as far back as the 1970s, although interest greatly increased starting in the 1980s (Alvarado, Gutch, & Wollen, 1987; Brown, 1991; Manley-Casimir & Luke, 1987; Masterman, 1985; Ploghoft & Anderson, 1982). Consistent with recent theory and research on mass communication, the contemporary emphasis is more on empowerment for choice rather than "protection from the dangerous influence." No one can be realistically shielded from media; they are omnipresent and enduring parts of our lives. Rather, we must learn to live with not only traditional print and electronic media, but also with all the new technologies of mass and personal media (Dorr & Kunkel, 1990; Ganley, 1992).

BOX 12.1: DOES TV WATCHING INTERFERE WITH READING SKILLS?

A common concern of many parents is that their children watch too much television and do not read enough. Beentjes and van der Voort (1989) identified several hypotheses about the effect of watching TV on reading and looked at the support for each of them.

A *stimulation hypothesis* argues that watching television stimulates or enhances reading. Not a theory that is widely held, only two small pieces of evidence support it, namely reading subtitles on foreign TV (see Box 12.2) and reading a book directly based on a TV show after watching the show.

More widely believed and scientifically studied is some sort of *reduction hypothesis*, with TV watching having a negative impact on reading. There are five variations of this hypothesis. First, the *passivity hypothesis* argues that TV causes children to become more mentally lazy and less prepared to invest the mental effort necessary for reading. Although it is true that TV requires less mental effort than reading (Salomon, 1984, 1987), viewers are far from totally passive. A second variety of reduction hypothesis is *concentration-deterioration*, which says that TV weakens a child's ability to concentrate. There is really no support for this either. The least promising of the reduction hypotheses is probably the *retardation hypothesis*, which argues that TV deteriorates or rots the brain. The active verbal and visual information processing required in watching TV or any other medium makes this untenable. The *anti-school hypothesis* argues that TV leads children to expect school to be as entertaining as "Sesame Street" or "Barney and Friends" and, when it is not, they lose motivation. This is a difficult hypothesis to study empirically, and the evidence that does exist is inconclusive. Finally, the *displacement hypothesis* argues that television hurts reading but only when it takes away time from reading. Although all the research is not entirely consistent (see Mutz, Roberts, & van Vuuren, 1993; Ritchie, Price, & Roberts, 1987), this hypothesis has the most support. If children watch TV instead of reading, it may diminish their reading skills. If they watch TV in addition to reading, there probably is no detrimental effect.

Part of media literacy involves learning the formal features of each particular medium. For example, as children mature and experience more TV, part of the perceived reality naturally arising from that experience is the knowledge of how to interpret the cuts, fades, dissolves, and general montage techniques used in the editing of film to make a TV show. Very young children may misinterpret things that they see on television because they fail to understand such techniques. Merely having acquired such television literacy, however, does not insure a critical processing of program content or a careful comparison of such material with external reality. These skills must be taught more intentionally, either in the school or the home.

BOX 12.2: READING, IGNORING, OR NOT HAVING TO DEAL WITH SUBTITLES

In much of the world a considerable amount of television is imported from some-place where a different language is spoken. Thus the program is either dubbed or subtitled in the local language. Dubbing allows one to hear one's own language, even though it does not match the lips of the characters on the screen. However, reading subtitles while simultaneously processing the visual content and ignoring the sound track in an unfamiliar language involves a set of cognitive skills that requires some practice to do effectively. Belgian psychologist Gery d'Ydewalle and his colleagues (e.g., d'Ydewalle, Praet, Verfaillie, & Van Rensbergen, 1991) did a series of studies measuring eye movements as indicators of people's relative attention to subtitles and visual content. They found that people look at subtitles in their own language and may find them distracting in cases where they know both the languages involved. Belgians are familiar with reading subtitles; most of their movies and much television is foreign and subtitled, sometimes bilingually in two subtitled parallel lines in French and Dutch (the country's two languages).

Subtitling, dubbing, and the original language can interact in some interesting ways in the mind of a multilingual viewer. For example, I remember once in Brazil seeing an Ingmar Bergman film with lips moving in Swedish but dubbed in English and subtitled in Portuguese! On other occasions I saw French films subtitled in Portuguese; my intermediate-level knowledge of both languages allowed me to pick up most of the story from simultaneously processing the French sound track and the Portuguese subtitles, although my mind was pretty exhausted after 2 hours!

The United States is unusual among nations in having virtually no subtitled television available. Presumably because so much domestic programming, almost all in English, is available, U.S. audiences have never had to become used to reading subtitles. Subtitled foreign films are shown, but only as "art" films to highly restricted audiences. The conventional industry wisdom, accurate or not, is that American audiences will not watch foreign language subtitled films or television. Some (e.g., Zoglin, 1992) have argued that this assumption excludes much high-quality and potentially popular television from U.S. screens.

Curriculum Development

Numerous attempts have been made to develop curricula for use in schools to help children become more critical viewers of television. For an extensive review and careful evaluation of these projects in the United States and elsewhere, see Brown (1991). Such curricula have been developed by school districts (e.g., Idaho Falls, Idaho, New York City, Eugene, Oregon), universities (e.g., Yale, Boston University), religious organizations (e.g., U.S. Catholic Conference, Media Action

Research Center), private companies (e.g., The Learning Seed Co., Television Learning, Ltd.), United Nations/UNESCO, and other governmental or public interest groups (e.g., Scottish Film Council, Western Australia Ministry of Education, National Congress of Parents and Teachers).

Although even a superficial examination of the different media literacy curricula is beyond the scope of this book, as an example we examine briefly the program developed by Dorothy and Jerome Singer and their colleagues at Yale University starting in the late 1970s. They offer eight lessons to be taught twice a week over a 4-week period to third-, fourth-, and fifth-grade children. Topics included reality and fantasy on TV, camera effects, commercials, stereotypes, identification with TV characters, and violence and aggression. Evaluation studies showed sizable increases in knowledge by the experimental group, particularly at immediate testing. The program was then extended to kindergarten, first-, and second-grade children; extensive pilot testing suggested that such children could be taught considerable amounts about the nature of television through such a curriculum (Singer & Singer, 1981, 1983; Singer, Singer, & Zuckerman, 1981; Singer, Zuckerman, & Singer, 1980).

A second sample project is that of Dorr, Graves, and Phelps (1980). Their materials used taped TV excerpts and group discussion, role playing, games, and teacher commentary. One emphasis was on the economic bases of the broadcasting industry, stressing, for example, that the "bottom-line" purpose of television is to sell advertising time to make money. A second emphasis, very much in line with the theme of this book, stressed how TV programs vary greatly in realism. It encouraged children to critically evaluate the reality of each show in several ways. In evaluative research, Dorr et al.'s (1980) curriculum was shown to engender a questioning attitude about television and skepticism about its accurate reflection of reality.

One of the most recent efforts has been the Center for Media and Values Media Literacy Workshop Kits (Thoman, 1991). These packets of readings, group activities, videos, and discussion starters deal with such topics as images of war and peace, parenting and TV, advertising, citizenship and media, and news. At present these are too new to have been carefully evaluated.

What Can Be Done in the Home

Media education should not be limited only to the classroom, however. Whatever the negative effects of television on children, they can be mitigated, and perhaps even turned to positive changes, through dialogue in the home (Corder-Bolz, 1980), leading to development of what have sometimes been called "receivership skills" (Ploghoft & Anderson, 1982). Although it is obviously not possible to always be with the child when he or she is watching television, an effort to be there at least some of the time may pay off. As the family watches television together, conversation may occur about deceptive advertising, stereotyped group portrayals, antisocial values, or excessive sex or violence. Parents can question the children about their reactions to what is on TV, thus better understanding the perceived reality held by the child. They may comment about their own reactions, thus providing a balance to what may be a skewed portrayal on TV. For example, during my preteen period of being enamoured with game shows, I remember my father commenting, as I watched "The Price Is Right," that the winners had to pay lots of taxes on all of their prizes; it was Dad's way of doing some antimaterialism values teaching. Johnsson-Smaragdi (1983) found some evidence that family interaction, especially for children around 11 years old, was facilitated by television viewing, at least when it was seen as an important family interactive activity. Even sibling coviewing, without parents, may have some positive effects, e.g., in reducing fearful responses to suspenseful programs (Wilson & Weiss, 1993).

Such parental discussions may help the child deal with troubling material, such as extreme sex or violence, or with a theme that is cognitively too difficult to follow without some adult "translation." Such discussion during the news may help the child learn about events of the world. Television may be used as a catalyst for discussion of important issues within the family. Although it may be difficult for a parent and child to discuss sex or drugs, for example, it may be easier in the context of discussing a TV program on that theme. Even if the program was not particularly well done or consistent with the family's values, it still may serve as a relatively nonthreatening catalyst for discussing the issue.

Television need not be an antisocial medium that isolates one family member from another (the "shut-up-I'm-trying-to-watch" model). It can also be an activity that brings them together to watch, but also to talk about the content and other topics that leads to (the "hey-look-at-this" model). It can help family members learn each other's reactions to many topics and situations. It can be a stimulus to cognitive, emotional, and personal growth. All of this is not to say that it will be such a positive influence, just that it can be. The more carefully that programs are selected and the more intentional the parent is about discussing the content, the better the outcome. Austin, Roberts, and Nass (1990; see also Desmond, Singer, & Singer, 1990) developed and tested a model of how parent–child communication about TV and its portrayals can affect the children's construction of reality. Social, cultural, and family structure variables also have a role in determining the effect of family interactions on the impact of TV on children (Greenberg, Ku, & Li, 1992; Wright, St. Peters, & Huston, 1990).

Using television as a springboard for productive discussion and psychological growth is not limited to children and families. See Box 12.3 for a use of tapes of the show "thirtysomething" in psychotherapy.

Most of the focus in this book has been on the perceived reality that we construct through the interaction of our minds with the stimulus material from the TV, radio, magazines, or newspapers. If we want to change the reality of the

---

BOX 12.3: "THIRTYSOMETHING" AS PSYCHOTHERAPY

A few psychotherapists thought so highly of at least one former network TV show that they use tapes from it in their group and individual therapy. The ABC drama "thirtysomething" (1987–1991) featured seven urban upper middle-class characters in their 30s trying to make sense out of today's world. Although the show was criticized by some for being a tiresome and humorless display of self-indulgent yuppie angst, it struck a responsive chord with many more viewers and developed an extremely loyal following, as well as receiving critical praise for its scripts and acting.

Among those who were impressed were some therapists, who found "thirtysomething" episodes very useful in stimulating thought and discussion in clients. One family therapist had his therapy group for new fathers watch a segment where Michael tells his wife Hope that he has mixed feelings about the arrival of their baby. While he loves the little girl, he regrets some ways in which the marital relationship seems to have changed. Another episode, focusing on the nightmares of 7-year-old Ethan after his parents' separation, was used to help divorcing parents better understand the emotional effects of divorce on their children. Another scene, where one couple has an argument in front of another couple later "replays" the scene from the perspective of each of the four participants, was used by therapists to stress to clients how different parties interpret and remember the same interpersonal encounter so differently. Episodes dealing with Elliot and Nancy's on-again, off-again marriage were useful for clients who were trying to sort out similarly ambivalent relationships. Series characters express their feelings and can often effectively model such expression for client viewers. These clients thus receive some reassurance that they are not alone in their concerns and also receive some direction on how to deal with these concerns (Hersch, 1988). Brookfield (1990) argued that the unusually accurate depiction of adult life on "thirtysomething" and its portrayal and promotion of critical thinking makes it useful in adult education.

---

media, we can sometimes do that as well. Although not the focus of this book, this issue is worth examining briefly as a complement to our basic thesis.

INFLUENCING THE MEDIA

Very often when we critically examine media, we are left with the feeling that there is much we do not like, for whatever reason, but that there is little we can do about that state of affairs other than choose not to use the medium (e.g., watch the program, read the paper, etc.) we do not care for. This passive approach of person–media interaction is not entirely accurate, however. Just as we cognitively interact with the media in understanding it, so can we behaviorally interact with it to help effect change in areas we desire. Commercial and political interests have long been doing this, and it behooves concerned and interested individual media consumers to learn to do likewise.

Individual Efforts

Individual complaints do have disproportionate impact, in that those who receive them assume that each complaint represents a similar view of many others who did not write. Certain types of letters are more effective than others. A reasoned, logically argued case has a lot more impact than an angry tirade. For example, one brand of club cocktails once advertised in *Ms* magazine with the slogan "Hit me with a Club." The company received over 1,000 letters of protest, arguing that the ad contained a suggestion of violence toward women. The company responded that such a connection was never intended or imagined, yet they were concerned enough by the letters to withdraw the ad (Will, 1987). Responses do make a difference! Letters from Michigan homemaker Terry Rakolta and her supporters concerned about negative family values once caused Kimberly-Clark, McDonald's, and other sponsors to pull their ads from "Married . . . with Children."

Jamieson and Campbell (1992) suggested three types of arguments that are particularly effective when writing to a network, TV or radio station, or publication. First, a claim of inaccuracy or deception evokes immediate concern. Publishing or broadcasting inaccurate information is seldom intended and must be quickly corrected or balanced to avoid a loss of credibility and possibly legal trouble as well. Second, a claim that an item violates community standards or general good taste causes concern. The press is very loath to offend, for example, with overly explicit sex, violence, or raunchy language. A sufficient number of people with such concerns may lead to the fear of loss of advertising dollars, the lifeblood of the enterprise. See Box 12.4 for an example of an ad that offended people and was withdrawn due to their complaints. Third, a claim of lack of balance or fairness is serious. This includes obvious concerns like lack of fairness in covering a political campaign or the use of an unfairly misleading ad, but also claims such as unfairly stereotyping some group or unfairly exploiting the cognitive immaturity of children to encourage them to request certain products from their parents.

Once in a great while the efforts of a single individual can result in policy change or the emergence of organizations to counter heavy media use to promote particular views. For example, John Banzhaf III once persuaded the FCC that the Fairness Doctrine required television to run antismoking ads to counter cigarette ads on TV at the time. (They ended in the U.S. in 1971.) Pete Shields, who lost a son to a handgun homicide, and Sarah Brady, whose husband Jim was permanently brain-damaged in the assassination attempt on President Reagan in 1981, became active media users in gun control lobbying efforts through agencies like Handgun Control, Inc., founded by Shields. Millionaire heart-attack victim Phil Sokolof took out large newspaper ads targeting big food corporations to change their practice of cooking in cholesterol-rich tropical oils. This campaign and the ensuing media coverage helped cause 12 large food corpora-

---

BOX 12.4: CASE STUDY OF A COMMERCIAL KILLED BY COMPLAINTS

A syndicated Ann Landers column (6/13/88) told of a test market commercial that was dropped due to calls and letters to the company. The ad opened with two teenage boys on a cliff overlooking the ocean. One challenges the other to a game, whereby both drive their cars toward the cliff and the one who jumps out first is a "chicken." The boys start their race. The boy who made the dare at some point jumps out of his car. The other boy looks nervous and is shown panicking and pushing against the car door, which is stuck. We hear him screaming as his car goes over the cliff and crashes onto the rocks below, as the first boy watches in horror. Finally, the camera cuts to the ocean with a denim jacket and pair of jeans floating on the water with a caption on a black screen: "Union Bay—Fashion that Lasts."

The company marketing director told Ann Landers that the ad was chosen for its "impact" and its "dramatic" quality. The director further said she believed that teens did not take ads very literally and would think that it was funny. However, after "several" complaints by phone and letter, the company withdrew the ad.

---

tions to begin using healthier oils within 2 years. Sokolof then turned his campaign on McDonald's, to encourage them to reduce the fat content in their burgers (Dagnoli, 1990, in Jamieson & Campbell, 1992).

An excellent first outlet for media concerns is the editorial page of a local newspaper. Most are delighted to print letters to the editor or even guest columns. For some addresses of larger organizations and agencies to contact to express media concerns, see Box 12.5.

Group Efforts

Individuals working together can often have even more impact than isolated individuals. One corporate method is the *boycott*, whereby people refrain from buying some product or using some publication or station until changes are made. Even the threat of a boycott sends chills up the spines of advertisers, publications, or radio or TV stations. Newspapers have gone out of business when certain key economic interests have pulled their advertising. Convenience stores have stopped selling sex magazines in response to public complaints and threat of a boycott by the religious right. Nestle's changed its infant formula marketing in response to a public outcry and boycott. Fear of adverse and organized public reaction is a major reason that U.S. television stations are so slow to accept condom ads, even in the age of the AIDS scare when a majority of public opinion favors such ads.

In occasional cases a group may file legal action against a media organization. For example, when the FCC periodically reviews applications of radio and

---

BOX 12.5: ADDRESSES OF UNITED STATES GOVERNMENT AGENCIES, NETWORKS, AND CONSUMER GROUPS

Federal Trade Commission
Pennsylvania Avenue at Sixth
Avenue N.W.
Washington, DC 20580

Federal Communications Commission
Consumer Assistance Office
1919 M Street N.W.
Washington, DC 20554

National Advertising Division
Council of Better Business Bureaus
845 Third Avenue
New York, NY 10022

CBS
524 W. 57th St.
New York, NY 10019

ABC
7 West 66th St.
New York, NY 10023

NBC
30 Rockefeller Plaza
New York, NY 10012

Public Broadcasting Service (PBS)
1320 Braddock Place
Alexandria, VA 22314

National Public Radio (NPR)
2025 M St. NW
Washington, DC 20036

Cable News Network (CNN), TBS, TNT
Turner Broadcasting Center
One CNN Center
Box 105366
Atlanta, GA 30348

Associated Press (AP)
50 Rockefeller Plaza
New York, NY 10020

New York Times
229 W. 43rd St.
New York, NY 10036

USA Today
1000 Wilson Blvd.
Arlington, VA 22229

---

television stations for renewal, opportunity is available to challenge such renewal. Although the actual failure to renew is extremely rare in the United States, such pressure may have substantial effects on subsequent station policy. For example, civil rights groups in the 1960s used this approach to force broadcasters to become more responsive to African-American concerns in their communities. Sometimes the mere threat of legal or legislative action is enough to produce the desired change. For example, consumer groups like the now-defunct Action for Children's Television (ACT) have put pressure on the broadcast industry's National Association of Broadcasters (NAB) to limit the allowable number of minutes of commercials per hour on children's television. Their appeals to the FCC to regulate such numbers have led to the NAB limiting commercial time itself, a move it apparently considered preferable to government-mandated regulation.

Certain organizations have established themselves as watchdogs on certain kinds of issues. For example, the national PTA has at different times monitored children's advertising and violent and sexual content on television. Resulting public awareness, as well as the latent threat of a boycott, has probably had some subtle effects. Many local citizens' groups protesting pornography have pressured convenience stores to stop selling sex magazines. The Reverend Donald Wildmon has led boycotts against sponsors of television that contains "excessive, gratuitous sex, violence, profanity, [and] the negative stereotyping of Christians" (Winbush, 1989, p. 54). For example, a boycott of Pepsi in 1989 led to the company's cancellation of its sponsorship of a Madonna video and tour.

Sometimes follow-up monitoring is necessary, recognizing that unwanted regulation may sometimes be creatively circumvented. For example, the Children's Television Act of 1990 required TV stations to increase the number of hours of "educational" programming to children. In response to this, some stations redefined existing cartoons and syndicated sitcom reruns as "educational." For example, in its license-renewal application, one station described "G.I. Joe" as presenting a "fight against an evil that has the capabilities of mass destruction of society" ("School of Hard Knocks," 1992, p. 32). Truly educational shows like news shows for children ran at 5:30 in the morning, whereas "educational" programs like "The Jetsons" and "Leave It to Beaver" retained the better time slots. By early 1993, however, the FCC was looking askance at such practices.

Sometimes social science research itself may have important impact on policy making. For example, the laboratory research finding that people could not perceive or be affected by backward audio messages (Box 4.5) led several states to withdraw pending legislation requiring record companies to put warning labels on album jackets (Vokey & Read, 1985). The recent research on sexual violence (discussed in chapter 10) has tremendous potential impact on legal, policy, filmmaking, and even lifestyle issues. For a careful discussion of how research on sexual violence may be used to effect legal and policy change, see Penrod and Linz (1984) and Linz, Turner, Hesse, and Penrod (1984).

Before such research can have much impact on public opinion or public policy, however, the findings from that research must somehow be communicated to the world beyond the scientific community. This act in itself can often affect the perceived reality about that issue in the mind of the public.

REPORTING MEDIA RESEARCH TO THE PUBLIC

In the reporting of science, the scientist's "truth" and the reporter's "news" are often far from the same. For example, an editor may not consider a particular background feature story about pornography research as newsworthy because the paper has already carried two stories that week on that particular topic.

The scientist looking at the same situation may not be convinced of the overlap, in that one was a story about citizens seeking a ban on sales of *Playboy* in convenience stores and the other was a story about a woman involved in acting in pornographic videos, neither of which at all overlaps with a report of behavioral research on the topic.

In their desire to fairly present all sides of an issue, journalists may emphasize controversy and thus (perhaps inadvertently) play up and legitimatize a fringe position given little credibility in the scientific community. As discussed in chapter 7, conflict and controversy are highly newsworthy. For example, subliminal advertising greatly intrigues and even alarms the general public, whereas the research community realizes that its feared effects are vastly overrated or nonexistent (Moore, 1982; Pratkanis, 1992; Saegert, 1987). Such a topic may make good journalism but it is bad science. The perceived reality of readers of such stories may be significantly at variance with the scientific reality.

Journalists and scientists use language in very different ways. As Tavris (1986) said:

> To the academician, the language of the reporter is excessively casual, trivializing, and simple-minded, if not downright wrong or silly. To the journalist, the language of the academicians is excessively passive, technical, and complicated, if not downright wordy or pompous. . . . Academic language strives to be informative and accurate. . . . To the reporter, though, the result sounds like nit-picking; it encumbers the research with so many qualifications and exceptions that the results seem meaningless. (p. 25)

It is not unusual to encounter the feeling that social science is inferior, immature science. Not surprisingly, this feeling is common among journalists trained in science. More surprising, however, is that this view is also not unusual among social scientists themselves, some of whom see themselves as doing work that is inferior to that of their colleagues in physics or biology. If many social scientists do not see themselves as true scientists, is it surprising that others do not so perceive them? This collective feeling of inferiority may stem from the fact that social science is by its very nature probabilistic, not deterministic. One can never predict for sure the effect on a particular person of seeing a violent movie, in the sense that one can predict with absolute certainty that $2 + 2 = 4$.

Still, social science stories hold much interest for many readers and even journalists. In a study by Dunwoody (1986), newspaper editors actually reported a preference for social science topics over "hard" science. However, the reverse preference was found in reporters. Thus there may often be a situation of an editor selecting a social science topic but assigning it to a reporter who has less interest in it and thus may not treat it as "science," thereby resulting in more sloppy treatment than would be given a "real" science story. For a fascinating series of papers examining how the media report scientific research about media, see Goldstein (1986).

Throughout most of this book, we have focused on the perceived reality of the *receiver* of media input. It is even more magical to *appear* in the media (see Box 12.6).

LOOKING TOWARD THE FUTURE

One of the most difficult aspects of writing this book is that mass communication is a constantly changing arena. Today's blockbuster miniseries is barely a memory in 3 months. The next new trend of hit TV shows are now but an idea in some producer's mind. Broader trends are ephemeral as well. In early 1984 pundits were saying that the sitcom was a dying genre; a few months later "The Cosby Show" turned that around and 2 or 3 years later almost all of the top-10 Nielsen shows in the United States were sitcoms. In the early 1990s this trend had started reversing again. In the early 1980s many people scorned the introduction of *USA Today*, saying that a national paper using such a colorful magazine format could never last; they were wrong.

No place is beyond the reach of mass communication. For political reasons South Africa was for a long time the last large nation without TV, until 1976 (Mutz, Roberts, & van Vuuren, 1993). Isolated and mountainous Nepal (1985)

BOX 12.6: BEING ON TELEVISION
AS A MAGICAL EXPERIENCE

There is something magical for most people about being on television. Because it is a very intrusive medium, being on television makes someone either very excited or very uncomfortable or perhaps both. The importance seems to be more in the act of being on TV than in what one does there. People are very happy to look perfectly foolish singing a song on a talk show or even exposing personally embarrassing information on "The Newlywed Game." Over the years we have seen shows of people in the "real world," often doing very strange things (e.g., "Candid Camera," "Real People," "That's Incredible," "America's Funniest Home Videos").

It is hard to "act natural" if the cameras are running, sometimes even if the camera is a family member's camcorder. Anthropologist Edmund Carpenter reported an interesting example of what happened when Lowell Thomas visited a remote New Guinean village some years ago: "The instant they saw cameras they rushed about for props, then sat in front of the cameras, one chopping with a stone axe, another finger-painting on bark, a third starting a fire with bamboo—Santa's workshop" (Kenner, 1973, p. 7).

It will be interesting to see if, over the years, the use of camcorders and home videos removes some of the "magic" from being on TV, because children will grow up seeing themselves on the TV screen frequently.

and the Cook Islands (1989) were two of the last small countries to introduce television, with Bhutan being one of the only nations without TV as of 1992. Even the isolated valley town unable to receive TV as late as the 1970s is virtually nonexistent today. Satellite dishes and VCRs running off generators now allow video experiences in places out of the normal reach of broadcast signals. See Williams (1986) for a collection of papers studying the effects of the late introduction of television in the mid-1970s to an otherwise normal Canadian town. Such a study can probably never be done again, because no such TV-less place would exist.

An important emphasis in future media research, as indeed in all social science research, will be on cross-cultural aspects. Virtually every society in the world is becoming increasingly multicultural, in part due to the communications revolution. We are all exposed to media communications from many different national and cultural sources, and it is necessary to understand how different cultures perceive the same message differently. For excellent collections of papers on comparative and cross-cultural media research, see Korzenny and Ting-Toomey (1992), Lull (1988), and Blumler, McLeod, and Rosengren (1992).

Changing technology is accelerating more fundamental structural changes in television and other media. The slow but sure decline in the audience percentage for network TV (down from 90% to 66% from 1978 to 1990; Zoglin, 1990a) relative to cable will have an enormous, but still unclear, effect on TV programming, economics, and viewing habits. Proliferating cable channels and satellite technology are vastly increasing the number of offerings available. The psychological impact of all these choices is less clear; it is not obvious how receiving 100 or even 500 channels will change one's TV viewing. VCRs have greatly increased audience control in program selection and timing; the total effects of VCRs on quantity and quality of viewing are just starting to emerge (Gunter & Levy, 1987; Levy, 1987; Lindlof & Shatzer, 1990). Pay-per-view television is beginning to catch on, especially for major events like boxing matches, although the "Triplecast" of the 1992 Summer Olympics offering three 24-hour channels of Olympic coverage for around $125 brought far fewer takers than anticipated. High-definition television (HDTV) is on the horizon, promising a whole new level of technology for television. Experimental interactive TV projects like Montreal's Videoway (Came, 1991) allow viewers to press one button to see the original live feed and another to call up additional background information during newscasts or sports events. Pressing yet another button can bring up a closeup shot of an athlete during a ball game, whereas another can provide an instant replay.

It is also becoming increasingly difficult to identify exactly what is mass communication and what is not. Technology has blurred distinctions between mass and personal media (Ganley, 1992). For example, the advent of the VCR allows us to watch home movies using the technology of mass communication (television). The widespread use of the television set as a medium for viewing films has further blurred this distinction. The computer has also complicated the issue. For example, computer bulletin boards and networks (Rafaeli & LaRose, 1993; Trevino & Webster, 1992) have been used as quasi-mass communication for spreading news during insurrections and revolution. The government of the city-state nation of Singapore has initiated the National Information Infrastructure, a project to link all households in the country to a network of fiber-optic cables allowing high-speed exchanges of text, sound, video, and other information; there will also be a wireless communication network for mobile computer users ("Twenty-First-Century Singapore," 1992). Similar projects are underway or are being seriously discussed elsewhere, including France, Japan, Germany, Canada, and the United States.

Although electronic, and to a lesser extent print, media can be controlled by an authoritarian government, computers and VCRs are much more difficult to suppress. Groups like the Palestinian intifada, Afghan mujahedin, and Burmese Karen rebels routinely use videotaping of their activities to document actions against them and to recruit and motivate new members (Zoglin, 1989). When Boris Yeltsin and the democratic protesters took refuge in the Russian Parliament building during the abortive August 1991 coup in Moscow, they kept in touch with the world through fax and computer lines.

The worldwide fax revolution of Chinese students (43,000 studying in the United States alone in 1989) in response to the 1989 Tiananmen Square massacre and subsequent crackdown has already become legendary (Ganley, 1992). The estimated 10,000 fax numbers in China were jammed for weeks with reports from abroad about what had really happened in Beijing. Much of the communication among those sending the fax messages was by the academic computer mail system BITNET, usually available for free to any student or staff at a university that subscribes to the service. Taped newscasts out of Hong Kong circulated widely on the 2 million or more VCRs in China. The democratic uprising in China was suppressed but it will never again be possible to so totally isolate a society from the news of its own oppression. Electronic information in all its forms is not easily controlled.

Although most of the discussion of television in this book has focused on network television, such stations are already a minority of the channels offered in most markets. The network share of the viewing audience is still a majority but has been rapidly falling in recent years. Interactive television has already arrived in children's TV, where full enjoyment may require purchase of an interactive toy like the Power Jet weapon for "Captain Power and the Soldiers of the Future." Rapid proliferation and dissemination of such interactive media could totally revolutionize the psychological experience of mass communication in ways only vaguely imagined today.

All of this brings us back to the question of "why study the *psychology*, especially cognitive psychology, of the media?" At heart media offers an experience that emerges from the interaction of our minds with the content of the communication. Media affect our minds—they give us ideas, change our attitudes, tell us what the world is like. These mind changes (i.e., our perceived reality) then become the framework around which we interpret the totality of experience. Thus media consumption is very much a cognitive phenomenon.

In one sense media production is art, a creation, a fabrication, but yet, as Picasso once said, "Art is a lie through which we can see the truth." The same is often true of media. Performing in media is acting, pretending, taking a role, yet as Oscar Wilde once said, "I love acting. It is so much more real than life." One might say the same about media. Life imitates art, and art imitates life. After a while, it becomes hard to tell which is which.

REFERENCES

Abel, E. (1984). Television in international conflict. In A. Arno & W. Dissayanake (Eds.), *The news media and national and international conflict* (pp. 63–70). Boulder, CO: Westview Press.

Abel, G. G., Barlow, D. H., Blanchard, E. B., & Guild, D. (1977). The components of rapists' sexual arousal. *Archives of General Psychiatry, 34,* 895–903.

Abel, G. G., Becker, J., & Skinner, L. (1980). Aggressive behavior and sex. *Psychiatric Clinics of North America, 3,* 133–151.

Abelman, R. (1989). From here to eternity: Children's acquisition of understanding of projective size on television. *Human Communications Research, 15,* 463–481.

Abernethy, A. M. (1992). The information content of newspaper advertising. *Journal of Current Issues and Research in Advertising, 14*(2), 63–68.

Abramson, P. R., & Hayashi, H. (1984). Pornography in Japan: Cross-cultural and theoretical considerations. In N. M. Malamuth & E. Donnerstein (Eds.), *Pornography and sexual aggression* (pp. 173–183). Orlando: Academic Press.

Abramson, P. R., Perry, L., Seeley, T., Seeley, D., & Rothblatt, A. (1981). Thermographic measurement of sexual arousal: A discriminant validity analysis. *Archives of Sexual Behavior, 10*(2), 175–176.

Ahn, W.-K., Brewer, W. F., & Mooney, R. J. (1992). Schema acquisition from a single example. *Journal of Experimental Psychology: Learning, Memory, and Cognition, 18,* 391–412.

Alali, A. O., & Eke, K. K. (Eds.). (1991). *Media coverage of terrorism: Methods of diffusion.* Newbury Park, CA: Sage.

Alesandrini, K. L. (1983). Strategies that influence memory for advertising communications. In R. J. Harris (Ed.), *Information processing research in advertising* (pp. 65–82). Hillsdale, NJ: Lawrence Erlbaum Associates.

Alsop, R. (1988, January 26). Advertisers retreat from making direct pitch to the gay market. *Wall Street Journal,* p. 33.

Altheide, D. L. (1976). *Creating reality: How TV news distorts events.* Beverly Hills: Sage.

Alvarado, M., Gutch, R., & Wollen, T. (1987). *Learning the media: An introduction to media teaching.* London: Macmillan.

Alwitt, L. F., Deighton, J., & Grimm, J. (1991). Reactions to political advertising depend on the nature of the voter–candidate bond. In F. Biocca (Ed.), *Television and political advertising: Vol. 1. Psychological processes* (pp. 329–350). Hillsdale, NJ: Lawrence Erlbaum Associates.

Amador, O. G. (1988). Latin lovers, Lolita, and *La Bamba. Americas, 40*(4), 2–9.

Andersen, P. A., & Kibler, R. J. (1978). Candidate valence as a predictor of voter preference. *Human Communication Research, 5*, 4–14.

Anderson, D. R. (1985). Online cognitive processing of television. In L. F. Alwitt & A. A. Mitchell (Eds.), *Psychological processes and advertising effects* (pp. 177–199). Hillsdale, NJ: Lawrence Erlbaum Associates.

Anderson, D. R., & Burns, J. (1991). Paying attention to television. In J. Bryant & D. Zillmann (Eds.), *Responding to the screen: Reception and reaction processes* (pp. 3–25). Hillsdale, NJ: Lawrence Erlbaum Associates.

Anderson, D. R., & Field, D. E. (1991). Online and offline assessment of the television audience. In J. Bryant & D. Zillmann (Eds.), *Responding to the screen: Reception and reaction processes* (pp. 199–216). Hillsdale, NJ: Lawrence Erlbaum Associates.

Andison, F. S. (1977). TV violence and viewer aggression: A cumulation of study results: 1956–1976. *Public Opinion Quarterly, 41*, 314–331.

Andreasen, M. S. (1990). Evolution of the family's use of television: Normative data from industry and academe. In J. Bryant (Ed.), *Television and the American family* (pp. 3–55). Hillsdale, NJ: Lawrence Erlbaum Associates.

Apter, M. J. (1982). *The experience of motivation: The theory of psychological reversals.* San Diego: Academic Press.

Arias, M. B. (1982). Educational television: Impact on the socialization of the Hispanic child. In G. L. Berry & C. Mitchell-Kernan (Eds.), *Television and the socialization of the minority child* (pp. 203–211). New York: Academic Press.

Arlen, M. J. (1969). *Livingroom war.* New York: Viking Press.

Arms, R. L., Russell, G. W., & Sandilands, M. L. (1979). Effects on the hostility of spectators of viewing aggressive sports. *Social Psychology Quarterly, 42*, 275–279.

Armstrong, G. B., Neuendorf, K. A., & Brentar, J. E. (1992). TV entertainment, news, and racial perceptions of college students. *Journal of Communication, 42*(3), 153–176.

Aronoff, C. (1974). Old age in prime time. *Journal of Communication, 24*(1), 86–87.

Assman, H. (1987a). *La iglesia electronica y su impacto en America latina* [The electronic church and its impact in Latin America]. San Jose, Costa Rica: DEI.

Assman, H. (1987b). Phenomenal growth of sects, electronic church related to continent's poverty. *Latinamerica Press, 19*(16), 5–6.

Atkin, C., & Arkin, E. B. (1990). Issues and initiatives in communicating health information. In C. Atkin & L. Wallack (Eds.), *Mass communication and public health* (pp. 13–40). Newbury Park, CA: Sage.

Atkin, C., Greenberg, B., & McDermott, S. (1983). Television and race role socialization. *Journalism Quarterly, 60*(3), 407–414.

Austin, E. W., Roberts, D. F., & Nass, C. I. (1990). Influences of family communication in children's television-interpretation processes. *Communication Research, 17*, 545–564.

Bacchetta, V. (1987). Brazil's soap operas: "Huge dramas where the country portrays itself." *Latinamerica Press, 19*(9), 5–6.

Bachy, V. (1976). Danish "permissiveness" revisited. *Journal of Communication, 26*, 40–43.

Baehr, H., & Dyer, G. (Eds.). (1987). *Boxed in: Women and television.* London: Pandora.

Baggaley, J. P. (1988). Perceived effectiveness of interactional AIDS campaigns. *Health Education Research: Theory and Practice, 3*, 7–17.

Baggett, P. (1979). Structurally equivalent stories in movie and text and the effect of the medium on recall. *Journal of Verbal Learning and Verbal Behavior, 18*, 333–356.

Ball, S., & Bogatz, G. A. (1970). *The first year of Sesame Street: An evaluation.* Princeton, NJ: Educational Testing Service.

Ball, S., & Bogatz, G. A. (1973). *Reading with television: An evaluation of The Electric Company.* Princeton, NJ: Educational Testing Service.

Bancroft, J., & Mathews, A. (1971). Autonomic correlates of penile erection. *Journal of Psychosomatic Research, 15,* 159–167.

Bandura, A. (1965). Influence of models' reinforcement contingencies on the acquisition of imitative responses. *Journal of Personality and Social Psychology, 1,* 585–595.

Bandura, A. (1977). *Social learning theory.* Englewood Cliffs, NJ: Prentice-Hall.

Bandura, A., Ross, D., & Ross, S. A. (1961). Transmission of aggression through imitation of aggressive models. *Journal of Abnormal and Social Psychology, 63,* 575–582.

Bandura, A., Ross, D., & Ross, S. A. (1963). Imitation of film-mediated aggressive models. *Journal of Abnormal and Social Psychology, 66,* 3–11.

Bandura, A., & Walters, R. H. (1963). *Social learning and personality development.* New York: Holt, Rinehart & Winston.

Barach, J. A. (1984, July/August). Applying marketing principles to social causes. *Business Horizons,* pp. 65–69.

Barbaree, H. E., Marshall, W. L., & Lanthier, R. D. (1979). Deviant sexual arousal in rapists. *Behaviour Research and Therapy, 17,* 215–222.

Barcus, F. E. (1980). The nature of television advertising to children. In E. L. Palmer & A. Dorr (Eds.), *Children and the faces of television: Teaching, violence, and selling* (pp. 273–285). New York: Academic Press.

Barcus, F. E. (1983). *Images of life on children's television.* New York: Prager.

Barnett, M. A., Klassen, M., McMinimy, V., & Schwarz, L. (1987). The role of self- and other-oriented motivation in the organ donation decision. *Advances in Consumer Research, 14,* 335–337.

Baron, R. A. (1979). Heightened sexual arousal and physical aggression: An extension to females. *Journal of Research in Personality, 13,* 91–102.

Basil, M., Schooler, C., & Reeves, B. (1991). Positive and negative political advertising: Effectiveness of ads and perceptions of candidates. In F. Biocca (Ed.), *Television and political advertising: Vol. 1. Psychological processes* (pp. 245–262). Hillsdale, NJ: Lawrence Erlbaum Associates.

Bateman, T. S., Sakano, T., & Fujita, M. (1992). Roger, me, and my attitude: Film propaganda and cynicism toward corporate leadership. *Journal of Applied Psychology, 77,* 768–771.

Beagles-Roos, J., & Gat, I. (1983). Specific impact of radio and television on children's story comprehension. *Journal of Educational Psychology, 75,* 128–137.

Beeman, W. O. (1984). The cultural role of the media in Iran: The revolution of 1978–1979 and after. In A. Arno & W. Dissayanake (Eds.), *The news media and national and international conflict* (pp. 147–165). Boulder, CO: Westview Press.

Beentjes, J. W. J., & van der Voort, T. H. A. (1989). Television and young people's reading behaviour: A review of research. *European Journal of Communication, 4,* 451–477.

Berelson, B. (1942). The effects of print on public opinion. In D. Waples (Ed.), *Print, radio, and film in a democracy* (pp. 41–64). Chicago: University of Chicago Press.

Berelson, B. R., Lazarsfeld, P. F., & McPhee, W. N. (1954). *Voting.* Chicago: University of Chicago Press.

Berkowitz, L. (1965). Some aspects of observed aggression. *Journal of Personality and Social Psychology, 2,* 359–369.

Berkowitz, L. (1984). Some effects of thoughts on anti- and prosocial influences of media events: A cognitive neoassociation analysis. *Psychological Bulletin, 95,* 410–427.

Bernstein, C. (1990, December 24). The leisure empire. *Time,* pp. 56–59.

Berry, G. L. (1980). Television and Afro-Americans: Past legacy and present portrayals. In S. B. Withey & R. P. Abeles (Eds.), *Television and social behavior* (pp. 231–247). Hillsdale, NJ: Lawrence Erlbaum Associates.

Berry, G. L., & Asamen, J. K. (Eds.). (1993). *Children and television: Images in a changing sociocultural world.* Newbury Park, CA: Sage.

Berry, V. T. (1992). From *Good Times* to *The Cosby Show:* Perceptions of changing televised images among black fathers and sons. In S. Craig (Ed.), *Men, masculinity, and the media* (pp. 111–123). Newbury Park, CA: Sage.

Beuf, A. (1974). Doctor, lawyer, household drudge. *Journal of Communication, 24*(2), 142–145.

Bever, T., Smith, M., Bengen, B., & Johnson, T. (1975). Young viewers' troubling responses to TV ads. *Harvard Business Review, 53*(6), 109–120.

Biocca, F. (1990). Semiotics and mass communication: Points of intersection. In T. Sebeok & J. Umiker-Sebeok (Eds.), *Semiotic web*. The Hague: Mouton.

Biocca, F. (Ed.). (1991a). *Television and political advertising, Vol. 1: Psychological processes*. Hillsdale, NJ: Lawrence Erlbaum Associates.

Biocca, F. (1991b). Viewers' mental models of political messages: Toward a theory of the semantic processing of television. In F. Biocca (Ed.), *Television and political advertising, Vol. 1: Psychological processes* (pp. 27–89). Hillsdale, NJ: Lawrence Erlbaum Associates.

Blatt, J., Spencer, L., & Ward, S. (1972). A cognitive developmental study of children's reactions to television advertising. In E. A. Rubinstein, G. A. Comstock, & J. P. Murray (Eds.), *Television and social behavior: Vol. 4. Television in everyday life: Patterns of use* (pp. 452–467). Washington, DC: U.S. Government Printing Office.

Block, C. (1972). White backlash to Negro ads: Fact or fantasy? *Journalism Quarterly, 49*(2), 253–262.

Bloom, P. N., & Novelli, W. D. (1981). Problems and challenges in social marketing. *Journal of Marketing, 45*(2), 79–88.

Blumler, J. G. (1979). The role of theory in uses and gratifications research. *Communication Research, 6*, 9–36.

Blumler, J. G., McLeod, J. M., & Rosengren, K. E. (Eds.). (1992). *Comparatively speaking: Communication and culture across space and time*. Newbury Park, CA: Sage.

Blumler, J. G., & Katz, E. (Eds.). (1974). *The uses of mass communications: Current perspectives on gratifications research*. Beverly Hills: Sage.

Blumler, J. G., & McQuail, D. (1969). *Television in politics: Its uses and influences*. Chicago: University of Chicago Press.

Boeckmann, K., & Hipfl, B. (1987). How can we learn about children and television? *Journal of Educational Television, 13*, 217–229.

Bogart, L. (1980). Television news as entertainment. In P. H. Tannenbaum (Ed.), *The entertainment functions of television* (pp. 209–249). Hillsdale, NJ: Lawrence Erlbaum Associates.

Bogart, L. (1981). *Press and public*. Hillsdale, NJ: Lawrence Erlbaum Associates.

Bogatz, G. A., & Ball, S. (1972). *The second year of Sesame Street: A continuing evaluation*. Princeton, NJ: Educational Testing Service.

Bogle, D. (1973). *Toms, coons, mulattoes, and bucks: An interpretive history of blacks in American films*. New York: Viking.

Boiney, J., & Paletz, D. L. (1991). In search of the model model: Political science versus political advertising perspectives on voter decision making. In F. Biocca (Ed.), *Television and political advertising, Vol. 1: Psychological processes* (pp. 3–25). Hillsdale, NJ: Lawrence Erlbaum Associates.

Bollen, K. A., & Phillips, D. P. (1982). Imitative suicides: A national study of the effects of television news stories. *American Sociological Review, 47*, 802–809.

Bordeaux, B. R., & Lange, G. (1991). Children's reported investment of mental effort when viewing television. *Communication Research, 18*, 617–635.

Bower, G. H., Black, J. B., & Turner, T. J. (1979). Scripts in memory for text. *Cognitive Psychology, 11*, 177–220.

Bowes, J. E., & Strentz, H. (1978). Candidate images: Stereotyping and the 1976 debates. In B. D. Ruben (Ed.), *Communication yearbook 2* (pp. 391–406). New Brunswick, NJ: Transaction.

Brabant, S., & Mooney, L. (1986). Sex role stereotyping in the Sunday comics. *Sex Roles, 14*(3/4), 141–148.

Breslow, L. (1978). Risk factor intervention for health maintenance. *Science, 200*, 908–912.

Brewer, W. F., & Nakamura, G. V. (1984). The nature and functions of schemas. In R. S. Wyer & T. K. Srull (Eds.), *Handbook of social cognition*. Hillsdale, NJ: Lawrence Erlbaum Associates.

Brockhoff, W. (1988, February). Magazine not negligent in running ad. *KSU Collegian*, p. 2.

Brookfield, S. (1990, September). Using TV drama to teach adults: Realness, recognition, and critical thinking in *thirtysomething. Adult Learning*, pp. 20–22.

Brosius, H.-B. (1993). The effects of emotional pictures in television news. *Communication Research, 20*, 105–124.

Brosius, H.-B., & Kepplinger, H. M. (1990). The agenda-setting function of television news: Static and dynamic views. *Communication Research, 17*, 183–211.

Brown, D., & Bryant, J. (1983). Humor in mass media. In P. E. McGhee & J. H. Goldstein (Eds.), *Handbook of humor research* (Vol. 2). New York: Springer-Verlag.

Brown, D., & Bryant, J. (1990). Effects of television on family values and selected attitudes and behaviors. In J. Bryant (Ed.), *Television and the American family* (pp. 227–251). Hillsdale, NJ: Lawrence Erlbaum Associates.

Brown, J. A. (1991). *Television "critical viewing skills" education: Major media literacy projects in the United States and selected countries.* Hillsdale, NJ: Lawrence Erlbaum Associates.

Brown, J. D., & Campbell, K. (1986). Race and gender in music videos: The same beat but a different drummer. *Journal of Communication, 36*(1), 94–106.

Brown, J. D., & Einsiedel, E. F. (1990). Public health campaigns: Mass media strategies. In E. B. Ray & L. Donohew (Eds.), *Communication and health: Systems and applications* (pp. 153–170). Hillsdale, NJ: Lawrence Erlbaum Associates.

Brown, W. J., & Cody, M. J. (1991). Effects of a prosocial television soap opera in promoting women's status. *Human Communication Research, 18*, 114–142.

Brown, W. J., & Singhal, A. (1990). Ethical dilemmas of prosocial television. *Communication Quarterly, 38*, 268–280.

Brown, W. J., Singhal, A., & Rogers, E. M. (1989). Pro-development soap operas: A novel approach to development communication. *Media Development, 36*(4), 43–47.

Bruce, S. (1990). *Pray TV: Televangelism in America.* London: Routledge.

Bruno, K. J., & Harris, R. J. (1980). The effect of repetition on the discrimination of asserted and implied claims in advertising. *Applied Psycholinguistics, 1*, 307–321.

Bryant, J. (1989). Viewers' enjoyment of televised sports violence. In L. A. Wenner (Ed.), *Media, sports, and society* (pp. 270–289). Newbury Park, CA: Sage.

Bryant, J. (Ed.). (1990). *Television and the American family.* Hillsdale, NJ: Lawrence Erlbaum Associates.

Bryant, J., Alexander, A. F., & Brown, D. (1983). Learning from educational television programs. In M. J. A. Howe (Ed.), *Learning from television: Psychological and educational research* (pp. 1–30). London: Academic Press.

Buchholz, M., & Bynum, J. (1982). Newspaper presentation of America's aged: A content analysis of image and role. *The Gerontologist, 22*, 83–88.

Buerkel-Rothfuss, N. L., & Mayes, S. (1981). Soap opera viewing: The cultivation effect. *Journal of Communication, 31*, 108–115.

Burke, R. R., DeSarbo, W. S., Oliver, R. L., & Robertson, T. S. (1988). Deception by implication: An experimental investigation. *Journal of Consumer Research, 14*, 483–494.

Busby, L. J. (1985). The mass media and sex-role socialization. In J. R. Dominick & J. E. Fletcher (Eds.), *Broadcasting research methods* (pp. 267–295). Boston: Allyn & Bacon.

Caird, W., & Wincze, J. P. (1977). *Sex therapy: A behavioral approach.* New York: Harper & Row.

Calvert, S. L. (1988). Television production feature effects of children's comprehension of time. *Journal of Applied Developmental Psychology, 9*, 263–273.

Came, B. (1991, April). Do-it-yourself television. *World Press Review*, p. 42.

Camels for kids. (1991, December 23). *Time*, p. 52.

Campbell, A., Gurin, G., & Miller, W. E. (1954). *The voter decides.* Evanston, IL: Row, Peterson.

Cannon, C. M. (1989). Prime-time violence and dramatized murder figure. *Washington Post.*

Cantor, J. (1991). Fright responses to mass media productions. In J. Bryant & D. Zillmann (Eds.), *Responding to the screen: Reception and reaction processes* (pp. 169–197). Hillsdale, NJ: Lawrence Erlbaum Associates.

Cantor, J., & Sparks, G. G. (1984). Children's fear responses to mass media: Testing some Piagetian predictions. *Journal of Communication, 34*, 90–103.

Cantor, J., & Venus, P. (1980). The effect of humor on recall of a radio advertisement. *Journal of Broadcasting, 24*(1), 13–22.

Cantor, M. G., & Cantor, J. M. (1986). American television in the international marketplace. *Communication Research, 13*, 509–520.

Canzoneri, V. (1985, January 28). TV's feminine mistake. *TV Guide*, pp. 14–15.

Carlson, M. (1990, September 10). A new ball game. *Time*, pp. 40–41.

Carlsson-Paige, N., & Levin, D. E. (1990). *Who's calling the shots? How to respond effectively to children's fascination with war play and war toys.* Philadelphia: New Society Publishers.

Carroll, J. S., Kerr, N. L., Alfini, J. J., Weaver, F. M., MacCount, R. J., & Feldman, V. (1986). Free press and fair trial: The role of behavioral research. *Law and Human Behaviour, 10*, 187–202.

Carveth, R., & Alexander, A. (1985). Soap opera viewing motivations and the cultivation process. *Journal of Broadcasting & Electronic Media, 29*, 259–273.

Cassata, B., Anderson, P., & Skill, T. (1980). The older adult in daytime serial drama. *Journal of Communication, 30*, 48–49.

Centerwall, B. S. (1989a). Exposure to television as a cause of violence. In G. Comstock (Ed.), *Public communication and behavior* (Vol. 2, pp. 1–58). New York: Academic Press.

Centerwall, B. S. (1989b). Exposure to television as a risk factor for violence. *American Journal of Epidemiology, 129*, 643–652.

Chaffee, S. H., & Choe, S. Y. (1980). Times of decision and media use during the Ford–Carter campaign. *Public Opinion Quarterly, 44*, 53–69.

Chandler, J. M. (1977, April). TV and sports: Wedded with a golden hoop. *Psychology Today*, pp. 64–66, 75–76.

Chaffee, S. H., Nass, C. I., & Yang, S. M. (1990). The bridging role of television in immigrant political socialization. *Human Communication Research, 17*, 266–288.

Check, J. V. P. (1985). *The effects of violent and nonviolent pornography.* Ottawa: Department of Justice for Canada.

Check, J. V. P., & Guloien, T. H. (1989). Reported proclivity for coercive sex following repeated exposure to sexually violent pornography, nonviolent pornography, and erotica. In D. Zillmann & J. Bryant (Eds.), *Pornography: Research advances and policy considerations* (pp. 159–184). Hillsdale, NJ: Lawrence Erlbaum Associates.

Child's play: Violent videos lure the young. (1987, June 1). *Time*, p. 31.

Christenson, P. G. (1992). The effects of parental advisory labels on adolescent music preferences. *Journal of Communication, 42*(1), 106–113.

Christenson, P. G., & Roberts, D. F. (1983). The role of television in the formation of children's social attitudes. In M. J. A. Howe (Ed.), *Learning from television: Psychological and educational research* (pp. 79–99). London: Academic Press.

Christianson, S., & Loftus, E. F. (1987). Memory for traumatic events. *Applied Cognitive Psychology, 1*, 225–239.

Clark, C. (1969). Television and social controls: Some observation of the portrayal of ethnic minorities. *Television Quarterly, 8*(2), 18–22.

Clarke, G. (1988, July 4). A reluctance to play gay. *Time*, p. 61.

Coakley, J. J. (1986). *Sport in society: Issues and controversies.* St. Louis: Times Mirror/Mosby.

Coates, T. J. (1990). Strategies for modifying sexual behavior for primary and secondary prevention of HIV disease. *Journal of Consulting and Clinical Psychology, 58*, 57–69.

Colfax, D., & Steinberg, S. (1972). The perpetuation of racial stereotypes: Blacks in mass circulation magazine advertisements. *Public Opinion Quarterly, 35*, 8–18.

Collins, A. M., & Loftus, E. F. (1975). A spreading activation theory of semantic processing. *Psychological Review, 82*, 407–428.

Comstock, G. (1985). Television and film violence. In S. J. Apter & A. P. Goldstein (Eds.), *Youth violence: Programs and prospects.* New York: Pergamon Press.

Comstock, G., Chaffee, S., Katzman, N., McCombs, M., & Roberts, D. (1978). *Television and human behavior*. New York: Columbia University Press.

Condry, J. C. (1989). *The psychology of television*. Hillsdale, NJ: Lawrence Erlbaum Associates.

Condry, J. C., Bence, P., & Scheibe, C. (1988). Non-program content of children's television. *Journal of Broadcasting and Electronic Media, 32*, 255–270.

Conway, J. C., & Rubin, A. M. (1991). Psychological predictors of television viewing motivation. *Communication Research, 18*, 443–463.

Cook, G. (1992). *Discourse of advertising*. London: Routledge.

Cook, T. D., Appleton, H., Conner, R. F., Shaffer, A., Tabkin, G., & Weber, J. S. (1975). *Sesame Street revisited*. New York: Sage.

Corcoran, F. (1986). KAL 007 and the evil empire: Mediated disaster and forms of rationalization. *Critical Studies in Mass Communication, 3*, 297–316.

Corder-Bolz, C. R. (1980). Mediation: The role of significant others. *Journal of Communication, 30*, 106–118.

Corliss, R. (1988, July 11). Born in East L.A. *Time*, pp. 66–67.

Corliss, R. (1989, January 9). Fire this time. *Time*, pp. 56–62.

Court, J. H. (1977). Pornography and sex crimes: A re-evaluation in the light of recent trends around the world. *International Journal of Criminology and Penology, 5*, 129–157.

Court, J. H. (1982). Rape trends in New South Wales: A discussion of conflicting evidence. *Australian Journal of Social Issues, 17*, 202–206.

Court, J. H. (1984). Sex and violence: A ripple effect. In N. M. Malamuth & E. Donnerstein (Eds.), *Pornography and sexual aggression* (pp. 143–172). Orlando: Academic Press.

Courtney, A. E., & Whipple, T. W. (1983). *Sex stereotyping in advertising*. Lexington, MA: D. C. Heath.

Crimmins, C. (1991, January). Sexism in cartoonland. *Working Mother*, pp. 37–41.

Croteau, D., & Hoynes, W. (1992). Men and the news media: The male presence and its effect. In S. Craig (Ed.), *Men, masculinity, and the media* (pp. 154–168). Newbury Park, CA: Sage.

Culley, J. D., & Bennett, R. (1976). Selling women, selling blacks. *Journal of Communication, 26*(4), 160–174.

Cumberbatch, G., & Howitt, D. (1989). *A measure of uncertainty: The effects of the mass media*. London: John Libbey.

Cumberbatch, G., & Negrine, R. (1991). *Images of disability on television*. London: Routledge.

Cumings, B. (1992). *War and television*. New York: Verso.

Cuperfain, R., & Clarke, T. K. (1985). A new perspective on subliminal perception. *Journal of Advertising, 14*(1), 36–41.

Dagnoli, J. (1990, April). Sokolof keeps thumping away at food giants. *Advertising Age*, pp. 3, 63.

Dan Quayle vs. Murphy Brown. (1992, June 1). *Time*, p. 50.

Davis, D. K., & Baran, S. J. (1981). *Mass communication and everyday life: A perspective on theory and effects*. Belmont, CA: Wadsworth.

Davis, M. H., Hull, J. G., Young, R. D., & Warren, G. G. (1987). Emotional reactions to dramatic film stimuli: The influence of cognitive and emotional empathy. *Journal of Personality and Social Psychology, 52*, 126–133.

Davis, R. H. (1983). Television health messages: What are they telling us? *Generations, 3*(5), 43–45.

Davis, R. H., & Davis, J. A. (1985). *TV's image of the elderly*. Lexington, MA: Lexington Books/ D. C. Heath.

Day, G., & Bloom, C. (Eds.). (1988). *Perspectives on pornography: Sexuality in film and literature*. London: Macmillan.

Demers, D. P., Craff, D., Choi, Y.-H., & Pessin, B. M. (1989). Issue obtrusiveness and the agenda-setting effects of national network news. *Communication Research, 16*, 793–812.

Dermer, M., & Pyszczynski, T. A. (1978). Effects of erotica upon men's loving and liking responses. *Journal of Personality and Social Psychology, 36*, 1302–1309.

Dershowitz, A. (1985, May 25). These cops are all guilty. *TV Guide*, pp. 4–7.

Desmond, R. J., Singer, J. L., & Singer, D. G. (1990). Family mediation: Parental communication patterns and the influences of television on children. In J. Bryant (Ed.), *Television and the American family* (pp. 293–309). Hillsdale, NJ: Lawrence Erlbaum Associates.

Devlin, L. P. (1987). Campaign commercials. In A. A. Berger (Ed.), *Television in society* (pp. 17–28). New Brunswick, NJ: Transaction Books.

Diamond, D. (1987, June 13). Is the toy business taking over kids' TV? *TV Guide*, pp. 4–8.

Diamond, E., & Noglows, P. (1987, June 20). When network news pulls its punches. *TV Guide*, pp. 2–9.

Diaz-Guerrero, R., Reyes-Lagunes, I., Witzke, D. B., & Holtzman, W. H. (1976). *Plaza Sesamo* in Mexico: An evaluation. *Journal of Communication, 26*, 109–123.

Diener, E., & DeFour, D. (1978). Does television violence enhance program popularity? *Journal of Personality and Social Psychology, 36*, 333–341.

Dietz, P. E., & Evans, B. (1982). Pornographic imagery and prevalence of paraphilia. *American Journal of Psychiatry, 139*, 1493–1495.

Dietz, P. E., Harry, B., & Hazelwood, R. R. (1986). Detective magazines: Pornography for the sexual sadist? *Journal of Forensic Sciences, 31*(1), 197–211.

DiFranza, J. R., & Tye, J. B. (1990). Who profits from tobacco sales to children? *Journal of the American Medical Association JAMA, 263*, 2784–2787.

Dobrow, J. R. (1990). Patterns of viewing and VCR use: Implications for cultivation analysis. In N. Signorielli & M. Morgan (Eds.), *Cultivation analysis: New directions in media effects research* (pp. 71–84). Newbury Park, CA: Sage.

Dominick, J. R., & Rauch, G. E. (1972). The image of women in network TV commercials. *Journal of Broadcasting, 16*, 259–265.

Donnerstein, E. (1980). Aggressive erotica and violence against women. *Journal of Personality and Social Psychology, 39*, 269–277.

Donnerstein, E., & Berkowitz, L. (1981). Victim reactions in aggressive erotic films as a factor in violence against women. *Journal of Personality and Social Psychology, 41*, 710–724.

Donnerstein, E., Donnerstein, M., & Evans, R. (1975). Erotic stimuli and aggression: Facilitation or inhibition? *Journal of Personality and Social Psychology, 32*, 237–244.

Donnerstein, E., & Hallam, J. (1978). Facilitating effects of erotica on aggression against women. *Journal of Personality and Social Psychology, 36*, 1270–1277.

Donnerstein, E., Linz, D., & Penrod, S. (1987). *The question of pornography: Research findings and policy implications.* New York: Free Press.

Donohew, L., Helm, D., & Haas, J. (1989). Drugs and (Len) Bias on the sports page. In L. A. Wenner (Ed.), *Media, sports, and society* (pp. 225–237). Newbury Park, CA: Sage.

Doob, A. N., & Macdonald, G. E. (1979). Television viewing and fear of victimization: Is the relationship causal? *Journal of Personality and Social Psychology, 37*, 170–179.

Dorr, A. (1980). When I was a child I thought as a child. In S. B. Withey & R. P. Abeles (Eds.), *Television and social behavior* (pp. 191–229). Hillsdale, NJ: Lawrence Erlbaum Associates.

Dorr, A. (1982). Television and the socialization of the minority child. In G. L. Berry & C. Mitchell-Kernan (Eds.), *Television and the socialization of the minority child.* New York: Academic Press.

Dorr, A., Graves, S. B., & Phelps, E. (1980). Television literacy for young children. *Journal of Communication, 30*, 71–83.

Dorr, A., & Kunkel, D. (1990). Children and the media environment: Change and constancy amid change. *Communication Research, 17*, 5–25.

Dorr, A., & Kovaric, P. (1980). Some of the people some of the time—but which people? Televised violence and its effects. In E. Palmer & A. Dorr (Eds.), *Children and the faces of television* (pp. 183–199). New York: Academic Press.

Dorris, M. (1988, May 28). Why Mister Ed still talks good horse sense. *TV Guide*, pp. 34–36.

Drabman, R. S., & Thomas, M. H. (1974). Does media violence increase children's toleration of real-life aggression? *Developmental Psychology, 10*, 418–421.

Drabman, R. S., & Thomas, M. H. (1976). Does watching violence on television cause apathy? *Pediatrics, 57*, 329–331.

Duncan, M. C. (1992). Gender bias in televised sports [Special issue]. *Extra!*, p. 27.

Duncan, M. C., Messner, M. A., & Williams, L. (1990). *Gender stereotyping in televised sports*. Los Angeles: The Amateur Athletic Association of Los Angeles.

Dunwoody, S. (1986). When science writers cover the social sciences. In J. H. Goldstein (Ed.), *Reporting science: The case of aggression* (pp. 67–81). Hillsdale, NJ: Lawrence Erlbaum Associates.

Durkin, K. (1985a). Television and sex-role acquisition 1: Content. *British Journal of Social Psychology, 24*, 101–113.

Durkin, K. (1985b). Television and sex-role acquisition 2: Effects. *British Journal of Social Psychology, 24*, 191–210.

d'Ydewalle, G., Praet, C., Verfaillie, K., & Van Rensbergen, J. (1991). Watching subtitled television: Automatic reading behavior. *Communication Research, 18*, 650–666.

Easterbrook, G. (1989, February 20). *Satanic Verses* as Muslims see it. *Manhattan Mercury*, p. A5.

Eastman, H. & Liss, M. (1980). Ethnicity and children's preferences. *Journalism Quarterly, 57*(2), 277–280.

Eban, A. (1983). *The new diplomacy: International affairs in the modern age*. New York: Random House.

Eccles, A., Marshall, W. L., & Barbaree, H. E. (1988). The vulnerability of erectile measures to repeated assessments. *Behavior Research and Therapy, 26*, 179–183.

Edelstein, A. S. (1993). Thinking about the criterion variable in agenda-setting research. *Journal of Communication, 43*(2), 85–99.

Edwards, H. (1987). Race in contemporary American sports. In A. Yiannakis, T. McIntyre, M. Melnick, & D. Hart (Eds.), *Sport sociology: Contemporary issues* (pp. 194–197). Dubuque, IA: Kendall/Hunt.

Egly, M. (1973). Teleniger. *Dossiers Psychologiques, 1*, 2–5.

Einsiedel, E. F. (1988). The British, Canadian, and U.S. pornography commissions and their use of social science research. *Journal of Communication, 38*(2), 108–121.

Entman, R. M. (1991). Framing U.S. coverage of international news: Contrasts in the narratives of the KAL and Iran Air incidents. *Journal of Communication, 42*(1), 6–27.

Eron, L. D., Huesmann, L. R., Lefkowitz, M. M., & Walder, L. O. (1972). Does television violence cause aggression? *American Psychologist, 27*, 253–263.

Esslin, M. (1982). *The age of television*. San Francisco: Freeman.

Evans, J. S. B. (1982). *The psychology of deductive reasoning*. London: Routledge & Kegan Paul.

Eysenck, H. J., & Nias, D. K. B. (1978). *Sex, violence, and the media*. New York: Harper.

Fabes, R. A., & Strouse, J. S. (1984). Youth's perception of models of sexuality: Implications for sexuality education. *Journal of Sex Education and Therapy, 10*, 33–37.

Fabes, R. A., & Strouse, J. S. (1987). Perceptions of responsible and irresponsible models of sexuality: A correlational study. *Journal of Sex Research, 23*, 70–84.

Faber, R. J. (1992). Advances in political advertising research: A progression from if to when. *Journal of Current Issues and Research in Advertising, 14*(2), 1–18.

Fayol, M., & Monteil, J.-M. (1988). The notion of script: From general to developmental and social psychology. *Cahiers de Psychologie Cognitive/European Bulletin of Cognitive Psychology, 8*, 335–361.

Fejes, F. J. (1989). Images of men in media research. *Critical Studies in Mass Communication, 6*(2), 215–221.

Fejes, F. J. (1992). Masculinity as a fact: A review of empirical mass communication research on masculinity. In S. Craig (Ed.), *Men, masculinity, and the media* (pp. 9–22). Newbury Park, CA: Sage.

Fellner, C. H., & Marshall, J. R. (1981). Kidney donors revisited. In J. P. Rushton & R. M. Sorrentino (Eds.), *Altruism and helping behavior*. Hillsdale, NJ: Lawrence Erlbaum Associates.

Fenigstein, A., & Heyduk, R. G. (1985). Thought and action as determinants of media exposure. In D. Zillmann & J. Bryant (Eds.), *Selective exposure to communication* (pp. 113–139). Hillsdale, NJ: Lawrence Erlbaum Associates.

Fernandez-Collado, C., & Greenberg, B. S. (1978). Sexual intimacy and drug use in TV series. *Journal of Communication, 28*(3), 30–37.

Ferrante, C. L., Haynes, A. M., & Kingsley, S. M. (1988). Image of women in television advertising. *Journal of Broadcasting & Electronic Media, 32,* 231–237.

Feshbach, N. D. (1988). Television and the development of empathy. In S. Oskamp (Ed.), *Television as a social issue* (pp. 261–269). Newbury Park, CA: Sage.

Feshbach, S. (1955). The drive-reducing function of fantasy behavior. *Journal of Abnormal and Social Psychology, 50,* 3–11.

Feshbach, S. (1976). The role of fantasy in the response to television. *Journal of Social Issues, 32,* 71–85.

Feshbach, S., & Singer, R. (1971). *Television and aggression.* San Francisco: Jossey-Bass.

Final report of the attorney general's commission on pornography. (1986). Nashville, TN: Rutledge Hill Press.

Findahl, O., & Hoijer, B. (1981). Media content and human comprehension. In K. E. Rosengren (Ed.), *Advances in content analysis.* Beverly Hills, CA: Sage.

Findahl, O., & Hoijer, B. (1982). The problem of comprehension and recall of broadcast news. In J. F. LeNy & W. Kintsch (Eds.), *Language and comprehension* (pp. 261–272). Amsterdam: North-Holland.

Fine, S. M. (1981). *The marketing of ideas and social issues.* New York: Praeger.

Fiske, J. (1987). *Television culture.* London: Methuen.

Flay, B. R., & Burton, D. (1990). Effective mass communication strategies for health campaigns. In C. Atkin & L. Wallack (Eds.), *Mass communication and public health* (pp. 129–146). Newbury Park, CA: Sage.

Flora, J. A., & Maibach, E. W. (1990). Cognitive responses to AIDS information: The effects of issue involvement and message appeal. *Communication Research, 17,* 759–774.

Ford, G. T., & Calfee, J. E. (1986). Recent developments in FTC policy on deception. *Journal of Marketing, 50,* 82–103.

Fore, W. F. (1987). *Television and religion: The shaping of faith, values, and culture.* Minneapolis, MN: Augsburg Publishing House.

Freedman, D. H. (1988, February). Why you watch commercials—whether you mean to or not. *TV Guide,* pp. 4–7.

Freedman, J. L. (1984). Effects of television violence on aggressiveness. *Psychological Bulletin, 96,* 227–246.

Freedman, J. L. (1986). Television violence and aggression: A rejoinder. *Psychological Bulletin, 100,* 372–378.

Freedman, J. L. (1988). Television violence and aggression: What the evidence shows. In S. Oskamp (Ed.), *Television as a social issue* (pp. 144–162). Newbury Park, CA: Sage.

Freimuth, V. S., Hammond, S. L., Edgar, T., & Monahan, J. L. (1990). Reaching those at risk: A content-analytic study of AIDS PSAs. *Communication Research, 17,* 775–791.

Freuh, T., & McGhee, P. E. (1975). Traditional sex-role development and time spent watching television. *Developmental Psychology, 11*(1), 109.

Friedrich, O. (1987, August, 17). Edging the government out of TV. *Time,* p. 58.

Friedrich-Cofer, L., & Huston, A. C. (1986). Television violence and aggression: The debate continues. *Psychological Bulletin, 100,* 364–371.

Fuchs, D. A. (1966). Election-day radio-television and Western voting. *Public Opinion Quarterly, 30,* 226–236.

Funabiki, J. (1992). "Asian invasion" cliches recall wartime propaganda. *Extra!, 5*(5), 13–14.

Ganley, G. D. (1992). *The exploding political power of personal media.* Norwood, NJ: Ablex.

Gans, H. (1979). *Deciding what's news.* New York: Pantheon.

Gardner, D. M., & Leonard, N. H. (1990). Research in deceptive and corrective advertising: Progress to date and impact on public policy. *Current Issues and Research in Advertising, 12,* 275–309.

Gardner, M. P., & Houston, M. J. (1986). The effects of verbal and visual components of retail communications. *Journal of Retailing, 62,* 64–78.

Garelik, G. (1985, April). The weather peddlers. *Discover*, pp. 18–29.

Garramone, G. M. (1984). Voter responses to negative political ads. *Journalism Quarterly, 61*(2), 250–259.

Garramone, G. M. (1985). Effects of negative political advertising: The role of sponsor and rebuttal. *Journal of Broadcasting and Electronic Media, 29*(2), 147–159.

Garramone, G. M., Atkin, C. K., Pinkleton, B. E., & Cole, R. T. (1990). Effects of negative political advertising on the political process. *Journal of Broadcasting and Electronic Media, 34*, 299–311.

Garramone, G. M., Steele, M. E., & Pinkleton, B. (1991). The role of cognitive schemata in determining candidate characteristic effects. In F. Biocca (Ed.), *Television and political advertising, Vol. 1: Psychological processes* (pp. 311–328). Hillsdale, NJ: Lawrence Erlbaum Associates.

Gebhard, P. (1977). The acquisition of basic sex information. *Journal of Sex Research, 13*, 148–169.

Geen, R. G., & Quanty, M. B. (1977). The catharsis of aggression: An evaluation of a hypothesis. In L. Berkowitz (Ed.), *Advances in experimental social psychology* (Vol. 10, pp. 1–37). New York: Academic Press.

Geiger, S. F., & Reeves, B. (1991). The effects of visual structure and content emphasis on the evaluation and memory for political candidates. In F. Biocca (Ed.), *Television and political advertising, Vol. 1: Psychological processes* (pp. 125–143). Hillsdale, NJ: Lawrence Erlbaum Associates.

Geiger, S., & Reeves, B. (1993a). The effects of scene changes and semantic relatedness on attention to television. *Communication Research, 20*, 155–175.

Geiger, S., & Reeves, B. (1993b). We interrupt this program . . . Attention for television sequences. *Human Communication Research, 19*, 368–387.

Geis, F., Brown, V., Jennings, J., & Porter, N. (1984). TV commercials as achievement scripts for women. *Sex Roles, 10*(7/8), 513–525.

Geis, M. L. (1982). *The language of television advertising.* New York: Academic Press.

Gelb, B. D., & Zinkhan, G. M. (1985). The effect of repetition on humor in a radio advertising study. *Journal of Advertising, 14*(4), 13–20.

Gerbner, G., & Gross, L. (1980). The violent face of television and its lessons. In E. Palmer & A. Dorr (Eds.), *Children and the faces of television: Teaching, violence, selling* (pp. 149–162). New York: Academic Press.

Gerbner, G., Gross, L., Morgan, M., & Signorielli, N. (1980). The mainstreaming of America: Violence profile No. 11. *Journal of Communication, 30*(3), 10–29.

Gerbner, G., Gross, L., Morgan, M., & Signorielli, N. (1981a). Health and medicine on television. *New England Journal of Medicine, 305*(15), 901–904.

Gerbner, G., Gross, L., Morgan, M., & Signorielli, N. (1981b). Scientists on the TV screen. *Society, 18*(4), 41–44.

Gerbner, G., Gross, L., Morgan, M., & Signorielli, N. (1982). Charting the mainstream: Television's contributions to political orientations. *Journal of Communication, 32*(2), 100–127.

Gerbner, G., Gross, L., Morgan, M., & Signorielli, N. (1984). Political correlates of television viewing. *Public Opinion Quarterly, 48*, 283–300.

Gerbner, G., Gross, L., Morgan, M., & Signorielli, N. (1986). Living with television: The dynamics of the cultivation process. In J. Bryant & D. Zillmann (Eds.), *Perspectives on media effects* (pp. 17–40). Hillsdale, NJ: Lawrence Erlbaum Associates.

Gerbner, G., Gross, L., Morgan, M., & Signorielli, N. (in press). Growing up with television: The cultivation perspective. In J. Bryant & D. Zillmann (Eds.), *Media effects: Advances in theory and research.* Hillsdale, NJ: Lawrence Erlbaum Associates.

Gerbner, G., Gross, L., Signorielli, N., & Morgan, M. (1980). Aging with television: Images on television drama and conception of social reality. *Journal of Communication, 30*(1), 37–47.

Gerbner, G., Gross, L., Signorielli, N., & Morgan, M. (1986). *Television's mean world: Violence profile No. 14–15.* Philadelphia: Annenberg School of Communication, University of Pennsylvania.

Gerbner, G., Gross, L., Signorielli, N., & Morgan, M., & Jackson-Beeck, M. (1979). The demonstration of power: Violence profile No. 10. *Journal of Communication, 29*(3), 177–195.

Gerbner, G. & Signorielli, N. (1979). *Women and minorities in television drama* (1969–1978). Philadelphia: Annenberg School of Communication, University of Pennsylvania.

Gilly, M. C. (1988). Sex roles in advertising: A comparison of television advertisements in Australia, Mexico, and the United States. *Journal of Marketing, 52,* 75–85.

Goldberg, M. (1988, February 20). Take two doses for Kildare and Casey and don't call me in the morning. *TV Guide,* pp. 12–13.

Goldstein, J. H. (Ed.). (1986). *Reporting science: The case of aggression.* Hillsdale, NJ: Lawrence Erlbaum Associates.

Goldstein, J. H., & Arms, R. L. (1971). Effects of observing athletic contests on hostility. *Sociometry, 34,* 83–90.

Goldstein, S., & Ibaraki, T. (1983). Japan: Aggression and aggression control in Japanese society. In A. Goldstein & M. Segall (Eds.), *Aggression in global perspective.* New York: Pergamon Press.

Gorn, G. I., Goldberg, M. E., & Kanungo, R. N. (1976). The role of educational television in changing intergroup attitudes of children. *Child Development, 47,* 277–280.

Graber, D. A. (1988). *Processing the news: How people tame the information tide.* New York: Longman.

Graber, D. A. (1989). Content and meaning: What's it all about? *American Behavioral Scientist, 33,* 144–151.

Graber, D. A. (1990). Seeing is remembering: How visuals contribute to learning from television news. *Journal of Communication, 40*(3), 134–155.

Graesser, A. C., & Bower, G. H. (Eds.). (1990). *Inferences and text comprehension.* San Diego: Academic Press.

Graves, S. B. (1980). Psychological effects of black portrayals on television. In S. B. Withey & R. P. Abeles (Eds.), *Television and social behavior* (pp. 259–289). Hillsdale, NJ: Lawrence Erlbaum Associates.

Gray, H. (1986). Television and the new black man: Black male images in prime-time situation comedy. *Media, Culture and Society, 8,* 223–242.

Greeley, A. M. (1988, July 9). In defense of TV evangelism. *TV Guide,* pp. 4–7.

Greenberg, B. S. (1980). *Life on television.* Norwood, NJ: Ablex.

Greenberg, B. S. (1982). Television and role socialization. In D. Pearl, L. Bouthilet, & J. Lazar (Eds.), *Television and behavior: Ten years of scientific progress and implications for the eighties: Vol. 2. Technical Reviews.* Rockville, MD: NIMH.

Greenberg, B. S. (1986). Minorities and the mass media. In J. Bryant & D. Zillman (Eds.), *Perspectives on media effects* (pp. 165–188). Hillsdale, NJ: Lawrence Erlbaum Associates.

Greenberg, B. S. (1988). Some uncommon television images and the Drench Hypothesis. In S. Oskamp (Ed.), *Television as a social issue* (pp. 88–102). Newbury Park, CA: Sage.

Greenberg, B. S., Abelman, R., & Neuendorf, K. (1981). Sex on the soap operas: Afternoon intimacy. *Journal of Communication, 31*(3), 83–89.

Greenberg, B. S., & Atkin, C. (1982). Learning about minorities from television: A research agenda. In G. Berry & C. Mitchell-Kernan (Eds.), *Television and the socialization of the minority child* (pp. 215–243). New York: Academic Press.

Greenberg, B. S., & Brand, J. E. (1993). Television news and advertising in schools: The "Channel One" controversy. *Journal of Communication, 43*(1), 143–151.

Greenberg, B. S., & Brand, J. E. (in press). Minorities and the mass media: 1970s to 1990s. In J. Bryant & D. Zillmann (Eds.), *Media effects: Advances in theory and research.* Hillsdale, NJ: Lawrence Erlbaum Associates.

Greenberg, B. S., Brown, J. D., & Buerkel-Rothfuss, N. L. (1993). *Media, sex, and the adolescent.* Cresskill, NJ: Hampton Press.

Greenberg, B. S., & D'Alessio, D. (1985). Quantity and quality of sex in the soaps. *Journal of Broadcasting & Electronic Media, 29,* 309–321.

Greenberg, B. S., & Gantz, W. (Eds.). (1993). *Desert Storm and the mass media.* Cresskill, NJ: Hampton Press.

Greenberg, B. S., Heeter, C., Graef, D., Doctor, K., Burgoon, J. K., Burgoon, M., & Korzenny, F. (1983). Mass communication and Mexican Americans. In B. S. Greenberg, M. Burgoon, J. K. Burgoon, & F. Korzenny (Eds.), *Mexican Americans and the mass media* (pp. 7–34). Norwood, NJ: Ablex.

Greenberg, B. S., Korzenny, F., & Atkin, C. (1979). The portrayal of the aging: Trends on commercial television. *Research on Aging, 1*, 319–334.

Greenberg, B. S., Ku, L., & Li, H. (1992). Parental mediation of children's mass media behaviors in China, Japan, Korea, Taiwan, and the United States. In F. Korzenny & S. Ting-Toomey (Eds.), *Mass media effects across cultures* (pp. 150–172). Newbury Park, CA: Sage.

Greenberg, B. S., Neuendorf, K., Buerkel-Rothfuss, N., & Henderson, L. (1982). The soaps: What's on and who cares? *Journal of Broadcasting, 26*(2), 519–535.

Greene, E., & Wade, R. (1987). Of private talk and public print: General pre-trial publicity and juror decision-making. *Applied Cognitive Psychology, 1*, 1–13.

Greenfield, J. (1985, March 2). Rich is in—and we may be the poorer for it. *TV Guide*, pp. 2–5.

Greenfield, P. M. (1984). *Mind and media*. Cambridge, MA: Harvard University Press.

Greenfield, P. & Beagles-Roos, J. (1988). Radio vs. television: The cognitive impact on different socioeconomic and ethnic groups. *Journal of Communication, 38*(2), 71–92.

Greenfield, P., Farrar, D., & Beagles-Roos, J. (1986). Is the medium the message? An experimental comparison of the effects of radio and television on imagination. *Journal of Applied Developmental Psychology, 7*, 201–218.

Greenwald, A. G., Spangenberg, E. R., Pratkanis, A. R., & Eskanazi, J. (1991). Double-blind tests of subliminal self-help audiotapes. *Psychological Science, 2*, 119–122.

Griggs, R. A. (1983). The role of problem content in the selection task and THOG problem. In J. St. B. T. Evans (Ed.), *Thinking and reasoning: Psychological approaches*. London: Routledge & Kegan Paul.

Grimes, T. (1990). Audio–video correspondence and its role in attention and memory. *Educational Technology, Research, and Development, 38*, 15–25.

Grimes, T. (1991). Mild auditory–visual dissonance in television news may exceed viewer attentional capacity. *Human Communication Research, 17*, 268–298.

Gross, L. (1984). The cultivation of intolerance: Television, blacks, and gays. In G. Melischek, K. E. Rosengren, & J. Stappers (Eds.), *Cultural indicators: An international symposium* (pp. 345–364). Vienna: Austrian Academy of Sciences.

Gumpert, G. (1987). *Talking tombstones and other tales of the media age*. New York: Oxford University Press.

Gunter, B. (1985). *Dimensions of television violence*. New York: St. Martin's Press.

Gunter, B. (1986). *Television and sex-role stereotyping*. London: John Libbey.

Gunter, B. (1987). *Poor reception: Misunderstanding and forgetting broadcast news*. Hillsdale, NJ: Lawrence Erlbaum Associates.

Gunter, B. (in press). The question of media violence. In J. Bryant & D. Zillmann (Eds.), *Media effects: Advances in theory and research*. Hillsdale, NJ: Lawrence Erlbaum Associates.

Gunter, B., Berry, C., & Clifford, B. (1982). Remembering broadcast news: The implications of experimental research for production technique. *Human Learning, 1*, 13–29.

Gunter, B., & Levy, M. M. (1987). Social contexts of video use. *American Behavioral Scientist, 30*, 486–494.

Gunter, B., & Svennevig, M. (1987). *Behind and in front of the screen: Television's involvement with family life*. London: John Libbey.

Guttman, A. (1986). *Sports spectators*. New York: Columbia University Press.

Hallin, D. C. (1992). Sound bite news: Television coverage of elections, 1968–1988. *Journal of Communication, 42*(2), 5–24.

Handler, D. (1987, April 18). TV finished first, friends second, helping others third. *TV Guide*, pp. 20–21.

Hanratty, M. A., O'Neal, E., & Sulzer, J. L. (1972). The effect of frustration upon imitation of aggression. *Journal of Personality and Social Psychology, 21*, 30–34.

Hansen, C. H., & Hansen, R. D. (1990). The influence of sex and violence on the appeal of rock music videos. *Communication Research, 17,* 212–234.

Hardaway, F. (1979). The language of popular culture: Daytime television as a transmitter of values. *College English, 40*(5), 517–521.

Harris, A., & Feinberg, J. (1977). Television and aging: Is what you see what you get? *Gerontologist, 17,* 464–468.

Harris, R. J. (1981). Inferences in information processing. In G. H. Bower (Ed.), *The psychology of learning and motivation* (Vol. 15, pp. 82–128). New York: Academic Press.

Harris, R. J., Dubitsky, T. M., & Bruno, K. J. (1983). Psycholinguistic studies of misleading advertising. In R. J. Harris (Ed.), *Information processing research in advertising* (pp. 241–262). Hillsdale, NJ: Lawrence Erlbaum Associates.

Harris, R. J., Pounds, J. C., Maiorelle, M. J., & Mermis, M. M. (1993). The effect of type of claim, gender, and buying history on the drawing of pragmatic inferences from advertising claims. *Journal of Consumer Psychology, 2,* 83–95.

Harris, R. J., Schoen, L. M., & Hensley, D. (1992). A cross-cultural study of story memory. *Journal of Cross-cultural Psychology, 23,* 133–147.

Harris, R. J., Sturm, R. E., Klassen, M. L., & Bechtold, J. I. (1986). Language in advertising: A psycholinguistic approach. *Current Issues and Research in Advertising, 9,* 1–26.

Harris, R. J., Trusty, M. L., Bechtold, J. I., & Wasinger, L. (1989). Memory for implied versus directly asserted advertising claims. *Psychology & Marketing, 6,* 87–96.

Hartmann, D. P. (1969). Influence of symbolically modelled instrumental aggression and pain cues on aggressive behavior. *Journal of Personality and Social Psychology, 11,* 280–288.

Harvey, M., & Rothe, J. (1986). Videocassette recorders: Their impact on viewers and advertisers. *Journal of Advertising Research, 25*(6), 19–27.

Harwood, J., & Giles, H. (1992). "Don't make me laugh": Age representations in a humorous context. *Discourse & Society, 3,* 403–436.

Hass, R. G. (1981). Effects of source characteristics on cognitive responses and persuasion. In R. E. Petty, T. M. Ostrom, & T. C. Brock (Eds.), *Cognitive responses in persuasion* (pp. 141–172). Hillsdale, NJ: Lawrence Erlbaum Associates.

Hausknecht, D., & Moore, D. L. (1986). The effects of time compressed advertising of brand attitude judgments. *Advances in Consumer Research, 13,* 105–110.

Hawkins, R. P., Kim, Y.-H., & Pingree, S. (1991). The ups and downs of attention to television. *Communication Research, 18,* 53–76.

Hawkins, R. P., & Pingree, S. (1981). Uniform messages and habitual viewing: Unnecessary assumptions in social reality effects. *Human Communication Research, 7,* 291–301.

Hawkins, R. P., & Pingree, S. (1990). Divergent psychological processes in constructing social reality from mass media content. In N. Signorielli & M. Morgan (Eds.), *Cultivation analysis* (pp. 35–50). Newbury Park, CA: Sage.

Hawkins, R. P., Pingree, S., & Adler, I. (1987). Searching for cognitive processes in the cultivation effect: Adult and adolescent samples in the United States and Australia. *Human Communication Research, 13,* 553–577.

Hayes, D., & Birnbaum, D. W. (1980). Preschoolers' retention of televised events: Is a picture worth a thousand words? *Developmental Psychology, 16,* 410–416.

Hearold, S. (1986). A synthesis of 1043 effects of television on social behavior. In G. Comstock (Ed.), *Public communication and behavior* (Vol. 1, pp. 65–133). Orlando: Academic Press.

Heath, R. L., & Bryant, J. (1992). *Human communication theory and research: Concepts, contexts, and challenges.* Hillsdale, NJ: Lawrence Erlbaum Associates.

Heath, T. B., Mothersbaugh, D. L., & McCarthy, M. S. (1993). Spokesperson effects in high involvement markets. *Advances in Consumer Research, 20,* 704–707.

Hebditch, D., & Anning, N. (1988). *Porn gold: Inside the pornography business.* London: Faber & Faber.

Heiby, E., & Becker, J. D. (1980). Effect of filmed modeling on the self-reported frequency of masturbation. *Archives of Sexual Behavior, 9,* 115–121.

Heiman, J., LoPiccolo, L., & LoPiccolo, J. (1976). *Becoming orgasmic: A sexual growth program for women.* Englewood Cliffs, NJ: Prentice-Hall.

Heller, M. S., & Polsky, S. (1975). *Studies in violence and television.* New York: American Broadcasting Companies.

Heritage, J. (1985). Analyzing news interviews: Aspects of the production of talk for an overhearing audience. In T. A. van Dijk (Ed.), *Handbook of discourse analysis* (Vol. 3, pp. 95–117). London: Academic Press.

Herman, E. S., & Chomsky, N. (1988). *Manufacturing consent: The political economy of the mass media.* New York: Pantheon.

Herman, E. S., & O'Sullivan, G. (1989). *The terrorism industry: The experts and institutions that shape our view of terror.* New York: Pantheon.

Hersch, P. (1988, October). Thirtysomething therapy. *Psychology Today,* pp. 62–64.

Hessing, D. J., & Elffers, H. (1986). Attitude toward death, fear of being declared dead too soon, and donation of organs after death. *Omega, 17*(2), 115–126.

Hickey, N. (1988, January 2). It's upbeat TV—or else! *TV Guide,* pp. 36–39.

Hicks, D. J. (1965). Imitation and retention of film-mediated aggressive peer and adult models. *Journal of Personality and Social Psychology, 2,* 97–100.

Hicks, D. J. (1968). Short- and long-term retention of affectively varied modeled behavior. *Psychonomic Science, 11,* 369–370.

Hiebert, E., & Reuss, C. (Eds.). (1985). *Impact of mass media: Current issues.* White Plains, NY: Longman.

Hill, C., Davis, H., Holman, R., & Nelson, G. (1984). *Video violence and children.* London: Report of a Parliamentary Group Video Enquiry.

Hill, R. P. (1991). Political advertising in the 1990s: Expected strategies, voter responses, and public policy implications. *Advances in Consumer Research, 18,* 715–719.

Himmelweit, H. (1978). Youth, television, and experimentation. In *Cultural role of broadcasting.* Tokyo: Hoso-Bunka Foundation.

Hinck, E. A. (1992). *Enacting the Presidency: Political argument, Presidential debates, and Presidential character.* Westport, CT: Praeger.

Hirsch, P. M. (1980). The "scary world" of the nonviewer and other anomalies: A reanalysis of Gerbner et al.'s findings on cultivation analysis, part I. *Communication Research, 7,* 403–456.

Hirschberg, M. S. (1993). *Perpetuating patriotic perceptions: The cognitive function of the Cold War.* Westport, CT: Greenwood.

Hoijer, B. (1989). Television-evoked thoughts and their relation to comprehension. *Communication Research, 16,* 179–203.

Hoover, S. M. (1988). *Mass media religion.* Newbury Park, CA: Sage.

Howell, F., Miracle, A., & Rees, R. (1984). Do high school athletics pay? The effects of varsity participation on socioeconomic attainment. *Sociology of Sport Journal, 1*(1), 15–25.

Howitt, D. (1982). *Mass media and social problems.* Oxford: Pergamon Press.

Hoy, M. G., Young, C. E., & Mowen, J. C. (1986). Animated host-selling advertisements: Their impact on young children's recognition, attitudes, and behavior. *Journal of Public Policy and Marketing, 5,* 171–184.

Huesmann, L. R., Eron, L. D., Klein, R., Brice, P., & Fischer, P. (1983). Mitigating the imitation of aggressive behaviors by changing children's attitudes about media violence. *Journal of Personality and Social Psychology, 44,* 899–910.

Huesmann, L. R., Eron, L. D., Lefkowitz, M. M., & Walder, L. O. (1984). Stability of aggression over time and generations. *Developmental Psychology, 20,* 1120–1134.

Huesmann, L. R., Lagerspetz, K., & Eron, L. D. (1984). Intervening variables in the TV violence–aggression relation: Evidence from two countries. *Developmental Psychology, 20,* 746–775.

Hughes, M. (1980). The fruits of cultivation analysis: A reexamination of some effects of television watching. *Public Opinion Quarterly, 44,* 287–302.

Husson, W., Stephen, T., Harrison, T. M., & Fehr, B. J. (1988). An interpersonal communication perspective on images of political candidates. *Human Communication Research, 14,* 397–421.

Huston, A. C., Donnerstein, E., Fairchild, H. H., Feshbach, N. D., Katz, P., Murray, J. P., Rubinstein, E. A., Wilcox, B. L., & Zuckerman, D. (1992). *Big world, small screen: The role of television in American society.* Washington, DC: American Psychological Association.

Huston, A. C., & Wright, J. C. (1987). The forms of television and the child viewer. In G. A. Comstock (Ed.), *Public communication and behavior* (Vol. 2, pp. 103–159). New York: Academic Press.

Iiyama, P., & Kitano, H. H. L. (1982). Asian-Americans and the media. In G. L. Berry & C. Mitchell-Kernan (Eds.), *Television and the socialization of the minority child* (pp. 151–186). New York: Academic Press.

Ilola, L. M. (1990). Culture and health. In R. W. Brislin (Ed.), *Applied cross-cultural psychology* (pp. 278–301). Newbury Park, CA: Sage.

Intons-Peterson, M. J., & Roskos-Ewoldsen, B. (1989). Mitigating the effects of violent pornography. In S. Gubar & J. Hoff-Wilson (Eds.), *For adult users, only.* Bloomington, IN: Indiana University Press.

Intons-Peterson, M. J., Roskos-Ewoldsen, B., Thomas, L., Shirley, M., & Blut, D. (1989). Will educational materials reduce negative effects of exposure to sexual violence? *Journal of Social and Clinical Psychology, 8,* 256–275.

Iyengar, S., & Simon, A. (1993). News coverage of the Gulf Crisis and public opinion. *Communication Research, 20,* 365–383.

Jackson, D. Z. (1989, January 22). Calling the plays in black and white. *The Boston Globe,* pp. A30–A33.

Jacoby, J., & Hoyer, W. D. (1987). *The comprehension and miscomprehension of print communication: A study of mass media magazines.* Hillsdale, NJ: Lawrence Erlbaum Associates.

Jakes, J. (1985, November 2). What? A successful media campaign without TV spots and Phil Donohue? *TV Guide,* pp. 12–15.

Jamieson, K. H., & Campbell, K. K. (1992). *The interplay of influence: News, advertising, politics, and the mass media.* (3rd ed.). Belmont, CA: Wadsworth.

Janis, I. L. (1980). The influence of television on personal decision making. In S. B. Withey & R. P. Abeles (Eds.), *Television and social behavior* (pp. 161–189). Hillsdale, NJ: Lawrence Erlbaum Associates.

Jennings, J., Geis, F., & Brown, V. (1980). Influence of television commercials on women's self-confidence and independent judgment. *Journal of Personality and Social Psychology, 38*(2), 203–210.

Jhally, S., & Lewis, J. (1992). *Enlightened racism: The Cosby Show, audiences, and the myth of the American dream.* Colorado: Westview Press.

Johnson, D. K., & Satow, K. (1978). Consumers' reaction to sex in TV commercials. *Advances in Consumer Research, 5,* 411–414.

Johnson-Cartee, K. S., & Copeland, G. A. (1991). *Negative political advertising: Coming of age.* Hillsdale, NJ: Lawrence Erlbaum Associates.

Johnsson-Smaragdi, U. (1983). *TV use and social interaction in adolescence: A longitudinal study.* Stockholm: Almqvist & Wiksell International.

Johnston, J., & Ettema, J. (1982). *Positive images: Breaking stereotypes with children's television.* Beverly Hills, CA: Sage.

Johnston, J., & Ettema, J. S. (1986). Using television to best advantage: Research for prosocial television. In J. Bryant & D. Zillmann (Eds.), *Perspectives on media effects* (pp. 143–164). Hillsdale, NJ: Lawrence Erlbaum Associates.

Jowett, G., & Linton, J. M. (1989). *Movies as mass communication* (2nd ed.). Newbury Park, CA: Sage.

Joy, L. A., Kimball, M. M., & Zabrack, M. L. (1986). Television and children's aggressive behavior. In T. M. Williams (Ed.), *The impact of television: A natural experiment in three communities* (pp. 303–360). Orlando: Academic Press.

Joyce, E. M. (1986). Reporting of hostage crises: Who's in charge of television? *SAIS Review, 6*(1), 169–176.

Just, M., Crigler, A., & Wallach, L. (1990). Thirty seconds or thirty minutes: What viewers learn from spot advertisements and candidate debates. *Journal of Communication, 40*(3), 120–133.

Kahle, L. R., & Homer, P. M. (1985). Physical attractiveness of the celebrity endorsers: A social adaptation perspective. *Journal of Consumer Research, 11,* 954–961.

Kaid, L. L., & Boydston, J. (1987). An experimental study of the effectiveness of negative political advertisements. *Communication Quarterly, 35,* 193–201.

Kaid, L. L., Gerstle, J., & Sanders, K. R. (Eds.). (1991). *Mediated politics in two cultures: Presidential campaigning in the United States and France.* New York: Prager.

Kaid, L. L., & Johnston, A. (1991). Negative versus positive television advertising in U.S. Presidential campaigns, 1960–1988. *Journal of Communication, 41*(3), 53–64.

Kalter, J. (1986a, May 11). Disability chic. *TV Guide,* pp. 40–44.

Kalter, J. (1987a, May 30). Exposing media myths: TV doesn't affect you as much as you think. *TV Guide,* pp. 2–5.

Kalter, J. (1987b, July 11). Guess right—or we'll throw you to the bees! *TV Guide,* pp. 26–28.

Kalter, J. (1988a, January 30). What working women want from TV. *TV Guide,* pp. 2–7.

Kalter, J. (1988c, July 23). How TV is shaking up the American family. *TV Guide,* pp. 4–11.

Kardes, F. R. (1992). Consumer inference: Determinants, consequences, and implications for advertising. In A. A. Mitchell (Ed.), *Advertising exposure, memory, and choice.* Hillsdale, NJ: Lawrence Erlbaum Associates.

Kassarjian, H. (1969). The Negro and American advertising: 1946–1965. *Journal of Marketing Research, 6,* 29–39.

Kelly, H. (1981). Reasoning about realities: Children's evaluations of television and books. In H. Kelly & H. Gardner (Eds.), *Viewing children through television.* San Francisco: Jossey-Bass.

Kendall, K. E., & Yum, J. O. (1984). Persuading the blue-collar voter: Issues, images, and homophily. In R. N. Bostrom (Ed.), *Communication yearbook 8* (pp. 707–722). Beverly Hills, CA: Sage.

Kenner, H. (1973, July 29). Review of E. Carpenter, *Oh, what a blow that phantom gave me. New York Times Book Review,* p. 7.

Kenrick, D. T., Gutierres, S. E., & Goldberg, L. L. (1989). Influence of popular erotica on judgments of strangers and mates. *Journal of Experimental Social Psychology, 25,* 159–167.

Key, W. B. (1974). *Subliminal seduction.* New York: Signet.

Key, W. B. (1976). *Media sexploitation.* New York: Signet.

Key, W. B. (1981). *The clam-plate orgy.* New York: Signet.

Key, W. B. (1989). *The age of manipulation.* New York: Holt.

Kilbourne, W. E., Painton, S., & Ridley, D. (1985). The effect of sexual embedding on responses to magazine advertisements. *Journal of Advertising, 14*(2), 48–56.

Kimball, M. M. (1986). Television and sex-role attitudes. In T. M. Williams (Ed.), *The impact of television: A natural experiment in three communities* (pp. 265–302). Orlando: Academic Press.

King, K. W., & Reid, L. N. (1990). Fear arousing anti-drinking and driving PSAs: Do physical injury threats influence young people? *Current Issues and Research in Advertising, 12,* 155–175.

Kintsch, W. (1977). On comprehending stories. In P. Carpenter & M. Just (Eds.), *Cognitive processes in comprehension.* Hillsdale, NJ: Lawrence Erlbaum Associates.

Kintsch, W., & van Dijk, T. A. (1978). Toward a model of text comprehension and production. *Psychological Review, 85,* 363–394.

Klapper, J. T. (1960). *The effects of mass communications.* Glencoe, IL: Free Press.

Klatell, D. A., & Marcus, N. (1988). *Sports for sale: Television, money, and the fans.* New York: Oxford University Press.

Kline, S. (1992). *Out of the garden: Toys, TV, and children's culture in the age of marketing.* New York: Verso.

Knill, B. J., Pesch, M., Pursey, G., Gilpin, P., & Perloff, R. M. (1981). Still typecast after all these years? Sex role portrayals in television advertising. *International Journal of Women's Studies, 4,* 497–506.

Kolatch, J. (1986a, May 31). Uprising in the Philippines: Could there have been a revolution without television? *TV Guide*, pp. 4–14.

Kolatch, J. (1986b, June 7). TV and the Philippines: For the first time the people could see what was happening. *TV Guide*, pp. 16–21.

Kolbe, R. H., & Muehling, D. D. (1992). A content analysis of the "fine print" in television advertising. *Journal of Current Issues and Research in Advertising, 14*(2), 47–61.

Kopkind, A. (1993, May/June). From Russia with love and squalor. *Utne Reader*, pp. 80–89.

Korzenny, F., & Ting-Toomey, S. (Eds.). (1992). *Mass media effects across cultures*. Newbury Park, CA: Sage.

Kosicki, G. M. (1993). Problems and opportunities in agenda-setting research. *Journal of Communication, 43*(2), 100–127.

Kottak, C. P. (1990). *Prime-time society: An anthropological analysis of television and culture*. Belmont, CA: Wadsworth.

Krafka, C. L. (1985). *Sexually explicit, sexually violent, and violent media: Effects of multiple naturalistic exposures and debriefing on female viewers*. Unpublished doctoral dissertation, University of Wisconsin, Madison.

Kraft, R. N., Cantor, P., & Gottdiener, C. (1991). The coherence of visual narratives. *Communication Research, 18*, 601–616.

Kraus, S. (Ed.). (1962). *The great debates*. Bloomington, IN: Indiana University Press.

Kraus, S. (Ed.). (1977). *The great debates: 1976, Ford vs. Carter*. Bloomington, IN: Indiana University Press.

Kraus, S. (1988). *Televised presidential debates and public policy*. Hillsdale, NJ: Lawrence Erlbaum Associates.

Kubey, R. (1980). Television and aging: Past, present, and future. *Gerontologist, 20*, 16–35.

Kubey, R. (1986). Television use in everyday life: Coping with unstructured time. *Journal of Communication, 36*, 108–123.

Kubey, R. (1992). A critique of *No Sense of Place* and the homogenization theory of Joshua Meyrowitz. *Communication Theory, 2*, 259–271.

Kubey, R., & Csikszentmihalyi, M. (1990). *Television and the quality of life: How viewing shapes everyday experience*. Hillsdale, NJ: Lawrence Erlbaum Associates.

Kunkel, D. (1988). Children and host-selling television commercials. *Communication Research, 15*(1), 71–92.

Kutchinsky, B. (1973). The effect of easy availability of pornography on the incidence of sex crimes: The Danish experience. *Journal of Social Issues, 29*(3), 163–181.

Kutchinsky, B. (1985). In R. F. Tomasson (Ed.), *Comparative social research* (Vol 8). Greenwich, CT: JAI Press.

Lambert, W. E., & Klineberg, O. (1967). *Children's views of foreign peoples: A cross-national study*. New York: Appleton-Century-Crofts.

Lang, A. (1990). Involuntary attention and physiological arousal evoked by structural features and emotional content in TV commercials. *Communication Research, 17*, 275–299.

Lang, A. (1991). Emotion, formal features, and memory for televised political advertisements. In F. Biocca (Ed.), *Television and political advertising: Vol. 1. Psychological Processes* (pp. 221–243). Hillsdale, NJ: Lawrence Erlbaum Associates.

Lang, A., Geiger, S., Strickwerda, M., & Sumner, J. (1993). The effects of related and unrelated cuts on television viewers' attention, processing capacity, and memory. *Communication Research, 20*, 4–29.

Lang, G. E., & Lang, K. (1984). *Politics and television re-viewed* Beverly Hills, CA: Sage.

Lang, K., & Lang, G. E. (1968). *Politics and television*. Chicago: Quadrangle Books.

Lapchick, R., & Rodriguez, A. (1990). Professional sports: The 1990 racial report card. *Center for the Study of Sport in Society Digest, 2*(2), 4–5.

Larsen, S. F. (1983). Text processing and knowledge updating in memory for radio news. *Discourse Processes, 6*, 21–38.

Larson, J. F. (1984). *Television's window on the world: International affairs coverage on the U.S. networks.* Norwood, NJ: Ablex.

Larson, J. F. (1986). Television and U.S. foreign policy: The case of the Iran hostage crisis. *Journal of Communication, 36*(4), 108–130.

Larson, J. F., McAnany, E. G., & Storey, J. D. (1986). News of Latin America on network television, 1972–1981: A northern perspective on the southern hemisphere. *Critical Studies in Mass Communication, 3,* 169–183.

Lasisi, M. J., & Onyehalu, A. S. (1992). Cultural influences of a reading text on the concept formation of second-language learners of two Nigerian ethnic groups. In R. J. Harris (Ed.), *Cognitive processing in bilinguals* (pp. 459–471). Amsterdam: Elsevier/North Holland.

Lasswell, H. D. (1927). *Propaganda technique in the world war.* New York: Knopf.

Lasswell, H. D. (1935). *World politics and personal insecurity: A contribution to political psychiatry.* New York: McGraw-Hill.

Lau, R. R. (1986). Political schemata, candidate evaluations, and voting behavior. In R. R. Lau & D. O. Sears (Eds.), *Political cognition* (pp. 95–126). Hillsdale, NJ: Lawrence Erlbaum Associates.

Lazarsfeld, P. F. (1941). Remarks on administrative and critical communications research. *Studies in Philosophy of Social Science, 9,* 2–16.

Lazarsfeld, P. F., Berelson, B., & Gaudet, H. (1948). *The people's choice.* New York: Columbia University Press.

Leavitt, L. A., & Fox, N. A. (Eds.). (in press). *The psychological effects of war and violence on children.* Hillsdale, NJ: Lawrence Erlbaum Associates.

Lee, C. C. (1980). *Media imperialism reconsidered.* Beverly Hills, CA: Sage.

Lee, M. A., & Solomon, N. (1991). *Unreliable sources: A guide to detecting bias in news media.* New York: Carol Publishing Group.

Lefkowitz, M. M., Eron, L. D., Walder, L. O., & Huesmann, L. R. (1977). *Growing up to be violent: A longitudinal study of the development of aggression.* New York: Pergamon.

Lemar, J. (1977). Women and blacks on prime-time television. *Journal of Communication, 27,* 70–80.

Lever, J., & Wheeler, S. (1993). Mass media and the experience of sport. *Communication Research, 20,* 125–143.

Levin, I. P., & Gaeth, G. J. (1988). How consumers are affected by the framing of attribute information before and after consuming the product. *Journal of Consumer Research, 15,* 374–378.

Levy, M. R. (1980). Program playback preferences in VCR households. *Journal of Broadcasting, 24,* 327–336.

Levy, M. R. (1982). Watching TV news as para-social interaction. In G. Gumpert & R. Cathcart (Eds.), *Inter/media* (2nd ed., pp. 177–187). New York: Oxford University Press.

Levy, M. R. (1987). Some problems of VCR research. *American Behavioral Scientist, 30,* 461–470.

Levy, M. R., & Windahl, S. (1984). Audience activity and gratifications: A conceptual clarification and exploration. *Communication Research, 11,* 51–78.

Lewy, G. (1978, February). Vietnam: New light on the question of American guilt. *Commentary, 65,* 29–49.

Leyens, J., Camino, L., Parke, R., & Berkowitz, L. (1975). The effects of movie violence on aggression in a field setting as a function of group dominance and cohesion. *Journal of Personality and Social Psychology, 32,* 346–360.

Liebert, R. M., & Sprafkin, J. (1988). *The early window: Effects of television on children and youth* (3rd ed.). New York: Pergamon.

Liebes, T., & Livingstone, S. M. (1992). Mothers and lovers: Managing women's role conflicts in American and British soap operas. In J. G. Blumler, J. M. McLeod, & K. E. Rosengren (Eds.), *Comparatively speaking: Communication and culture across space and time* (pp. 94–120). Newbury Park, CA: Sage.

Lindlof, T. R., & Shatzer, M. J. (1990). VCR usage in the American family. In J. Bryant (Ed.), *Television and the American family* (pp. 89–109). Hillsdale, NJ: Lawrence Erlbaum Associates.

Linz, D. (1985). *Sexual violence in the mass media: Effects on male viewers and implications for society.* Unpublished doctoral dissertation, University of Wisconsin, Madison.

Linz, D., & Donnerstein, E. (1988). The methods and merits of pornography research. *Journal of Communication, 38*(2), 180–184.

Linz, D., & Donnerstein, E. (1992, September 30). Research can help us explain violence and pornography. *Chronicle of Higher Education,* pp. B3–B4.

Linz, D., & Donnerstein, E., & Adams, S. M. (1989). Physiological desensitization and judgments about female victims of violence. *Human Communication Research, 15,* 509–522.

Linz, D., Donnerstein, E., Bross, M., & Chapin, M. (1986). Mitigating the influence of violence on television and sexual violence in the media. In R. Blanchard (Ed.), *Advances in the study of aggression* (Vol. 2, pp. 165–194). Orlando, FL: Academic Press.

Linz, D., Donnerstein, E., & Penrod, S. (1984). The effects of multiple exposures to filmed violence against women. *Journal of Communication, 34*(3), 130–147.

Linz, D., Donnerstein, E., & Penrod, S. (1987). The findings and recommendations of the Attorney General's Commission on Pornography: Do the psychological "facts" fit the political fury? *American Psychologist, 42,* 946–953.

Linz, D., Fuson, I. A., & Donnerstein, E. (1990). Mitigating the negative effects of sexually violent mass communications through preexposure briefings. *Communication Research, 17,* 641–674.

Linz, D., & Malamuth, N. (1993). *Pornography.* Newbury Park, CA: Sage.

Linz, D., Turner, C. W., Hesse, B. W., & Penrod, S. D. (1984). Bases of liability for injuries produced by media portrayals of violent pornography. In N. M. Malamuth & E. Donnerstein (Eds.), *Pornography and sexual aggression* (pp. 277–304). Orlando: Academic Press.

Lippmann, W. (1922). *Public opinion.* New York: Harcourt Brace and World.

Littwin, S. (1988, April 9). How TV Americanizes immigrants—for better or for worse. *TV Guide,* pp. 4–10.

Lobo, I. (1991, July). *Television: Ideologia y socializacion. Un estudio comparativo con ninos en edad preschollar* [Television: Ideology and socialization. A comparative study of preschool children]. Paper presented at meeting of the Interamerican Congress of Psychology, San Jose, Costa Rica.

Loftus, E. F., & Burns, T. E. (1982). Mental shock can produce retrograde amnesia. *Memory & Cognition, 10,* 318–323.

Long, D. L., & Graesser, A. C. (1988). Wit and humor in discourse processing. *Discourse Processes, 11,* 35–60.

Longford, L. (Ed.). (1972). *Pornography: The Longford Report.* London: Coronet.

Longmore, P. K. (1985, Summer). Screening stereotypes: Images of disabled people. *Social Policy,* pp. 31–37.

Lovaas, O. I. (1961). Effect of exposure to symbolic aggression on aggressive behavior. *Child Development, 32,* 37–44.

Lowery, S., & DeFleur, M. L. (1983). *Milestones in mass communication research.* New York: Longman.

Lowry, D. T., Love, G., & Kirby, M. (1981). Sex on the soap operas: Patterns of intimacy. *Journal of Communication, 31,* 90–96.

Lowry, D. T., & Towles, D. E. (1989). Soap opera portrayals of sex, contraception, and sexually transmitted diseases. *Journal of Communication, 39*(2), 76–83.

Loy, J. W., McPherson, B. D., & Kenyon, G. (1978). *Sport and social systems: A guide to the analysis, problems, and literature.* Reading, MA: Addison-Wesley.

Lozano, E. (1992). The force of myth on popular narratives: The case of melodramatic serials. *Communication Theory, 2,* 207–220.

Luebke, B. (1989). Out of focus: Images of women and men in newspaper photographs. *Sex Roles, 20*(3/4), 121–133.

Luke, C. (1987). Television discourse and schema theory: Toward a cognitive model of information processing. In M. E. Manley-Casimir & C. Luke (Eds.), *Children and television: A challenge for education* (pp. 76–107). New York: Praeger.

Lull, J. (Ed.). (1988). *World families watch television*. Newbury Park, CA: Sage.

Lyons, J. S., Anderson, R. L., & Larson, D. B. (1993). A systematic review of the effects of aggressive and nonaggressive pornography. In D. Zillmann, J. Bryant, & A. C. Huston (Eds.), *Media, family, and children: Social, scientific, psychodynamic, and clinical perspectives*. Hillsdale, NJ: Lawrence Erlbaum Associates.

Maccoby, N., & Solomon, D. S. (1981). The Stanford community studies in heart disease prevention. In R. Rice & W. Paisley (Eds.), *Public communication campaigns*. Beverly Hills, CA: Sage.

MacFarland, D. T. (1990). *Contemporary radio programming strategies*. Hillsdale, NJ: Lawrence Erlbaum Associates.

Madden, T. J., & Weinberger, M. G. (1982). The effects of humor on attention in magazine advertising. *Journal of Advertising, 11*(3), 8–14.

Madden, T. J., & Weinberger, M. G. (1984). Humor in advertising: A practitioner view. *Journal of Advertising Research, 24*(4), 23–29.

Magnuson, E. (1988, March 7). Search and seizure on Capitol Hill. *Time*.

Malamuth, N. M. (1981). Rape fantasies as a function of exposure to violent sexual stimuli. *Archives of Sexual Behavior, 10*, 33–47.

Malamuth, N. M. (1984). Aggression against women: Cultural and individual causes. In N. M. Malamuth & E. Donnerstein (Eds.), *Pornography and sexual aggression* (pp. 19–52). Orlando: Academic Press.

Malamuth, N. M., & Check, J. V. P. (1980a). Penile tumescence and perceptual responses to rape as a function of victim's perceived reactions. *Journal of Applied Social Psychology, 10*, 528–547.

Malamuth, N. M., & Check, J. V. P. (1980b). Sexual arousal to rape and consenting depictions: The importance of the woman's arousal. *Journal of Abnormal Psychology, 89*, 763–766.

Malamuth, N. M., & Check, J. V. P. (1983). Sexual arousal to rape depictions: Individual differences. *Journal of Abnormal Psychology, 92*, 55–67.

Malamuth, N. M., Check, J. V. P., & Briere, J. (1986). Sexual arousal in response to aggression: Ideological, aggressive, and sexual correlates. *Journal of Personality and Social Psychology, 50*, 330–340.

Malamuth, N. M., & Spinner, B. (1980). A longitudinal content analysis of sexual violence in the best selling erotica magazines. *Journal of Sex Research, 16*, 226–237.

Malamuth, N. M., Feshbach, S., & Heim, M. (1980). Ethical issues and exposure to rape stimuli: A reply to Sherif. *Journal of Personality and Social Psychology, 38*, 413–415.

Malamuth, N. M., Haber, S., & Feshbach, S. (1980). Testing hypotheses regarding rape: Exposure to sexual violence, sex differences, and the "normality" of rapists. *Journal of Research in Personality, 14*, 121–137.

Malamuth, N. M., Heim, M., & Feshbach, S. (1980). Sexual responsiveness of college students to rape depictions: Inhibitory and disinhibitory effects. *Journal of Personality and Social Psychology, 38*, 399–408.

Manhattan Mercury. (1987, May 4). Ivory Coast television, p. 5 (AP wire story).

Mankiewicz, F., & Swerdlow, J. (1978). *Remote control: Television and the manipulation of American life*. New York: Ballantine.

Manley-Casimir, M. E., & Luke, C. (Eds.). (1987). *Children and television: A challenge for education*. New York: Praeger.

Manrai, L. A., & Gardner, M. P. (1992). Consumer processing of social ideas advertising: A conceptual model. *Advances in Consumer Research, 19*, 15–20.

Marquez de Melo, J. (1991, May). *The presence of the Brazilian telenovelas in the international market: Case study of Globo network*. Paper presented at meeting of the International Communication Association, Chicago, IL.

Marty, M. (1983, December 24). We need more religion in our sitcoms. *TV Guide*, pp. 2–8.

Massing, H. H. (1987). Decoding "Dallas": Comparing American and German viewers. In A. A. Berger (Ed.), *Television in society* (pp. 96–103). New Brunswick, NJ: Transaction Books.

Masterman, L. (1985). *Teaching the media*. London: Comedia.

Matabane, P. W. (1988). Television and the black audience: Cultivating moderate perspectives on racial integration. *Journal of Communication, 38*(4), 21–31.

Maynard, J. (1987, May 9). Raising kids and having a career is a snap. *TV Guide*, pp. 4–7.

Mayo, J. K., Hornik, R. C., & McAnany, E. G. (1976). *Educational reform with television: The El Salvador experience*. Stanford: Stanford University Press.

McAlister, A. L., Puska, P., & Salonen, J. T. (1982). Theory and action for health promotion: Illustrations from the North Karelia project. *American Journal of Public Health, 72*, 43–50.

McAnany, E. G. (1983). Television and crisis: Ten years of network news coverage of Central America, 1972–1981. *Media, culture and society, 5*(2), 199–212.

McCarroll, T. (1992, June 22). A whole new ball game. *Time*, p. 63.

McChesney, R. W. (1989). Media made sport: A history of sports coverage in the United States. In L. A. Wenner (Ed.), *Media, sports, and society* (pp. 46–69). Newbury Park, CA: Sage.

McCombs, M. E. (1981). The agenda-setting approach. In D. D. Nimmo & K. R. Sanders (Eds.), *Handbook of political communication* (pp. 121–140). Beverly Hills: Sage.

McCombs, M. E., & Gilbert, S. (1986). News influence on our pictures of the world. In J. Bryant & D. Zillmann (Eds.), *Perspectives on media effects* (pp. 1–15). Hillsdale, NJ: Lawrence Erlbaum Associates.

McCombs, M. E., & Shaw, D. L. (1993). The evolution of agenda-setting research: Twenty-five years in the marketplace of ideas. *Journal of Communication, 43*(2), 58–67.

McDermott, S., & Greenberg, B. (1985). Parents, peers, and television as determinants of black children's esteem. In R. Bostrom (Ed.), *Communication yearbook 8*. Beverly Hills, CA: Sage.

McGhee, P. (1979). *Humor: Its origin and development*. San Francisco: Freeman.

McGuire, W. J. (1974). Psychological motives and communication gratification. In J. G. Blumler & E. Katz (Eds.), *The uses of mass communications: Current perspectives on gratifications research* (pp. 167–196). Beverly Hills, CA: Sage.

McGuire, W. J. (1985a). Attitudes and attitude change. In G. Lindzey & E. Aronson (Eds.), *Handbook of social psychology* (3rd ed.). Reading, MA: Addison-Wesley.

McGuire, W. J. (1985b). The myth of massive media impact: Savagings and salvagings. In G. Comstock (Ed.), *Public communication and behavior* (Vol. 1). New York: Academic Press.

McIntyre, P., Hosch, H. M., Harris, R. J., & Norvell, D. W. (1986). Effects of sex and attitudes toward women on the processing of television commercials. *Psychology and Marketing, 3*, 181–190.

McKenzie-Mohr, D., & Zanna, M. P. (1990). Treating women as sexual objects: Look to the (gender schematic) male who has viewed pornography. *Personality and Social Psychology Bulletin, 16*, 296–308.

McNeal, J. U. (1987). *Children as consumers: Insights and implications*. Lexington, MA: Lexington Books.

McNeal, J. U. (1990). From savers to spenders: How children became a consumer market. *Media & Values, 52*, 4–6.

Meadowcroft, J. M., & Reeves, B. (1989). Influence of story schema development on children's attention to television. *Communication Research, 16*, 352–374.

Mele, M. (1987, October). Joint TV programming. *World Press Review*, p. 57.

Melton, G., & Fowler, G. (1987). Female roles in radio advertising. *Journalism Quarterly, 64*(1), 145–149.

Mendelsohn, H. A. (1966). Election-day broadcasts and terminal voting decisions. *Public Opinion Quarterly, 30*, 212–225.

Mendelsohn, H. A., & O'Keefe, G. J. (1976). *The people choose a President: Influences on voter decision making*. New York: Praeger.

Merikle, P. M. (1988). Subliminal auditory messages: An evaluation. *Psychology & Marketing, 5*, 355–372.

Merikle, P. M., & Cheesman, J. (1987). Current status of research on subliminal advertising. *Advances in Consumer Research, 14*, 298–302.

Merikle, P. M., & Skanes, H. E. (1992). Subliminal self-help audiotapes: A search for placebo effects. *Journal of Applied Psychology, 77*, 772–776.

Meringoff, L. K. (1980). Influence of the medium on children's story apprehension. *Journal of Educational Psychology, 72*, 240–249.

Meringoff, L. K., Vibbert, M. M., Char, C. A., Fernie, D. E., Banker, G. S., & Gardner, H. (1983). In J. Bryant & D. R. Anderson (Eds.), *Children's understanding of television* (pp. 151–179). New York: Academic Press.

Merritt, S. (1984). Negative political advertising: Some empirical findings. *Journal of Advertising, 13*, 27–38.

Messner, M. A., Duncan, M. C., & Jensen, K. (1993). Separating the men from the girls: The gendered language of televised sports. *Gender & Society, 7*, 121–137.

Meyer, P. (1990). News media responsiveness to public health. In C. Atkin & L. Wallack (Eds.), *Mass communication and public health: Complexities and conflicts* (pp. 52–57). Newbury Park, CA: Sage.

Meyrowitz, J. (1985). *No sense of place: The impact of electronic media on social behavior*. New York: Oxford University Press.

Michaels, J. (1988, March). Soap dollars. *World Press Review*, p. 51.

Mielke, K. W., & Chen, M. (1983). Formative research for *3-2-1 Contact*: Methods and insights. In M. J. A. Howe (Ed.), *Learning from television: Psychological and educational research* (pp. 31–55). London: Academic Press.

Milavsky, J. R., Kessler, R., Stipp, H., & Rubens, W. (1982). Television and aggression: Results of a panel study. In D. Pearl, L. Bouthilet, & J. Lazar (Eds.), *Television and behavior: Ten years of scientific progress and implications for the eighties* (Vol. 2, pp. 138–157). Washington, DC: U.S. Government Printing Office.

Moore, D. L., Hausknecht, D., & Thamodaran, K. (1986). Time compression, response opportunity, and persuasion. *Journal of Consumer Research, 13*, 85–99.

Moore, T. E. (1982). What you see is what you get. *Journal of Marketing, 46*(2), 38–47.

Moore, T. E. (1988). The case against subliminal manipulation. *Psychology & Marketing, 5*, 297–316.

Morgan, M. (1982). Television and adolescents' sex-role stereotypes: A longitudinal study. *Journal of Personality and Social Psychology, 43*(5), 947–955.

Morgan, M. (1989). Television and democracy. In I. Angus & S. Jhally (Eds.), *Cultural politics in contemporary America* (pp. 240–253). New York: Routledge.

Morgan, M. (1990). International cultivation analysis. In N. Signorielli & M. Morgan (Eds.), *Cultivation analysis: New directions in media effects research* (pp. 225–247). Newbury Park, CA: Sage.

Morgan, M., & Gerbner, G. (1982). TV professions and adolescent career choices. In M. Schwarz (Ed.), *TV and teens: Experts look at the issues* (pp. 121–126). Reading, MA: Addison-Wesley.

Morgan, M., & Shanahan, J. (1991). Television and the cultivation of political attitudes in Argentina. *Journal of Communication, 41*(1), 88–103.

Morgan, M., & Shanahan, J. (1992). Comparative cultivation analysis: Television and adolescents in Argentina and Taiwan. In F. Korzenny & S. Ting-Toomey (Eds.), *Mass media effects across cultures* (pp. 173–197). Newbury Park, CA: Sage.

Morgan, M., & Signorielli, N. (1990). Cultivation analysis: Conceptualization and methodology. In N. Signorielli & M. Morgan (Eds.), *Cultivation analysis: New directions in media effects research* (pp. 13–34). Newbury Park, CA: Sage.

Morley, D. (1986). *Family television: Cultural power and domestic leisure.* London: Comedia.

Morley, D. (1988). Domestic relations: The framework of family viewing in Great Britain. In J. Lull (Ed.), *World families watch television* (pp. 22–48). Newbury Park, CA: Sage.

Morris, J. S. (1982). Television portrayal and the socialization of the American Indian child. In G. L. Berry & C. Mitchell-Kernan (Eds.), *Television and the socialization of the minority child* (pp. 187–202). New York: Academic Press.

Mowlana, H. (1984). The role of the media in the U.S.-Iranian conflict. In A. Arno & W. Dissayanake (Eds.), *The news media in national and international conflict* (pp. 71–99). Boulder, CO: Westview Press.

Mowlana, H., Gerbner, G., & Schiller, H. (Eds.). (1993). *Triumph of the image: The media's war in the Persian Gulf—A global perspective.* Boulder, CO: Westview Press.

Mundorf, N., Drew, D., Zillmann, D., & Weaver, J. (1990). Effects of disturbing news on recall of subsequently presented news. *Communication Research, 17,* 601–615.

Mundorf, N., Weaver, J., & Zillmann, D. (1989). Effects of gender roles and self-perceptions on affective reactions to horror films. *Sex Roles, 20,* 655–673.

Murray, J. P. (1980). *Television and youth: Twenty-five years of research and controversy.* Boys Town, NE: Boys Town Center for the Study of Youth Development.

Mutz, D. C., Roberts, D. F., & van Vuuren, D. P. (1993). Reconsidering the displacement hypothesis. *Communication Research, 20,* 51–75.

Myers, D. G. (1992). *Psychology* (3rd ed.). New York: Worth Publishers.

Myers, P. N., Jr., & Biocca, F. A. (1992). The elastic body image: The effect of television advertising and programming on body image distortions in young women. *Journal of Communication, 42*(3), 108–133.

Nelson, J. P., Gelfand, D. M., & Hartmann, D. P. (1969). Children's aggression following competition and exposure to an aggressive model. *Child Development, 40,* 1085–1097.

Newhagen, J. E., & Reeves, B. (1991). Emotion and memory responses for negative political advertising: A study of television commercials used in the 1988 Presidential election. In F. Biocca (Ed.), *Television and political advertising, Vol. 1: Psychological processes* (pp. 197–220). Hillsdale, NJ: Lawrence Erlbaum Associates.

Newhagen, J. E., & Reeves, B. (1992). The evening's bad news: Effects of compelling negative television news images on memory. *Journal of Communication, 42*(2), 25–41.

Nias, D. K. B. (1983). The effects of televised sex and pornography. In M. J. A. Howe (Ed.). *Learning from television: Psychological and educational implications* (pp. 179–192). London: Academic Press.

Nimmo, D., & Savage, R. L. (1976). *Candidates and their images.* Pacific Palisades, CA: Goodyear.

Northcott, H. C. (1975). Too young, too old: Aging in the world of television. *The Gerontologist, 15,* 184–186.

Nussbaum, J. F., & Robinson, J. D. (1986). Attitudes toward aging. *Communication Research Reports, 1,* 21–27.

O'Bryant, S. L., & Corder-Bolz, C. R. (1978). The effects of television on children's stereotyping of women's work roles. *Journal of Vocational Behavior, 12,* 233–244.

O'Connor, J. J. (1990, February 20). Cartoons teach children, but is the lesson good? *New York Times,* p. B1.

Oliver, M. B. (1993). Adolescents' enjoyment of graphic horror. *Communication Research, 20,* 30–50.

Olweus, D. (1979). The stability of aggressive reaction patterns in human males: A review. *Psychological Bulletin, 85,* 852–875.

Paletz, D. L. (1988). Pornography, politics, and the press: The U.S. attorney general's commission on pornography. *Journal of Communication, 38*(2), 122–136.

Paletz, D. L., & Schmid, A. P. (Eds.). (1992). *Terrorism and the media.* Newbury Park, CA: Sage.

Palmgreen, P. (1984). Uses and gratifications: A theoretical perspective. In R. N. Bostrom (Ed.), *Communication yearbook 8* (pp. 20–55). Newbury Park, CA: Sage.

Palys, T. S. (1986). Testing the common wisdom: The social content of video pornography. *Canadian Psychology, 27,* 22–35.

Panitt, M. (1988, June 4). In India, they'll trash a station . . . or worship an actor. *TV Guide,* pp. 44–45.

Parke, R., Berkowitz, L., Leyens, J., West, S., & Sebastian, R. (1977). Some effects of violent and non-violent movies on the behavior of juvenile delinquents. In L. Berkowitz (Ed.), *Advances in social psychology* (Vol. 10). New York: Academic Press.

Patterson, T. E., & McClure, R. D. (1976). *The unseeing eye: The myth of television power in national politics.* New York: Putnam.

Patton, G. W. R. (1978). Effect of party affiliation of student voters on the image of presidential candidates. *Psychological Reports, 43,* 343–347.

Pechmann, C., & Stewart, D. W. (1988). Advertising repetition: A critical review of wearin and wearout. *Current Issues and Research in Advertising, 11*, 285–329.

Peck, J. (1992). *The gods of televangelism: The crisis of meaning and the appeal of religious television.* Cresskill, NJ: Hampton Press.

Penrod, S., & Linz, D. (1984). Using psychological research on violent pornography to inform legal change. In N. M. Malamuth & E. Donnerstein (Eds.), *Pornography and sexual aggression* (pp. 247–265). Orlando: Academic Press.

Percy, L., & Rossiter, J. R. (1983). Mediating effects of visual and verbal elements in print advertising upon belief, attitude, and intention responses. In L. Percy & A. Woodside (Eds.), *Advertising and consumer psychology* (pp. 171–186). Lexington, MA: Lexington Books.

Perloff, R. M. (1989). Ego-involvement and the third person effect of television news coverage. *Communication Research, 16*, 236–262.

Perse, E. M. (1986). Soap opera viewing patterns of college students and cultivation. *Journal of Broadcasting & Electronic Media, 30*, 175–193.

Perse, E. M., & Rubin, R. B. (1989). Attribution in social and parasocial relationships. *Communication Research, 16*, 59–77.

Pezdek, K., & Hartman, E. F. (1983). Children's television viewing: Attention and comprehension of auditory versus visual information. *Child Development, 54*, 1015–1023.

Pezdek, K., Lehrer, A., & Simon, S. (1984). The relationship between reading and cognitive processing of television and radio. *Child Development, 55*, 2072–2082.

Pezdek, K., & Stevens, E. (1984). Children's memory for auditory and visual information on television. *Developmental Psychology, 20*, 212–218.

Phillips, D. P. (1977). Motor vehicle increase just after publicized suicide stories. *Science, 196*, 1464–1465.

Phillips, D. P. (1984). Teenage and adult temporal fluctuations in suicide and auto fatalities. In H. S. Sudak, A. B. Ford, & N. B. Rushforth (Eds.), *Suicide in the young* (pp. 69–80). Boston: John Wright.

Phillips, D. P., & Carstensen, L. L. (1986). Clustering of teenage suicides after TV news stories about suicides. *New England Journal of Medicine, 315*, 685–689.

Phillips, K. (1993, January–February). How *Seventeen* undermines young women. *Extra!, 6*(1), 14.

Picard, R. G. (1993). *Media portrayals of terrorism: Functions and meaning of news coverage.* Ames, IA: Iowa State University Press.

Pierce, C. M. (1980). Social trace contaminants: Subtle indicators of racism in TV. In S. B. Withey & R. B. Abeles (Eds.), *Television and social behavior* (pp. 249–257). Hillsdale, NJ: Lawrence Erlbaum Associates.

Pierce, M. C., & Harris, R. J. (1993). The effect of provocation, race, and injury description on men's and women's perception of a wife-battering incident. *Journal of Applied Social Psychology, 23*, 767–790.

Pierre, E. (1973). La communication class-ecran: Une relation d'apprentissage. *Dossiers Pedagogiques, 1*, 6–11.

Pingree, S., & Hawkins, R. (1981). U.S. programs on Australian television: The cultivation effect. *Journal of Communication, 31*(1), 97–105.

Pingree, S., & Thompson, M. E. (1990). The family in daytime serials. In J. Bryant (Ed.), *Television and the American family* (pp. 113–127). Hillsdale, NJ: Lawrence Erlbaum Associates.

Pitkanen-Pulkkinen, L. (1981). Concurrent and predictive validity of self-reported aggressiveness. *Aggressive Behavior, 7*, 97–110.

Ploghoft, M. E., & Anderson, J. A. (1982). *Teaching critical television viewing skills: An integrated approach.* Springfield, IL: Charles C. Thomas.

Poindexter, P. M., & Stroman, C. (1981). Blacks and television: A review of the research literature. *Journal of Broadcasting, 25*(2), 103–122.

Postman, N. (1982). *The disappearance of childhood.* New York: Delacorte.

Postman, N. (1985). *Amusing ourselves to death.* New York: Viking Penguin.

Potter, W. J. (1986). Perceived reality and the cultivation hypothesis. *Journal of Broadcasting & Electronic Media, 30*, 159–174.

Potter, W. J. (1988). Perceived reality in television effects research. *Journal of Broadcasting & Electronic Media, 32*, 23–41.

Potter, W. J. (1989). Three strategies for elaborating the cultivation hypothesis. *Journalism Quarterly, 65*, 930–939.

Potter, W. J. (1991a). Examining cultivation from a psychological perspective: Component subprocesses. *Communication Research, 18*, 77–102.

Potter, W. J. (1991b). The relationships between first- and second-order measures of cultivation. *Human Communication Research, 18*, 92–113.

Potter, W. J. (1993). Cultivation theory and research: A conceptual critique. *Human Communication Research, 19*, 564–601.

Powell, L. (1977). Voting intention and the complexity of political images: A pilot study. *Psychological Reports, 40*, 243–246.

Powers, R. (1984). *Supertube: The rise of television sports*. New York: Coward-McCann.

Pratap, A. (1990, August 13). Romance and a little rape. *Time*, p. 69.

Pratkanis, A. R. (1992). The cargo-cult science of subliminal persuasion. *Skeptical Inquirer, 16*, 260–272.

Pratkanis, A. R., & Aronson, E. (1992). *Age of propaganda: The everyday use and abuse of persuasion*. New York: W. H. Freeman.

Pratkanis, A. R., & Greenwald, A. G. (1988). Recent perspectives on unconscious processing: Still no marketing applications. *Psychology & Marketing, 5*, 339–355.

Preston, E. H. (1990). Pornography and the construction of gender. In N. Signorielli & M. Morgan (Eds.), *Cultivation analysis* (pp. 107–122). Newbury Park, CA: Sage.

Preston, I. L. (1975). *The great American blow-up: Puffery in advertising and selling*. Madison: University of Wisconsin Press.

Preston, I. L., & Richards, J. I. (1986). Consumer miscomprehension as a challenge to FTC prosecutions of deceptive advertising. *The John Marshall Law Review, 19*, 605–635.

Prottas, J. M. (1983). Encouraging altruism: Public attitudes and the marketing of organ donation. *Health and Society, 61*(2), 278–306.

Quinsey, V. L., & Marshall, W. (1983). Procedures for reducing inappropriate sexual arousal: An evaluation review. In J. G. Greer & I. Stuart (Eds.), *The sexual aggressor: Current perspectives on treatment*. New York: Van Nostrand Reinhold.

Rabinovitch, M. S., McLean, M. S., Markham, J. W., & Talbott, A. D. (1972). Children's violence perception as a function of television violence. In G. A. Comstock, E. A. Rubinstein, & J. P. Murray (Eds.), *Television and social behavior: Vol. 5. Television's effects: Further explorations*. Washington, DC: U.S. Government Printing Office.

Rachman, S. (1966). Sexual fetishism: An experimental analogue. *Psychological Record, 16*, 293–296.

Rachman, S., & Hodgson, R. J. (1968). Experimentally-induced "sexual fetishism": Replication and development. *Psychological Record, 18*, 25–27.

Radecki, T. (1984). Deerhunter continues to kill, 35th victim—31 dead. *NCTV News, 5*(3–4), 3.

Rader, B. G. (1984). *In its own image: How television has transformed sports*. New York: The Free Press.

Rafaeli, S., & LaRose, R. J. (1993). Electronic bulletin boards and "public goods" explanations of collaborative mass media. *Communication Research, 20*, 277–297.

Rainville, R., & McCormick, E. (1977). Extent of covert racial prejudice in pro football announcers' speech. *Journalism Quarterly, 54*(1), 20–26.

Raju, P. S., & Lonial, S. C. (1990). Advertising to children: Findings and implications. *Current Issues and Research in Advertising, 12*, 231–274.

Read, W. H. (1976). *America's mass media merchants*. Baltimore: Johns Hopkins University Press.

Real, M. R. (1989). Super Bowl football versus World Cup soccer: A cultural-structural comparison. In L. A. Wenner (Ed.), *Media, sports, and society* (pp. 180–203). Newbury Park, CA: Sage.

Reeves, B. (1989). Theories about news and theories about cognition: Arguments for a more radical separation. *American Behavioral Scientist, 33*, 191–197.

Reeves, B., Thorson, E., Rothschild, M., McDonald, D., Hirsch, J., & Goldstein, R. (1985). Attention to television: Intrastimulus effects of movement and scene changes on alpha variation over time. *International Journal of Neuroscience, 25*, 241–255.

Reid, P. T. (1979). Racial stereotyping on television: A comparison of the behavior of black and white television characters. *Journal of Applied Psychology, 64*(5), 465–489.

Report of the Special Committee on Pornography and Prostitution (Vol. 1). (1985). Ottawa: Minister of Supply and Services.

Rice, M. L., Huston, A. C., & Wright, J. C. (1986). Replays as repetitions: Young children's interpretation of television forms. *Journal of Applied Developmental Psychology, 7*, 61–76.

Richards, J. I. (1990). *Deceptive advertising.* Hillsdale, NJ: Lawrence Erlbaum Associates.

Riggs, M. (1992, June 15). *Color adjustment.* PBS documentary.

Ritchie, D., Price, V., & Roberts, D. F. (1987). Reading and television: A longitudinal investigation of the displacement hypothesis. *Communication Research, 14*, 292–315.

Rivera, G. (1987, April 18). There's Lt. Castillo, Sifuentes . . . and little else. *TV Guide,* pp. 40–43.

Roberts, D. F., & Maccoby, N. (1985). Effects of mass communication. In G. Lindzey & E. Aronson (Eds.), *Handbook of social psychology* (3rd ed.). New York: Random House.

Robertson, T. S., & Rossiter, J. R. (1974). Children and commercial persuasion: An attribution theory analysis. *Journal of Consumer Research, 1*(1), 13–20.

Robertson, T. S., Rossiter, J. R., & Gleason, T. C. (1979). *Televised medicine advertising and children.* New York: Praeger.

Robertson, T. S., Ward, S., & Gatignon, H., & Klees, D. M. (1989). Advertising and children: A cross-cultural study. *Communication Research, 16*, 459–485.

Robinson, J. D. (1989). Mass media and the elderly: A uses and dependency interpretation. In J. F. Nussbaum (Ed.), *Life-span communication* (pp. 319–337). Hillsdale, NJ: Lawrence Erlbaum Associates.

Robinson, J. P. (1990). Television's effects on families' uses of time. In J. Bryant (Ed.), *Television and the American family* (pp. 195–209). Hillsdale, NJ: Lawrence Erlbaum Associates.

Robinson, J. P., & Davis, D. K. (1990). Television news and the informed public: An information-processing approach. *Journal of Communication, 40*(3), 106–119.

Robinson, M. J., & Sheehan, M. A. (1983). *Over the wire and on TV: CBS and UPI in Campaign '80.* New York: Sage.

Rogers, E. M., & Dearing, J. W. (1988). Agenda-setting research: Where has it been, Where is it going? In J. A. Anderson (Ed.), *Communication yearbook 11* (pp. 555–594). Beverly Hills, CA: Sage.

Rogers, E. M., Dearing, J. W., & Bregman, D. (1993). The anatomy of agenda-setting research. *Journal of Communication, 43*(2), 68–84.

Rogers, E. M., & Singhal, A. (1989). Estrategias de educacion entretenimiento [Strategies for educating through entertainment]. *Chasqui, 31*, 9–22.

Rogers, E. M., & Singhal, A. (1990). The academic perspective. In C. Atkin & L. Wallack (Eds.), *Mass communication and public health* (pp. 176–181). Newbury Park, CA: Sage.

Rojahn, K., & Pettigrew, T. F. (1992). Memory for schema-relevant information: A meta-analytic resolution. *British Journal of Social Psychology, 31*, 81–109.

Rosencrans, M. A., & Hartup, W. W. (1967). Imitative influences of consistent and inconsistent response consequences to a model on aggressive behavior in children. *Journal of Personality and Social Psychology, 7*, 429–434.

Rosengren, K. E. (1992). The structural invariance of change: Comparative studies of media use (some results from a Swedish research program). In J. G. Blumler, J. M. McLeod, & K. E. Rosengren (Eds.), *Comparatively speaking: Communication and culture across space and time* (pp. 140–178). Newbury Park, CA: Sage.

Rosengren, K. E., Wenner, L. A., & Palmgreen, P. (Eds.). (1985). *Media gratifications research: Current perspectives.* Newbury Park, CA: Sage.

Ross, J. (1992, August). The cola war's new front. *World Press Review,* p. 45.

Rotfeld, H. J. (1988). Fear appeals and persuasion: Assumptions and errors in advertising research. *Current Issues and Research in Advertising, 11*, 21–40.

Rothenbuhler, E. W. (1988). The living room celebration of the Olympic games. *Journal of Communication, 38*(4), 61–81.

Rubin, A. M. (1981). An examination of television viewing motivations. *Communication Research, 8*, 141–165.

Rubin, A. M. (1983). Television uses and gratifications: The interactions of viewing patterns and motivations. *Journal of Broadcasting, 27*, 37–51.

Rubin, A. M. (1984). Ritualized and instrumental television viewing. *Journal of Communication, 34*(3), 67–77.

Rubin, A. M. (1986). Uses, gratifications, and media effects research. In J. Bryant & D. Zillmann (Eds.), *Perspectives on media effects* (pp. 281–301). Hillsdale, NJ: Lawrence Erlbaum Associates.

Rubin, A. M. (in press). Media uses and effects: A uses-and-gratifications perspective. In J. Bryant & D. Zillmann (Eds.), *Media effects: Advances in theory and research.* Hillsdale, NJ: Lawrence Erlbaum Associates.

Rubin, A. M., & Perse, E. M. (1987). Audience activity and television news gratifications. *Communication Research, 14*, 58–84.

Rubin, A. M., & Perse, E. M. (1988). Audience activity and soap opera involvement. *Human Communication Research, 14*, 246–268.

Rubin, A. M., Perse, E. M., & Powell, R. A. (1985). Loneliness, parasocial interaction, and local television news viewing. *Human Communication Research, 12*, 155–180.

Rubin, A. M., Perse, E. M., & Taylor, D. S. (1988). A methodological examination of cultivation. *Communication Research, 15*, 107–134.

Rubin, A. M., & Windahl, S. (1986). The uses and dependency model of mass communication. *Critical Studies in Mass Communication, 3*, 184–199.

Rubin, D. M., & Cummings, C. (1989). Nuclear war and its consequences on television. *Journal of Communication, 39*(1), 39–58.

Rubin, R. B., & McHugh, M. P. (1987). Development of parasocial interaction relationships. *Journal of Broadcasting & Electronic Media, 31*, 279–292.

Rumelhart, D. E. (1980). Schemata: Building blocks of cognition. In R. J. Spiro, B. C. Bruce, & W. F. Brewer (Eds.), *Theoretical issues in reading comprehension* (pp. 33–58). Hillsdale, NJ: Lawrence Erlbaum Associates.

Russo, J. E., Metcalf, B. L., & Stevens, D. (1981). Identifying misleading advertising. *Journal of Consumer Research, 8*, 119–131.

Sabo, D., & Jansen, S. C. (1992). Images of men in sport media. In S. Craig (Ed.), *Men, masculinity, and the media* (pp. 169–184). Newbury Park, CA: Sage.

Sabo, D., & Runfola, R. (Eds.). (1990). *Jock: Sports and male identity.* Englewood Cliffs, NJ: Prentice-Hall.

Saegert, J. (1987). Why marketing should quit giving subliminal advertising the benefit of the doubt. *Psychology & Marketing, 4*, 107–120.

Salomon, G. (1979). *Interaction of media, cognition, and learning.* San Francisco: Jossey-Bass.

Salomon, G. (1983). Television watching and mental effort: A social psychological view. In J. Bryant & D. Anderson (Eds.), *Children's understanding of television* (pp. 181–198). New York: Academic Press.

Salomon, G. (1984). Television is "easy" and print is "tough": The differential investment of mental effort in learning as a function of perceptions and attributions. *Journal of Educational Psychology, 76*, 647–658.

Salomon, G. (1987). Television and reading: The roles of orientations and reciprocal relations. In M. E. Manley-Casimir & C. Luke (Eds.), *Children and television* (pp. 15–33). New York: Praeger.

Sapolsky, B. S. (1984). Arousal, affect, and the aggression-moderating effect of erotica. In N. M. Malamuth & E. Donnerstein (Eds.), *Pornography and sexual aggression* (pp. 85–113). Orlando: Academic Press.

Savitsky, J. C., Rogers, R. W., Izard, C. E., & Liebert, R. M. (1971). Role of frustration and anger in the imitation of filmed aggression against a human victim. *Psychological Reports, 29*, 807–810.

Schachter, S., & Singer, J. E. (1962). Cognitive, social, and physiological determinants of emotional state. *Psychological Review, 69*, 379–399.

Schaefer, H. H., & Colgan, A. H. (1977). The effect of pornography on penile tumescence as a function of reinforcement and novelty. *Behavior Therapy, 8*, 938–946.

Schank, R., & Abelson, R. (1977). *Scripts, plans, goals, and understanding.* Hillsdale, NJ: Lawrence Erlbaum Associates.

Schement, J. R., Gonzalez, I. N., Lum, P., & Valencia, R. (1984). The international flow of television programs. *Communication Research, 11*, 163–182.

Schlesinger, P. (1978). *Putting "reality" together: BBC news.* London: Methuen.

Schlesinger, P. (1987). Ten years on. Reissue of Schlesinger, P. (1978). *Putting "reality" together: BBC news.* London: Methuen.

Schleuder, J., McCombs, M. E., & Wanta, W. (1991). Inside the agenda-setting process: How political advertising and TV news prime viewers to think about issues and candidates. In F. Biocca (Ed.), *Television and political advertising, Vol. 1: Psychological processes* (pp. 265–309). Hillsdale, NJ: Lawrence Erlbaum Associates.

Schlinger, M. J. (1976). The role of mass communications in promoting public health. *Advances in Consumer Research, 3*, 302–305.

Schlinger, M. J., & Plummer, J. (1972). Advertising in black and white. *Journal of Marketing Research, 9*, 149–153.

Schneider, J. A. (1987). Networks hold the line. In A. A. Berger (Ed.), *Television in society* (pp. 163–172). New Brunswick, NJ: Transaction Books.

Schneider, K. C., & Schneider, S. B. (1979). Trends in sex roles in television commercials. *Journal of Marketing, 43*(3), 79–84.

Schneider, S. L., & Laurion, S. K. (1993). Do we know what we've learned from listening to the news? *Memory & Cognition, 21*, 198–209.

Scholfield, J., & Pavelchak, M. (1985). *The Day After*: The impact of a media event. *American Psychologist, 40*, 542–548.

School of hard knocks. (1992, October 12). *Time*, pp. 31–32.

Schramm, W. (1977). *Big media, little media.* Beverly Hills, CA: Sage.

Schuman, H., & Presser, S. (1981). *Questions and answers in attitude surveys: Experiments on question form, wording, and context.* New York: Academic Press.

Schumann, D. W., Petty, R. E., & Clemons, D. S. (1990). Predicting the effectiveness of different strategies of advertising variation: A test of the repetition-variation hypotheses. *Journal of Consumer Research, 17*, 192–202.

Schwartz, T. (1981). *Media: The second god.* New York: Random House.

Seefeldt, C. (1977). Young and old together. *Children Today, 6*(1), 22.

Seggar, J. F., Hafen, J., & Hannonen-Gladden, H. (1981). Television's portrayal of minorities and women in drama and comedy drama, 1971–1980. *Journal of Broadcasting, 25*(3), 277–288.

Seifart, H. (1984). Sport and economy: The commercialization of Olympic sport by the media. *International Review for the Sociology of Sport, 19*, 305–315.

Selnow, G. W. (1990). Values in prime-time television. *Journal of Communication, 40*(2), 64–74.

Servaes, J. (1991). European press coverage of the Grenada crisis. *Journal of Communication, 42*(1), 28–41.

Shaheen, J. G. (1984a). *The TV Arab.* Bowling Green, OH: Bowling Green State University Popular Press.

Shaheen, J. G. (1984b, March–April). Arabs—TV's villains of choice. *Channels*, pp. 52–53.

Shaheen, J. G. (1984c, November 23). The Arabs and the moviemakers. *Middle East International*, pp. 15–16.

Shaheen, J. G. (1992). The Arab stereotype: A villain without a human face. *Extra!, 5*(5), 26.

Shanteau, J. (1988). Consumer impression formation: The integration of visual and verbal information. In S. Hecker & D. W. Stewart (Eds.), *Nonverbal communication in advertising* (pp. 43–57). Lexington, MA: Lexington.

Shanteau, J., & Harris, R. J. (Eds.). (1990). *Organ donation and transplantation: Psychological and behavioral factors.* Washington, DC: American Psychological Association.

Shapiro, M. A. (1991). Memory and decision processes in the construction of social reality. *Communication Research, 18*, 3–24.

Sheikh, A. A., Prasad, V. K., & Rao, T. R. (1974). Children's TV commercials: A review of research. *Journal of Communication, 24*(4), 126–136.

Sherif, C. W. (1980). Comment on ethical issues. *Journal of Personality and Social Psychology, 38*, 409–412.

Sherman, B. L., & Dominick, J. R. (1986). Violence and sex in music videos: TV and rock 'n' roll. *Journal of Communication, 36*(1), 79–93.

Sherman, B. L., & Etling, L. W. (1991). Perceiving and processing music television. In J. Bryant & D. Zillmann (Eds.), *Responding to the screen: Reception and reaction processes* (pp. 373–388). Hillsdale, NJ: Lawrence Erlbaum Associates.

Shimp, T. A., & Gresham, L. G. (1983). An information-processing perspective on recent advertising literature. *Current Issues and Research in Advertising, 5*, 39–75.

Siegel, A. N. (1956). Film-mediated fantasy aggression and strength of aggressive drive. *Child Development, 27*, 365–378.

Signorielli, N. (1990). Television's mean and dangerous world: A continuation of the Cultural Indicators perspective. In N. Signorielli & M. Morgan (Eds.), *Cultivation analysis: New directions in media effects research* (pp. 85–106). Newbury Park, CA: Sage.

Signorielli, N., & Morgan, M. (Eds.). (1990). *Cultivation analysis: New directions in media effects research.* Newbury Park, CA: Sage.

Simon, H. A., & Stern, F. (1955). The effect of television upon voting behavior in Iowa in the 1952 Presidential election. *American Political Science Review, 49*, 470–477.

Simon, R. (1985, July 13). What's red, white, and blue—and makes Madison Avenue see green? *TV Guide*, pp. 36–37.

Simon, R. J., & Fejes, F. (1987). Real police on television supercops. In A. A. Berger (Ed.), *Television in society* (pp. 63–69). New Brunswick, NJ: Transaction Books.

Singer, D. G., & Singer, J. L. (1983). Learning how to be intelligent consumers of television. In M. J. A. Howe (Ed.), *Learning from television: Psychological and educational research* (pp. 203–222). London: Academic Press.

Singer, D. G., Singer, J. L., & Zuckerman, D. M. (1981). *Getting the most out of TV.* Santa Monica, CA: Goodyear.

Singer, D. G., Zuckerman, D. M., & Singer, J. L. (1980). Helping elementary school children learn about TV. *Journal of Communication, 30*(3), 84–93.

Singer, J. L., & Singer, D. G. (1976). Can TV stimulate imaginative play? *Journal of Communication, 26*, 74–80.

Singer, J. L., & Singer, D. G. (1981). *Television, imagination, and aggression: A study of preschoolers.* Hillsdale, NJ: Lawrence Erlbaum Associates.

Singer, M. (1984). Inferences in reading comprehension. In M. Daneman & P. A. Carpenter (Eds.), *Reading research: Advances in theory and practice* (Vol. 6). New York: Academic Press.

Singhal, A., & Rogers, E. M. (1989a). Prosocial television for development in India. In R. E. Rice & C. Atkin (Eds.), *Public communication campaigns* (2nd ed., pp. 331–350). Newbury Park, CA: Sage.

Singhal, A., & Rogers, E. M. (1989b). Entertainment-education strategies for family planning. *Populi, 16*(2), 38–47.

Singhal, A., & Rogers, E. M. (1989c). *India's information revolution.* New Delhi: Sage.

Sintchak, G., & Geer, J. (1975). A vaginal plethysymograph system. *Psychophysiology, 12*, 113–115.

Skill, T., Lyons, J. S., & Larson, D. (1991, November). *Television and religion: Content analysis of the portrayal of spirituality in network primetime fictional programs.* Summary report to the American Family Association, Tupelo, MS.

Skill, T., Wallace, S., & Cassata, M. (1990). Families on prime-time television: Patterns of conflict escalation and resolution across intact, nonintact, and mixed-family settings. In J. Bryant (Ed.), *Television and the American family* (pp. 129–163). Hillsdale, NJ: Lawrence Erlbaum Associates.

Slater, D., & Elliott, W. R. (1982). Television's influence on social reality. *Quarterly Journal of Speech, 68,* 69–79.

Slater, M. D. (1990). Processing social information in messages: Social group familiarity, fiction versus nonfiction, and subsequent beliefs. *Communication Research, 17,* 327–343.

Smith, R., Anderson, D. R., & Fischer, C. (1985). Young children's comprehension of montage. *Child Development, 56,* 962–971.

Snyder, L., Roser, C., & Chaffee, S. (1991). Foreign media and the desire to emigrate from Belize. *Journal of Communication, 41*(1), 117–132.

Soap operas. (1981, September 28). *Newsweek,* p. 65.

Soley, L. (1983). The effect of black models on magazine ad readership. *Journalism Quarterly, 60*(4), 686–690.

Solomon, D. S., & Cardillo, B. A. (1985). The elements and process of communication campaigns. In T. A. van Dijk (Ed.), *Discourse and communication* (pp. 60–68). Berlin: de Gruyter.

Spangler, L. C. (1989). A historical overview of female friendships in prime-time television. *Journal of Popular Culture, 22*(4), 13–23.

Spangler, L. C. (1992). Buddies and pals: A history of male friendships on prime-time television. In S. Craig (Ed.), *Men, masculinity, and the media* (pp. 93–110). Newbury Park, CA: Sage.

Sparks, G. G. (1986). Developmental differences in children's reports of fear induced by the mass media. *Child Study Journal, 16*(1), 55–66.

Spencer, J. W., Seydlitz, R., Laska, S., & Triche, E. (1992). The different influences of newspaper and television news reports of a natural hazard on response behavior. *Communication Research, 19,* 299–325.

Sprafkin, J. N., Gadow, K. D., & Abelman, R. (1992). *Television and the exceptional child: A forgotten audience.* Hillsdale, NJ: Lawrence Erlbaum Associates.

Sprafkin, J. N., & Silverman, L. T. (1981). Update: Physically intimate and sexual behavior on prime-time television 1978–79. *Journal of Communication, 31*(1), 34–40.

Stall, R. D., Coates, T. J., & Hoff, C. (1988). Behavioral risk reduction for HIV infection among gay and bisexual men. *American Psychologist, 43,* 878–885.

Stayman, D. M., & Kardes, F. R. (1992). Spontaneous inference processes in advertising: Effects of need for cognition and self-monitoring on inference generation and utilization. *Journal of Consumer Psychology, 1,* 125–142.

Stein, B. (1979). *The view from Sunset Boulevard.* New York: Basic Books.

Stein, B. (1987). Fantasy and culture on television. In A. A. Berger (Ed.), *Television in society* (pp. 215–228). New Brunswick, NJ: Transaction Books.

Stempel, G. (1971). Visibility of blacks in news and news-picture magazines. *Journalism Quarterly, 48*(2), 337–339.

Stephens, N., & Stutts, M. A. (1982). Preschoolers' ability to distinguish between television programming and commercials. *Journal of Advertising, 11,* 16–26.

Stern, B. L., & Harmon, R. R. (1984). Disclaimers in children's advertising. *Journal of Advertising, 13,* 12–16.

Sternthal, B., & Craig, S. (1973). Humor in advertising. *Journal of Marketing, 37*(4), 12–18.

Stewart, L. (1988, February 18). For ABC, it's been all downhill in Winter Olympics. *Manhattan Mercury.* (*L.A. Times* wire)

Stone, G. (1987). *Examining newspapers: What research reveals about America's newspapers.* Newbury Park, CA: Sage.

Strate, L. (1992). Beer commercials: A manual on masculinity. In S. Craig (Ed.), *Men, masculinity, and the media* (pp. 78–92). Newbury Park, CA: Sage.

Straubhaar, J. D., Heeter, C., Greenberg, B. S., Ferreira, L., Wicks, R. H., & Lau, T.-Y. (1992). What makes news: Western, socialist, and Third-world newscasts compared in eight countries. In F. Korzenny & S. Ting-Toomey (Eds.), *Mass media effects across cultures* (pp. 89–109). Newbury Park, CA: Sage.

Strouse, J. A., & Fabes, R. A. (1985). Formal vs. informal sources of sex education: Competing forces in the sexual socialization process. *Adolescence, 78*, 251–263.

Stutts, M. A., & Hunnicutt, G. G. (1987). Can young children understand disclaimers in television commercials? *Journal of Advertising, 16*(1), 41–46.

Stutts, M. A., Vance, D., & Hudelson, S. (1981). Program-commercial separators in children's television: Do they help a child tell the difference between *Bugs Bunny* and *The Quik Rabbit? Journal of Advertising, 10*(2), 16–48.

Suleiman, M. W. (1988). *The Arabs in the mind of America.* Brattleboro, VT: Amana Books.

Suls, J. M. (1983). Cognitive processes in humor appreciation. In P. E. McGhee & J. H. Goldstein (Eds.), *Handbook of humor research: Basic issues* (Vol. 1, pp. 39–57). New York: Springer-Verlag.

Surlin, S. H. (1974). Bigotry on air and in life: The Archie Bunker case. *Public Telecommunications Review, 212*, 34–41.

Sutton, S. R. (1982). Fear-arousing communications: A critical examination of theory and research. In R. Eiser (Ed.), *Social psychology and behavioral medicine* (pp. 303–337). London: Wiley.

Tamborini, R. (1991). Responding to horror: Determinants of exposure and appeal. In J. Bryant & D. Zillmann (Eds.), *Responding to the screen: Reception and reaction processes* (pp. 305–328). Hillsdale, NJ: Lawrence Erlbaum Associates.

Tamborini, R., & Choi, J. (1990). The role of cultural diversity in cultivation research. In N. Signorielli & M. Morgan (Eds.), *Cultivation analysis: New directions in media effects research* (pp. 157–180). Newbury Park, CA: Sage.

Tamborini, R., & Stiff, J. (1987). Predictors of horror film attendance and appeal: An analysis of the audience for frightening films. *Communication Research, 14*, 415–436.

Tamborini, R., Stiff, J., & Heidel, C. (1990). Reacting to graphic horror: A model of empathy and emotional behavior. *Communication Research, 17*, 616–640.

Tamborini, R., Stiff, J., & Zillmann, D. (1987). Preference for graphic horror featuring male versus female victimization: Individual differences associated with personality characteristics and past film viewing experiences. *Human Communication Research, 13*, 529–552.

Tan, A. S. (1986). Social learning of aggression from television. In J. Bryant & D. Zillmann (Eds.), *Perspectives on media effects* (pp. 41–55). Hillsdale, NJ: Lawrence Erlbaum Associates.

Tan, A. S., Li, S., & Simpson, C. (1986). American TV and social stereotypes of Americans in Taiwan and Mexico. *Journalism Quarterly, 63*, 809–814.

Tannen, D. (1990). *You just don't understand: Women and men in conversation.* New York: Ballantine Books.

Tannenbaum, P. H. (1971). *Emotional arousal as a mediator of communication effects* (Technical reports of the Commission on Obscenity and Pornography, Vol. 8). Washington, DC: U.S. Government Printing Office.

Tannenbaum, P. H. (1980). Entertainment as vicarious emotional experience. In P. H. Tannenbaum (Ed.), *The entertainment functions of television* (pp. 107–131). Hillsdale, NJ: Lawrence Erlbaum Associates.

Tate, E., & Surlin, S. (1976). Agreement with opinionated TV characters across culture. *Journalism Quarterly, 53*(2), 199–203.

Tavris, C. (1986). How to publicize science: A case study. In J. H. Goldstein (Ed.), *Reporting science: The case of aggression* (pp. 23–32). Hillsdale, NJ: Lawrence Erlbaum Associates.

Tavris, C. (1988). Beyond cartoon killings: Comments on two overlooked effects of television. In S. Oskamp (Ed.), *Television as a social issue* (pp. 189–197). Newbury Park, CA: Sage.

Taylor, S. (1982). The availability bias in social perception and interaction. In D. Kahneman, P. Slovic, & A. Tversky (Eds.), *Judgment under uncertainty: Heuristics and biases* (pp. 190–200). Cambridge: Cambridge University Press.

Television: For gold or for broke? (1988, June 6). *Time*, p. 59.

Thoman, E. (1991, Winter). Media literacy for the '90s—U.S. style. *Media Development*, pp. 28–30.

Thomas, S. (1986). Gender and social-class coding in popular photographic erotica. *Communication Quarterly, 34*(2), 103–114.

Thomas, S., & Callahan, B. P. (1982). Allocating happiness: TV families and social class. *Journal of Communication, 32*, 184–190.

Thorndyke, P. W. (1984). Applications of schema theory in cognitive research. In J. R. Anderson & S. M. Kosslyn (Eds.), *Tutorials in learning and memory* (pp. 167–192). San Francisco: Freeman.

Thorson, E. (1990). Consumer processing of advertising. *Current Issues and Research in Advertising, 12*, 197–230.

Thorson, E., Christ, W. G., & Caywood, C. (1991). Selling candidates like tubes of toothpaste: Is the comparison apt? In F. Biocca (Ed.), *Television and political advertising, Vol. 1: Psychological processes* (pp. 145–172). Hillsdale, NJ: Lawrence Erlbaum Associates.

Tower, R. B., Singer, D. G., & Singer, J. L. (1979). Differential effects of television programming on preschoolers' cognition, imagination, and social play. *American Journal of Orthopsychiatry, 49*, 265–281.

Townley, R. (1988, February 27). Daniel Striped Tiger . . . Meet Stepashka the brash rabbit. *TV Guide*, pp. 12–17.

Trenaman, J., & McQuail, D. (1961). *Television and the political image: A study of the impact of television on the 1959 general election*. London: Methuen.

Trevino, L. K., & Webster, J. (1992). Flow in computer-mediated communication: Electronic mail and voice mail evaluation and impacts. *Communication Research, 19*, 539–573.

Tuchman, G. (1978). *Making news: A study in the construction of reality*. New York: Free Press.

Tuchman, G. (1987). Mass media values. In A. A. Berger (Ed.), *Television in society* (pp. 195–202). New Brunswick, NJ: Transaction Books.

Tuchman, S., & Coffin, T. E. (1971). The influence of election nights television broadcasts in a close election. *Public Opinion Quarterly, 35*, 315–326.

Tulloch, J. (1989). Australian television and the representation of AIDS. *Australian Journal of Communication, 16*, 101–124.

Tulloch, J., & Chapman, S. (1992). Experts in crisis: The framing of radio debate about the risk of AIDS to heterosexuals. *Discourse and Society, 3*, 437–467.

Tulloch, J., Kippax, S., & Crawford, J. (1993). *Television, sexuality, and AIDS*. Sydney: Allen & Unwin.

Tunstall, J. (1977). *The media are American*. New York: Columbia University Press.

Tversky, A., & Kahneman, D. (1973). Availability: A heuristic for judging frequency and probability. *Cognitive Psychology, 5*, 207–232.

Tversky, A., & Kahneman, D. (1974). Judgment under uncertainty: Heuristics and biases. *Science, 185*, 1124–1131.

Twenty-first century Singapore. (1992, August). *World Press Review*, p. 45.

Tye, J. B., Warner, K. E., & Glantz, S. A. (1987, Winter). Tobacco advertising and consumption: Evidence of a causal relationship. *Journal of Public Health Policy*, pp. 492–508.

Ume-Nwagbo, E. N. E. (1986). "Cock Crow at Dawn": A Nigerian experiment with television drama in development communication. *Gazette, 37*(4), 155–167.

U.S. Commission on Obscenity and Pornography. (1970). *The report of the Commission on Obscenity and Pornography*. New York: Bantam.

Van der Voort, T. H. A. (1986). *Television violence: A child's eye view*. Amsterdam: North-Holland.

van Dijk, T. A. (Ed.). (1985a). *Discourse and communication*. Berlin: De Gruyter.

van Dijk, T. A. (1985b). Introduction: Discourse analysis in (mass) communication research. In T. A. van Dijk (Ed.), *Discourse and communication* (pp. 1–9). Berlin: De Gruyter.

van Dijk, T. A. (1988). *News as discourse.* Hillsdale, NJ: Lawrence Erlbaum Associates.

Van Evra, J. (1990). *Television and child development.* Hillsdale, NJ: Lawrence Erlbaum Associates.

Vidmar, N., & Rokeach, M. (1974). Archie Bunker's bigotry: A study in selective perception and exposure. *Journal of Communication, 24*(1), 35–47.

Vincent, R. C., Davis, D. K., & Boruszkowski, L. A. (1987). Sexism on MTV: The portrayal of women in rock videos. *Journalism Quarterly, 64*(4), 750–755.

Vokey, J. R., & Read, J. D. (1985). Subliminal messages: Between the devil and the media. *American Psychologist, 40*, 1231–1239.

Volgy, T. J., & Schwarz, J. E. (1980). TV entertainment programming and sociopolitical attitudes. *Journalism Quarterly, 57*, 150–155.

von Feilitzen, C., Strand, H., Nowak, K., & Andren, G. (1989). To be or not to be in the TV world: Ontological and methodological aspects of content analysis. *European Journal of Communication, 4*, 11–32.

Wallack, L. (1990). Improving health promotion: Media advocacy and social marketing approaches. In C. Atkin & L. Wallack (Eds.), *Mass communication and public health* (pp. 147–163). Newbury Park, CA: Sage.

Walters, R. H., & Willows, D. C. (1968). Imitative behavior of disturbed and nondisturbed children following exposure to aggressive and nonaggressive models. *Child Development, 39*, 79–89.

Ward, S., Wackman, D., & Wartella, E. (1977). *How children learn to buy: The development of consumer information-processing skills.* Beverly Hills, CA: Sage.

Wartella, E. (1980). Individual differences in children's responses to television advertising. In E. L. Palmer & A. Dorr (Eds.), *Children and the faces of television: Teaching, violence, and selling* (pp. 307–322). New York: Academic Press.

Wartella, E., Heintz, K. E., Aidman, A. J., & Mazzarella, S. R. (1990). Television and beyond: Children's video media in one community. *Communication Research, 17*, 45–64.

Wason, P. C., & Johnson-Laird, P. N. (1972). *Psychology of reasoning.* Cambridge, MA: Harvard University Press.

Waters, H. F., & Huck, J. (1988, January 25). TV's new racial hue. *Newsweek*, pp. 52–54.

Watkins, B. (1988). Children's representations of television and real-life stories. *Communication Research, 15*, 159–184.

Watkins, B. A., Huston-Stein, A., & Wright, J. C. (1980). Effects of planned television programming. In E. L. Palmer & A. Dorr (Eds.), *Children and the faces of television* (pp. 49–69). New York: Academic Press.

Watt, J. H., Mazza, M., & Snyder, L. (1993). Agenda-setting effects of television news coverage and the effects delay curve. *Communication Research, 20*, 408–435.

Weaver, J. B. (1991). Responding to erotica: Perceptual processes and dispositional implications. In J. Bryant & D. Zillmann (Eds.), *Responding to the screen* (pp. 329–354). Hillsdale, NJ: Lawrence Erlbaum Associates.

Weaver, J. B. (in press). The impact of exposure to horror film violence on perceptions of women: Is it the violence or an artifact? In B. Austin (Ed.), *Current research in film* (Vol. 5). Norwood, NJ: Ablex.

Weaver, J. B., Masland, J. L., & Zillmann, D. (1984). Effects of erotica on young men's aesthetic perception of their female sexual partners. *Perceptual and Motor Skills, 58*, 929–930.

Weaver, J., & Wakshlag, J. (1986). Perceived vulnerability to crime, criminal victimization experience, and television viewing. *Journal of Broadcasting & Electronic Media, 30*, 141–158.

Webster, J. G., & Wakshlag, J. (1985). Measuring exposure to television. In D. Zillmann & J. Bryant (Eds.), *Selective exposure to communication* (pp. 35–62). Hillsdale, NJ: Lawrence Erlbaum Associates.

Weigel, R. H., Loomis, J., & Soja, M. (1980). Race relations on prime time television. *Journal of Personality and Social Psychology, 39*(5), 884–893.

Weimann, G., & Brosius, H.-B. (1991). The newsworthiness of international terrorism. *Communication Research, 18*, 333–354.

Wenner, L. A. (1989). The Super Bowl pregame show: Cultural fantasies and political subtext. In L. A. Wenner (Ed.), *Media, sports, & society* (pp. 157–179). Newbury Park, CA: Sage.

Wenner, L. A., & Gantz, W. (1989). The audience experience with sports on television. In L. A. Wenner (Ed.), *Media, sports, & society* (pp. 241–269). Newbury Park, CA: Sage.

Weymouth, L. (1981, January–February). Walter Cronkite remembers. *Washington Journalism Review*, p. 23.

Whannel, G. (1992). *Fields in vision: Television sport and cultural transformation*. London: Routledge.

White, L. A. (1979). Erotica and aggression: The influence of sexual arousal, positive affect, and negative affect on aggressive behavior. *Journal of Personality and Social Psychology, 37*, 591–601.

Whitman, W., & Quinsey, V. L. (1981). Heterosexual skills training for institutionalized rapists and child molesters. *Canadian Journal of Behavioral Science, 13*, 105–114.

Wilcox, B. L. (1987). Pornography, social science, and politics: When research and ideology collide. *American Psychologist, 42*, 941–943.

Wilhoit, G. C., & de Bock, H. (1976). "All in the Family" in Holland. *Journal of Communication, 26*(1), 75–84.

Will, E. (1987). Women in media. *The Other Side, 23*(4), 44–46.

Williams, B. (1979, November). *Report of the Departmental Committee on Obscenity and Film Censorship*. London: Her Majesty's Stationery Office. Command 7772.

Williams, F., Phillips, A., & Lum, P. (1985). Gratifications associated with new communication technologies. In K. Rosengren, L. Wenner, & P. Palmgreen (Eds.), *Media gratifications research: New perspectives*. Beverly Hills, CA: Sage.

Williams, T. M. (Ed.). (1986). *The impact of television*. Orlando: Academic Press.

Wilson, B. J. (1987). Reducing children's emotional reactions to mass media through rehearsed explanation and exposure to a replica of a fear object. *Human Communication Research, 14*, 3–26.

Wilson, B. J. (1989). Desensitizing children's emotional reactions to the mass media. *Communication Research, 16*, 723–745.

Wilson, B. J. (1991). Children's reactions to dreams conveyed in mass media programming. *Communication Research, 18*, 283–305.

Wilson, B. J., & Cantor, J. (1987). Reducing fear reactions to mass media: Effects of visual exposure and verbal explanation. In M. McLaughlin (Ed.), *Communication yearbook 10* (pp. 553–573). Newbury Park, CA: Sage.

Wilson, B. J., Hoffner, C., & Cantor, J. (1987). Children's perceptions of the effectiveness of techniques to reduce fear from mass media. *Journal of Applied Developmental Psychology, 8*, 39–52.

Wilson, B. J., Linz, D., Donnerstein, E., & Stipp, H. (1992). The impact of social issue television programming on attitudes toward rape. *Human Communication Research, 19*, 179–208.

Wilson, B. J., & Weiss, A. J. (1993). The effects of sibling coviewing on preschoolers' reactions to a suspenseful movie sequence. *Communication Research, 20*, 214–248.

Winbush, D. (1989, June 19). Bringing Satan to heel. *Time*, pp. 54–55.

Windahl, S. (1981). Uses and gratifications at the crossroads. In G. C. Wilhoit & H. de Bock (Eds.), *Mass communication review yearbook* (Vol. 2, pp. 174–185). Newbury Park, CA: Sage.

Winn, M. (1977). *The plug-in drug: Television, children, and the family*. New York: Viking Penguin.

Witte, K. (1992). Preventing AIDS through persuasive communications. In F. Korzenny & S. Ting-Toomey (Eds.), *Mass media effects across cultures* (pp. 67–86). Newbury Park, CA: Sage.

Wittebols, J. H. (1991). The politics and coverage of terrorism: From media images to public consciousness. *Communication Theory, 1*, 253–266.

Wober, J. M. (1978). Televised violence and paranoid perception: The view from Great Britain. *Public Opinion Quarterly, 42*, 315–321.

Wober, J. M. (1986). The lens of television and the prism of personality. In J. Bryant & D. Zillmann (Eds.), *Perspectives on media effects* (pp. 205–231). Hillsdale, NJ: Lawrence Erlbaum Associates.

Wober, J. M. (1988). *The use and abuse of television: A social psychological analysis of the changing screen*. Hillsdale, NJ: Lawrence Erlbaum Associates.

Wober, J. M., & Gunter, B. (1986). Television audience research at Britain's Independent Broadcasting Authority, 1974–1984. *Journal of Broadcasting & Electronic Media, 30*, 15–31.

Wood, W., Wong, F. Y., & Chachere, J. G. (1991). Effects of media violence on viewers' aggression in unconstrained social interaction. *Psychological Bulletin, 109*, 371–383.

Wright, C. R. (1986). *Mass communication: A sociological perspective* (3rd ed.). New York: Random House.

Wright, J. C., Kunkel, D., Pinon, M., & Huston, A. C. (1989). How children reacted to televised coverage of the space shuttle disaster. *Journal of Communication, 39*(2), 27–45.

Wright, J. C., St. Peters, M., & Huston, A. C. (1990). Family television use and its relation to children's cognitive skills and social behavior. In J. Bryant (Ed.), *Television and the American family* (pp. 227–251). Hillsdale, NJ: Lawrence Erlbaum Associates.

Wroblewski, R., & Huston, A. C. (1987). Televised occupational stereotypes and their effects on early adolescence: Are they changing? *Journal of Early Adolescence, 7*, 283–297.

Wurtzel, A., & Lometti, G. (1987a). Researching television violence. In A. A. Berger (Ed.), *Television in society* (pp. 117–131). New Brunswick, NJ: Transaction Books.

Wurtzel, A., & Lometti, G. (1987b). Smoking out the critics. In A. A. Berger (Ed.), *Television in society* (pp. 143–151). New Brunswick, NJ: Transaction Books.

Wyer, R. S., & Collins, J. E. (1992). A theory of humor elicitation. *Psychological Review, 99*, 663–688.

Yang, N., & Linz, D. (1990). Movie ratings and the content of adult videos: The sex-violence ratio. *Journal of Communication, 40*(2), 28–32.

Yorke, D., & Kitchen, P. (1985). Channel flickers and video speeders. *Journal of Advertising Research, 25*(2), 21–25.

Young, B. M. (1991). *Television advertising and children*. New York: Oxford University Press.

Zechmeister, E. B., & Johnson, J. E. (1992). *Critical thinking: A functional approach*. Pacific Grove, CA: Brooks-Cole.

Zelizer, B. (1992). CNN, the Gulf War, and journalistic practice. *Journal of Communication, 42*(1), 66–81.

Zillmann, D. (1978). Attribution and mis-attribution of excitatory reactions. In J. H. Harvey, W. J. Ickes, & R. F. Kidd (Eds.), *New directions in attribution research* (Vol. 2). Hillsdale, NJ: Lawrence Erlbaum Associates.

Zillmann, D. (1980). Anatomy of suspense. In P. H. Tannenbaum (Ed.), *The entertainment functions of television* (pp. 133–163). Hillsdale, NJ: Lawrence Erlbaum Associates.

Zillmann, D. (1983). Transfer of excitation in emotional behavior. In J. T. Cacioppo & R. E. Petty (Eds.), *Social psychophysiology* (pp. 215–240). New York: Guilford Press.

Zillmann, D. (1984). *Connections between sex and aggression*. Hillsdale, NJ: Lawrence Erlbaum Associates.

Zillmann, D. (1991a). Television viewing and physiological arousal. In J. Bryant & D. Zillmann (Eds.), *Responding to the screen: Reception and reaction processes* (pp. 103–133). Hillsdale, NJ: Lawrence Erlbaum Associates.

Zillmann, D. (1991b). Empathy: Affect from bearing witness to the emotions of others. In J. Bryant & D. Zillmann (Eds.), *Responding to the screen: Reception and reaction processes* (pp. 135–167). Hillsdale, NJ: Lawrence Erlbaum Associates.

Zillmann, D. (1991c). The logic of suspense and mystery. In J. Bryant & D. Zillmann (Eds.), *Responding to the screen: Reception and reaction processes* (pp. 281–303). Hillsdale, NJ: Lawrence Erlbaum Associates.

Zillmann, D., & Bryant, J. (1982). Pornography, sexual callousness, and the trivialization of rape. *Journal of Communication, 32*(4), 10–21.

Zillmann, D., & Bryant, J. (1983). Selective-exposure phenomena. In D. Zillmann & J. Bryant (Eds.), *Selective exposure to communication* (pp. 1–10). Hillsdale, NJ: Lawrence Erlbaum Associates.

Zillmann, D., & Bryant, J. (1984). Effects of massive exposure to pornography. In N. M. Malamuth & E. Donnerstein (Eds.), *Pornography and sexual aggression* (pp. 115–141). Orlando: Academic Press.

Zillmann, D., & Bryant, J. (1988a). Pornography's impact on sexual satisfaction. *Journal of Applied Social Psychology, 18*, 438–453.

Zillmann, D., & Bryant, J. (1988b). Effects of prolonged consumption of pornography on family values. *Journal of Family Issues, 9*, 518–544.

Zillmann, D., & Bryant, J. (1988c). A response to Linz and Donnerstein. *Journal of Communication, 38*(2), 185–192.

Zillmann, D., & Bryant, J. (Eds.). (1989). *Pornography: Research advances and policy considerations.* Hillsdale, NJ: Lawrence Erlbaum Associates.

Zillmann, D., & Bryant, J. (1991). Responding to comedy: The sense and nonsense in humor. In J. Bryant & D. Zillmann (Eds.), *Responding to the screen: Reception and reaction processes* (pp. 261–279). Hillsdale, NJ: Lawrence Erlbaum Associates.

Zillmann, D., Bryant, J., Comisky, P. W., & Medoff, N. J. (1981). Excitation and hedonic valence in the effect of erotica on motivated intermale aggression. *European Journal of Social Psychology, 11*, 233–252.

Zillmann, D., Bryant, J., & Sapolsky, B. S. (1979). The enjoyment of watching sport contests. In J. H. Goldstein (Ed.), *Sports, games, and play: Social and psychological viewpoints* (pp. 297–355). Hillsdale, NJ: Lawrence Erlbaum Associates.

Zillmann, D., & Mundorf, N. (1987). Image effects in the appreciation of video rock. *Communication Research, 14*, 316–334.

Zillmann, D., Weaver, J. B., Mundorf, N., & Aust, C. F. (1986). Effects of opposite-gender companion's affect to horror on distress, delight, and attraction. *Journal of Personality and Social Psychology, 51*, 586–594.

Zoglin, R. (1988a, July 11). Awaiting a gringo crumb. *Time*, p. 76.

Zoglin, R. (1988b, May 30). Heady days again for cable. *Time*, pp. 52–53.

Zoglin, R. (1989, September 11). Subversion by cassette. *Time*, p. 80.

Zoglin, R. (1990a, November 19). Goodbye to the mass audience. *Time*, pp. 122–123.

Zoglin, R. (1990b, March 26). The great TV takeover. *Time*, pp. 66–68.

Zoglin, R. (1991, March 11). It was a public relations rout too. *Time*, pp. 56–57.

Zoglin, R. (1992, June 29). What Americans never see. *Time*, pp. 72–73.

Zohoori, A. R. (1988). A cross-cultural analysis of children's TV use. *Journal of Broadcasting & Electronic Media, 32*(1), 105–113.

AUTHOR INDEX

Subject Index